The Alberta Supreme Court at 100
History & Authority

PATRONS OF THE OSGOODE SOCIETY

David Asper
Blake, Cassels & Graydon LLP
Gowlings
McCarthy Tétrault LLP
Osler, Hoskin & Harcourt LLP
Paliare Roland Rosenberg Rothstein LLP
Torkin Manes Cohen Arbus LLP
Torys LLP
WeirFoulds LLP

 The Osgoode Society is supported by a grant from The Law Foundation of Ontario.

The Society also thanks The Law Society of Upper Canada for its continuing support.

The *Alberta Supreme Court* at *100*

History & Authority

edited by
JONATHAN SWAINGER

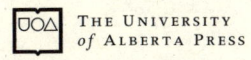
THE UNIVERSITY of ALBERTA PRESS

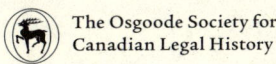
The Osgoode Society for Canadian Legal History

Published by
The University of Alberta Press
Ring House 2
Edmonton, Alberta, Canada
T6G 2E1

A co-publication of The University of Alberta Press and the Osgoode Society for Canadian Legal History
Copyright © 2007
 The Osgoode Society for Canadian Legal History

ISBN-10: 0-88864-493-0
ISBN-13: 978-0-88864-493-0

LIBRARY AND ARCHIVES CANADA
CATALOGUING IN PUBLICATION

The Alberta Supreme court at 100 : history and authority / Jonathan Swainger, editor.
Includes index.
Co-published by: Osgoode Society for Canadian Legal History.

ISBN 978-0-88864-493-0

1. Alberta. Supreme Court--History.
I. Swainger, Jonathan Scott, 1962-
II. Osgoode Society for Canadian Legal History

KEA535.4.A78 2007
347.7123'03509
C2007-903959-6
KF8764.ZA3A53 2007

All rights reserved.
First edition, first printing, 2007.

Printed and bound in Canada
by Kromar Printing Ltd.,
Winnipeg, Manitoba.

Copyediting by Brendan Wild.
Indexing by Judy Dunlop.
Book design & typesetting by Jason Dewinetz.

No part of this publication may be produced, stored in a retrieval system, or transmitted in any forms or by any means, electronic, mechanical, photocopying, recording, or otherwise, without the prior written consent of the copyright owner or a licence from The Canadian Copyright Licensing Agency (Access Copyright). For an Access Copyright license, visit *www.accesscopyright.ca* or call toll free: 1-800-893-5777.

The University of Alberta Press is committed to protecting our natural environment. As part of our efforts, this book is printed on EnviroPaper: it contains 100% post-consumer recycled fibres and is acid- and chlorine-free.

The University of Alberta Press gratefully acknowledges the support received for its publishing program from The Canada Council for the Arts. The University of Alberta Press also gratefully acknowledges the financial support of the Government of Canada through the Book Publishing Industry Development Program (BPIDP) and from the Alberta Foundation for the Arts for its publishing activities.

Contents

- vii   Contributors
- ix   Foreword
- xi   Acknowledgements
- xv   Photographs

INTRODUCTION

1   *History and Authority: The Past and Present in the Supreme Court of Alberta*
    Jonathan Swainger

Part One: Overviews

ONE
27   *The Supreme Court of Alberta: The Formative Years, 1905–1921*
    Louis A. Knafla

TWO
69   *The Power of Law: Judicial Independence and the Supreme Court of Alberta, 1918*
    Wayne N. Renke

THREE
99   *The Supreme Court of Alberta Meets the Supreme Law of Canada*
    Dale Gibson

Part Two: Specific Issues and Areas of Law

FOUR
133   *The Supreme Court of Alberta and First Nations Treaty Hunting Rights: Federalism and Respect for "the Queen's Promises"*
    Brian Calliou

FIVE
159 *Space for Religion: Regulation of Hutterite Expansion and the Superior Courts of Alberta*
     Jonnette Watson Hamilton

SIX
193 *The Supreme Court of Alberta and Water Law*
     Arlene J. Kwasniak

SEVEN
227 *Energy Law: The Court and the Prosperity Bonus*
     Alastair R. Lucas

EIGHT
261 *The Marriage of Law and History: Family Law Cases in the Alberta Supreme Court, 1907–2006*
     Marie L. Gordon

NINE
297 *The Province of Persons: The Alberta Supreme Court and Women's Equality*
     Jennifer Koshan and Elizabeth Whitsitt

APPENDIX
333 *Judges of the Supreme Court of Alberta, 1907–2007*

345 Index

Contributors

BRIAN CALLIOU holds a Bachelor of Laws and Master of Laws from the University of Alberta and was appointed program director for The Banff Centre's Aboriginal Leadership and Management programs in August 2003. In various academic journals and books, he has published works centred on First Nations peoples and the law.

DALE GIBSON, Distinguished Professor Emeritus, University of Manitoba, is currently a consulting barrister in the area of public law, after a career in law at the University of Manitoba and the University of Alberta during which he authored several books and many articles on constitutional law and legal history.

MARIE L. GORDON, Q.C., is a family law practitioner with the Gordon Zwaenepoel firm in Edmonton and teaches as a sessional instructor in family law at the University of Alberta. She has published a number of articles on topics related to spousal support, child support, access and gender bias in family law.

LOUIS A. KNAFLA is Professor Emeritus in the Department of History and Director of Socio-Legal Studies at the University of Calgary where he established himself as one of the leaders of western Canadian legal history while also publishing and editing numerous books, essay collections, and articles on English and European legal history.

JENNIFER KOSHAN is an Associate Professor in the Faculty of Law at the University of Calgary where her teaching and research interests have produced numerous articles in the areas of constitutional law, equality and human rights, violence against women, legal theory, and public interest advocacy.

ARLENE J. KWASNIAK is an Associate Professor in the Faculties of Environmental Design and Law at the University of Calgary where her research interests and numerous publications have centred on environmental conservation, natural resources, and municipal law and policy.

ALASTAIR R. LUCAS, Q.C., is a founding member of the Faculty of Law at the University of Calgary where he is currently acting Dean. His academic interests concentrate on regulatory issues related to energy and environmental law, oil and gas law, constitutional law, and judicial review.

WAYNE N. RENKE is Associate Dean of the Faculty of Law at the University of Alberta. He has published on a wide range of topics, including criminal procedure, sexual assault, judicial independence, counter-terrorism, and privacy.

JONATHAN SWAINGER is an Associate Professor and the Chair of the History program at the University of Northern British Columbia and has published articles on the crime history of central Alberta and northeastern British Columbia. He has also published a book on the Canadian Department of Justice and edited two essay collections on western Canadian legal history.

JONNETTE WATSON HAMILTON is an Associate Professor in the Faculty of Law at the University of Calgary where her research interests have been in the areas of dispute resolution, legal theory, legal reasoning, and negotiable instruments.

ELIZABETH WHITSITT graduated from the University of Calgary's law school in 2004 and was admitted to the Alberta Bar in 2005. After working at Borden Ladner Gervais LLP for two years, she obtained an LLM in international legal studies from NYU.

Foreword

THE CENTENARY OF THE SUPREME COURT OF ALBERTA provides an excellent occasion for reflection on its history, and we are grateful to this volume's editor, Jon Swainger, for putting together this collection. The first two chapters provide an overview of the institutional history, and the remainder examine the court's jurisprudence in its historical context, exploring the relationship between the court and the province as both moved through the twentieth century. The collection examines the extent to which the Court articulated a specifically Albertan response to the varied legal questions of the past century, analysing First Nations' hunting rights, oil and gas law, water law, gender, the Hutterites and religious freedom, and the constitution. This volume contributes substantially to our growing knowledge of the history of Canada's superior courts.

The purpose of The Osgoode Society for Canadian Legal History is to encourage research and writing in the history of Canadian law. The Society, which was incorporated in 1979 and is registered as a charity, was founded at the initiative of the Honourable R. Roy McMurtry, formerly attorney general for Ontario and chief justice of the province, and officials of the Law Society of Upper Canada. The Society seeks to stimulate the study of legal history in Canada through supporting researchers, collecting oral histories, and publishing volumes that contribute to legal-historical scholarship. It has published 70 books on the courts, the judiciary, and the legal profession, as well as on the history of crime and punishment, women and law, law and economy, the legal treatment of ethnic minorities, and famous cases and significant trials in all areas of the law.

Current directors of The Osgoode Society for Canadian Legal History are Robert Armstrong, Kenneth Binks, Patrick Brode, Michael Bryant, Brian Bucknall, David Chernos, Kirby Chown, J. Douglas Ewart, Martin Friedland, John Honsberger, Horace Krever, C. Lankyer, Gavin MacKenzie, Virginia MacLean, Roy McMurtry, Brendan O'Brien, Jim Phillips, Paul Reinhardt, Joel Richler, William Ross, Robert Sharpe, James Spence, Mary Stokes, Richard Tinsley, and Michael Tulloch.

The annual report and information about membership may be obtained by writing: The Osgoode Society for Canadian Legal History, Osgoode Hall, 130 Queen Street West, Toronto, Ontario, M5H 2N6. Telephone: 416-947-3321. Email: *mmacfarl@lsuc.on.ca* Website: *Osgoodesociety.ca*

R. ROY MCMURTRY
President

JIM PHILLIPS
Editor-in-Chief

Acknowledgements

MY INVOLVEMENT WITH THIS PROJECT marking the centenary of the Supreme Court of Alberta began with a telephone call from fellow legal historian Rod Macleod in January 2005, during which he asked whether I was interested in editing a proposed collection on the Court's first hundred years. The appeal of reconnecting with the legal history of Alberta, the place I started my career as a legal historian, was considerable. Yet at the same time, I had no illusions about the challenges that such an undertaking would involve. In the space of approximately two and a half years, essays on the Court and its role in Alberta's history were solicited, drafts produced, scholarly review was completed and revisions made, and then the manuscript was brought into production, a final phase that was miraculously completed in well under one year. Hitting the difficult deadlines and finding time, resources, and energy was an extraordinary effort powered by many hands. And for the fact they weathered the stream of email messages exhorting them to find the necessary time to shape their essays and then undertake revisions, I cannot say enough about the contributors to this volume. For their labours, persistence, and good humour in tolerating my demands, I extend my genuine thanks.

Throughout my work as editor I have benefited greatly from the heartfelt enthusiasm of Mr. Justice Ernest Marshall who, on behalf of the Supreme Court of Alberta's Historical Committee, insisted that the volume be a sound analysis of the court and its history. Mr Justice Marshall helped frame possible topics and themes, solicited contributors, and championed our cause in seeking out and securing financial support. In a fundamental way this essay collection exists because of his commitment. At the same time, as individuals and as a group, the Historical Committee also provided valuable support and guidance while also working to secure funding for the project. The committee was composed of Chief Justice A.H.J. Wachowich, Mr Justice J.L. Foster, Mr Justice A.W. Germain, Mr Justice W.V. Hembroff, Mr Justice A.G. Park, Madam Justice D.C. Read, Mr. Justice A.B. Sulatycky, Mr Justice W.E. Wilson, Mr Justice T.W. Gallant, J.K. Holmes, Q.C., Edith Delanghe, Peggy Kobly, Wayne Samis, Michelle Somers, Brenda Davis and Linda Cathrea. Special thanks also goes out to Robert Maybank, Q.C., Executive Director Court Services and Strategic Initiatives, Alberta Justice, a member of the Court's Historical Committee, who shared our vision along with the Hon. Ron Stevens, Alberta Minister of Justice and Attorney General, who has backed the entire project from the outset.

In managing the work as editor, I called on Jim Phillips of the Osgoode Society for Canadian Legal History on numerous occasions and throughout he provided sound counsel and welcomed encouragement. Michael Luski of the University of Alberta Press invested a great deal of time keeping us on track while providing the room to make the substantive decisions on how the essays worked. Both Jim and Michael have made the task of bringing together a joint publication a rewarding experience. I also acknowledge the support for both the Osgoode Society for Canadian Legal History and the University of Alberta Press for their willingness to publish the essay collection. And when it comes to working with the Osgoode Society one cannot overstate the many contributions of Marilyn MacFarlane.

On behalf of all the contributors I would also like to acknowledge the efforts of the external reviewers whose commitment to quality scholarship certainly helped us produce a better collection of essays. In the course of deciding on the photographs, we were fortunate to draw upon the good will and energy of Stacy Kaufield, Brenda McCafferty, and Kendra Drever of the Legal Archives Society of Alberta and Peter Enman at the University of Calgary Press. Colleagues in History at the University of Northern British Columbia, specifically Jacqueline Holler, Gordon Martel and Ted Binnema were called upon too often as unwilling audiences for the editor's lament. For their patience and good humor, I could not be more grateful. Others who made an important contribution included Brendan Wild, Jason Dewinetz, Cathie Crooks, Judy Dunlop, Bonita Dueck, Barb Noon, and Alex Lester.

Finally, for 25 years I have relied upon Jennifer Sauvé, first as a great friend and then later as my wife and the mother of our two sons, Matthew and Thomas. Throughout she has suffered through the uncertainties of academic life and tolerated the hours dedicated to research, writing and editing. Despite the fact her name does not appear in the table of contents, it is beyond doubt that she was a key contributor to this essay collection.

JONATHAN SWAINGER

Photographs

1 Nicholas D. Beck, Supreme Court of Alberta, 1907–1921. (Legal Archives of Alberta, LAS-5-G-33)

2 Horace Harvey, Supreme Court of Alberta, 1907–1921. (Legal Archives of Alberta, LAS-5-G-36)

3 William C. Ives, Supreme Court of Alberta 1914–1921. (Legal Archives of Alberta, LAS-5-G-35)

4 David L. Scott, Supreme Court of Alberta, 1907–1921. (Legal Archives of Alberta, LAS-5-G-34)

5 Charles A. Stuart, Supreme Court of Alberta, 1907–1921. (Legal Archives of Alberta, LAS-5-G-32)

6 Calgary Territorial courthouse, c. 1890s. (Glenbow Archives, NA-1497-13)

7 Fort Macleod Provincial courthouse, c. 1903. (National Archives of Canada, PA-53102)

8 Edmonton courthouse, 1912. (Glenbow Archives, NC-6-324)

9 Medicine Hat courthouse, 1913. (Provincial Archives of Alberta, 10.593)

10 Lethbridge courthouse, *c.* 1914. (Legal Archives of Alberta, LAS-5-G-72)

11 Criminal trial at Lethbridge courthouse, 1914. (Legal Archives of Alberta, LASA 61-G-39)

12 Calgary courthouse, 1914. (Glenbow Archives, NA-1667-1)

13 Grande Prairie courthouse, *c.* 1929. (Grand Prairie Regional Museum, 1993.40.1D)

14 Wetaskiwin courthouse, 1930. (City of Wetaskiwin Archives, 88.7/197P)

15 Red Deer courthouse, 1933. (Red Deer and District Archives, 90-81-1)

16 New Grand Prairie courthouse, 1957. (Grand Prairie Regional Museum, 050.08.02.35)

17 Supreme Court of Alberta, Appellate Division, 1922.
(Legal Archives of Alberta, LAS-62-G-14)

18 Supreme Court in session, Edmonton, 1925. (Glenbow Archives, ND-3-2911)

19 Judges conference at Edmonton, 1946. (Legal Archives of Alberta, LAS-5-G-57)

20 Supreme Court of Alberta Appellate Division, c. 1946. (Legal Archives of Alberta, LAS-62-G-6)

21 A.J. Cullen, Harry Slater Rowbotham, J.V.H. Milvain, Francis (Frank) Quigley, and L.S. (Louis Sherman) Turcotte, c. 1970s. (Legal Archives of Alberta, LAS-47-G-15)

22 Judges of the Supreme Court of Alberta, Calgary, 1973. (Legal Archives of Alberta, LAS-62-G-32)

23 Court of Queen's Bench judges, 1991. (Legal Archives of Alberta, LAS-65-G-5)

INTRODUCTION
History and Authority
The Past and Present in the Supreme Court of Alberta

JONATHAN SWAINGER

ACKNOWLEDGING A COURT'S ANNIVERSARY is tricky business. Not only is the enterprise hobbled by the suspicion that celebration rather than reflection will carry the day, the supposedly "natural" association between law and history obscures the tangles that lie in wait. Admittedly, the coupling does have its appeal. Legal practitioners, scholars, and historians are often portrayed as "intellectual cousins" well attuned to easy connections between the courts, law, and history.[1] Indeed, we are told that an adherence to past decisions in the form of precedent is an inherently historical method that guides legal practitioners as they grapple with contemporary conflicts and disputes. Lawyers and judges are often perceived as exploring history as a matter of daily practice. Yet at the same time, a generation of legal historical scholarship has made it abundantly clear that beneath these apparent similarities, lawyers, legal scholars, and historians ask rather different questions of the past.[2] Ultimately this difference rests in the lawyerly inclination to view the past as a source of authority and legitimacy, while historians have become increasingly sceptical that such promises can be kept.[3] Indeed, as American legal historian Robert Gordon has argued, "lawyers want to discover a single authoritative meaning from a past act or practice, while historians look for plural, contested, or ambiguous meanings."[4] And it is this difference that renders a court's anniversary tricky business.

But to the degree that such milestones offer challenges, they fail to explain the idiosyncrasies of our court histories. As recently as 1997 it was noted that "the history of the courts is a subject that has never really gotten off the ground in Canada."[5] For beyond the institutional histories of the Canadian Supreme Court, studies of the bench and judiciary in Canada have been "few and far between."[6] Yet at the same time, Canadian legal historians have authored a broad assortment of court-centred histories using biographical approaches, studies centred on specific eras or themes, histories exploring the interaction of courts and law in the creation of communities and identities, case studies, and examinations of how ethnic and religious minorities have fared in the courts.[7] The results have been uneven, though not so much in quality as in coverage. While a number of courts in the colonial and post-Confederation era have been studied in some form or for specific periods, the gaps in our knowledge are considerably larger than are the areas that have been staked out. Recognizing this inclination should allow us to deepen our enquiries so that we might pursue a more thorough-going understanding of the entirety of our legal histories as they moved through time.

Such an approach obliges us to rein in our dependence on case studies as being necessarily more interesting and instructive than an exploration of how and why, within a broadly defined institutional or doctrinal history, a court acted as it did. This is not news. Writing of the state of criminal law history in Canada 25 years ago, Louis Knafla tersely noted that "the basic research is still to be done."[8] Returning to the topic years later, Knafla suggested "that Canadian legal historians were not interested in analyzing court records the way that English and French legal historians do: the process of examining litigation from pleading to factums to examinations to jury selection and verdicts; and then assessing how judges make their decisions and write up their legal reasoning by actually reading their judgments... Canadians study court functions only by examining the select case, or a particular kind of suit, and generalize the 'system' from that limited and isolated perspective."[9] If Knafla is correct, we have seemingly given judicial decision-making short shrift.

A change in course might be ushered in with a challenging question: how did the creation of courts, their structures, their workings, their interactions, the way they were perceived, and the roles attributed to the courts, shape our historic and contemporary communities? At its very heart, it is an enquiry into the assumptions that were woven into the creation of courts and then the subsequent playing out of those notions as communities moved through time.[10] What was it that courts were supposed to do, how was it they were expected to achieve these ends, and what role did judges and judging play in those processes? Admittedly, this quest will be sure to raise alarms that such an emphasis will drive Canadian research towards "internal legal history," but this need not be the case.[11] This is not a retreat to "law office history" but, rather, a reorientation aimed at capturing and exploring those ideas at the very core of the Canadian legal system and to then unravel how such notions were understood (or misunderstood), acted upon, glossed over, and, ultimately, the extent to which those notions corresponded with our varied identities.[12] The key is to recognize the notions at play *and* to discern the degree to which they were contested inside *and* outside the institutions and structures those ideas spawned. We need not proceed as if our only option is all or nothing. Just as case studies can be used to illuminate the ideas at the heart of our courts and their operation in both historic and contemporary society, a more fully grounded understanding of the courts, their genesis, and their evolution will surely provide insight into the meanings of law as demonstrated in case studies. By asking these questions within the framework provided by a court and its history, we launch our enquiry in a primary theatre where these notions came into play.

And it is this arena where the distinctions between a formalistic and historical view of the past is invariably cast into sharp relief. On the one side, formalistic lawyers and scholars working as historians conceive of the playing out of legal disputes within a court system as an inherently legal event shaped by the internal rationale of a legal world. Indeed, the privileging of that rationale stands to reason; from the formalistic perspective it is self-evident. Historians view such exclusively legalistic claims—especially those with the patina of being self-evident—as suspect in the extreme. Not only is the privilege rejected, but its very existence stands as an open invitation to examine the historical origins of such pretensions. That this conflict exists beneath the surface of the supposed fellowship between lawyers and historians is hardly a novel realization. Indeed, as Robert Gordon has succinctly put it, "Lawyers and historians have always cohabited in a relationship of intimate antagonism."[13] The substance of the difference has been articulated in many ways. In reviewing John Phillip Reid's book *In Defiance of the Law: The Standing Army Controversy, the Two Constitutions, and the Coming of the American Revolution,* historian J.M. Sosin voiced an oft-repeated critique: "Lawyers as adversaries strive not to present a balanced, objective solution, one which reconciles all the available evidence, but rather to marshall that which favors one side, ignoring or minimizing that which reflects adversely for their side."[14] Sosin's review is especially intriguing because it is

Reid who has articulated a particularly thoughtful examination of how formalists and historians view the past.[15]

At its core, Reid's exploration of the distinctions between the formalistic and historical views of the past is rooted in what we might perceive as differing standards of practice. Or to draw upon the work of American legal historian Mark Tushnet, our perspective should reflect an awareness of the differences in what constitutes sound scholarship and good practice in history and law.[16] Historians and lawyers do not share a methodology or a set of expectations about what that methodology ought to produce. Offering a valuable phrasing to illuminate the nature of this departure, Tushnet writes of lawyers practicing *history in law* as opposed to historians pursuing *law in history*.[17] Tushnet, Laura Kalman, and Robert Gordon have all used this distinction to great effect, while Reid has portrayed it as a substantive difference between using evidence from the past (the formalist's use) and practicing scientific history (the historian's approach).[18] Although many historians will be uneasy with the "scientific" label, the substance of the distinction is a useful one and offers a solvent for the largely unhelpful critique of how formalistic lawyers and scholars, as historians, have used and abused history.

If we shift our discussion to one that recognizes the great difference between "the past" and historical writing about that past, we avoid a fairly pointless argument comparing the fundamentally different notions obscured by this supposed fellowship. As Reid points out, the use of forensic history is not the same as "scientific history" or what we might now refer to as professional history, and thus comparisons across the disciplines will surely emphasize points of disagreement and conflict. Again, Tushnet's phrasing, that of *history in law* as compared with *law in history*, is helpful especially when we tie it to William Nelson's characterization—that history in law generates "data and interpretations that are of use in resolving modern legal controversies," while law in history provides and supports "new and interesting interpretations and bodies of data to advance the exploration of the past."[19] In drawing our eyes to this summary of Nelson, Laura Kalman argues that lawyers are interested in data first, whereas historians privilege interpretations. But regardless of which goal takes precedence, both lawyers and historians are pursuing data and interpretation, and this, for Kalman, is common ground.[20]

In the end Reid has provided us with the language to better understand the distinctions and move beyond squabbles rooted in different standards of practice. On the one hand, we see forensic history delves into the past in search of evidence to support a given position. It is an approach that, in Reid's estimation, simply cannot (and cannot be expected to) answer to the standards of scholarly history. The formalistic lawyer's view of history is forensic; it is aimed at establishing the timelessness of legal principles, which is admittedly an ahistorical pursuit.[21] Specifically, "Law and lawyers seek out continuity between past and present in an attempt to imbue the past with prescriptive authority."[22] In contrast, history pursues the complexity of the human experience—a past that is indeterminate.[23] Reid remarks: "The distinction to be underlined is utility. The forensic historian, in contrast to the non-forensic historian, searches the past for material applicable to a current issue. The purpose of the advocate, unlike that of the historian, is to use the past for the elucidation of the present, to solve some contemporary problem or, most often, to carry an argument. It is the past put to the service of winning the case at the bar."[24]

Even if historians and formalists disagree about how the past ought to be approached, the two camps can offer a great deal to each other. Sound legal scholarship provides historians with a glimpse of a legal world, its rationale, and an entrée into notions of what courts and laws were supposed to do. It is a particular mentalité that, even if it does not accord with the historian who wishes to ground an understanding of the past in a heavily contextualized environment, nonetheless provides a perspective that must be accounted for if we are to obtain a fuller sense of the varied meanings of law, legal remedy, and courts. At the same time, sound historical scholarship offers a wealth of subtleties, conditions, and contexts. The historical perspective articulates the distance that may exist between those ideals that founded the legal system and the manner in which it functions on the ground. For in as much as a legal system is expected to sort through the complexities of the human experience within an environment coloured by notions of responsibility, duty, and rights, surely a perspective well-attuned to these contrasts is of considerable value. Further, the awareness that courts, notions of judging, and expectations of the law are very much rooted in a time and place provides a crucial underpinning for an appreciation of what a particular line of cases meant in historic society and what they might then mean in contemporary society. Admittedly, moving towards taking courts as institutions more seriously while, in equal measure, placing those institutions within a context of their times may not render less tricky the acknowledgement of a court's anniversary, but it can provide us with the means to understand the varied roles that courts have played in our legal history.²⁵

THE ALBERTA SUPREME COURT AT 100

What follows is an attempt to pursue some of these questions and interpretative perspectives within the context of the historic Supreme Court of Alberta (SCA) and its more recent forms, the Court of Queen's Bench and Court of Appeal for Alberta.²⁶ The contributing authors were asked to reflect upon the relationship between these courts and Albertan society through the twentieth century, and to ask if there was anything particularly Albertan about the courts and their jurisprudence. We were also challenged to wonder about the extent to which Albertans reflected upon the role that the Supreme Court, Queen's Bench, and the Court of Appeal ought to have played (or continue to play) in shaping the province, its development, and its path to the future. It was the idea of capturing a sense of the relationship between Alberta, its history, and the Supreme Court that provided the point of departure for the essays in this volume. In its broadest sense, the Court's centenary signalled the opportunity to reflect on the role that it has played in Alberta and to begin teasing out those areas where we might profitably combine forensic and professional history to explore the meanings of courts, judging, and law in Alberta. What was it that courts were supposed to do in early Alberta and to what extent did the possibilities to fulfill these objectives depend on who was providing the answer? How did these notions change as Alberta grew from a settler society to one buffeted by war, economic hardship and depression, economic windfalls, modernity, jurisdictional clashes and conflicts, emergent rights consciousness, and, most recently, a combination of an economic and demographic explosion? Where did Albertans locate the Court in all this and, just as importantly, how did the Court perceive itself as the province moved through the twentieth century? Although largely centred on questions of doctrine, the results nonetheless illuminate changing notions about courts and how expectations borne of those notions ushered in institutional adaptation over the course of the century since the SCA was unveiled in 1907.²⁷

As detailed in this volume by Louis A. Knafla, the Court's original five members sat individually as trial judges in eleven communities throughout the province's original five judicial districts, and *en banc* to hear appeals in Calgary and Edmonton.²⁸ Although the 1907 legislation is entirely silent on the question of residency, it was probably assumed that the judges would reside in or around either Calgary or Edmonton.[29] Appeal hearings rotated on a monthly basis between Calgary and Edmonton, excepting the latter half of June and during July and August when the Court was on its summer break. Regular sessions for civil and criminal matters were scheduled for twice a year. So, for example, in 1916 criminal cases were heard in the Macleod district on the first Tuesday in March and the third Tuesday in October, while civil matters were heard on the third Tuesday in May and the first Tuesday in December.[30] By the mid-1940s, the number of sessions in Calgary and Edmonton had increased to a point that the calendar from January to June was almost entirely filled, and trials outside the two major cities were held only twice yearly. Three decades later, the emphasis on Calgary and Edmonton remained, while the volume of court business in centres such as Lethbridge, Medicine Hat, Red Deer, Wetaskiwin, Peace River, and Grande Prairie echoed a growing and developing province.[31]

The number of sitting judges on the original Supreme Court was gradually increased to nine and, following a pattern set in Manitoba and Saskatchewan, a separate five judge appellate division was established in 1919, and the trial division counted six judges.[32] The change sparked an eruption of judicial personalities and claims to the title of Chief Justice of Alberta. The contest matched Horace Harvey and David Lynch Scott in a clash that, despite a Judicial Committee of the Privy Council ruling in Scott's favour, was only truly settled with his death on 26 July 1924 and Harvey's elevation to Chief Justice of Alberta, sitting on the Appeal Court.[33] Harvey would remain Chief Justice until his passing on 9 September 1949.[34] Although Harvey's death severed the last link with the original SCA and its predecessor, the Supreme Court of the North-West Territories, little else changed because the Court continued with the judicial complement established in 1919 while the post-war oil boom signalled that the province's future would be fundamentally different from its immediate past.

Although the Court's jurisdiction expanded in some areas and contracted in others during the half century after 1919, the Court's structure remained largely intact until the mid-1970s. The *Revised Statutes* of 1922, 1942, 1955, and 1970 recorded the accumulated changes of intervening years, but beyond the creation of provincial courts for handling divorce and matrimonial questions or juvenile justice, the organization of the Supreme Court remained constant although, by 1970, the trial division had increased to eleven sitting judges while the appeal bench had grown to eight. Perhaps it was the growing realization that the Court had changed little for over half a century, combined with the electoral victory of Peter Lougheed's Progressive Conservatives in 1971 and the demographic shift, that may have facilitated the victory that created the impetus for a thorough-going review of Alberta's courts. Unveiled on 30 June 1973, the Kirby Board of Review was led by Mr Justice W.J.C. Kirby of the then SCA Trial Division, along with Dr M. Wyman, President of the University of Alberta, and J.E. Bower, editor of the *Red Deer Advocate* newspaper.[35] Charged with the task of reviewing the provincial court system, the "Kirby Commission" began with 18 separate questions ranging from whether or not court facilities were accessible throughout the province to what constituted the most effective roles for all the officials connected with the administration of justice. Although a number of reforms followed the release of interim reports, the largest recommendation was that the old Supreme Court Trial Division be reconstituted and combined with the old District Court of Alberta as a newly styled Court of Queen's Bench of Alberta. The new Court, headed by Chief Justice William Robert Sinclair, combined 24 judges from the old Trial Division, 22 judges from the old District Court, and two new appointees. The former Appellate Division was renamed the Court of Appeal and comprised ten sitting judges, including Chief Justice William Alexander McGillivray.[36]

That Alberta is a very different place than it was when the superior court system was first instituted is beyond question. For example, the original Supreme and District Courts counted only 14 members when they were established in 1907 and, as the Court now marks its centenary, there are 88 judges on the superior court bench in Alberta. Obviously, such a simple numerical comparison hardly does justice to either the historic bench or the contemporary courts. After all, in 1911, only four years after the superior courts had been created, the province boasted a population slightly under 375,000 people, and Calgary, its largest city, had fewer than 90,000 residents.[37] The Court of Queen's Bench and Court of Appeal in 2007 serve a province of 3.1 million people, and in 2005 Calgary's population topped 1 million. And to the extent that population numbers signal but one element of the enormous difference between Alberta in the first decade of the twentieth century and the province as it now stands, the intervening century has also witnessed an enormous expansion in court business. Although Alberta might not be described as a particularly litigious society, there is little question that the eruption of "ordinary" litigation, framed in part against the backdrop of rising rights consciousness of the post-World War II era, has created a demand on the court system that was inconceivable in the province's early history.

Not surprisingly, the Court's first century reveals that the all too easy caricatures of Alberta as the Wild West, peopled with red-neck cowboys, sharp-eyed oil men, social conservatives, and true-believers on the political fringe, find limited purchase within the Court's legal history and jurisprudence. It's not that Alberta has been without its share of social conservatives and political rebels; rather, their presence has done more to obscure than forward a thorough-going understanding of Alberta as a place of diverse perspectives and outlooks. Concentrating solely on a political culture or a strident social conservatism, or emphasizing such factors to the exclusion of all others, ignores the genuine complexities of the province and the legal issues at hand.[38] For example, when in 1992 Madam Justice Anne Russell of the Court of Queen's Bench supported Delbert Vriend's claim that he had been dismissed from his job at a private Christian college in Edmonton because he was gay, and that protection against such discrimination ought to be read into s. 15 (1) of the Canadian Charter of Rights and Freedoms, it was Mr Justice John W. McClung's reversal at the Alberta Court of Appeal that garnered most of the attention. And while McClung's subsequent comments served only to fuel the fire and lend weight to the image of Alberta and Albertans as being staunchly anti-homosexual, his judicial reversal had been based on a principled objection to courts legislating in the place of elected representatives.[39] As political scientist Allan Tupper has pointed out, the "national media paid extraordinary attention to the views of religious minorities and to homophobic sentiment in Alberta" while giving less coverage to the fact that ultimately "Alberta embraced the Canadian norm."[40] While there is ample room to question what truly shaped the ruling, proceeding as if an Albertan court would have been incapable of ruling otherwise simply ignores Russell's decision at the Court of Queen's Bench and Madam Justice Constance Hunt's dissent in the Court of Appeal.

Yet at the same time, rulings that are suggestive of a more comprehensive image of the province, its history and identities, must also be subjected to an engaged interpretation. For example, the Albertan origins of the "Persons case" have been seen as an indication that the province, and indeed the prairie west, was particularly amenable to a more equitable treatment of Canadian women. Still, while Mr Justice Charles Stuart of the appellate division in 1917 determined in *R. v. Cyr* that there was "no legal disqualification for holding public office arising from any distinction of sex"—a decision described as one where "the superior judges of Alberta joined hands with the executive of the province and thrust the full weight of judicial authority into the proposition that Alberta women were indeed full legal persons"—it would not be until the Judicial Committee of the Privy Council decided the matter in the so-called "Persons case" that the historical marker was recognized.[41] The emphasis on the JCPC decision has meant that with the exception of David Bright's 1998 examination of *Cyr*, no one has considered the broader possibilities of what that 1917 decision meant in terms of the Court's sense of its role in addressing the issues at play.[42] Indeed, the background to the Persons case provided in *Cyr* indicates that any broad characterisation of Alberta and its courts as either the Wild West or the home of far-sighted visionaries tends to obscure a historically grounded understanding of how the courts, Albertans generally, and Albertan women specifically, viewed women's roles in public and private spheres.

Further, in those areas where the Court did act, the weight of evidence suggests that while some aspects of Alberta's jurisprudential path have been creative and forward looking, in others they were less inclined to strike out in new directions. This is hardly peculiar to Alberta or its judges. Akin to the judiciary across the nation, Alberta's judges wrestled with thorny, often seemingly intractable questions in an ever changing environment. Not surprisingly, ready-made solutions were no more in the offing in Alberta than elsewhere. And if the Court's jurisprudence in a given area might appear tentative or tightly prescribed, in others we find indications of a distinctive "made in Alberta" flavour that did not necessarily tread expected paths. And in all these instances there were detractors from the view espoused from the bench. There was nothing peculiar in that Albertans, in some instances, were disinclined to accept judicial definitions of the province's best interests or what it meant to be Albertan.

Informed by both a forensic and professional approach to the past, what follows is a legal historical exploration of some of the key disputes, questions, and concerns of the Supreme Court of Alberta's first century. While in no way exhaustive, this canvas nonetheless provides an entrée into both a serious consideration of the Court as an institution on the one hand, and on the other provides a record of some of the defining moments in the province's history. Divided into two sections, the essays first examine broad institutional themes relating to the Court's early personnel and identity paired with the question of how the Court addressed constitutional law. In detailing the Supreme Court's early personnel, the adventuresome streak that brought them to the prairie west, and a sense that many of the judges felt a genuine connection to Alberta, its peoples and communities, Louis Knafla's portrait of the Supreme Court's early years suggests a trigger for some of its judicial creativity.[43] The lived experiences of being Albertans during the first decade and a half of provincehood, experiences gathered from the vantage point of the bench, may have encouraged a distinctive jurisprudence. Further, limited in number and thus examining a broad assortment of questions, individual judges exerted considerable influence in shaping the contours of the province's economic, social, and, ultimately, political character. Indeed, the early judges became entwined in almost every aspect of provincial life. According to Knafla, the heart of the early Court comprised Chief Justice Horace Harvey, Mr Justice Charles Stuart, and Mr Justice Nicholas DuBois Dominic Beck, all of whom held in common a belief in Alberta, its success, and the Court's role in forwarding that promise.

This confidence was perhaps nowhere in greater evidence than in the conscription troubles of the summer of 1918. Explored in detail by Wayne Renke, and noted by both Knafla and Dale Gibson as a watershed moment in the Supreme Court's early history, the cases of *In re Lewis* and *Re Gray* ignited a tense standoff between the Canadian state and Alberta's Supreme Court. Renke's detailed interpretation of the impasse indicates that the Supreme Court, and Chief Justice Horace Harvey in particular, harboured no doubts about his and their responsibilities to the law, Albertans, and Canadians.[44] Framed by the increasingly politicized pressures of maintaining Canadian manpower contributions to the Allied war effort, the two cases served to cast the Court, and especially Chief Harvey, in the role of principled defenders of judicial independence. Asked to consider whether the federal Order-in-Council 919 could institute a regulation that was inconsistent with the Military Service Act of 1917 and, in so doing call up exempted individuals, the Court ruled that O.C. 919 was *ultra vires* and the exempted men were not obliged to report. Instructing the military and the recruits to ignore the Court's ruling, the federal government sent a chilling message. Despatching the civilian sheriff to secure the local commanding officer at Calgary's Sarcee Barracks, the Court refused to back down in the face of federal intransigence. Harvey's stance was particularly notable because he had opposed the Court's ruling but then found himself defending it as a proper exercise of judicial authority. Tested, the Court's authority emerged unscathed.

Dale Gibson's survey of the Supreme Court of Alberta and constitutional law opens with the acknowledgment that given Canada's judicial structure, the province's judges have not always been afforded the opportunity to decide matters of constitutional importance. For example, the Social Credit legislation of the late 1930s and 1940s, with the exception of the Treasury Branch legislation and the 1946 Alberta Bill of Rights, was never considered by the Supreme Court of Alberta.[45] But while the Court, like all Canadian courts, was not provided those opportunities, it became increasingly involved in cases rooted in the rights consciousness of the post-World War II era. Arguing that on balance there has not been an Albertan approach to constitutional law, Gibson qualifies his conclusion by noting that while the Alberta Court of Appeal has revealed "less ardour for the *Charter*" than did the Canadian Supreme Court, Alberta's Court of Queen's Bench has been more open to Charter claims. That such a conclusion might be drawn, even if it is an impressionistic observation, demonstrates the point that Albertans, their government, and their courts are home to significant difference of opinion.

The second section of essays emphasizes how the Supreme Court has, during its first century, examined a series of specific legal, constitutional, social, and economic questions. Akin to Gibson's impression, these essays locate the Supreme Court's jurisprudence more comfortably within the broader Canadian stream than in one that was particularly Albertan. This did not mean that the provincial environment and the specifics of the issues at hand did not matter; rather, the developing jurisprudence revealed stresses and strains similar to those in evidence elsewhere in the nation. Still, when taken together with Knafla's examination of the early Court and Renke's study of the wartime conscription stalemate, it is hard to come away from these essays without the impression that the Court's first four decades were characterized by a somewhat more venturous spirit than that in effect after World War II. For example, in Brian Calliou's treatment of the Court's interpretation of First Nations' treaty hunting rights prior to World War II, Mr Justice Charles Stuart in *R. v. Stoney Joe,* and Mr Justice William Lunney and Mr Justice Alexander McGillvray in *R. v. Wesley,* demonstrated both judicial self-confidence and a notable inclination to take treaty promises seriously, in direct opposition to the federal Department of Indian Affairs.[46] The stance not only reveals the willingness to adopt a principled path, it also reflects the Court's self-perception as a legitimate voice in shaping policy and its application. Still, it is difficult not to recognize these particular decisions as exceptions to prevailing attitudes, and the fact that neither exerted a great deal of influence exposes the limits of a court's ability to mould public and governmental opinion. To the extent that Stuart's, Lunney's, and McGillivray's lived experiences provided them with a particular sense of Alberta's First Nations communities and the importance of taking treaty promises seriously, their perspective was not shared.

That identifiable groups or communities were singled out for popular or official discrimination was hardly a reality limited to Alberta during the twentieth century. Yet at the same time, as a settler society formed within a context shaped by a massive immigration influx that began in the late 1890s and that crested on the eve of World War I, Alberta wrestled with self-image. Central to this history is the tension between the notion that Alberta, as a space, needed to be populated and the desire, also at work, that it should be populated with the "right" kind of people.[47] And as often as this particular contest was played out in public debate in the first half of the century, the shifting values of the post-World War II era infused the matter with increasing urgency. By drawing a bead on the treatment of Hutterian Brethren colonies in Alberta's courts, Jonnette Watson Hamilton provides insight into a particular chapter of a story that played itself out across the prairies. That Albertan politicians and segments of the population were hostile to the Hutterites is beyond doubt, as was the concerted effort to prevent the Hutterite colonies from managing both internal and external affairs in ways consistent with their religious beliefs. Admittedly, the Supreme Court had limited opportunities to address the so-called "Hutterite problem" because the province had created administrative boards to manage the type of land questions that were at the forefront of concerns about the Hutterites. It was only when the constitutionality of the provincial Communal Property Act was challenged that the Supreme Court became involved. Disinclined to see questions of how Hutterite land management was a manifestation of religious belief, the Court construed the Act as being primarily concerned with property and not religion. In this instance, the Court altered its views only with a change in governmental (and to some extent popular) attitudes concerning the supposed threat posed by the Hutterites.

Resting more fully in the category of cases wherein the Court was actively engaged in balancing contradictory interests and perspectives and thus provided a measure of leadership, the area of water law was one in which the historic ties to England, the physical and geologic realities of the province, and the challenge of shaping contemporary and future opportunity and development all entwined.[48] Obviously, the task was not a simple one, for the Court was faced with the common law doctrine of accretion that eroded Crown ownership of river and stream beds, shores, and waterways in contrast with the dictates of the Torrens land registry system, preferred by the provincial government. Beginning from the proposition that developing Alberta and its economy were inherently desirable aims, the Court's jurisprudence ultimately favoured private interests over those of the Crown. While this may have been true to the individualist ethic often associated with the province, the view revealed the Court's attempt to advance the province's interests while reconciling legal precedent and legislative markers. Indeed, Arlene Kwasniak argues that had the Court rejected English common law riparian rights at the outset (a real possibility given the vast difference between England and the Canadian prairies), fashioning a water law for Alberta would have been significantly easier. The result would have, at the very least, favoured public ownership and development over that of private interests, but that was not to be the case.

A similar struggle of private and public interests infused the Court's approach to energy law but, as Alastair Lucas indicates, in this instance the Court encouraged a co-operative environment wherein private industry developed provincially owned resources.[49] Within the context of Alberta's energy industry, there was nothing natural about such notions for, perhaps more so than in any other chapter in the province's history, individualism and the unfettered race for results characterized the early energy industry. But with the ultimate goal of sustained development for the benefit of the industry, the provincial government, and, of course, Albertans, the industry had to be saved from itself on more than one occasion. While not always successful in creating the preferred co-operative environment, the Court nonetheless held to the proposition that the province as a whole would benefit from a locally controlled and regulated industry. While the Court's record on energy law might appear to resonate with notions about Alberta's free enterprise ethic, such a gloss fails to credit their efforts to fashion an approach true to the common law, legislation, and the contemporary and future needs of Albertans. There may be nothing particularly "Albertan" about this desire, but like their brethren elsewhere in Canada, Alberta's judges were striving to articulate what they believed to be sound legal principles.

Ideas about the elements crucial to a functioning society and what role the courts and the state ought to play in their protection are central to Marie Gordon's survey of family law in the Supreme Court of Alberta. Touching on questions of access to and grounds for divorce, along with the issues of alimony, support, children's rights, and the meaning of family in Alberta, Gordon's account illuminates the complicated tangle of morality, ideals, and the role of the state in the family sphere. Gordon demonstrates that Albertan and prairie judges generally revealed a notable willingness to level the field in terms of access to divorce proceedings prior to the 1960s and especially before World War II.[50] Yet at the same time, while equality of access to divorce proceedings was expanded, those same judges demonstrated little inclination to fashion a similar equity for women and men when it came to grounds for divorce. Indeed, the Court of the pre-1960s era demonstrated a number of steps forward in certain areas, although their reticence was always apparent. Interestingly, as the rights consciousness of the post-World War II era became increasingly prominent, family law cases expanded in scope and theme, and the Court cautiously worked its way through uncharted waters. Gordon argues that these cases contain insights into notions of gender, morality, economics, religion, power, and the role of the individual within the family unit; in equal measure, these cases reveal Alberta's judiciary seeking solid ground in a constantly shifting environment. The result has been the articulation of what Gordon described as "some of the most purposive and principled findings in the nation" and a firm rejection of stereotypical labels about the province and its attitudes.

Connected in a number of ways to the survey of family law is the line of Alberta Supreme Court cases relating to women's equality jurisprudence. By asking "the woman question," Jennifer Koshan and Elizabeth Whitsitt launch their essay by asking how effectively Alberta's courts have fared in taking women's circumstances, realities, and inequalities into account, and to what extent they have supported women in making progress toward equality.[51] Constructed upon a historical foundation beginning with Alberta's connection to the "Persons case" and moving forward to the Charter jurisprudence of the 1980s and beyond, Koshan and Whitsitt identify an uneven record for women's equality in Alberta's courts. At least part of this path has been determined by a broader national journey centred on how equality for women was to be understood and measured. Pressed forward by first- and second-wave feminism, the debate mirrored crucial changes in how Albertans and Canadians constructed citizenship as we moved through the twentieth century. To the extent that advances were made, Koshan and Whitsitt point to the presence of women on the bench as one of the key indicators in what emerged as an increasingly sophisticated attempt to recognize and account for the real obstacles placed in front of women seeking formal equality. Among the many questions at the heart of the issue is one that connects the "woman question" to the broader field of family law and to that of minors and the law. For it is here we see the particular historical constructions of the male-dominated family and the challenge presented to legislatures and courts to see women's rights and those of children as something other than a product of their membership (or non-membership) in the traditional family.

Although this collection of essays is not an exhaustive doctrinal or complete institutional history of the Alberta Supreme Court since 1907, it provides a series of images that illustrate how the Court perceived itself and how, in turn, Albertans embraced the Court as an integral element in shaping the province's character, development, and path forward. In one sense the Court's idea of the role it ought to play in Alberta has been a constant: from the outset the Court revealed itself as being comfortable with the task of fashioning a link with the broader stream of British and Canadian jurisprudence while, at the same time, it recognized that the province's realities would not always allow for strong and immediate ties. The confidence with which the Court went about this task is striking, and while some might suggest that the verities of early Alberta rendered it easier in those times than it would be for later courts, one would be hard pressed to view Chief Justice Harvey's role in the wartime conscription stand-off, Justice Beck's role in the *Board* divorce case, or Justice McGillivray's defence of First Nations treaty hunting rights in *R. v. Wesley* as anything other than statements of deeply held principle. And in the post-World War II era when rights-based claims did create novel situations, demands, and responsibilities, the Court did not blanch, and individual judges as dissimilar as Madam Justice Joanne Veit and Justice John McClung demonstrated that confidently standing behind one's rulings was not a behaviour restricted to the Court's early history.

The Court's continuity with its past is also revealed in the fact that until the appointment of Madam Justice Elizabeth McFadyen to the District Court of Edmonton in 1976, and then to the new Court of Queen's Bench in 1979, Alberta's superior courts remained a male bastion.[52] Counted amongst a number of appointments of women judges to Alberta's bench in the mid-1980s, Madam Justice Mary Hetherington's elevation to the Court of Appeal in 1985 brought to a close the male exclusivity of that Court and, less than a decade latter in 1992, Madam Justice Catherine Fraser of the Court of Appeal became the first woman to be appointed Chief Justice of Alberta.[53] Since the 1980s, and especially after 1990, the over-representation of men in Alberta's superior courts has become less pronounced, with an even split between men and women on the Court of Appeal prior to the elevation of Mr Justice Jack Watson in the place of Madam Justice E.I. Picard.[54] At the Court of Queen's Bench, women currently occupy one-third of the seats on the bench. Certainly these represent important advances, for as Jennifer Koshan and Elizabeth Whitsitt point out in this volume, the central role of women judges in framing women's equity decisions in the post-Charter era is readily apparent. Yet while the Court has moved a significant distance from its all-male composition prior to the late 1970s, other challenges remain for the federal government in making its judicial appointments, not the least of which will be finding a genuine way to represent people of colour within Alberta's judiciary. This task still awaits as the Court marks its centenary and turns to the future.

As much as continuity characterized a great deal of how the Court was constituted and conceived of its duties, it is equally true that the public view of the Court remained remarkably constant. For despite the periodic eruption of grumbling about judges making law or the supposed lack of accountability of federally appointed judges, most Albertans have rarely questioned the idea that the Supreme Court ought to actively shape the province's character. In simple terms the Court was, and continues to be considered, a legitimate participant in considering all manner of disputes, ranging from the heart of family and personal life to broad constitutional questions that reach well beyond the province's borders. Such an observation might easily be dismissed as a given, but within the context of Alberta's history as a settler society that was nourished at both an ideological and mundane level as a community suspicious of elites and privilege, we see little scepticism about the Court or its ability to truly understand the province and its peoples. Certainly the degree to which the Court, at any given time, actually captured the interests of all Albertans or found the means to represent and acknowledge those Albertans on the outside of dominant opinion, is a separate question. Indeed, these essays reveal that there were, and remain, real limits to how far the Court has been willing to move in recognizing voices and perspectives beyond the broad centre of provincial opinion. Our acknowledgement that such boundaries existed in the past and will continue to exist in the future does not diminish the reality that as a community and as individuals Albertans have had little hesitation in turning to the Supreme Court in search of answers. And further, that while Albertans turned to the Court with that expectation, it does not seem to have been invariably connected to the idea that a particular Albertan turn on the law was required. Albertans expected the Supreme Court to fashion the "right" decision regardless of whether the result resonated with provincial home truths.

Of course Alberta of 2007 shares a decreasing number of similarities with its former self of 100 years ago. Despite the mythology of ranching and small towns serving the surrounding family farms, Alberta is an urban society. It is a province where the vast majority of residents live in communities of over 5,000 people. That seemingly inexorable drift toward the cities has played itself out in the type of matters brought to the Court and will continue to exert a growing influence in the future. That the contest over Hutterite land seemingly ran out of fuel as Alberta modernized and urbanized during the 1970s provides a window into how the province's changing face found its way into the province's courts. We are left to wonder what the future might bring in this regard. Will the Supreme Court's future in Alberta be shaped by disputes over land, resources, rights and responsibilities only when those questions become relevant to an increasingly urbanized province? If it were to come to pass, such a possibility would be, in its own way, true to the history of both the province and the Supreme Court.

The Alberta Supreme Court at 100 bears the marks of a century-long contest between history and authority. Standing upon a foundation of British common law with its centuries of precedent, rule, interpretation, and evasion, the view from the bench in Alberta took in a place and people entirely familiar yet quite distinct from that found anywhere else. Given such a setting, and sustained by that legal history, the task for the Court was maddeningly simple: find substance and authority in the law so that it might provide those people and that place with a means to create communities and fashion a route to the future. By any measure the Court's success in this sense has been worthy of note. And while the playing out of the province's history has sometimes undercut the Court's efforts to provide the authoritative voice that law and legal remedy promises, that same history suggests the Court will invariably reset its markers, confidently step forward, and once again offer its voice in shaping the province, its legal history, and its place in the nation.

AUTHOR'S NOTE: I would like to acknowledge the two external readers who appraised the entire essay collection on behalf of the University of Alberta Press and the Osgoode Society for Canadian Legal History. Their comments strengthened this introduction and all of the essays. I would also like to thank Jim Phillips and Michael Luski for their encouragement, good humour, patience, and wise counsel. Additional assistance was provided by both Stacey Kaulfeld and Brenda McCafferty of the Legal Archives Society of Alberta, Bonita Dueck, Director, Judicial Administration, Alberta Court of Queen's Bench in Calagary, and Mr Justice E.A. Marshall of the Alberta Court of Queen's Bench, Edmonton, along with all the members of the Court's historical committee.

NOTES

1 Graeme Davison, "History on the Witness Stand: Interrogating the Past," in *Proof & Truth: The Humanist as Expert*, eds. Iain McCalman and Ann McGrath (Canberra: The Australian Academy of the Humanities, 2003), 53.
2 Robert Gordon, "The Past as Authority and as Social Critics: Stablizing and Destabalizing Functions of History in Legal Argument," in *The Historic Turn in the Human Sciences*, ed. Terrence J. McDonald (Ann Arbor: The University of Michigan Press, 1996), 339. The increasingly critical and sceptical view of the past as it pertains to historians generally, and to legal history in particular, is addressed in William F. Fisher, "Texts and Contexts: The Application to American Legal History of the Methodologies of Intellectual History," in *Stanford Law Review* 49, no. 5 (May 1997): 1065-1110. Also see Michael Lobban, "Introduction: The Tools and the Tasks of the Legal Historian," and David Ibbetson, "What is Legal History a History Of," in *Law and History: Current Legal Issues* 6, eds. Andrew Lewis and Michael Lobban (Oxford: Oxford University Press, 2004): 1-32 and 32-40, respectively.
3 On this legal view see Robert Gordon, "Foreward: The Arrival of Critical Historicism," in *Stanford Law Review* 49, no. 5 (May 1997): 1023.
4 Ibid., 1024-25. Also see Mr Justice Michael Kirby, "Alex Castles, Australian Legal History and the Courts," in *Australian Journal of Legal History* 9 (2005): 11.
5 "Introduction," *Lords of the Western Bench: A Biographical History of the Supreme Court and District Courts of Alberta, 1876–1990*, Louis A. Knafla and Richard Klumpenhouwer (Calgary: The Legal Archives Society of Alberta, 1997), 8.
6 Philip Girard, Jim Phillips, and Barry Cahill, eds., *The Supreme Court of Nova Scotia, 1754–2004* (Toronto: The Osgoode Society for Canadian Legal History and University of Toronto Press, 2004), 11. On the Canadian Supreme Court, see James G. Snell and Frederick Vaughan, *The Supreme Court of Canada* (Toronto: The Osgoode Society for Canadian Legal History and University of Toronto Press, 1985), and Ian Bushnell, *The Captive Court: A Study of the Supreme Court of Canada* (Montreal and Kingston: McGill-Queen's University Press, 1992). For the Federal Court, see Bushnell, *The Federal Court of Canada* (Toronto: The Osgoode Society for Canadian Legal History and University of Toronto Press, 1997).

7 See David R. Williams, *"...The Man For A New Country": Sir Matthew Baillie Begbie* (Sidney: Gray's Publishing, 1977); Kathryn Bindon, "Hudson's Bay Company Law: Adam Thom and the Institution of Order in Rupert's Land, 1839-54," in *Essays in the History of Canadian Law* 1, ed. Flaherty (Toronto: Osgoode Society for Canadian Legal History and University of Toronto Press, 1981), 43-87; Paul Craven, "Law and Ideology: The Toronto Police Court 1850-80," in *Essays in the History of Canadian Law* 2, ed. Flaherty, 248-307; Hamar Foster, "The Struggle for the Supreme Court: Law and Politics in British Columbia, 1871-1885," in *Law and Justice in a New Land*, ed. Louis A. Knafla (Toronto: The Carswell Company, 1986), 167-214; Paul Romney, *Mr Attorney: The Attorney General for Ontario in Court, Cabinet, and Legislature, 1791–1899* (Toronto: The Osgoode Society for Canadian Legal History and University of Toronto Press, 1986); William Kaplan, *State and Salvation: The Jehovah Witnesses and their fight for Civil Rights* (Toronto: University of Toronto Press, 1989); Clara Greco, "The Superior Court Judiciary of Nova Scotia, 1754-1900: A Collective Biography," in *Essays in the History of Canadian Law* vol. 3, *Nova Scotia*, eds. Philip Girard and Jim Phillips (Toronto: The Osgoode Society for Canadian Legal History and University of Toronto Press, 1990), 42-79; Hamar Foster, "Long Distance Justice: The Criminal Jurisdiction of Canadian Courts West of the Canadas, 1763-1859," in *American Journal of Legal History* 34 (1990): 1-48; John McLaren, "The Early British Columbia Judges, the Rule of Law and the 'Chinese Question': The Californian and Oregon Connection," in *Law for the Elephant, Law for the Beaver—Essays in the Legal History of the North American West*, eds. John McLaren, Hamar Foster, and Chet Orloff (Regina: Canadian Plains Research Centre and Pasadena: Ninth Judicial District Historical Society, 1992), 237-73; Tina Loo, *Making Law, Order, and Authority in British Columbia, 1821–1871* (Vancouver: UBC Press, 1994); Jan Grabowski, "French Criminal Justice and Indians in Montreal, 1670-1760," *Ethnohistory* 43, no. 3 (Summer 1996): 405-29; Mark Walters, "Criminal Jurisdiction over the Aboriginal Peoples of Upper Canada: Reconsidering the Shawanakiskie Case (1822-26)," *University of Toronto Law Journal* 46 (1996): 273-310; Russell Smandych and Rick Linden, "Administering Justice without the State: A Study of the Private Justice System of the Hudson's Bay Company to 1800," *Canadian Journal of Law and Society* 11 (1996): 21-61; R.C. Macleod and Heather Rollason, "'Restrain the Lawless Savages': Native Defendants in the Criminal Courts of the Northwest Territories, 1878-1885," *Journal of Historical Sociology* 10, no. 2 (June 1997): 157-84; James W. St. G. Walker, *"Race," Rights and the Law in the Supreme Court of Canada* (Toronto: The Osgoode Society for Canadian Legal History and Wilfred Laurier University Press, 1997); Constance Backhouse, *Colour-Coded: A Legal History of Racism in Canada, 1900–1950* (Toronto: The Osgoode Society for Canadian Legal History and University of Toronto Press, 1999); Robert J. Sharpe and Kent Roach, *Brian Dickson: A Judge's Story* (Toronto: The Osgoode Society for Canadian Legal History and University of Toronto Press, 2003); Paul C. Nigol, "Discipline and Discretion in the Mid-Eighteenth-Century Hudson's Bay Company Private Justice System," in *Laws and Societies in the Canadian Prairie West, 1670–1940*, eds. Louis A. Knafla and Jonathan Swainger (Vancouver: UBC Press, 2005), 150-84; Nina Jane Goudie, "The Supreme Court on Circuit: Northern District,

Newfoundland, 1826-33," in *Essays in the History of Canadian Law*, vol. IX, *Two Islands: Newfoundland and Prince Edward Island*, ed. Christopher English (Toronto: The Osgoode Society for Canadian Legal History and University of Toronto Press, 2005), 115-46; Christopher English, "The Judges go to Court: The Cashin Libel Trial of 1947," in *Essays in the History of Canadian Law* vol. IX, ed. Christopher English, 357-90; Dale Brawn, *The Court of Queen's Bench of Manitoba: A Biographical History* (Toronto: The Osgoode Society for Canadian Legal History and University of Toronto Press, 2006); and Donald Fyson, *Magistrates, Police, and People: Everyday Criminal Justice in Quebec and Lower Canada, 1764-1837* (Toronto: The Osgoode Society for Canadian Legal History and University of Toronto Press, 2006).

8 Louis A. Knafla, "Introduction: Aspects of the Criminal Law, Crime, Criminal Process and Punishment in Europe and Canada, 1500-1935," in *Crime and Criminal Justice in Europe and Canada*, rev. ed., ed. Louis A. Knafla (Waterloo: Wilfrid Laurier University, 1985), p. 4.

9 Knafla to author; this line of argument was played out in a paper presented to the Canada's Legal History: Past, Present, Future Conference at the Faculty of Law, University of Manitoba, 2 October 1997.

10 A compelling example of the work that such enquiries can produce is displayed in the recent collection of R.C.B. Risk's scholarship, edited by G. Blaine Baker and Jim Phillips. See R.C.B. Risk, *A History of Canadian Legal Thought—Collected Essays* (Toronto: The Osgoode Society for Canadian Legal History and University of Toronto Press, 2006).

11 For the distinction between internal and external legal history, see Robert W. Gordon, "J. Willard Hurst and the Common Law Tradition in American Legal Historiography," *Law and Society Review* 10 (1975): 9-11.

12 The phrase "law office history" was coined by Alfred H. Kelly in "Clio and the Court: An Illicit Love Affair," *Supreme Court Review* 119 (1965): 122.

13 Gordon, "The Past as Authority and as Social Critics," 339.

14 J.M. Sosin, "Historian's History or Lawyer's History?" in *Reviews in American History* 10, no. 1 (March 1982): 38.

15 See John Phillip Reid, "The Touch of History—The Historical Method of a Common Law Judge," in *The American Journal of Legal History* 8, no. 2 (April 1964): 157-71; "Law and History," in *Loyola of Los Angeles Law Review* 27 (1993): 193-223; and "The Jurisprudence of Liberty—The Ancient Constitution in the Legal Historiography of the Seventeenth and Eighteenth Centuries," in *The Roots of Liberty—Magna Carta, Ancient Constitution, and the Anglo-American Tradition of Rule of Law*, ed. Ellis Sandoz (Columbia: University of Missouri Press, 1993), 147-231.

16 Mark Tushnet, "Interdisciplinary Legal Scholarship: The Case of History-in-Law," *Chicago Kent Law Review*, no. 71 (1996): 909-10.

17 The distinctions between law in history and history in law are developed throughout Tushnet, "Interdisciplinary Legal Scholarship," pp. 909-35. A year later Laura Kalman offered a turn on Tushnet, in Laura Kalman, "Border Patrol: Reflections on the Turn to History in Legal Scholarship," *Fordham Law Review*, no. 66 (1997): 114. Here Kalman distinguished lawyers' legal history and historians' legal history. See, more generally, Laura Kalman, *The Strange Death of Legal Liberalism* (New Haven and London: Yale University Press, 1996).

18 Reid, "The Jurisprudence of Liberty," pp. 165-66.
19 This depiction of Reid's views are cited in Kalman, "Border Patrol," p. 115, and are taken from Richard B. Bernstein, "Charting the Bicentennial," *Columbia Law Review*, no. 87 (1987): 1578.
20 Kalman, "Border Patrol," p. 115.
21 Reid, "The Jurisprudence of Liberty," p. 153. I would like to thank Robert Gordon for directing my attention to Reid's notion of forensic history. Also see Reid, "Law and History," pp. 193-223. Reid began exploring these notions over 30 years ago; see, for example, Reid, "The Touch of History," pp. 157-71
22 Kalman, "Border Patrol," p. 103.
23 The distinctions between law in history and history in law (to use Tushnet's phrasing) is captured by Gordon in "The Past as Authority and as Social Critic," pp. 339-77.
24 Reid, "The Jurisprudence of Liberty," p. 167.
25 For some of the very best scholarship in Canada on the relationships between courts and the wider community, see Constance Backhouse, *Petticoats and Prejudice: Women and the Law in Nineteenth-Century Canada* (Toronto: The Osgoode Society for Canadian Legal History and Women's Press, 1991); Backhouse, *Colour-Coded: A Legal History of Racism in Canada, 1900-1930*, (Toronto: The Osgoode Society for Canadian Legal History and University of Toronto Press, 1999); G. Blaine Baker and Jim Phillips, eds., *Essays in the History of Canadian Law in Honour of R.C.B. Risk* (Toronto: The Osgoode Society for Canadian Legal History, 1999); and Baker and Phillips eds., *R.C.B. Risk, A History of Canadian Legal Thought*.
26 Although the Court of Queen's Bench and Court of Appeal are two distinct bodies, this essay employs a shorthand reference to the Supreme Court of Alberta unless specifically detailing one of the Courts or their membership.
27 "An Act Respecting the Supreme Court," *Statutes of Alberta*, (1907), c. 3.
28 The original judicial districts established in 1906 were Lethbridge, Macleod, Calgary, Wetaskiwin, and Edmonton. See "New Judicial Districts," *The Alberta Gazette—Extra*, 17 September 1906: 1-4. The Wetaskiwin district was divided into the new Red Deer judicial district, the Lacombe sub-district, and the newly configured Wetaskiwin judicial district in 1916; see "Alterations in Boundaries of Judicial Districts," *Alberta Gazette* 12, no. 20, 31 October 1916: 619-21.
29 The residency question was clarified in 1919 when it was specified that all of the judges were to reside at or in the cities of Edmonton or Calgary. See "An Act Respecting the Supreme Court and the Administration of Justice," *Statutes of Alberta* (1919), c. 3, s. 8.
30 "Sittings of Supreme Court," *Alberta Gazette* 12, no. 24, 27 December 1916: 771-72.
31 See "The Supreme Court of Alberta, 1946," *Alberta Gazette* 41, no. 22, 30 November 1945: 1218-19 and "The Supreme Court of Alberta, 1971," *Alberta Gazette* 66, no. 21, 14 November 1970: 2234-36.
32 "An Act Respecting the Supreme Court and the Administration of Justice," *Statutes of Alberta* (1919), c. 3.
33 W.F. Bowker, "Which is the Chief Justice: David Lynch Scott or Horace Harvey?" *Alberta Law Review* [cited hereafter *Alta LR*] 30, no. 4 (1992): 1179-1199.

34 See W.F. Bowker, "The Honourable Horace Harvey, Chief Justice of Alberta," *Canadian Bar Review* 32 (1954): 933-981; 1118-1139.
35 See "Commission," *The Alberta Gazette* 69, no. 12, 30 June 1973: 1345-47. Also see "William John Cameron Kirby," in *Lords of the Western Bench*, Knafla and Klumpenhouwer, p. 83.
36 "The Court of Appeal Act," *Statutes of Alberta* (1978) and "The Court of Queen's Bench Act," *Statutes of Alberta* (1978), c. 50 and 51, respectively. The changes took effect on 30 June 1979.
37 Alberta population urban and rural, *http://www40.statcan.ca/101/cst01/demo62j.htm*, accessed 19 September 2006.
38 See Roger Epp, "1996—Two Albertas: Rural and Urban Trajectories," in *Alberta Formed Alberta Transformed*, vol. 2, eds. Michael Payne, Donald Wetherell, and Catherine Cavanaugh (Edmonton and Calgary: University of Alberta Press and University of Calgary Press, 2006), 727-47
39 Knafla and Klumpenhouwer, "Introduction," *Lords of the Western Bench*, p. 6. On Mr Justice McClung's later inflammatory comments, see Dale Gibson, "The Supreme Court of Alberta Meets the Supreme Law of Canada."
40 Alan Tupper, "Uncertain Future: Alberta in the Canadian Community," in *Forging Alberta's Constitutional Framework*, eds. Richard Connors and John M. Law (Edmonton: University of Alberta Press, 2005), 489.
41 See R v. Cyr, *Alberta Law Reports* 12, (1917-18): 336; Catherine Cavanaugh, "Out of the West: History, Memory and the 'Persons Case,' 1919-2000," in *Forging Alberta's Constitutional Framework*, ed. Connors and Law, pp. 136-63; David Bright, "The Other Woman: Lizzie Cyr and the Origins of the Persons Case," *Canadian Journal of Law and Society* 13, no. 2 (1998): 99-115; and Olive Stone, "How Alberta Combined Judicial, Executive, and Legislative Powers to Win Full Legal Personality for all Canadian Women," *Alta LR* 17 (1979): 331-71.
42 Bright, "The Other Woman."
43 See Louis A. Knafla, in this volume.
44 See Wayne N. Renke, in this volume.
45 For Gibson's treatment of the Social Credit legislation, see "Bible Bill and the Money Barons: The Social Credit Court References and their Constitutional Consequences," in *Forging Alberta's Constitutional Framework*, ed. Connors and Law, pp. 191-236.
46 See Brian Calliou, , in this volume.
47 For the tension over peopling Alberta and which groups constituted the "best" mix for the province, see Howard and Tamara Palmer, eds., *Peoples of Alberta—Portraits of Cultural Diversity* (Saskatoon: Western Producer Prairie Books, 1985).
48 See Arlene J. Kwasniak, in this volume.
49 See Alastair R. Lucas, in this volume.
50 See Marie L. Gordon, in this volume.
51 See Jennifer Koshan and Elizabeth Whitsitt, in this volume.
52 See "Elizabeth Ann McFadyen," in *Lords of the Western Bench*, Knafla and Klumpenhouwer, pp. 119-20.
53 See "Mary Margaret McCormick Hetherington" and "Catherine Anne

Fraser," in ibid., pp. 71 and 46–47, respectively.
54 "Alberta Judicial Appointments Announced," 18 September 2006, *http://www.justice.gc.ca/en/news/ja/2006/doc_31886.html* accessed 28 September 2006.

ONE

The Supreme Court of Alberta
The Formative Years, 1905–1921

LOUIS A. KNAFLA

AS THE LATE HONOURABLE JUSTICE J.W. McCLUNG wrote, "Alberta's substantial contribution to the development of Canadian law has been unique and colourful."[1] This contribution has been made by lawyers and judges, and their premiere stage has been in the courtrooms of the Supreme Court of Alberta (SCA), whether on assize, at trial, or sitting *en banc*. This essay provides a substantive history of the SCA from its origins in the North-West Territories through what is characterized as its first generation: from its creation in 1907 to the judicial reorganization of 1921. The study has been organized as follows: the significance of the Territorial era; the making of the first court in 1907 and the building of its institutional structure; biographical studies of the first generation of judges; and the work of the Court, which includes the clash and accommodation of legal minds, caseloads for the province and its major centres, a changing judicial mindset that was shaped by the First World War, the legal sources used by legal counsel and judges and the libraries that were created to house and perpetuate them, and the growth of law reporting that published their judgments. Finally, the legacy of the Court will be addressed: making a western Canadian law for the peoples of Alberta.

§ ORIGINS

The Supreme Court of Alberta had its origins in the North-West Territories (NWT), where judges were first appointed in 1876 following the surrender of the Royal Charter of 1670 of the Hudson's Bay Company to the British Crown in 1869 and the subsequent transfer of its lands and authority under the Charter to the Dominion of Canada in 1870.[2] The first judges were stipendiary magistrates (SMs) appointed by the lieutenant-governor of the Territories, and they applied the law of England as of 15 July 1870 according to the English Judicature Act of 1873.[3] The application of this law fell to Colonel James F. Macleod, founder of Fort Macleod in 1874, the first judge for the District of Bow River in 1876, assize judge of the southern Alberta district in 1880, and judge of the territorial Supreme Court 1887–94.[4] It meant that the first judges of the future province of Alberta administered law and equity according to the most modern form of British law in North America. Chief Justice Horace Harvey recognized this when he wrote, later, that the territorial ordinance styled the court they presided over as "The High Court of Justice," with reference to the new English high judiciary.[5]

The initial Supreme Court of the NWT was created by the Dominion Parliament in 1886, and proclaimed on 18 February 1887.[6] The Supreme Court of the North-West Territories (SCNWT) was modelled upon England's new Supreme Court of 1873.[7] Assize circuits for Commissions of Gaol Delivery and Nisi Prius were created, with the five "puisne" (junior) judges riding on specific circuits and sitting twice a year in the territorial capital of Regina *en banc* for reserved cases and appeals. The Court had a rigorous schedule as judges travelled their large circuits and met where they sat *en banc*. While they attempted to be creative in making law for a new land, their decisions are best defined as "circumscribed judicial activism."[8] They relied heavily on English law, pre- and post-1870, with Canadian and American precedents becoming increasingly persuasive. They also had a strong sense of custom.[9] Their guiding principle was to seek out and apply "the customs of the country" in a diverse pioneer society.[10]

The promoter of this vision was Lieutenant-Governor Edgar Dewdney, an English civil engineer and a devoted exponent of English common law.[11] The Court's legal mind was Edward Ludlow Wetmore, an original member who became Chief Justice of the Supreme Court of Saskatchewan when the territorial court split between the two new provinces in 1907.[12] Wetmore is a critical figure in that his activities, judgments, and legal reasoning on the court set the tone for, and presaged, the judicial history of the SCA. According to the highest regarded legal counsel of his era, C.C. McCaul, he was "quite the strongest member of the court."[13]

A distinguished jurist of New Brunswick, Wetmore was in the process of consolidating that province's statutes in 1887 when the federal Minister of Justice, J.S.D. Thompson, offered a judicial posting in western Canada. Residing at Moosomin in southeastern Saskatchewan, Wetmore travelled the assize circuit to Fort Macleod and Calgary by canoe and scow. His assize circuit was a model of proficiency. He ran a tight and punctual court, writing clear and cogent judgments. A strong proponent of reviewing the work of magistrates, he made certain that the court stamp his vision of the law on the land. In the famous case of *The Queen v. Charcoal*, on appeal he overturned a jury verdict of guilty for murder on the English common law principle that the confession was not free and voluntary.[14] Of more than 100 cases he heard, only twenty were appealed and only four reversed.[15] Sitting *en banc* he wrote voluminous opinions, whether for the majority or minority. Possessing a classic knowledge of English law, he was not unwilling to write a treatise when a judgment required it. A historic landmark was his opinion that Hudson's Bay Company employees were subject to Native customs such as their law of marriage when Company men practised them.[16] When it came down to a thorny question such as this, he relied not on case law but on legal books, digests, and treatises to extract the legal principle.[17]

He was also decisive on questions of procedure and legislative interpretation. Articulating a perspective for the future history of courts in the prairies, and federal-provincial constitutional battles, Wetmore upheld the legislature's "Prairie Fire Ordinance" against the Canadian Pacific Railway—a national company under federal legislation—on the basis that there was a parliamentary "intent" under section 92 of the British North America Act of 1867 to give local assemblies authority to legislate on any local or private matter and that the City of London's law of *scienter* to prevent the spread of fires was part of common law custom inherited in Alberta.[18] Setting the tone for the legislature, a number of his decisions critical of their enactments resulted in the legislature's review and passage of revised ordinances.[19] His consolidation of the laws of Saskatchewan in 1908 served as the benchmark for the accumulated jurisprudence of the SCNWT.[20] As will be seen in the following sections, the idea of a strong judiciary was deeply engrained in the SCNWT. The judges saw their role as making law for a new land with as few federal shackles as possible—a vision that accounts for why so many other lawyers became politicians.[21]

The court was highly regarded. According to Harvey, who knew all its members and was writing just prior to retirement, within a decade it was "equal in dignity and authority to that of the Provinces."[22] Its calendar was dominated by civil actions, which composed 85 per cent of the caseload. Wetmore was the most frequent writer of judicial opinions, followed by David Lynch Scott. Scott, along with Nicholas Du Bois Dominic Beck (editor of the *Territories Law Reports* from 1900), became the key transition figures from the territorial to the provincial superior court. With the appointments of Harvey and Charles Allan Stuart to the territorial court in 1904 and 1906, respectively, the new court would not miss a beat when it sat for the first time in September 1907.

§ THE MAKING OF THE FIRST SUPREME COURT OF ALBERTA

The Alberta and Saskatchewan Acts of 1905 continued the law, courts, circuits, and judicial districts of the NWT until such time as the new provincial legislatures changed them.[23] Alberta was proclaimed as a province on 1 September 1905 by Governor General Sir George Grey, who read King Edward VII's proclamation at Fort Edmonton at 12:00 noon on a bright, sunny day. With Prime Minister Wilfrid Laurier in attendance, A.C. Rutherford was sworn in as premier on the next day. It took some time to establish the cabinet, call elections, and form a legislature, which sat for the first time in April 1906. The legislature confirmed the provincial capital at Edmonton after long debate, enacted legislation to create departments of state, government offices, Crown corporations, and schools, and passed incorporation acts for the private sector.[24] That autumn the cabinet created the judicial districts of Lethbridge, Macleod, Calgary, Wetaskiwin, and Edmonton.[25] It was not until the following year that an act instituting new courts was passed.[26]

The major concern of provincial legislators was to continue the governance and legal customs of their past and to use the banner of provincial rights to enshrine them. The memories of Ottawa's interventions in the territorial period were still fresh.[27] Given that Ottawa still controlled the land, natural resources, immigration, homesteading, and Native policies, these concerns were not unjustified. Thus the new provincial Supreme Court replaced the territorial one in September 1907.[28] An Act respecting the Supreme Court was enacted on 11 February 1907. It provided for a chief justice styled "The Chief

Justice of Alberta," and up to eight "puisne" justices. These officers were given the same powers held by all the superior and appeal court judges of England as of 15 July 1870, and jurisdiction over all legal matters at common law and equity. The rules of court and court officials remained those of the SCNWT until changed. While the justices would sit as trial judges on circuit, each December they would appoint four of themselves to sit as an Appellate Division in either Calgary or Edmonton to hear appeals *en banc*.[29]

Serving the interests of continuity with the previous high court, there was a chief justice—Arthur Lewis Sifton—and four puisne judges—Harvey, Scott, Stuart, and Beck—all of whom were federal appointments. A proclamation of 17 September 1906 organized the province into five judicial regions, with assize courts held at nine locales.[30] New judicial districts were established at Athabaska in 1909, Red Deer in 1914, Acadia in 1919, and Peace River in 1920, reflecting population growth in new areas of the province.[31] In northern Alberta, trials were held initially by Beck or Harvey at Peace River, Athabaska, Edmonton, Wetaskiwin, Hanna, and Red Deer. In southern Alberta, they were held by Scott, Sifton, or Stuart at Medicine Hat, Lethbridge, Macleod, Stettler, and Calgary. Each district also had its own district court. The SCA sat *en banc* in Calgary and Edmonton, where it was housed in the Sandison Block on Jasper Avenue just east of the MacDonald Hotel. When Sifton resigned to become premier in 1910, he was replaced by William Charles Simmons, and Harvey became chief justice.

The provincial Supreme Court, however, was clear in recognizing its independence from its territorial predecessor. As Justice Beck wrote in 1908, the SCA was "in no legitimate sense a successor of the Territorial Court," although its decisions were accorded the same respect as those of other superior courts.[32] This view was confirmed later by Harvey and Stuart, who reiterated that their court was not bound by its predecessor regardless of "the great weight which should be given to the opinion of the Territorial Court."[33] These statements were made to publicize the view that the new court, while following in the traditions of its predecessor, would be just as free in making new law.

The Appellate Division of the court remained unseparated from the Trial Division. With the trial judge of a case vacant on appeal, a three-quarters majority was required. The judges also thought that it was advantageous for all of them to have experience with appeal cases, and for appellate judges to be experienced at trials.[34] A sixth judge, William L. Walsh, was appointed by statute in 1913.[35] When three more judges were added by legislation the following year—James Duncan Hyndman, William Carlos Ives, and Maitland Stewart McCarthy—the Appellate Division remained at four, but the judges themselves would decide on an annual basis who would sit in that capacity.[36] In 1919, however, following changes in Saskatchewan, Manitoba, and British Columbia, the legislature made the two divisions distinct. Proclaimed on 15 September 1921, Scott was appointed Chief Justice of Alberta, with Beck, Hyndman, Stuart, and a new appointee, Alfred Henry Clarke, joining them on the Appellate Division, and Harvey was made Chief Justice of the Trial Division, sitting with Ives, McCarthy, Simmons, Walsh, and a new appointee, Thomas Mitchell Tweedie.[37]

Albertans had been the most vocal in insisting that the NWT be divided into two provinces and not kept as one. They had also clamoured for public space to identify their new status, from the building of new schools and government offices to courthouses. The courthouse symbolized not just the law, but also the local community and its government.[38] Politicians responded, and by 1921 imposing structures had been built in each assize town, as well as in others. The most splendid one was constructed in the new capital, Edmonton, in 1912. Designed in the Beaux-Arts classical tradition, it truly resembled a temple of justice. Housing separate grand oak-panelled rooms for the Supreme Court Civil, Criminal, and Appeal (and a room for the local District Court), as well as a magnificent library, it was the grandest building in the province.[39] Its imposing rotunda and marble staircase with ornate iron railings took litigants and onlookers up the stairs of justice. [See Illustration 8, p. *xix*]

This bastion was followed in 1914 with a second courthouse for Calgary, its first being over twenty years old and an insignificant, overcrowded structure. The new courthouse was an elongated sandstone edifice that personified austerity and dignity. Minimalist, only the entrance had a hint of ostentation. City councillors and the press decried its lack of splendour. While part of the design rationale was cost-saving (although it cost more than Edmonton's), the building represented a mood of self-confidence and accomplishment. Containing a large library and public museum, a yard was also added for the execution of murderers.[40] As it turned out, that was the year of the last hanging in Calgary, at the police barracks, and the yard eventually became a playground. [See Illustration 12, p. *xxi*.]

§ JUDGES: THE LIFE OF THE COURT

Of the five judges appointed to the SCA in 1907—Scott, Sifton, Harvey, Stuart, and Beck—all but Beck were from the previous territorial court. The court's pioneer judge was Scott, who had sat since 1894. While Sifton had a short career on the bench awaiting high political office, Harvey, Stuart, and Beck were each on the bench for more than two decades. The later appointees had similar careers. Simmons, appointed to replace Sifton in 1910, would sit for twenty-five years. Walsh, an additional appointment in 1912, would sit for twenty years; the three additional appointees in 1914—prominent Conservatives Hyndman, Ives, and McCarthy—were on the bench for an average of more than twenty years each. Indeed, taken as a whole, the average tenure of the ten judges was twenty-four years.

A similar factor of continuity came in to play in the formal split of the Trial and Appeal Divisions in 1921. Scott, Stuart, and Beck, who formed three of the four-person Appeal Division, had an average tenure of nineteen years on the bench upon their appointment. Federal judgeships were political appointments. However, apart from the overtly political appointment of Sifton, and the relatively light-weighted Simmons, politics seems to have had little role in the quality of federal appointments to the first Supreme Court of Alberta. This stands in some contrast to British Columbia, where James Alexander Macdonald was appointed Chief Justice of the Court of Appeal in 1909 for strictly patronage reasons and was quite undistinguished in almost twenty years on the bench.[41]

The brief biographies below are organized sequentially, according to the chronology of the justices' appointments from 1894 to 1921. Geographical origins, education, law practice, political and business interests, religious affiliation, and community activities compose the major biographical facts. Their judicial careers are assessed according to the published law reports, private papers, and bench-books. The purpose of this section is to provide a living portrait of each judge from which general conclusions can be drawn about the work of the court and its significance in the succeeding section of the chapter.

David Lynch Scott

The eldest of the first generation appointed to the bench, Scott was born in Upper Canada in 1845 of Scottish parents.[42] He studied law at Osgoode Hall and worked in his brother's law office in Orangeville until called to the bar in 1870. He served as mayor from 1878–80 before moving to Regina in 1882, where he was called to the Territorial bar and elected the town's first mayor that year.[43] Scott began his Regina career as a law partner of W.C. Hamilton in 1882 and was the first person enrolled as an Advocate in the new Law Society of the North-West Territories on 11 January 1885. Created Queen's Counsel, he was appointed Crown counsel for the District of Western Assiniboia in the same year. After prosecuting a number of minor crimes, his first major work was as junior counsel for the treason trial of Louis Riel, and the August–September 1885 trials of Poundmaker, Big Bear, and other participants from the Frog Lake Massacre and the clashes at Duck Lake and Batoche. Scott not only took depositions for the trials in June and July, but in court he conducted the examinations of the accused. The jurors found all the accused guilty. Some writers, however, have assessed his performance as clumsy, confused, and lacking knowledge of the rules of evidence.[44] After his 1885 trial experiences, he had gained a reputation in Regina as a man experienced in the real world, possessed with a high moral character and a learned legal mind in spite of his overbearing personality and controversial political behaviour.[45] Appearing frequently before the Supreme Court as counsel for private parties in both civil and criminal matters, Scott became legal advisor to the lieutenant-governor in 1887. His law partnerships expanded, becoming Scott and White in 1890, and Scott, Hamilton and Robinson in 1896.[46]

Scott was appointed Judge of the Supreme Court of the North-West Territories, District of Northern Alberta, seated at Calgary, on 28 September 1894, replacing Justice Macleod. He also continued to serve some of his clients in Regina through 1896 after being appointed to the Supreme Court. In numerous cases from 1894–98 he had to recuse himself from appearing in the court *en banc* because he had represented a party at trial.[47] After joining the new SCA at Edmonton in 1907, he was appointed to the Appellate Division in 1921 and became Chief Justice of Alberta in the same year.

As a judge, Scott was one of the most active writers of judicial opinions to 1910. He became a master of short, incisive judgments with pithy summaries of the legal issues. During this period he established major precedents on enforcing city bylaws, expanding the interpretation of legislative enactments, and pushing the court *en banc* to hear all the circumstances of any case on the full record that came before it.[48] Like Justice Macleod whom he succeeded, he wrote often of developing a "law of the west."[49] He cited Blackstone frequently on the concept of common law as common custom and the role of judges in defining it for their region.[50] He envisioned a legal culture moulded by a collective vision from lower to higher courts. His bench-books contain trial notes that reveal both his legal research and judicial reasoning.[51] Scott also enjoyed an active social and cultural life. Known as having a striking personality, he was prominent in community and charitable affairs. While he stayed out of politics in Alberta, he headed several royal commissions, the most prominent of which was his chairmanship of the commission to investigate the Great Waterways Railway contract in March 1910. He died at his South Cooking Lake cottage soon after the end of summer term on 26 July 1924.[52]

Arthur Lewis Watkins Sifton

Born in a farming community of Upper Canada in 1858, Sifton migrated with his Anglo-Irish family across the Great Shield as his father had a contract to build the telegraph line from Toronto to Winnipeg. Graduating from Victoria College in 1880, he articled in Winnipeg for two years and then moved with his family to Brandon, where he speculated in real estate with his father and was elected to the town's first city council. Called to the bar in 1883, he opened a law practice with his brother Clifford before moving on to Prince Albert as a notary public in 1885. Called to the territorial bar in the next year, he earned his LLB from the University of Toronto in 1888 and moved to Calgary for his wife's health, where he became a city solicitor, Crown prosecutor, and joined the firm of Sifton, Short and Stuart. Utilizing the patronage of his brother, who was then the Liberal Minister of the Interior in Ottawa, he was appointed Commissioner of Public Works and Treasurer for the NWT in 1901. Offered the chief justiceship in the same year, he thought it was too soon, stating that he would like it later. Thus he was appointed puisne justice upon Thomas Horace McGuire's retirement in 1903, and then Chief Justice of the SCA in 1907.[53]

Sifton's role on the bench was insignificant. Sitting with the full court as chief justice, in only two cases did he write the majority opinion.[54] A pragmatist, he sat sphinx-like, cynical in expression, smoking his cigar. On the trial division in southern Alberta he gave judgments instantly, even when the issues were so complex that normally they would have taken several days of legal argument. Most of his judgments were given orally, and not written.[55] Thus when he was appealed, his brethren had difficulty evaluating the appeal because he rarely provided any reasons for his judgment.[56] His bench-books, which survive, have simply the basic facts of the case with no legal authorities or precedents.[57] A Methodist, he often based his decisions on morality. When lumber companies were accused of price-fixing in restraint of trade, he called the defendants criminals, warning them not to interfere with the rights of the community in this province.[58] He levied harsh sentences for cattle rustling, often giving three years' hard labour. Ranchers themselves were not exempted, as he sentenced one to four years at Stony Mountain penitentiary for changing brands on cattle.[59] The press reported that he told them that he would put fear into the hearts of the wicked.

The Chief Justice's original appointment had been attributed by one Regina newspaper to "nepotism, the sacrifice of judicial honour, treachery toward Judge Richardson and the turning of the Judiciary into a part of the political machinery."[60] Thus when Rutherford's Liberal government imploded under financial scandals in 1909, the Laurier government turned to Sifton to save Alberta's provincial Liberal Party by having him resign the chief justiceship in favour of the premiership a year later. Many of his views expressed on the bench became reality in his premiership. Sifton's government introduced Prohibition, as well as women's suffrage, and unsuccessfully tried to convert corporate bonds to the use of the province.

Horace Harvey

Born in Upper Canada in 1863, the son of a Liberal MP, Harvey, a Quaker, graduated from the University of Toronto with a BA in 1886 and an LLB two years later. Called to the bar in the next year, he practised in Toronto until he heard the call west to Calgary in 1893. Practising with Peter McCarthy, he was appointed Registrar of Land Titles for southern Alberta in 1896, and then Deputy Attorney General of the Territories in 1900 when he moved to Regina. Appointed to the SCNWT in 1904, he first moved to Fort Macleod that year and then to Calgary in 1905 and Edmonton in 1907. Harvey was the longest serving Chairman of the Board of Governors of the University of Alberta (1917-40) and, when he died in 1949, he had been on the SCA longer than any other judge.[61]

Harvey took a very strict view of common and statute law. He believed that judges should unflinchingly adhere to judicial precedent and interpret statutes literally, word by word in plain meaning, and not seek to enter the minds of their makers. Harvey insisted on courtroom decorum and believed that the rules of court should be observed without question. Indeed, the rules of court that he authored in 1914 stood unrevised for three decades. Whenever there were conflicting interests at law, he believed that it was the role of legislators to resolve them and not the courts. A formidable figure *en banc*, contemporary lawyers felt that he intimidated his fellow judges. The case reports, however, show otherwise. For example, when four of his brethren ruled with conviction that the SCA did not have to follow either the Supreme Court of Nova Scotia or Harvey's earlier decision in the SCA to allow a magistrate to try the accused for possession of an unlicensed still, Harvey's stern dissent that such a decision "throws the door of uncertainty wide open" fell on deaf ears.[62]

Many of Harvey's decisions in the trial division were in criminal cases. He had a textbook knowledge of criminal law and applied it rigidly. While he was careful in following due process, he had no sympathy for the human pathos exhibited in the cases before him and delivered severe punishments for guilty verdicts. His major contribution to the law in this area, however, was his development of rules for the admissibility of evidence. Since the judges preferred dispassionate proceedings, they obtained the right for any SCA judge to try an indictable offence with consent of the accused.[63] Another major contribution of the Chief Justice was his acceptance of female magistrates. This occurred in 1917, when he disagreed with Justice Scott by holding that women could sit as magistrates.[64] Alice Jamieson in Calgary and Emily Murphy in Edmonton thus became the first female magistrates in the British Empire.[65] This was a unique decision that led to the famous "Persons case" of 1928-29 that granted women the right to sit in the Senate.[66]

Perhaps the most significant challenge he faced in court was a test of the federal government's Order in Council of April 1918 under the War Measures Act to remove exemptions from the Military Service Act of 1917. The SCA held that there was no such power and ordered the release of the farmer who had been seized by the local military authority. Harvey dissented in the face of strong popular support for the farmer's release.[67] The federal Cabinet then directed that the order be enforced regardless of the Alberta court's decision. Soon afterwards Norton, a conscript, applied to the SCA for a writ of *habeas corpus* to be discharged from military custody at Calgary's Sarcee Barracks. The Cabinet advised the commanding officer to evade the writ, and had his troops set up machine guns to thwart the sheriff. The SCA held that the writ must be served, and here Harvey spoke for his brethren when he stated that "the executive government have set at defiance the highest court in this province."[68] For Harvey, the rule of law had to be obeyed. The issue was resolved when the Supreme Court of Canada (SCC) held the federal order valid.[69] [See Illustration 2, p. *xvii*.]

Charles Allan Stuart

Born of English immigrants in Upper Canada in 1864, Stuart graduated with a BA from the University of Toronto with a gold medal in Classics, and an LLB from Osgoode Hall in 1896. Called to the bar in the same year, he lectured at Toronto in constitutional history. Due to a health problem, he went to Mexico, where he practised for a year before moving north to Calgary in 1897, and he was called to the territorial bar the next year. He joined Peter McCarthy and, when McCarthy died in 1901, Stuart joined Arthur Sifton and James Short. Living on a small farm near Gleichen, Stuart ran unsuccessfully as a Liberal against Richard B. Bennett for West Calgary in 1900 but later won when he ran to represent Gleichen in the first provincial legislature in 1905. Active in constitutional affairs in the legislature, he was appointed the fourth member of the new SCA in 1907.[70]

Stuart was a judicial activist who did not hesitate to make new law. A highly accomplished jurist, his judgments were rich in legal and historical authorities. He led the court against Chief Justice Harvey in holding that provincial courts of appeal did not have to follow decisions of other provincial courts.[71] A critic of corporate lawyers and railroad interests against the public good, he sparred continually with CPR counsel R.B. Bennett in a number of cases. In one instance he researched all of Bennett's references and concluded that two thirds of them were irrelevant.[72] Stuart was also a strong supporter of the early "rights" cases. For example, he gave judgment against the City of Edmonton for firing an employee without cause, commenting that he had been reduced to "the humblest navvy in the city sewers."[73] Later, he upheld the appointments as police magistrates of Alice Jamieson of Calgary and Emily Murphy of Edmonton by tracing the history of female office-holding in England from medieval times. Reversing the trial judgment of Justice Scott, Stuart acknowledged that while women were losing such rights in the course of nineteenth-century England, recently they were regaining them; legal history was important.[74] Equally significant, he prepared the opinion in *Board v. Board* (1918) that reviewed the history of divorce and separation in English and colonial law to dismiss an appeal that challenged the right of the court to decide actions for divorce.[75] His argument that the English Divorce and Matrimonial Causes Act of 1857 was part of the law of Alberta, even though it had never been invoked there, was upheld by the Judicial Committee of the Privy Council.[76]

The underlying jurisprudence of Justice Stuart was that local custom was the essence of the common law. Judges were obliged to look at how the issue was framed by customary usage before coming to judgment, no matter how much searching was involved to ascertain the custom. Moreover, he would not rush to judgment with any point of law unresolved.[77] He did this in a famous case where he wrote a judgment granting an appeal of uttering seditious words against a defendant who had expressed joy at the sinking of the *Lusitania*, a pivotal case in the history of the court that will be discussed in greater detail in the next section of this essay.[78] And, in an unreported case, he recognized the right of an Aboriginal to hunt and take game regardless of federal or provincial laws. The case was not reported until sixty years later because the federal government considered it too controversial and against its Native policies.[79] The first Chancellor of the University of Alberta in 1908, his dedication to education and the pursuit of knowledge saw him re-elected to that position continuously until his death in 1926.

Nicholas Du Bois Dominic Beck

Born in Upper Canada in 1857, his father an American-born Anglican rector, Beck studied law at Osgoode Hall and graduated with an LLB from the University of Toronto in 1881. Practising in Peterborough, he joined a group of Ontario lawyers who headed west on the CPR in 1883. He partnered with James Émile Pierre Prendergast—a Catholic and later judge of the SCNWT, Saskatchewan, and Chief Justice of Manitoba in Winnipeg—and converted to Catholicism. In 1889 he left for Calgary to join James Alexander Lougheed's firm. A founding member of the Calgary Bar Association in 1890, he left in 1891 to boost the settlement of Edmonton, where he became the town's first solicitor and Crown prosecutor. Forming a partnership with Edward Corrigan Emery, he drafted many of Edmonton's city bylaws, and was elected by the Benchers of the Law Society of the North-West Territories as its first vice-president in 1899, and president from 1901–7. His keen interest in developing the law of the new territory led him to become the editor of the *Territories Law Reports* from 1900 to 1910. Throughout the territorial years he fought against Clifford Sifton's efforts to disestablish the separate school system, and worked diligently to assist the construction of hospitals and churches. In time these issues caused him to switch his political affiliation from Conservative to Liberal in 1900.[80]

Beck was appointed as the fifth member of the SCA at its inception in 1907, holding what was regarded as the "Catholic Seat." An expert in corporate and financial law, he was ideally suited for the appointment. A thoughtful, meticulous judge, impassive on the bench, he allowed legal counsel to take as much time as needed to make and support their arguments. He was also willing to engage them in the interpretation of their sources. Beck was a judge who sought to get everything right, even if he had to postpone judgment to find a relevant case that would guide him to his conclusion.[81] Thus it was not accidental that he was cited frequently throughout the history of the court for both his minority and majority opinions. He also sat on numerous royal commissions, often as chair, because of his reputation for being politically unbiased.

His bench-books were voluminous, revealing a wealth of research and thought on the legal issues that he confronted. It is not surprising, therefore, that his judgments stood the test of time. He did not hesitate to cross out and revise his opinions in his bench-books, writing not only between the crabbed lines but also down the sides of pages. When it came to financial matters, the pages were replete with mathematical figures and modelling. The books also reveal an interest in human psychology, as he made doodles of people and objects throughout.[82]

William Charles Simmons

Born in an Upper Canadian farming community in 1865, Simmons graduated with a BA from the University of Toronto in 1895 and promptly sought out life in the west by moving to Lethbridge as Principal of Schools. He resigned in 1899 to article with R.B. Bennett in Calgary, where he acquired his legal skills. Admitted to the bar the next year, he practised first in Cardston and then in Lethbridge with S.J. Shepherd, acquiring a ranching clientele. Elected to the first provincial legislature in 1906, he resigned from his practice to run as a Liberal candidate in the 1908 federal election and lost. Perhaps his appointment to the SCA the next year was a result of Liberal patronage. A most popular judge, Simmons wrote many judicial opinions, even though he was overshadowed on the bench by Harvey, Beck, and Stuart. He was an outspoken critic of the CPR in a few notable recorded judgments.[83] What is interesting is that Simmons appears in few cases or judgments in his last decade when he was Chief Justice of the Trial Division 1924-36. More often than not he continued his active interest in politics and local promotional affairs. A devout Presbyterian, he contributed much of his time to promoting progressive labour laws, the development and welfare of Lethbridge, and, with his wife Mary, founded the "Nursing Mission" for hungry children.[84]

William Legh Walsh

The son of a pioneer legislator, Walsh was born in Upper Canada in 1857, and graduated with an LLB from the University of Toronto in 1878. Called to the bar in 1880, he practised first in his hometown of Simcoe and then in Orangeville, where he partnered with D'Alton McCarthy for nineteen years. A failed Conservative provincial politician, he was elected mayor of Orangeville three times. Boredom, however, led him to the Yukon gold rush in 1900, where he practised in Dawson City until the economic decline of 1904 and was acclaimed as "one of the most able barristers the Yukon ever produced." An avid sportsman, his curling rink won the championship in 1902, and in summers the hard-hitting centre-fielder on the baseball diamond was known as the "Orangeville Cyclone." He also played competitive lacrosse, cricket, and golf. Like other opportunists, he lost money in the Yukon gold fields before moving on to Calgary.[85] The first President of the Alberta Conservative Party, he was never successful in elections. The senior partner of Walsh, McCarthy and Carson, he was appointed to the SCA in 1912 as its seventh judge. A devout Anglican, Walsh served as Chancellor of the Diocese of Calgary for nineteen years. He was also the first non-Native to be made an Honorary Chief of the Blood Indian tribe. A popular figure known as "Big Daddy," he became lieutenant-governor of the province in 1931.[86]

Walsh was a highly competent judge with a great sense of humour and an affinity for "getting it right." Energetic and enthusiastic, he was interested in all aspects of the law, but especially criminal law. A supporter of capital punishment, he was said to have sentenced eighteen men and women to their deaths. Walsh was not, however, meticulous in handling details. In the famous case of the Crowsnest Pass rumrunners, where the jury found them guilty, upon appeal

Walsh was alleged to have made thirty-three points of trial misconduct in the original proceedings, but nonetheless appeals to the SCA and SCC failed.[87] His "loose" interpretations also allowed him to gain convictions of "nightwalkers" and "prostitutes."[88] His judgments were successful because they worked for jurors on socially sensitive issues. A devotee of English culture and society, Walsh's opinions were ensconced in a concept of "empire" where strong men and unflappable values held together a multiracial society where discord was always just around the corner. According to later Chief Justice Bruce Smith, who witnessed all the judges of the first court, Walsh was simply outstanding as a trial judge.[89]

James Duncan Hyndman

The youngest appointment to the bench, Hyndman was born in Prince Edward Island in 1874, attended the Prince of Wales College, and articled with Angus McLean, MP. Called to the bar in 1899, he left immediately to join his uncle's practice in Portage La Prairie. Moving to Edmonton in 1903, he ran unsuccessfully for the Conservatives in the federal election of 1906 and fell short again provincially in 1913. Elected to the Edmonton City Council in 1910, he was one of the three new appointments to the SCA in 1914. Retiring early in 1931, his later career brought him to Ottawa, first as Controller, then as Deputy Judge of the Exchequer Court of Canada, Chairman of the War Claims Commission, and vice-president and director of several corporations. Becoming an Officer of the Order of the British Empire, he had the most prestigious career of the first generation of Supreme Court judges.[90]

Hyndman was more active in hearing appeals than sitting on trials. His specialty was business and mortgage law, where he established a number of judicial precedents in the province. A student of English and Canadian case and statute law in these areas, his opinions were well-prepared and eloquent. He was a master of detail, which was revealed in a number of prominent decisions.[91] He was also strong on the punishment of violent crime and supported the death penalty. In contrast to some of his brethren, however, he had a more stringent definition of the criminal law, that it should be narrowly confined to clearly harmful actions and not extended to the regulation of morality.[92]

William Carlos Ives

Born in Quebec in 1873, his father was an original member of the RCMP in the march west that year. The family travelled west by muletrain along the Missouri River via Fort Benton. Ives left the family ranch at age fourteen to work as a cowhand, and was running over 1,500 head of cattle on the Cochrane Ranch by age seventeen. Having saved up money, he attended Coaticook College in Quebec, and he graduated with an LLB from McGill University in 1899. Called to the Quebec bar, he practised in Montreal for two years before returning west, where he settled in Lethbridge and partnered with Charles Conybeare. He ran for the Conservatives unsuccessfully in the federal elections of 1905 and 1909, and he was one of the three new appointees to the SCA in 1914. His family dynasty was centred in the ranching community.[93]

The "cowboy judge" was a placid figure on the bench, poker-faced. Legal counsel would seldom know which way the cause was headed. He listened carefully, never intervened with counsel, and on occasion would make a remark of dry humour. Since he knew his mind by the end of the trial, cases were seldom reserved. He gave judgment immediately, and his written reasons were short and cogent. By the years 1919–21, when sitting *en banc*, he was writing full opinions for the majority.[94] A man who believed in human nature, he thought that if a lawyer brought more than two books into court that his case must be weak. Noted for impartiality, his strength was in assessing the character of the parties and witnesses. Ives sat on a number of celebrated cases and handed down many controversial decisions. One of the most notable involved the trial of Ontario stockbrokers who were arrested in Alberta for running stockbroker "bucket shops," where they took short shares of stock and sold them long to customers without delivering the shares. The cowboy judge had no use for "white collar" crime. He convicted them on four counts of conspiracy and fined them $275,000 with four months' hard labour.[95]

Ives was a genuine character. Wilbur Bowker, who was admitted to the bar by Ives in 1933, wrote that the judge was quite interested in why he was so optimistic as to enter the law profession in the midst of a depression. He advised Bowker, "Don't cut corners." Ives was always encouraging to younger practitioners. As he told them in court one day, "I don't try to correct the bad habits of older lawyers because they're beyond redemption, but maybe I can do something for the young ones."[96]

Maitland Stewart McCarthy

McCarthy was born of Irish parents in 1872, his father an Ontario judge. He was also the nephew of the famous Ontario lawyer and politician D'Alton McCarthy.[97] A graduate of the University of Toronto in 1896, he practised in Ontario until moving to Calgary in 1903, where he joined the future Supreme Court Justice William Walsh in the firm of Walsh and McCarthy. A prominent Conservative MP from 1904–11, he relocated to Edmonton where he joined the firm of Eddinton, Hanna and Maitland. He became one of the leading members of the Bar Association and revelled in its social affairs.[98] He maintained his political interests until he was appointed to the Appellate Division of the SCA on 11 July 1914.[99]

On the bench, McCarthy was regarded as a wise observer of human action, and spoke slowly with a sense of humour. A generalist, he gave more weight to common sense than he did to legal technicalities. According to one of his associates, he became a heavy drinker and forgot his excellent legal training when he sat on the bench.[100] According to another, he could have been one of the most brilliant lawyers of his time.[101] While he did not write extensive judgments frequently, he authored several major legal precedents.[102] These included the extent of contributory negligence in personal accidents, corporate negligence, and rules of evidence.[103] Several of his major decisions involved the Canadian Pacific and Grand Trunk railways. He held a high opinion of precise judicial writing and did not hesitate to dissent from his colleagues. Indeed, in these years nearly one half of his written judgments were made in dissent.[104] One of his most noteworthy judgments was *Rex v. Wilson* (1919), where he overturned a lower court decision for wilful misconduct against an automobile driver and established more narrow parameters of personal liability for drivers encountering cyclists and pedestrians on the roadways.[105] Active in sports, church, and community throughout his legal career, he was a prominent volunteer. McCarthy retired from the bench due to health problems in May 1926, and died in Montreal while vacationing there in May 1930.[106]

§ THE WORK OF THE COURT

At the heart of the Supreme Court throughout this first era were Harvey, Stuart, and Beck, who sat continuously from 1906 until the deaths of Stuart and Beck in 1926 and 1928, respectively. All three men were well grounded in the law. For their roles on the bench, Harvey was the judge of character, Stuart the legal philosopher, and Beck the reform jurist.[107] What they had in common was a belief in Alberta, in its success, and in their role (tempered by Harvey) of making laws that would assist the new province in achieving that success. This role can be seen in the manner in which they handled the briefs of legal counsel. Counsel would refer to numerous authorities, few of which would be mentioned by the judge. In these early years, judges might prefer referring to other cases that they had researched personally, whether or not they had sought counsel's submissions.

In this, and other ways, judges did not envision themselves as "newcomers." As men experienced in law and politics, they had left the east to shape a new countryside. Thus when Beck was challenged in court on a point of law in 1919, he defended his view as one rooted in "thirty years experience as a practitioner and a Judge in this jurisdiction."[108] He was not about to be questioned on the bench. The concentration of Ontario lawyers in Alberta who left their home province, never to return, was not unique. By 1924 over 44 per cent of all professionals in Alberta were from Ontario, rising to 70 per cent for the major cities.[109] Ontario lawyers brought their professional knowledge and experience to create a legal culture that was in harmony with their new habitat, one that featured "the big sky," open spaces, ranching culture, individualism, and a more casual and egalitarian lifestyle.[110]

The ten judges who sat on the new court in this era shared a great deal in common. Eight of them were born in Upper Canada or Ontario, five received their LLB from the University of Toronto, and two from Osgoode Hall. All but Scott left Ontario soon after completing their degrees, or after a few years of practice. A youthful court, six were in their 40s when Alberta was created a province, and three in their 30s—only Scott was an older man, aged 60, at its inception. Eight were active in politics—one half Conservative and one half Liberal; and six were active in their churches. Personalities, however, did clash with differing views of the law. In full court, sitting *en banc*, Beck had an acrimonious relationship with Scott. Often he would dissent from Scott's opinions, and Scott would do likewise.[111] Sifton often agreed with Scott, and at times with Harvey.

There were major differences among the judges in their interpretation of statutes. Harvey saw a statute in its explicit words, and did not believe that one could get into the minds of the legislators who framed it. Beck, however, believed that judges had to go behind the words and into the thoughts that framed it. Since many Canadian statutes were based on English ones, Beck opined that a Canadian statute must be read in light of the English one, and in the case law and customary usages that lay behind it.[112] Beck also did not hesitate to criticize a legislature for drafting doubtful laws, or doing so poorly, much to McCarthy's exasperation.[113]

There were also occasional conflicts over personal advancement. A major conflict of the era was reminiscent of the past judicial wars in British Columbia, where Justices Martin and Hunter vied for supremacy.[114] An initial crisis occurred in 1910 when Horace Harvey, a Liberal, was appointed Chief Justice of Alberta. The displeasure of David Lynch Scott, a long-serving Conservative, was marked by his refusal to sit on the court's appeals *en banc*. For the next decade, his name was absent on such cases although he continued to sit as a judge alone at the trial and appeal levels.[115] Conflict between the two men sparked again when separate trial and appellate divisions were created by the Supreme Court acts of 1919-20.[116] Scott was appointed in 1921 to head the newly separated Appellate Division of the Court, and was titled Chief Justice of Alberta. Harvey, who was made Chief Justice of the Trial Division, claimed that he was still Chief Justice of Alberta and had the Governor General of Canada file on his behalf a reference case to the Supreme Court of Canada.[117] The SCC upheld Harvey's position, but Scott's appeal to the Judicial Committee of the Privy Council in 1923 was successful.[118] Championed in court by R.B. Bennett, Scott ended his career secure in the belief that he was the premier judge of the province. When Scott opened the spring term of the court *en banc* on 8 May 1923, Harvey was absent and did not return to the court *en banc* until after Scott's death in the following year.[119]

The judges were quite agreed, however, on accepting statutes regardless of their geographical or national origin. Thus Harvey expressed the view of the court when he opined that in rulings on statutory interpretation there was "a long line of decisions in the Upper Canada and Ontario courts which are entitled to the greatest respect in this Court."[120] It was equally important to observe how their brethren in Saskatchewan applied federal statutes so that "there should be a uniformity of interpretation of Dominion legislation" in the region.[121] Indeed, the court was eager to keep abreast with what was happening next door. Harvey expressed this desire on an occasion when he noted that "Only last month the Court of Appeal of Saskatchewan held..."[122]

Personalities aside, there was considerable camaraderie in the Court. It arose when there was difficulty in locating sources to make judgment, when judges parted company on precedent and the interpretation of statutes, and when they disagreed on the decision itself. Beck and Stuart, in particular, either reflected this view of accommodation or tried to promote it among their brethren. In some instances, judges who were not of the same mind often sought out common ground. Thus Harvey sitting on trial would at times express doubts about his finding, and Stuart on appeal would use this opening as a means to dissent.[123] This approach may have worked well because there is evidence that the judges did confer about cases before they were heard.[124]

The matters that the Court handled in the early years were primarily civil: commerce and land. Commercial cases were largely bills of exchange, chattel mortgages, creditor executions, mechanics' liens, and promissory notes. Land cases were largely fraudulent conveyances, sales, and restrictive covenants. Within a few years, railroad cases became prominent on the civil side, involving the CPR, Grand Trunk, and Canadian Northern in matters ranging from trespass to derailments, loss of goods, and torts. Criminal cases also began to appear with the growth of population, as did damage claims from automobile accidents after 1912.[125] [See Illustration 11, p. xx] Increasing the size of the Court from the original five judges in 1907 to eleven in 1921 reflected its rising workload. This work was caused by the great immigration of 1896-1921, when the population of the region of Alberta doubled from 1896 to 1906, and more than tripled from 1906 to 1921. Over 40 per cent were Canadian-born, with approximately 20 per cent American, 18 per cent British and Irish, and 15 per cent continental European.[126]

The caseload of the trial judges of the SCA rose significantly, in general terms, with the growth of population across the province. As Table 1 reveals, civil litigation suits rose 140 per cent from 1908 to 1921, while criminal prosecutions rose 232 per cent, making a total caseload increase of 165 per cent. Some areas, however, had very disparate figures (See also Tables 2-4). Combining civil and criminal caseloads in the judicial districts where the evidence is extant, there were rises of 340 per cent in Lethbridge, 297 per cent in Edmonton and Wetaskiwin combined, 174% in Red Deer, and 114 per cent in Calgary, with declines of 36 per cent in Macleod and 21 per cent in Grand Prairie. Most of the large increase was in the period 1908 to 1915, which explains why the government raised the number of judges from five to nine in 1913-1914. Other jurisdictions, especially on the eastern prairie where there was major growth in agriculture, the caseload rose significantly in the war years of 1915–1921 from 42 per cent in Stettler to 479 per cent in Hanna. The older settlement of Medicine Hat had a declining caseload of 20 per cent. Overall, the figures were slightly up for the war era, where civil suits rose modestly by 1 per cent while criminal prosecutions rose by 27 per cent—reflecting the growth of crime with the creation of new criminal offences and the Alberta Provincial Police.[127]

A different reality appears when we look at caseloads per capita. While the population of the province tripled from 1908 to 1921, the number of SCA cases per capita actually declined in this period from 76 to 63 per 1,000 people due to the appointment of additional judges. However, the rate varied for individual judicial districts (Tables 1–4). For example, cases per capita in the combined judicial districts of Edmonton and Wetaskiwin rose by 20 per cent, and in Lethbridge increased by 85 per cent, while Calgary declined by 5 per cent and in Macleod by 59 per cent. Criminal prosecutions remained around the rate of 2 cases per 1,000 people, while in civil suits it dropped from 5.5 to 4.2. For individual districts, on the civil side the rate in Wetaskiwin rose by 15 per cent and Lethbridge by 127 per cent, while the rate declined in Medicine Hat by 21 per cent, Calgary by 24 per cent, and Macleod by 39 per cent. On the criminal side, the rate dropped in Lethbridge by 31 per cent, in Medicine Hat by 33 per cent, in Calgary by 48 per cent, and in Macleod by 90 per cent. However, the rate rose significantly in the north, by 42 per cent in Edmonton and 69 per cent in Red Deer, substantiating the high rate of crime noted by historians of those regions.[128]

These distinctions can be seen more clearly in the litigation statistics for Calgary (See Table 2). Using tabulations for the Calgary Police Court and Justices of the Peace compiled by Thomas Thorner and Neil Watson, we can see that in the fastest-growing judicial district in the province, the number of civil suits before the Supreme Court justices in Calgary grew at a rate less than half that of the population, while the growth rate of all criminal prosecutions was higher than that of civil suits. The difference in criminal prosecutions was due largely to police courts, where the bulk of prosecutions were laid. The growth rate of prosecutions before the Police Court was more than five times that of the Supreme Court. The problem of crime and disorder, however, was not Calgary's alone, as seen above. The court records of other judicial districts reveal that most judges sat in trial at the southern Alberta sessions, the other busy assize towns being Edmonton and Wetaskiwin. As historians have noted, crimi-

Table 1: Supreme Court of Alberta Case Files, 1908-1921

TRIAL COURT	1908	1911	1915	1918	1921
Calgary civil	722	1,318	1,614	1,408	1,588
Calgary criminal	69	77	162	96	101
Edmonton criminal	191	491	703	837	1,001
Grand Prairie civil	28	27	26	22	18
Hanna civil			19	57	110
Hanna criminal					14
Lethbridge civil	70	288	356	369	374
Lethbridge criminal	24	35	29	55	40
Macleod civil	117	130	120	108	95
Macleod criminal	79	51	10	17	11
Medicine Hat civil			176	163	144
Medicine Hat criminal			33	18	23
Peace River civil					21
Red Deer criminal	19	34	40	58	52
Stettler criminal			19	29	27
Wetaskiwin civil	89	146	124	116	110
TOTAL CIVIL	1,026	1,909	2,435	2,243	2,460
% increase over 1908		86%	137%	119%	140%
TOTAL CRIMINAL	382	688	996	1,110	1,269
% increase over 1908		80%	161%	191%	232%
TOTAL CASES	1,408	2,597	3,431	3,353	3,729
% increase over 1908		85%	144%	138%	165%
POPULATION	185,000	374,663	496,525[a]		588,454
% increase over 1908		103%	168%		218%
TOTAL PER CAPITA	.0076	.0069	.0069		.0063

a) This figure is for the year 1916.

NOTE: These figures come from the docket books that accompany the case files for the judicial districts in the Provincial Archives of Alberta as follows. Calgary civil and criminal: fonds 79.285, Edmonton criminal: 83.1, Grand Prairie civil: 84.255, Hanna civil and criminal: 79.126, Lethbridge civil and criminal: 83.238, Macleod civil and criminal: 78.233, Medicine Hat civil and criminal: 83.168 & 77.318, Peace River civil: 80.320, Red Deer criminal: 79.220, Stettler criminal: 79.220, Wetaskiwin civil: 81.198. These are the only districts where the evidence was sufficiently complete to record the number of case files for the period. Population figures come from the *Census of Population and Agriculture of the Northwest Provinces: Manitoba, Saskatchewan, Alberta. 1906* (Ottawa: S.E. Dawson, 1907), 80; *Census of Prairie Provinces: Population and Agriculture. Manitoba, Saskatchewan, Alberta. 1916* (Ottawa: King's Printer, 1918), xvi; and *Census of the Prairie Provinces 1936, Vol. I: Population and Agriculture* (Ottawa: King's Printer, 1938), 833.

Table 2: Case Load at Calgary, 1908-1921

COURT	1908	1911	1915	1918	1921	% change 1908 to 1921
Supreme Court civil	722	1,318	1,614	1,408	1,588	+120%
Supreme Court criminal	69	77	162	96	101	+46%
Calgary Police Court	510	2,912	2,302	1,697	1,861	+265%
Population	22,000	43,704	56,514	59,910	63,305	+188%
Civil per capita	.033	.030	.028	.024	.025	-24%
Supreme Court criminal per capita	.0031	.0018	.0029	.0016	.0016	-48%
Calgary Police Court per capita	.023	.067	.041	.028	.029	+26%
TOTAL CRIMINAL per capita	.026	.068	.044	.030	.031	+19%
TOTAL SUPREME COURT per capita	.036	.032	.031	.025	.027	-25%
TOTAL CASES per capita	.059	.099	.072	.053	.056	-5%

NOTE: The Supreme Court figures are based on the docket books in the PAA, fonds 79.285. The Calgary police court and RCMP prosecutions, with the population figures for Calgary, are drawn from Neil Watson and Thomas Thorner, "Patterns of Prairie Crime: Calgary, 1875-1939," in *Crime and Criminal Justice in Europe and Canada*, ed. Louis A. Knafla (Waterloo: Wilfrid Laurier University press, 2nd ed., 1985), 248-53. The number of police rose from 14 to 68 in the period.

nal activity was also rife in the towns and rangelands of the south.[129] Criminal prosecutions occupied a lot of the Court's time compared with most civil suits. Thus the arduous working judges were Beck, McCarthy, Simmons, and Stuart, who sat in six of the nine judicial districts. Indeed, most judges traversed the province from end to end dispensing the law of the land. (See Table 5.) While the Supreme Court's caseload lessened during the war years, the impact of war itself brought contentious problems to diverse ethnicities.

The distinctions between north and south were prominent in the province, as seen in Tables 3 and 4. The total caseload increased fourfold in Lethbridge but declined by almost one-half in Macleod (Table 3). But on a per capita basis the rate rose almost twofold in Lethbridge but declined by more than one-half in Macleod. The

Table 3: Case Load at Lethbridge and Macleod, 1908–1921

COURT	1908	1911	1915	1918	1921	% change 1908 to 1921
Lethbridge civil	70	288	356	369	374	+434%
Civil per capita	.015	.036	.038		.034	+127%
Lethbridge criminal	24	35	29	55	40	+67%
Criminal per capita	.0052	.0043	.0031		.0036	-31%
Population[a]	4,600	8,050	9,436[b]		11,097	+380%
TOTAL per capita	.020	.040	.041		.037	+85%
Macleod civil	117	130	120	108	95	-19%
Civil per capita	.09	.071	.066		.055	-39%
Macleod criminal	79	51	10	17	11	-86%
Criminal per capita	.061	.028	.0055		.0064	-90%
Population	1,300	1,844	1,811[a]		1,723	+51%
TOTAL per capita	.151	.098	.072		.062	-59%

a) Population figure estimated from the *Census of the Prairie Provinces* (1938), I, 233.
b) The population figure is for 1916.

NOTE: The Supreme Court figures are based on the docket books in the PAA, fonds 79.285. The Calgary police court and RCMP prosecutions, with the population figures for Calgary, are drawn from Neil Watson and Thomas Thorner, "Patterns of Prairie Crime: Calgary, 1875–1939," in Crime and Criminal Justice in Europe and Canada, ed. Louis A. Knafla (Waterloo: Wilfrid Laurier University press, 2nd ed. 1985), 248–53. The number of police rose from 14 to 68 in the period.

northern urban centres, however, were much more litigious, with a combined civil and criminal caseload of 71 per thousand people by 1921 in Wetaskiwin and Edmonton, compared to 62 for Macleod, 56 for Calgary, 37 for Lethbridge, and 17 for Medicine Hat. Since the records are not as complete for counting case files here, Table 4 provides the data only for civil litigation in Wetaskiwin and only criminal prosecutions in neighbouring Edmonton. While civil suits increased by one-quarter in Wetaskiwin, the rise on a per capita basis was much less. However, in Edmonton criminal prosecutions increased tenfold, while rising by barely one-half on a per capita basis. Since the population of the province was more than 60 per cent rural in the period,[130]

Table 4: Case Load at Wetaskiwin and Edmonton, 1908–1921

COURT	1908	1911	1915[b]	1918	1921	% change from 1908 to 1921
Wetaskiwin[a] civil	89	146	124	116	110	+24%
Population[b]	1,950	2,411	2,048c		2,061	+6%
TOTAL per capita	.046	.061	.061		.053	+15%
Edmonton[d] criminal	191	491	703	837	1,001	+424%
Population[b]	16,600	24,900	53,846b		58,821	+254%
TOTAL per capita	.012	.020	.013		.017	+42%
Edmonton & Wetaskiwin TOTAL cases per capita	.015	.023	.015		.018	+20%

a) There are incomplete records for Wetaskiwin criminal cases.
b) Population figure estimated from the *Census of the Prairie Provinces* (1938), I, 233.
c) The population figure is for 1916.
d) There are incomplete records for Edmonton civil cases.

NOTE: Case files are drawn from the PAA, Supreme Court of Alberta, Wetaskiwin (81.198) and Edmonton (83.1) judicial districts. Population figures are from the Census cited in the note to Table 3.

the provincial average of 7 SCA cases per 1,000 suggests that rural society, apart from eastern townships such as Hanna, avoided the SCA at virtually every turn. Litigation in the superior courts, obviously, was not in the makeup of this agrarian society. The courts would fill their calendars with the activities of the mercantile society and the legal problems of integrating a mixed ethnic population into an English common law regime.

Perhaps the defining moment of the Court was its handling of dissent in the First World War, where it established a new standard for civil liberties in Canada. The judges, under the leadership of Stuart and Beck, expanded the ambit of permissible political dissent such that by the war's close, few individuals could be convicted. Creating a strict definition of "intent," it broke from the wide definition adopted by the Supreme Court of the United States that allowed the state a wide berth in prosecuting and convicting persons for seditious words.[131] Reflecting the diverse ethnic structure of the new

Table 5: Trial Judges of the Supreme Court of Alberta, by Judicial District, 1907-1921

JUDGE	Edmonton	Wetaskiwin	Red Deer	Hanna	Stettler	Calgary	Macleod	Lethbridge	Medicine Hat
Beck	×	×				×	×	×	×
Harvey	×	×	×				×		×
Hyndman	×					×			×
Ives	×	×				×	×		
McCarthy	×	×				×	×	×	×
Scott						×	×	×	×
Sifton	×					×	×		×
Simmons	×	×		×	×	×	×		×
Stuart	×		×	×	×	×			×
Walsh	×	×					×	×	

NOTE: These are the towns of the judicial districts where judges sat on trial. The attributions are derived from the case files at the PAA given in the notes to Table 1. It should be mentioned that the case files for the judicial districts of Athabaska, Grande Prairie, and Peace River were too incomplete to make a determination of who sat in those districts.

province and the customary norms of its society, the Court exhibited tolerance of working-class European immigrants who settled the farming communities of central Alberta. It held that their pro-German and anti-British stance "entitled them to opinions that were not actionable unless there was evidence that the expression of those opinions in public places could be tied directly to hindering the prosecution of the war in Europe."[132] Perhaps the judges developed a recognition of social reality in hearing cases when the continental European population was almost as large as that from the British Isles.[133]

Four cases of seditious utterances faced Justice McCarthy at the Red Deer assizes in September 1915.[134] Some of the accused were socialists, who saw the Allied war effort as the work of capitalists who strove for profit on the backs of dead soldiers. These cases led to public debate about the boundaries of free speech. Earlier in August,

Table 6: Legal Resources Frequently Used by SCA Judges

PUBLICATION TITLE	AUTHOR/PUBLISHER	EDITION
DIGESTS		
Digest	William Cassell	1908
Ruling Cases	R. Campbell	1894 to 1908 (27 volumes)
Leading Cases in Various Branches of the Law	John W. Smith	1903
TREATISES		
Annual Practice of the Supreme Court		1st ed. 1883
Law relating to Vendors and Purchasers of Real Estate	J.H. Dart	7th ed. 1905
Conflict of Laws	A.V. Dicey	2nd ed. 1908
Law of Fraud and Mistake	W.W. Kerr	4th ed. 1910
Equity Jurisprudence	Pomeroy	3rd ed. 1908
Treatise on the Anglo-American System of Evidence in Trials at Common Law	John H. Wigmore	10 vols. 1905
Law relating to Vendors and Purchasers of Real Estate and Chattels Real	T.C. Williams	1st ed. 1904–6

NOTE: Many other legal resources were used occasionally throughout the period. Judges may also have had their own libraries, but I have been unable to find any information on that for these judges.

in the trial of *R. v. Felton,* Justice Walsh found the defendant guilty of seditious language, which was affirmed upon appeal *en banc* by Chief Justice Harvey. Justice Stuart, however, voiced a concern about such a broad interpretation of seditious intent. After later riots in Calgary over seditious utterances, Simmons upheld a guilty verdict upon appeal and, with Stuart again voicing his concerns, was joined by Beck and Stuart. Another round of convictions was handed down by Harvey in Red Deer in September 1916. The final case was Arthur Trainor's conviction by Simmons in Calgary for suggesting in a Strathmore drugstore that the sinking of the *Lusitania* was no worse than the British starving German civilians. Found guilty by Simmons, the appeal was drafted by Stuart, who held for the majority that Trainor had not raised disaffection against the government and that such words were morally bankrupt, not seditious.[135] He closed with his general observations on how such recent prosecutions had brought a lack of dignity to the law. While such offences continued to be prosecuted throughout 1917 and 1918, none brought convictions. Both Stuart and Beck believed in putting the public welfare above partisanship, and believed that the rule of law should promote amity between peoples rather than unbridled zeal.

§ EXPANDING LEGAL RESOURCES

Challenging interpretations of the law required wide reading, and the prairies were not known as a centre of higher education. But the judges carried their educational experiences with them, and through the Law Society ensured that significant legal resources would be made available. The Law Society of the North-West Territories had gathered a rich collection of English sources that was housed in the court libraries of the assize towns. By 1921 the judges insisted to the Benchers that they must have subscriptions to the major sources at their front-line courthouses at Calgary, Edmonton, Lethbridge, Medicine Hat, Fort Macleod, Red Deer, and Wetaskiwin. These libraries became the major venues for Beck, Stuart, and Scott, who, in an extreme example, cited twenty-one English cases in assessing whether an Ontario judgment should be enforced in Alberta.[136] Harvey was more interested in Canadian cases—especially those from Ontario and the Supreme Court of Canada.

Thus the new Law Society of Alberta was concerned with the provision of legal sources from its inaugural meeting. While its predecessor Law Society of the North-West Territories had been generous with its allowances, there had been a hiatus with the transfer of authority. Therefore, at the Benchers' meeting of 4 December 1907, $8,400 was allocated to books and journals for the courthouse libraries noted above.[137] Acquisitions continued to occupy an important part of the Benchers' semi-annual meetings throughout the period, although financial problems caused a new policy to be set in 1909. There would be first-class libraries for every circuit court town, second-class libraries wherever there was a resident justice, and small reference libraries where there were deputy clerks. In addition, limits were set for library holdings in any new judicial district.[138]

The major works used by the judges were primarily of English common law, not only because the judges had knowledge of it, but also because the final court of appeal was Great Britain's Judicial Committee of the Privy Council. As the Chief Justice put it, in any conflict "we must be bound by the decision of the Privy Council."[139] The common law, however, was more than England's. As he wrote in another case, an English judgment "should not be binding on us, and should not be followed unless it approves itself as reasonable."[140] Gradually Canadian and American sources were cited with greater frequency, especially as litigation concerning railways and automobiles increased.

Key sources for the Supreme Court were its own reports. While the predecessor court was well served with Beck as its editor, he was now a judge and the new province required law reporting. The first publisher of Alberta decisions was the *Western Law Reporter* (*WLR*), which was founded by Carswell in 1905 to publish western Canadian reports including those of the new provinces. Edited in Winnipeg, the *WLR* published thirty-four volumes (three a year) through 1916. A new entrant, however, arrived in 1910 when W. Kent Power, law teacher and author, Haligonian and graduate of Dalhousie Law School, who had worked as a law writer in New York, moved to Calgary to take up the editorship of the new *Western Weekly Reports* (*WWR*) in 1910. The internal evidence suggests that Power allied with the local Calgary publisher Burroughs to launch this competitor to Carswell's *WLR*. Power was styled Editor-in-Chief, appointed associate editors for each province, and enlarged its size and coverage. The result was that Carswell closed down the *WLR* in 1916. Power himself left the *WWR*, which became the dominant law reporter in the west, in 1918 to focus his energies on the *Alberta Law Reports* and the writing of legal texts and treatises.[141]

Power had a vision for creating a western Canadian law and soon became a major figure in the legal world of the province. The Law Society of Alberta had hired William Pentlowe Taylor as the first editor of the *Alberta Law Reports* (*ALR*) in 1907–8. After slow progress and uneven quality, the Society dismissed him in 1912 and brought in Power to co-edit volume three, and then take over volume four, both volumes being published in 1913. His appointment not only brought up-to-date volumes in a timely fashion, it also brought a departure by focussing his text on decisions made in chambers, for the instruction of the practising bar. Having established himself as editor, in 1914 Power wrote to the Benchers objecting to their expectation that all of the Court's decisions *en banc* ought to be published *verbatim*. Preferring shorter versions, his caveat was to raise his salary if they did not agree with the request. The Benchers eagerly participated in critiquing his work by examining texts of sample cases, shortened and un-shortened. Their final agreement was to allow abridgment on a case by case basis with the assent of the Chief Justice. Power's salary remained the same.[142] Despite this disagreement, the Law Society's Convocation commended his work in 1917, when Power brought in his Calgary publisher, Burroughs, to take over from the Canada Law Book Company, and he remained editor through 1922.

Power also filled the need for local legal publishing. Believing that legal identity came from compilations of legal learning and legal treatises, he compiled a mammoth seven-volume *Canadian Encyclopedic Digest* for the four western provinces (Calgary: Burroughs, 1919–1925), accompanied by *Power's Western Practice Digest: An Index-Digest of Western Practice Cases in Civil Actions to the end of 1920* (Calgary: Burroughs, 1921). His purpose was to put together the case law of the four western provinces because, in his mind, this was a new law for a new country.[143] Original subscribers included prairie law libraries and Supreme Court justices Stuart and Walsh. And when Powers had a hand in Burroughs taking over the publication of the ALR, the Canada Law Book Company of Toronto censured the University of Alberta Law Faculty for its discrimination against central Canadian publishers, which University President Tory called "a fiction of your imagination." Clearly, the law made by the SCA, as well as its publication, was going to remain western Canadian. Later on, when the possibility of discontinuing the ALR was debated in 1925–28, members strongly objected on the grounds that it represented Alberta's legal history and was more accurate and informative than those of competitors.[144]

Possessing an unflagging interest in legal education, Power played a prominent role in its development and acted as Registrar of the ill-fated Faculty of Law for the University of Calgary in 1912. When students in Calgary petitioned for lectures in the city, Power and others organized sixty lectures. He personally delivered thirty lectures to Calgary students in autumn 1912, and sixty in 1913. They were considered, however, to be of poor quality, read largely from texts with little advance preparation.[145] Hearing the complaints, he promised Convocation that he had no ambition to be a law teacher. Named King's Counsel in 1936, he died in 1961 at the age of 76.

Reading the Supreme Court judges' bench-books, written opinions, and published reports, one can summarize how the judges used these resources in their research process as follows.[146] Taking into consideration the cases, statutes, and legal writings cited by counsel, they turned to legal encyclopaedias, digests, and treatises to identify what additional original sources they wished to consult. The most often used were the *American and English Encyclopedia of Law* (2nd ed., 32 vols. 1896–1905), the *Cyclopedia of Procedure and Practice* (40 vols. 1905–12), and Halsbury's *Laws of England,* which were used and cited as its thirty-one volumes appeared from 1907 to 1917. The *Cyclopedia,* published in New York, traced its origins to Sir Francis Bacon and contained cases from all common law countries. The *American and English,* also published in New York, was a more complete textbook for British, American, and Canadian cases. Halsbury, however, published in London, became the judges' touchstone for English law by 1921. They did not much use the new American encyclopedia, or the *Corpus Juris* that came out with volume one in 1914 and took twenty-five years to produce seventy-two volumes. The judges' most commonly used digests and treatises are listed in Table 6.

The original sources were primarily cases and statutes. Most courthouse libraries had the *English Reports Annotated* (10 vols. 1866–69), and subscribed to the *English Reports Reprint,* which contained all the original English published law reports from the sixteenth century in 178 volumes from 1900 to 1932. Some libraries also had the *Lawyer's Reports Annotated,* a 70-volume edition (1888–1906) of U.S. state and territorial cases. The Calgary and Edmonton courthouse libraries had all the English *Statutes at Large,* in addition to the Canadian federal and provincial statutes, and the United States federal enactments. They seemed to have little need, however, of American state statutes and law reports, which were infrequently acquired. The judges appeared to gain access to these other works quite swiftly. Harvey, giving judgment in a case on estoppel, wrote that the latest word was contained in volume 13 of Halsbury's *Laws,* which was published "within the last few months."[148] Scott referred to a case decided by the Judicial Committee of the Privy Council within two months of its writing.[149] And in 1920, the Court referred to Hogg's *Registration of Title to Land Throughout the Empire* that was published in that year.[150]

§ THE LEGACY

The first Supreme Court of Alberta can be seen as trying to preserve the rule of law that it inherited from the Supreme Court of the North-West Territories and, at the same time, adapting the law to a rapidly growing, ethnically diverse society. The judges were well aware of new social and cultural demands emerging against the backdrop of the horrendous carnage of the World War in concert with the rise of new industries; new social, economic, and moral concerns; and split families. While judges are often accused of being passive in the face of rapid change, to their credit the judges of the SCA sought to respond, albeit in a limited manner. While economic issues dominated the Court's agenda from 1907 to 1914, social ones emerged in the war years, such as divorce and ethnicity. A burgeoning caseload could be met by additional appointments to the Court, coupled with new judicial districts for growing settlements. But rendering decisions that alleviated problems rather than assuaging them was more difficult. Justice William George Morrow, later judicial reformer and visionary who studied the early courts, noted this distinction: the original Supreme Court had to wrestle with new social and economic problems, and in doing so the judges had the perspicacity to establish a jurisprudence that served the needs of the people.[151] [See Illustration 17]

The problem, as one author put it, was that by the war's height in 1917, "Men came home slowly and haphazardly to an economy that often could not facilitate them, to a society that could not understand them, and wives who no longer loved them."[152] Thus legal issues such as ownership of property and goods, debt, mortgages, mechanic's liens, alcohol, prostitution, separation, and divorce became more exacerbated. A sign of the times was when Justice Beck, a Roman Catholic, went out of his way in *Board v. Board* to state unequivocally that his religion did not bar him from hearing petitions for divorce: "my duty is to find the true facts and to declare the *civil law* applicable to those facts."[153] The Alberta legislature could change and make new provincial laws, and create a police force to enforce them, but it was up to the courts to determine how such laws would be interpreted and applied.

The evidence in this essay suggests that the SCA adapted common law principles to the situations that it confronted, and provided an "Alberta" solution to problems that were germane not only to the province, but to other regions of the country as well. This included being receptive to legal remedies found elsewhere in the common law world, a liberal interpretation of statutes to apply to local situations, the protection of individual over corporate rights, and the promotion of civil liberties. Reaching majority decisions, moreover, resorted at times to intellectual currents that were adrift south of the border. Initially, the early judges of the United States Supreme Court held that law was not just its black letters, but the philosophical mindset that lay behind it.[154] Later, in the early twentieth century, that Court's judges became more cognizant of moral science and philosophy, and applied their larger understanding of the world in which they lived to the cases that came before them.[155] Judges, authoritative with a sense of independence from the executive and legislature, eschewing formalities and pretension, were confident of their abilities to interpret the law within the context of the values of the community as they perceived them. They were not tied to business interests, and they sought to have their opinions respected in the communities they served. These attributes fit the judges of Alberta. The provincial bar, however, would not admit of such intellectual excursions. As the Society's Benchers put it in 1912, before Walsh's appointment, the qualities required in judges of appeal were simply "a profound knowledge of law and the ability to apply legal principles to an admitted state of facts."[156] What the Benchers actually got, however, was much more than that. The judges, committed to provide law for a new people moving onto an old land, and combative in personalities, politics, and legal reasoning, were also, as Justice McClung put it, "unique and colourful."

AUTHOR'S NOTE: I wish to thank Jim Philips and Jonathan Swainger, and the anonymous readers of the manuscript, for their astute criticisms and suggestions, and my wife Maggie for her painstaking editing, leaving all errors and misunderstandings to myself. I also wish to thank the librarians and archivists at the Glenbow-Alberta Institute, the Legal Archives Society of Alberta, the Provincial Archives of Alberta, and the University of Calgary Law and Mackimmie Libraries for their assistance, and the LASA for accessing and providing permission to publish the illustrations.

NOTES

1 Louis Knafla and Richard Klumpenhouwer, *Lords of the Western Bench: A Biographical History of the Supreme and District Courts of Alberta, 1876–1990* (Calgary: Legal Archives Society of Alberta, 1997), ix.
2 British North America Act (GB 1871), 34 & 35 Victoria, c. 28. Appointed by the Commissioner of the North-West Mounted Police, the first justices were police magistrates, an office having its origins in London in the 1690s and extended to other English boroughs by the 1830s. See J.M. Beattie, *Policing and Punishment in London, 1660–1750—Urban Crime and the Limits of Terror* (Oxford: Oxford University Press, 2001), 91–100, and Roderick G. Martin, "The North-West Mounted Police and Frontier Justice, 1874-1898" (PHD dissertation, University of Calgary, 2005), 161–71.
3 North-West Territories Act (CAN 1875), c. 49, in the *Revised Statutes of Canada* (1886), c. 50, s.48; a discussion is in S.M. Jackson, "Stipendiary Magistrates and Lay Justices," *Modern Law Review* 9, no.1 (1946): 1–12. The first police magistrates for what would become Alberta were Colonel James F. Macleod and L.F.N. Crozier: Knafla and Klumpenhouwer, *Lords of the Western Bench*, 92–94; R.C. Macleod, "Macleod, James Farquharson," *Dictionary of Canadian Biography* [cited hereafter DCB], vol. XII, *1891 to 1900* (Toronto: University of Toronto Press, 1990), 672–75; and Bob Beal, "Crozier, Lief Newry Fitzroy," DCB, vol. XIII, *1901 to 1910*, 232–35.
4 Roderick G. Martin, "Macleod at Law: A Judicial Biography of James Farquharson Macleod, 1874-94," in *People and Place: Historical Influences on Legal Culture*, ed. Jonathan Swainger and Constance Backhouse (Vancouver: UBC Press, 2003), 37–59.
5 Horace Harvey, "The Early Administration of Justice in the North West," *Alberta Law Quarterly* 1 (1954): 13. See Harvey's analysis (pp. 1–15) of the British and Canadian legislation concerning the NWT from 1690.
6 Administration of Justice Act (CAN 1885), and An Act further to amend the law respecting the North-West Territories (CAN 1886), c. 25.
7 Supreme Court of Judicature Act, 38 & 39 Victoria (GB 1873), c. 77.
8 The assessment of Roderick G. Martin in "The Common Law and Justices of the Supreme Court of the North-West Territories: The First Generation, 1887-1907," in *Laws and Societies in the Canadian Prairie West, 1670–1940*, ed. Louis A. Knafla and Jonathan Swainger (Vancouver: UBC Press, 2005), 211–31 at 225.
9 J.E. Cote, "The Introduction of English Law into Alberta," *Alberta Law Review* [cited hereafter *Alta LR*] 3 (1964): 266–74.

10 Louis A. Knafla, "Introduction: Law and Societies in the Anglo-Canadian North-West Frontier and Prairie Provinces, 1670-1940," in *Laws and Societies*, Knafla and Swainger, 31.
11 See Brian Titley, *The Frontier World of Edgar Dewdney* (Vancouver: UBC Press, 1999).
12 Louis A. Knafla, "Law and Justice," in *The Encyclopedia of Saskatchewan: A Living Legacy* (Regina: Canadian Plains Research Center, 2005), 537-38.
13 C.C. McCaul, "Precursors of the Bench and Bar," *Canadian Bar Review* 3 (1925): 39.
14 NWT, *Territorial Law Reports* 3 (1897): 7-13.
15 Provincial Archives of Alberta [cited hereafter PAA], 78.235, case files for the judicial district of southern Alberta.
16 *R. v. Nan-E-Quis-A-Ka*, NWT, *Territories Law Reports* [cited hereafter TLR] 1 (1889): 211.
17 TLR 3: 319, writing for the court *en banc*.
18 *Rex v. Canadian Pacific Railway*, NWT, TLR 7 (1904-05): 286-87. The provincial Railway Act (1907 [AB] c.8 s.192) was upheld by Harvey in *R. v. C.P.R.*, AB, TLR 7 (1907): 443, and reversed by the SCC in *C.P.R. v. R.*, *Supreme Court Reports* [cited hereafter SCR] 39 (1907): 476. For the larger subject see Roderick Graham Martin, "The Common Law and the Justices of the Supreme Court of the North-West Territories, 1887-1907" (MA thesis, University of Calgary, 1997), 118-21.
19 Martin, "Common Law and Justices," 68-72.
20 Knafla and Klumpenhouwer, *Lords of the Western Bench*, 189-90.
21 See Michael Payne, "A Very Political Profession," a study of lawyers as politicians in the *Centennial History of the Law Society of Alberta* (Irwin Law, 2006), forthcoming.
22 Harvey, "Early Administration," 15.
23 1906 (AB), cc. 3, 6, 13, 15, 17; 1906 (SA), cc. 7, 19-21, 23, 45.
24 *The Formation of Alberta: A Documentary History*, ed. Douglas Owram (Edmonton: Alberta Records Publication Board, 1979), 372-86.
25 Order-in-Council, 17 September 1906, PAA file 6910-8-9-2.
26 1905 (AB), c. 3 s. 16(2).
27 See, for example, *Correspondence, Reports...Dominion and Provincial Legislation 1867-1895*, ed. W.E. Hodgins (Ottawa, 1896), 1236-79.
28 Supreme Court Act (AB 1907), c. 3.
29 *Public Statutes of Alberta 1906-15, Consolidated* (1907), cap 3, ss. 5-32.
30 The original judicial districts established in 1906 were Lethbridge, Macleod, Calgary, Wetaskiwin, and Edmonton. See "New Judicial Districts," *The Alberta Gazette—Extra*, 17 September 1906, 1-4.
31 Orders-in-Council, PAA, file 6910-8-9-2. Sub-judicial districts were established at Bassano and Taber in 1914, Lacombe in 1916, Camrose in 1918, and Grand Prairie in 1920.
32 *Reeves v. Chase*, Alberta Law Reports [cited hereafter ALR] 1 (1908): 277.
33 *R. v. Thompson*, ALR 4, no. 18 [1912]: the quote at 25.
34 Horace Harvey, "Formerly Rupert's Land," *Obiter Dicta* (Fall 1948): 37.
35 An Act to amend the Statute Law (AB 1913), c. 9 s. 38.
36 Ibid., the judges *en banc* to be known as Appellate Judges.

37 The Judicature Act (1919) c. 3, and *An Act respecting the Supreme Court and the Administration of Justice* (1920) ss. 2-4. The proclamation is in *The Alberta Gazette*, vol. 17 (1921), 472-73.
38 David Mittelstadt, *Foundations of Justice: Alberta's Historic Courthouses* (Calgary: University of Calgary Press, 2005), xix-xxiv.
39 Ibid., 151-55.
40 Ibid., 195-209.
41 Louis A. Knafla, "Macdonald, James Alexander (1858-1939)," in DCB, vol. XVI, *1931 to 1940* (forthcoming).
42 The terms *Upper* and *Lower Canada* have been used for Canada West and East for the period 1841-67 throughout the chapter as the legal terms for the colonies: Margaret A. Banks, "Upper and Lower Canada or Canada West and East, 1841-67?" *Canadian Historical Review* LIV, no. 4 (1973), 473-80.
43 Scott also saw considerable military service, defending against the Fenian invasion of 1866 and becoming a lieutenant-colonel in 1879. Retiring from service in 1883, he retained his rank and organized a volunteer company in Regina for the Indian and Métis rising in 1884, and a militia company to put down the uprising in April-May 1885.
44 See *The Queen v. Louis Riel*, ed. Desmond Morton (Toronto, 1974), and Bob Beal and Rod Macleod, *Prairie Fire—The 1885 North-West Rebellion* (Edmonton: Prairie Books, 1984), 321-22.
45 *Regina Leader Post*, October 1894.
46 For general biographical details, see Louis A. Knafla, "Scott, David Lynch," DCB, vol. XV, *1921 to 1930* (2005), 910-11; and Knafla and Klumpenhouwer, *Lords of the Western Bench*, 163-64.
47 Ibid.
48 *R. v. Banks*, TLR 2 (1894): 8; *Cragg v. Lamarsh*, TLR 3, (1898): 91; and *R. ex Rel. Thompson v. Dinnin*, TLR 3 (1898): 112.
49 Knafla and Klumpenhouwer, *Lords of the Western Bench*, 163-64.
50 A theme throughout his judicial decisions, especially in his judgments contained in the civil trial books of the Northern District, Supreme Court of Alberta: PAA, Fonds 79.266.
51 Scott's judicial letter and notebooks for 1894-1899, and 1902-1904: PAA, Fonds 69.310.
52 Biographical details in Knafla and Klumpenhouwer, *Lords of the Western Bench*, 163-64, and *The Calgary Daily Herald*, 18 July 1924.
53 For biographical details, see David J. Hall, "Sifton, Arthur Lewis Watkins," DCB, vol. XV, *1921 to 1930* (2005), 937-41; and Knafla and Klumpenhouwer, *Lords of the Western Bench*, 165-67.
54 *Rex v. Clark*, ALR, 1st ser., 1 (1907): 358 at 361-68 (oral), and *Great West Implement Co. v. Grams*, ALR, 1st ser., 1 (1908): 411 at 414-15
55 For example, at Calgary, PAA 79.285 *passim*, and at Macleod, PAA 78.233 *passim*, 1907-9.
56 See ALR 1-2 (1907-09), *passim*.
57 Legal Archives Society of Alberta [cited hereafter LASA], Arthur Lewis Sifton fonds 11-00-00.
58 *R. v. Clarke*, ALR, 1st ser., 1 (1908): 358.
59 *R. v. Lawrence* (1904), unreported.

60 *Canadian Annual Review* (1903), 195, quoting the *Regina West*.
61 Knafla and Klumpenhouwer, *Lords of the Western Bench*, 68-71. Harvey is the only early justice to receive a full biographical and judicial study: William Bowker, "The Honourable Horace Harvey, Chief Justice of Alberta," *The Canadian Bar Review* 32, no. 9 (Nov. 1954): 933-81, 1118-39. While noteworthy, there is an insufficient critical focus.
62 *R. v. Schmolke*, ALR 14 (1919): 601 (Harvey's decision), and *R. v. Hartfeil*, ALR 16 (1920): 22.
63 Harvey's contributions here are well examined by Bowker, *Legal Writings*, 943-51.
64 *R. v. Cyr*, ALR 1st ser., 12 (1917): 320.
65 David Mittelstadt, "Calgary's Early Courts," in *Remembering Chinook Country*, ed. Chinook Country Historical Society (Calgary: Detselig Enterprises Ltd., 2005), 203-4.
66 Denied by the SCC in *Reference as to Meaning of the Word "Persons" in Section 24 of the British North America Act, 1867*, SCR (1928): 276; but allowed by the Judicial Committee of the Privy Council: *Edwards v. Attorney General for Canada* [1930], *Appeal Cases* 124. See Catherine Cavanaugh, "Out of the West: History, Memory, and the 'Persons' Case, 1919-2000," in *Forging Alberta's Constitutional Framework*, ed. Richard Connors and John M. Law (Edmonton: University of Alberta Press, 2005), 137-64.
67 *Re. Lewis*, ALR 1st ser., 13 (1918): 411.
68 *Re. Norton, Western Weekly Reports* [cited hereafter WWR] 2 (1918): 865.
69 *Re. Gray*, SCR 57 (1918): 150. For the most recent discussion of the controversy surrounding the Norton and Gray cases, see Wayne Renke, "The Power of Law: Judicial Independence and the Supreme Court of Alberta," in this volume.
70 For general biographical information, see Knafla and Klumpenhouwer, *Lords of the Western Bench*, 176-78.
71 *R. v. Hartfeil*, ALR 1st ser., 16 (1920): 19.
72 *The International Coal and Coke Co. v. Trelle*, ALR 1st ser., 1 (1907): 178.
73 *Gallagher v. Armstrong*, ALR 1st ser., 3 (1911): 443.
74 *R. v. Cyr (alias Waters)*, WWR 3 (1917): 849.
75 *Board v. Board*, WWR 2 (1918): 633. For a similar result in British Columbia, see *M., Falsely called S. v. S., British Columbia Law Reports* 1 (1877): 25.
76 For a discussion of the case see Allison Rankin, "Rescinding the Vow: Divorce in Alberta and Prairie Canada, 1905-1930" (MA thesis, University of Calgary, 1998), Chap. 5.
77 In *Gallagher v. Armstrong*, ALR 1st ser., 3 (1911): 443, he apologized for his delay in giving judgment as there were "four or five grave points of law on which there is little authority or precedent."
78 *R. v. Trainor*, WWR 1 (1917): 415.
79 *R. v. Stoney Joe, Canadian Native Law Reports* 1 (1981): 117. For a discussion of how the early Supreme Court of Alberta approached Aboriginal hunting cases, see Douglas Sanders, "The Queen's Promises," in Knafla, *Law & Justice in a New Land*, 101-27; and Brian Calliou, "The Supreme Court of Alberta and First Nations Treaty Hunting Rights: Federalism and Respect for 'the Queen's Promises,'" in this volume.

80 For general biographical information, see Richard A. Willie, "Beck, Nicholas Du Bois Dominic," DCB, vol. XV, *1921 to 1930* (2005), 69-71; and Knafla and Klumpenhouwer, *Lords of the Western Bench*, 17-18.
81 *Miner v. Canadian Pacific Railway*, ALR 1st ser., 3 (1911): 408, where he found in Australia "a case of very great important [sic] in connection with the subject under discussion."
82 LASA, Fonds 12-00-01 (1907-28).
83 See, for example, his notable opinions in *Alfred and Wickham v. Grand Trunk Pacific Railway Company*, WWR 1 (1911): 624, and on streetcar liability in *Harnovis v. City of Calgary*, WWR 4 (1913): 263; as well as throughout ALR 1st ser., 2-15 (1909-21), *passim*.
84 For biographical information, see Knafla and Klumpenhouwer, *Lords of the Western Bench*, 167-68.
85 Burt Harris, "Fighting Spirits: The Yukon Legal Profession, 1898-1912," in *British Columbia and the Yukon: Essays in the History of Canadian Law*, vol. VI, ed. Hamar Foster and John McLaren (Toronto: The Osgoode Society, 1995), 474-78, the quote at 476.
86 For biographical information, see Knafla and Klumpenhouwer, *Lords of the Western Bench*, 187-89.
87 *R. v. Picariello and Lassandro*, WWR 2 (1922): 872.
88 For example, *R. v. Brady*, ALR 1st ser., 5 (1913): 400; and *R. v. Jackson*, WWR 5 (1914): 1286.
89 Bruce Smith, "The Superior Courts of Alberta," *Alberta Law Review*. Anniversary Issue (1980), 3.
90 For general biographical information, see Knafla and Klumpenhouwer, *Lords of the Western Bench*, 74-75.
91 For example, *Royal Trust Company v. Fraser et al.*, ALR 1st ser., 12 (1917): 109; and *Crump et al v. McNeill et al.*, ALR 1st ser., 14 (1918): 206.
92 *R. v. Rose*, WWR 3 (1918): 950, where he upheld, reluctantly, the Liquor Act.
93 For general biographical information, see Knafla and Klumpenhouwer, *Lords of the Western Bench*, 76-77.
94 ALR 1st ser., 14-16 (1919-1921), *passim*.
95 *R. v. Solloway*, and *R. v. Mills*, WWR 1 (1930): 486, 779.
96 Bowker, *Legal Writings*, 618.
97 Larry L. Kulisek, "McCarthy, D'Alton," DCB, vol. XII, *1891 to 1900* (1990), 578-88.
98 Edmonton Bar Association papers, Fonds CB.1.E243A, Glenbow-Alberta Institute, Calgary [cited hereafter GAI].
99 Knafla and Klumpenhouwer, *Lords of the Western Bench*, 114-15. His legal career in Edmonton is summarized in the *Edmonton Journal*, 19 May 1930.
100 Oral interview of John Macleod, 21 May 1964, by May Harbin: GAI, Tape Fonds D920/H255.
101 Oral interview of George Skene, 17 Aug. 1964, by May Harbin: GAI, Tape Fonds D920/H255.
102 The civil trial books of the Northern District, Supreme Court of Alberta, Fonds 79.266, PAA, Edmonton.
103 *R. v. Wilson*, WWR 15 (1919): 159; *White and Walker v. Grand Trunk Pacific Company*, ALR 1st ser., 11 (1916): 260, and *McLean v. C.P.R.*, WLR 1 (1917): 1466; *Denmore v.*

       Trusts and Guarantee Company, ALR 1st ser., 1 (1919): 32, and *Simpson v. Tasker Grain Company*, ALR 1st ser., 15 (1920): 138.
104 See especially the cases in ALR 1st ser., 14 (1919): 416 at 427–32, ALR 1st ser., 14 (1919): 534 at 537–41 and 512 at 580–82; ALR 1st ser., 15 (1919): 17 at 25–30, and 31 at 39–43, and ALR 1st ser., 15 (1920): 537 at 543–46.
105 *R. v. Wilson*, WWR 15 (1919): 159.
106 For biographical details see Louis A. Knafla, "McCarthy, Maitland Stewart," *DCB*, vol. XV, *1921 to 1930* (2005), 618–19.
107 This view coincides with that of Bowker, *Legal Writings*, 624.
108 *Northern Crown Bank v. Woodcrafts*, ALR 1st ser., 14 (1919): 480.
109 Douglas Francis, "'Rural Ontario West': Ontarians in Alberta," in *Peoples of Alberta: Portraits of Cultural Diversity*, ed. Howard & Tamara Palmer (Saskatoon: Western Producer Prairie Books, 1985), 131–35.
110 Louis A. Knafla, "Introduction: Laws and Societies in the Anglo-Canadian North-West Frontier and Prairie Provinces, 1670-1940," in *Laws and Societies in the Canadian Prairie West, 1670–1940*, ed. Knafla and Jonathan Swainger (Vancouver: UBC Press, 2005), 30–32.
111 For example, Beck, in *The Canadian Pacific Railroad Company v. Meadows*, ALR 1st ser., 1 (1908): 344, and *Colonial Investment Company v. Borland*, ALR 1st ser., 5 (1912): 13; and Scott in *Ross v. Gorman*, ALR 1st ser., 1 (1908): 109 and the appeal *en banc* at 516.
112 *Risler v. Alta. Newspapers Ltd.*, ALR 1st ser., 14 (1919): 464.
113 *Colonial Investment Co. v. Borland*, ALR 1st ser., 5 (1911): 71.
114 David R. Williams, "Judges at War: Mr Justice Martin vs. Chief Justice Hunter," *The Gazette* 16 (1982), 295–333.
115 ALR, 1st ser.
116 See n. 42 above.
117 Bowker, "The Honourable Horace Harvey," in *Legal Writings*, 59–117 at 66.
118 *Scott v. A.-G. for Canada*, Dominion Law Reports 4 (1923): 647, reversing SCR 64 (1922): 135.
119 Justice Ronald Martland interview, Calgary Bar Association Oral History Project, 19 May 1983, LASA fonds 09-00-05, vol. 12, file 56.
120 *McNiven v. Smith*, ALR 1st ser., 14 (1919): 550.
121 *R. v. Schmolke*, ALR 1st ser., 14 (1919): 602.
122 *McCormack v. McCormack*, ALR 1st ser., 15 (1920): 490.
123 *Ellis v. Fruchtman*, ALR 1st ser., 5 (1912): 456.
124 *Alfred & Wickham v. Grand Trunk Pacific Railway Co.*, ALR 1st ser., 5 (1912): 447; and *R. v. O'Brien*, ALR 1st ser., 15 (1919): 64.
125 See Justice W.G. Morrow, "An Historical Examination of Alberta's Legal System—The First Seventy-Five Years," *Alta LR* 1 (1981): 148–70.
126 Howard Palmer, "Patterns of Immigration and Ethnic Settlement in Alberta, 1880-1920," in his *Peoples of Alberta*, xiv-xv, 1–23.
127 Zhiqui Lin and Augustine Brannigan, "The Implications of a Provincial Police Force in Alberta and Saskatchewan," in Knafla and Swainger, *Laws and Societies*, 237–49 for Alberta in this period.
128 For Edmonton and northern Alberta see J.W. McClung, *Law West of the Bay* (privately printed, 1997); and for Red Deer, Jonathan Swainger, "Law in the Parkland: A History of the Red Deer Judicial District, 1907-1920" (University

of Calgary, MA thesis, 1987), which is still an unsurpassed study of the subject.
129 Louis A. Knafla, "Violence on the Western Canadian Frontier: A Historical Perspective," in *Violence in Canada: Sociopolitical Perspectives*, ed. Jeffrey Ian Ross (Somerset, NJ: Transaction Publishers, 2nd ed., 2004), 10–39, and the authors cited in *Violent Crime in North America*, ed. Louis A. Knafla (Westport: Praeger, 2003), xi–xiv.
130 *Census of Population and Agriculture of the Northwest Provinces: Manitoba, Saskatchewan, Alberta. 1906* (Ottawa: S.E. Dawson, 1907), 101; *Census of Prairie Provinces. Population and Agriculture: Manitoba, Saskatchewan, Alberta. 1916* (Ottawa: King's Printer, 1918), xx; and *Census of the Prairie Provinces 1921*, vol. I: *Population and Agriculture* (Ottawa: King's printer, 1922), 223.
131 *Schenck v. United States*, US 249 (1919): 47.
132 Louis A. Knafla and Susan W.S. Binnie, "Beyond the State: Law and Legal Pluralism in the Making of Modern Societies," in their edited *Law, Society, and the State: Essays in Modern Legal History* (Toronto: University of Toronto Press, 1995), 19–20.
133 The 1906 Census recorded 13.1 per cent of British descent, and 15 per cent of continental European; the divergence would have been even larger by 1916: David Hall, "1904-1905 Alberta Proclaimed," in *Alberta Formed Alberta Transformed*, ed. Michael Payne, Donald Wetherell, and Catherine Cavanagh (Edmonton: University of Alberta Press, 2006), vol. 1, 335.
134 A major study of these cases that supersedes all previous work and is summarized here is Jonathan Swainger, "Wagging Tongues and Empty Heads: Seditious Utterances and the Patriotism of Wartime in Central Alberta, 1914-1918," in *Law, Society, and the State*, Knafla and Binnie, 263–89.
135 *R. v. Trainor*, ALR 1st ser., 10 (1916): 171–74. Only Walsh dissented.
136 *Mills v. McGrath*, ALR 1st ser., 1 (1907): 32.
137 LASA, Minute Books, Fonds 5/1, p. 7.
138 Ibid., Fonds 5/3, p. 151.
139 *Miner v. Canadian Pacific Railway*, ALR 1st ser., 3 (1911): 408.
140 *R. v. Girvin*, ALR 1st ser., 3 (1911): 387.
141 This description is based on my reading of the law reports through the years under discussion.
142 Ibid., Fonds 5/12, pp. 46–49.
143 From the introduction, p. 1. This was first suggested by myself, before I saw Power's book, in "From Oral to Written Memory: The Common Law Tradition in Western Canada," in *Law & Justice in a New Land: Essays in Western Canadian Legal History* (Toronto, Calgary, Vancouver: Carswell, 1986), 67–68.
144 Peter M. Sibenik, "The Doorkeepers: The Governance of Territorial and Alberta Lawyers, 1885-1928" (MA thesis, University of Calgary, 1984), 25, 51–60, the quote at 80, n. 176.
145 Sibenik, "Doorkeepers," 116–19.
146 I wish to thank Lillian MacPherson, whose paper on "The Supreme Court of Alberta: The First Fifteen Years" (1984), written for me in a Directed Research course for the Faculty of Law, University of Calgary, sparked my original interest in this subject. Later seminars devoted to the early legal history of

Alberta, both in the Law Faculty and History Department, allowed me to expand this area.
147 Many others were used occasionally throughout the period. Judges may also have had their own libraries, but I have been unable to find any information on that for these judges.
148 *Hatfield v. Canadian Pacific Railway Co.*, ALR 1st ser., 3 (1911): 309.
149 *Smith v. Doll*, ALR 1st ser., 3 (1911): 383.
150 *Brogden v. Brogden*, ALR 1st ser., 15 (1920): 494.
151 W.G. Morrow, "An Historical Examination of Alberta's Legal System—The First Seventy-Five Years," *Alta LR* 19 (1980): 148–50.
152 Rankin, "Divorce in Alberta," 121.
153 *Board v. Board*, WWR 2 (1918): 662.
154 See in general, Adrienne Siegel, *The Marshall Court, 1801–1835* (Associated Press, 1987).
155 Mark Warren Bailey, *Guardians of the Moral Order: The Legal Philosophy of the Supreme Court, 1860–1910* (De Kalb: Northern Illinois University Press, 2004).
156 LASA, Minute Books, Fonds 5/9, p. 42.

TWO

The Power of Law
Judicial Independence and the Supreme Court of Alberta, 1918

WAYNE N. RENKE

THE SUPREME COURT OF CANADA developed a robust jurisprudence concerning judicial independence around the close of the twentieth century. For the most part, the cases have centred on the provincial courts and, more recently, justices of the peace, in their relations with provincial governments. The following principles have been established: Judicial independence has both an express and unwritten constitutional foundation. It is justified because it is necessary to protect the constitution and constitutional rights, and because it ensures public confidence in the administration of justice. It has two dimensions—individual, relating to the independence of particular judges; and institutional, relating to the independence of the court from other branches of government and other public and private interests. Both dimensions are assessed objectively. Further, judicial independence has three core characteristics—security of tenure, protecting judges from arbitrary dismissal; financial security, preserving judges from financial manipulation; and administrative independence, ensuring that judges control practical aspects of hearing cases.[1]

In the early jurisprudence of the Supreme Court of Alberta, judicial independence was more implicit than explicit. But in June and July 1918, a set of events occurred that threw the Court's conception of judicial independence into sharp relief.[2] From our perspective in the early twenty-first century, the Court's conception included both familiar and surprisingly unfamiliar elements. I shall discuss (1) the setting against which the events of the summer of 1918 played out; (II) the events of the summer of 1918; (III) familiar aspects of judicial independence that emerged through those events; and (IV) unfamiliar aspects of the Court's conception of judicial independence.

(I)

The setting for the events of the summer of 1918 was a shortfall in enlistments for the Canadian Expeditionary Force. The Militia Act (1906) established Canadians' duty to serve. Section 10 provided that "All the male inhabitants of Canada, of the age of eighteen years and upwards, and under sixty, not exempt or disqualified by law and being British subjects, shall be liable to service in the Militia: Provided that the Governor General may require all the male inhabitants of Canada, capable of bearing arms, to serve in the case of a *levée en masse*."[3] Under s. 16, "[t]he Militia of Canada shall be divided into Active and Reserve Militia," which was to consist of a corps raised by voluntary enlistment and a corps raised by ballot. Sections 26 and 27 dealt with raising corps by ballot. Section 26 provided that "[w]hen men are required to organize or complete a corps at any time…and enough men do not volunteer to complete the quota required, the men liable to serve shall be drafted by ballot." Section 27 authorized the Governor in Council to make regulations concerning notifications to men balloted for service and for deciding exemptions. Finally, s. 69 provided that "[t]he Governor in Council may place the Militia… on active service anywhere in Canada, and also beyond Canada, for the defence thereof, at any time when it appears advisable so to do by reason of emergency."

Canada joined the Great War on 4 August 1914.[4] The War Measures Act, 1914, passed shortly after Canada entered the war, granted sweeping powers to the executive.[5] This statute did not expressly deal with the raising of military forces, although section six provided that:

> The Governor in Council shall have power to do and authorize such acts and things, and to make from time to time such orders and regulations, as he may by reason of the existence of real or apprehended war, invasion or insurrection deem necessary or advisable for the security, defence, peace, order and welfare of Canada; and for greater certainty, but not so as to restrict the generality of the foregoing terms, it is hereby declared that the powers of the Governor in Council

shall extend to all matters coming within the classes of subjects hereinafter enumerated, that is to say:

(a) censorship and the control and suppression of publications, writings, maps, plans, photographs, communications and means of communications;[6]
(b) arrest, detention, exclusion and deportation;
(c) control of the harbours, ports and territorial waters of Canada and the movements of vessels;
(d) transportation by land, air, or water and the control of the transport of persons and things;
(e) trading, exportation, importation, production and manufacture;
(f) appropriation, control, forfeiture and disposition of property and of the use thereof.

Conservative Prime Minister Robert Borden assured the public in December 1914 that Canada would not resort to conscription. At that time the promise was unnecessary. Enthusiasm for the cause was high and the nation was unified. Anglo Canadians and French Canadians made common cause against the Hun. Volunteers flowed into the ranks of the Canadian Expeditionary Force, with Alberta having one of the highest enlistment rates in the country.[7] According to one historian, "The enthusiastic support for the war was almost universal among the majority of Albertans, who were British by birth or descent."[8]

The readiness to volunteer was the product of several factors. First, it was widely believed that the war would be brief and that victory was sure. A front-page *Calgary Daily Herald* editorial on 5 August 1914 made the following pronouncement: "That success will crown our banners no Britisher doubts, for God is with the right. The star of Britain's empire, which has lit the path of civilization for a thousand years, will shine all the more brightly once these clouds are past."[9] A day later the same newspaper quoted a British attaché who claimed that "the week between August 16 and August 23 would determine in great measure whether Germany and Austria are to be dominate powers or be reduced to a condition of inferiority." "And of course," he added, "you know what we of England expect to happen."[10] These favourable odds fed into the romanticization of military service.[11] Further, many volunteers were recent immigrants from Britain and were inclined to join Britain's war effort for personal, familial, and cultural connections.[12] Finally, volunteers desired work. In 1914 Canada had been suffering from economic depression and the rate of unemployment was high. Soldiering provided a ready means of earning a living.[13]

On New Year's Day 1916, Prime Minister Borden pledged to raise the size of the Canadian Expeditionary Force to 500,000, although, at the time, Canada's population was only about 8 million. Yet within months recruiting had slowed dramatically as the unity of the late summer of 1914 was lost. French Canada had been alienated as the linguistic and cultural needs of French Canadian volunteers were systematically ignored. French Canadians lacked their English neighbours' ties of blood and memory to Britain. Conditions on the home front, including the eruption of the Ontario Schools conflict over French language education, eroded French Canada's motivation to participate in a war for the Empire. And despite war-time censorship, the story of the real war had come to Canada, and with the news an expectation of a rapid and easy victory evaporated. Not only were Canadian casualties high, but the pool of British-born volunteers had been exhausted. Lastly, by 1916 the war had energized the Canadian economy which, in turn, demanded greater agricultural and industrial production. The farms and factories needed workers. Wages and working conditions had improved and young men no longer needed military service to earn a living.[14]

Still, for the Prime Minister, reducing Canada's military contribution was unthinkable. There was a real risk that the war would be lost. The French army was close to mutiny, Russia was collapsing, and the German submarine offensive was enjoying troubling success. Borden may have believed that Canada itself was in danger. Having visited France, camps in England, and military hospitals, Borden resolutely believed that Canada could not break faith with its fighting men.[15] Therefore, on 18 May 1917, the Prime Minister presented Canadians with this message:

> All citizens are liable for the defence of their country and I conceive that the battle for Canadian liberty and autonomy is being fought today on the plains of France and Belgium....I know from my personal experience that [our soldiers] cannot realize the thought that their country, which summoned them to her service, will be content to desert and humiliate them.[16]

Men were needed, volunteers were no longer fulfilling the need, and conscription was therefore required.[17] The legislative foundation for conscription would be the Military Service Act, 1917.

The Military Service Act, 1917 was patterned on the United States' selective service law. In its preamble, the Act quoted ss. 10 and 69 of the Militia Act, referred to its s. 26, and asserted that the Canadian Expeditionary Force required reinforcements but that an insufficient number of men had volunteered. The preamble recognized that while many men had already volunteered, to sustain the "productivity of the Dominion," further men would be secured for military service "not by ballot as provided in the Militia Act, but by selective draft." To this end, s. 2 provided that (generally) all male British subjects ordinarily resident in Canada, under the age of 45, falling within one of six classes, and not falling within an exception set out in the Schedule to the Act, were liable to be called out to active service in the Canadian Expeditionary Force. Section 3 established the classes. Pursuant to s. 4, men falling within the classes were to be called out on active service by proclamation of the Governor in Council. The primary exception set out in the Schedule was for men who held a certificate of exemption granted under the Act.

The Act balanced the draft provisions with extensive provisions for exemptions. Section 11 allowed applications for exemptions on grounds that included the following: "it is expedient in the national interest that the [applicant] should, instead of being employed in military service, be engaged in other work in which he is habitually engaged;" "serious hardship...owing to his exceptional financial or business obligations or domestic position;" and conscientious objection.[18] Applications were made to "local tribunals," constituted under s. 6 of the Act and empowered to grant certificates of exemption. Rights of appeal were recognized under s. 10. Appeals went to "Appeal Tribunals" constituted under s. 7 of the Act. Under s. 8, the final appeal was to the "Central Appeal Judge," Mr Justice Lyman Duff of the Supreme Court of Canada.[19] The Act did not purport to replace the Militia Act but rather—under s. 13 (1)—the Militia Act, "so far as not inconsistent therewith," formed part of the Act.

Opposed by farmers, trade union leaders, and nearly unanimously by French Canada, the prospect of conscription threatened to fracture the country. To avoid this fate and to mend divisions within his own party, on 25 May 1917 Borden sought out Liberal leader Wilfrid Laurier in an attempt to bring him into a wartime coalition government. Laurier refused. Borden then set about the task of creating the

Union coalition (including Conservatives, non-Laurier Liberals, and Independents) and marshalling support for conscription. The coalition and its platform were finally unveiled in early October. In the midst of these efforts and confident of success thanks to its majority in the House of Commons, Borden's Conservatives introduced the Military Service Act, 1917 on 11 June. After "long and heated debate," the Act was passed and received royal assent on 29 August 1917. The first conscripts were summoned on 13 October 1917 and ordered to report in January 1918.[20]

Having pushed the conscription bill through the House, Borden then led the Union coalition to the national polls on a platform of conscription, an end to political patronage, and women's suffrage. The election was tremendously important and decisive. It certainly contributed to the persisting divisions between French and English Canada. The editor ("Politicus") of the *Calgary Daily Herald* claimed that there "never was an election in Canada of such importance as the present one."[21] The focus of this editorial, however, was not on conscription, but on the perils of subordination to Laurier and his French Canadian compatriots. They were "opposed to military service, opposed to western development, opposed to religious tolerance, indifferent to everything except the narrow sectional interests of their own province."[22] Politicus went on: "We in Western Canada, if we would save our country from the terrible evils of racial domination, must vote on behalf of English-speaking Canada."[23] Cartoons in the *Calgary Daily Herald* showed that Fritz was pleased with Laurier's policies.[24] On 15 December the *Calgary Daily Herald* ran a story claiming that "Hun Writer Says Laurier Will Succeed."[25] When the votes were counted, the Unionists had won handily, carrying 11 of 12 seats in Alberta.[26]

The passage of the Military Service Act, 1917 and the Union coalition victory at the polls did little to settle the national debate over conscription. Indeed, events were seemingly conspiring against Borden. In early 1918 no one could have predicted the imminent end of the war. The Germans had launched a successful offensive in March 1918 and the government was uncertain whether a sufficient number of conscripts would be called up.[27] Fearing such a shortfall, in April 1918 the Union government moved to revoke the Act's exemptions.[28]

On 20 April 1918, the Governor in Council passed two orders-in-council under the War Measures Act, 1914. The first, P.C. 919, effectively repealed the exemptions established under the Military Service Act, 1917. P.C. 919 recited that given the "urgent need of reinforcements" it was deemed "essential" that "a substantial number of men should be withdrawn forthwith from the civil life for the purpose of serving in a military capacity." Further, the pressing need did not allow the "examination by exemption tribunals of the value in civil life, or the position, of the individuals called up for duty." Therefore, all exemptions were cancelled as of the date that each individual was ordered to report and no further requests for exemptions would be entertained or considered.[29] The second order-in-council, P.C. 962, directed certain men to report for duty, notwithstanding any prior exemptions.[30] The two orders-in-council were submitted to both Houses of Parliament on 20 April 1918, and were approved and came into force by resolutions of both Houses. This resolution process did not transform the orders-in-council into Acts of Parliament; and this process was not equivalent to the process used to pass Acts.

The elimination of the conscription exemptions ignited protest across the nation. Beginning on 29 March and continuing until Easter Monday two days later, Quebec City witnessed growing unrest and eventually riot when, on the evening of 1 April, troops fired upon the crowds, killing four. On 15 May 1918 farmers marched on Ottawa in protest:[31] "Just as seeding time began, farmers watched sons depart to the military depots and cursed the lying Unionist politicians."[32]

(11)

Against this backdrop, the events of the summer of 1918 in Alberta unfolded in two phases and involved three cases. The first phase concerned Norman Earl Lewis, a 21-year-old unmarried farmer, and the second concerned Lieutenant Colonel Philip Moore, the officer in command of First Alberta Depot Battalion at Calgary.[33] Lewis's circumstances were considered in the eponymous *In re Lewis* case heard by the five-judge panel of Chief Justice Harvey and Justices Beck, Hyndman, Simmons, and Stuart.[34] Lt. Col. Moore played the pivotal role in the subsequent *In re Norton* case, heard by the Chief Justice and Justices Beck and Stuart.[35] The third case, *Re Gray*, was taken to the Supreme Court of Canada on facts similar to those in *Lewis*.[36] *Gray* overruled *Lewis*, but was decided some two weeks later. In the interval between *Lewis* and *Gray*, the events figuring in *Norton* unfolded.

Lewis was called for service and fell under Class 1 of the Military Service Act, 1917. He applied for and was granted an exemption by a local tribunal, but on 8 May 1918, under the authority of the orders-in-council, he was recalled to report for active service. Although he complied with the order to report, Lewis applied to the Court by way of habeas corpus for a discharge from military custody and service. His counsel was R.B. Bennett. Lewis's application was not unique. By July 1918, similar requests for habeas corpus from formerly exempted draftees had been brought in Quebec City, Montreal, and Toronto.[37] The Court took jurisdiction, on the basis that "orders and regulations made by virtue of a delegated authority from a Legislature are open to review by the Courts and are invalid if they do not come within the powers conferred by the legislative enactment."[38]

A four-judge majority of the Court (Beck, Hyndman, Simmons, and Stuart JJ.) held that P.C. 919 was invalid for two main reasons.[39] First, P.C. 919 was *ultra vires* because it was made without statutory authorization. The War Measures Act, 1914 did not authorize the Governor in Council to make regulations respecting the raising of military forces. These matters were dealt with in the Militia Act.[40] Mr Justice William Simmons observed that this was evident because Parliament passed the Military Service Act, 1917 to modify the Militia Act and Parliament therefore did not consider the earlier War Measures Act, 1914 to "[cover] the ground in question."[41] More precisely, the War Measures Act, 1914 had not authorized the Governor in Council to make regulations inconsistent with the Militia Act.[42] The list of subjects did not support a power to create regulations inconsistent with any statute passed before or after the regulations or the War Measures Act, 1914.[43] Subsection 13(5) of the Military Service Act, 1917, which provided that nothing in that Act "shall limit or affect the powers of the Governor in Council under the War Measures Act, 1914," did not assist the opposing position: the Military Service Act, 1917 did not confer an authority that was otherwise absent from the War Measures Act, 1914.[44] Furthermore, "Parliament never dreamed that it would be even suggested that the powers of the Governor in Council" under the War Measures Act, 1914 would be so extensive that regulation could undo the provisions of the Military Service Act, 1917—"which...was the occasion of such fierce antagonisms both within and without Parliament."[45]

Second, the resolutions of 20 April 1918 did not confer validity on P.C. 919. Mere parliamentary resolutions "cannot take away the right of the liberty of the subject unless some valid statute of Parliament has declared that it shall do so."[46] Properly passed statutes may limit subjects' liberty, but resolutions may not: "a right derived by statute... can only be taken away by statute."[47] Mr Justice Nicholas Beck wrote that the resolutions were not passed in the form or under the procedural safeguards which, in the course of constitutional development, parliamentary custom, tradition and rules have imposed for the protection of the lives, liberties and property of the subjects of the Crown, with the view to full discussion and consideration of the measures proposed...The Bill of Rights (1 W. & M., c. 2) expressly rejects the assumed power of the Crown of "dispensing with and suspending of laws and the execution of laws" without the consent of parliament. There was not then, nor has there since been any mode known to the law whereby the consent of parliament can be declared save by an Act expressly declaring it to be enacted by the Sovereign "by and with the advice and consent" of both Houses. An Act of Parliament requires no proof. A resolution of one or both Houses of Parliament is a matter solely of the internal economy of the body which passes it.[48]

Chief Justice Horace Harvey dissented. He reasoned as follows: Parliament has the power to delegate some of its authority. This is what it did under the War Measures Act, 1914, which permitted the Governor in Council to make regulations necessary or advisable for the security, defence, peace, order, and welfare of Canada, by reason of the existence of real or apprehended war, invasion or insurrection. In the Chief Justice's estimation, P.C. 919 was "clearly...in relation to the war and the security of Canada" and the Governor in Council manifestly considered it "necessary or advisable."[49] The enumeration of particular subjects of regulation did not restrict the authority of the Governor in Council. The Military Service Act, 1917 did not restrict that authority, because that Act expressly confirmed the authority of the Governor in Council under the War Measures Act, 1914. The Chief Justice agreed that the resolutions did not have the status of an Act and did not add to the legitimacy of P.C. 919. Nonetheless, P.C. 919 was *intra vires* and legally effective.[50]

Since the Court held that P.C. 919 was *ultra vires,* Lewis was entitled to an order for his discharge and release from military service. The Court, however, stayed the order for two weeks so an appeal could be taken to the Supreme Court of Canada.[51] Other litigation respecting the same issues was also working its way through the courts, however. The Supreme Court issued its decision in *Gray* on 19 July 1918 and, in so doing, overruled the Alberta majority's decision in *Lewis. Gray,* an appeal from Ontario, turned on facts similar to *Lewis. Gray,* too, was a young unmarried farmer, called up through the elimination of his exemption under the Military Service Act, 1917. The Supreme Court majority essentially adopted Chief Justice Harvey's reasoning. Parliament could delegate legislative authority to the Governor in Council. According to Mr Justice Francis Anglin, "[s]hort of [a complete abdication by Parliament of its legislative functions], any limited delegation would seem to be within the ambit of a [plenary and ample] legislative jurisdiction."[52] Parliament did delegate. Nothing in the language of the War Measures Act, 1914 restricted the authority of the Governor in Council to pass P.C. 919.[53] Hence, P.C. 919 was *intra vires*. While the decision in *Gray* settled the legal issues, it came too late to prevent a second series of events.

In the two weeks between the Alberta Court's ruling in *Lewis* and the Supreme Court's decision in *Gray,* some twenty draftees, including Marvin Chester Norton, applied for habeas corpus. The draftees' personal circumstances soon faded into the background. Mr Justice Charles Stuart granted an order restraining Colonel George Macdonald, the District Officer Commanding, along with Lt. Col. Phillip Moore from removing the draftees from Alberta pending disposition of the habeas corpus applications. Counsel for the draftees returned to Court before Chief Justice Harvey on 8 July, alleging that the draftees had been transported from the province in violation of Justice Stuart's order.[54] Counsel asked for a writ of attachment against Lt. Col. Moore, based on contempt of court.[55] Chief Justice Harvey adjourned the application to 10 July and ordered Lt. Col. Moore to appear with the draftees.

The *Calgary Daily Herald* headline, "CRISIS IN HABEAS CORPUS CASES," of 10 July, indicated that the situation had further deteriorated.[56] Lt. Col. Moore had not complied with Chief Justice Harvey's order. He did not appear before the Chief Justice or produce the draftees.[57] The Court was informed by Major J.M. Carson, counsel for the military, that Lt. Col. Moore had been instructed by the Adjutant-General in Ottawa, Col. O.M. Biggar, to disregard any court orders compelling a court appearance.[58] Major Carson argued that Lt. Col. Moore lacked the *mens rea* for contempt because he was following a superior's orders. The Major then produced a "surprise" July 5 order-in-council, P. C. 1697, which he had received by telegram. The order-in-council caused "a sensation" in court.[59] It directed "that men whose exemptions were cancelled pursuant to the provisions of the orders in council of the 20th of April, 1918, above referred to, be dealt with in all respects as provided by the said orders in council notwithstanding the judgment and notwithstanding any judgment or any order that may be made by any Court and that instructions be sent accordingly to the general and other officers commanding military districts in Canada." The order failed to move the Court. The Chief Justice responded that since *Lewis* held that the Governor in Council could not cancel the exemptions by order-in-council, the more recent order-in-council was equally ineffective. The Chief Justice would write in his reasons in *Norton* that the order-in-council "can be deemed only a notice that the decisions of the Courts of Canada are to be ignored and treated with contempt and that the military authorities are to be so instructed."[60] In the course of argument, the Chief Justice observed that if the military persisted in defying the Court's orders, "he would not be surprised if a rebellion did take place."[61]

At 3 o'clock in the afternoon of July 10, the Court directed Sheriff F.M. Graham to execute the writ of attachment and apprehend Lt. Col. Moore. The attempt to locate Lt. Col. Moore brought John McCaffray, assistant Sheriff of the Calgary Judicial District, and Detective Sergeant Waugh of the Alberta Provincial Police to the Sarcee Camp and the Victoria Barracks, where they met "armed military resistance."[62] The Victoria Park Barracks had been "turned into an armed camp" with the Strathcona Horse standing guard.[63] Two machine guns were emplaced to cover the front entrance to the headquarters building.[64]

According to the *Calgary Daily Herald*, by these actions the authorities of military district No. 13 had "completely defied the civil courts of the province of Alberta."[65] The officers were met at the Victoria Barracks by Major R.B. Eaton, who uttered the words immortalized in Wilbur Bowker's portrait of Chief Justice Harvey: "Who started this thing anyway? Why don't they leave us alone and go about their business? Who is going to run this country, the chief justice or the government?"[66] Major Eaton then "firmly informed the court officers that they would not be permitted to arrest Col. Moore."[67] The officers then talked to Col. Macdonald, who confirmed that he had instructions from his superiors "to offer all necessary resistance to any attempt to arrest Col. Moore."[68] Sheriff Graham offered his assessment of the situation:

> we could lay our hands on him [Lt. Col. Moore] in five minutes, but [I] have no doubt we would meet forcible resistance. It means that if one man goes he will get

kicked out; if two men go they would get kicked out; and if a thousand men were sworn in as deputies there would probably be bloodshed, as both sides would be very much inclined to follow orders.[69]

So grave was the situation that Sheriff Graham contemplated posting the proclamations and requiring every able-bodied man in the community to assemble, "bringing what arms they have."[70] Events had reached such a pitch that the *Calgary Daily Herald* reported that an anonymous source indicated that the "situation, it is unofficially stated, is rapidly reaching that acute point which may render the necessity of martial law in the province."[71] Acting Mayor Frank Freeze of Calgary issued a public appeal to citizens to "remain calm and be discreet in their acts and utterances."[72]

Having learned of the situation, the Court ordered all parties and their counsel to appear at 2 o'clock the following day and adjourned the matter until that time.[73] Upon reconvening on 11 July, the Court heard from James Muir, K.C., speaking on behalf of the Honourable Charles Doherty, Minister of Justice and Attorney General, who offered a way out of the mounting crisis. Minister Doherty suggested that the contempt and habeas corpus matters be held over pending the decision of the Supreme Court on the *Lewis* issues.[74] The Court indicated that it would comply with the request, but it wanted its orders to be obeyed and the applicants protected; and it still wanted Lt. Col. Moore.[75]

Lt. Col. Moore once again failed to appear on 12 July and the draftees were not produced. Further, the Minister of Justice indicated by telegram that he refused to consent to any conditions. Chief Justice Harvey thereupon read the Court's decision in *Norton*, in which he confirmed the Court's decision in *Lewis*, catalogued the government's resistance to court-ordered process in the *Norton* proceedings, marked the government's defiance of the Court and its rulings, and granted the relief sought in the habeas corpus applications: "The order should therefore go directing the Sheriff to obtain the persons of the applicants...and to bring them before the Court and that they then be discharged from military custody and control without further order."[76] The Chief Justice reminded the Sheriff of his duties, "which included the swearing-in of men to enforce the order."[77]

Counsel for acting Mayor Freeze and city councillors of Calgary was permitted to address the Court. He asked that the order not be acted on until the next day, 13 July, in the hope that a solution still might be worked out. The Court agreed to delay execution of the order. On 13 July a meeting was held. In attendance were Chief Justice Harvey, Sheriff Graham, Col. Macdonald, Major Carson, Mayor Freeze, Alderman Mahaffey, and the City Solicitor.[78] On his own initiative, Col. Macdonald agreed not to remove the applicants from the judicial district without 24 hours notice to the sheriff. The Chief Justice agreed to instruct the sheriff not to execute the orders to bring Lt. Col. Moore and the draftees before the Court unless notice was given.[79] The Honourable Martin Burrell, acting Minister of Militia, sent a telegram confirming that the Militia Department would honour Col. Macdonald's undertaking.[80] "At last the government had capitulated," but the Court had not.[81] Throughout the crisis the Court had maintained its integrity and independence.

(III)

On one reading, in that summer of 1918 the Court displayed a conception of judicial independence similar to our own. The Court's conception was less elaborate, refined, and variegated than ours, but still contained the persistent core of independence. Similarities are not surprising. The Court relied on a tradition of judicial independence dating from the first half of the eighteenth century in England that continues to feed our current jurisprudence.[82] Chief Justice Harvey was content simply to gesture toward this tradition: "These Courts grew up and acquired their powers not merely by legislation but through exercise for centuries."[83] The circumstances called for actions, not words.

Three features of the *Lewis/Norton* circumstances enhance the familiarity of the Court's conception of judicial independence. First, the Court found itself in an archetypal conflict. On the one hand, it confronted the State, motivated by serious national security concerns. On the other hand, the Court's protection was sought by individuals, whose rights and interests were threatened by the State's planned actions. As Wilbur Bowker noted, when President Abraham Lincoln suspended habeas corpus during the American Civil War, the United States courts faced a situation similar to that in *Norton*.[84] Thankfully, our courts have not yet been tested to this high degree in our war against terrorism, although rhetoric and speculation have sometimes been pitched very high.[85]

Second, within this conflict the Court anchored its independence on the law. The Court demonstrated its independence from political influence. The Court was subject to considerable pressure, as Chief

Justice Harvey intimated: "In deciding to pursue its proper functions this Court is not unmindful of the fact which the Minister of Justice desires to press on us that the need of Canada for soldiers is very great and urgent, but it is apparent that to allow such a consideration to be our guiding principle would be to substitute expediency for law as the basis of the judicial decision."[86] We should not underestimate the level of pressure. Canada was in a world war. Tens of thousands of Canadian men had died. So far as could have been apparent to the members of the Court, there was a reasonable prospect that the war could be lost. More men were needed to fight. Only six months before, the country had gone through a bitterly contested election in which conscription had divided the electorate. The gravity of the situation was echoed in the preamble to P.C. 919. After the Court decided *Lewis*, the federal government expressly declared that it would ignore the ruling. It would have been easy—doubtless the path of least resistance—to find a way to favour State over individual interests. Sir Charles Fitzpatrick, Chief Justice of the Supreme Court of Canada, was evidently prepared to adopt such a course in reference to the conscription exemptions: "Our legislators were no doubt impressed in the hour of peril with the conviction that the safety of the country is the supreme law against which no other law can prevail. It is our clear duty to give effect to their patriotic intention."[87] The Court displayed its independence precisely by refusing to substitute patriotic duty for the duty to apply the law. Whatever may have been the legitimate concerns of Parliament and the executive, the Court's responsibilities were to the law itself. Mr Justice Stuart argued that, "[n]o consideration other than the pure question of the law...can be for a moment entertained upon such an application, as this," while fellow judge Mr Justice William Simmons confirmed that "[t]he question before the Court, however, is one of the legality or constitutionality of the order in council in question."[88] Echoing his brethren, Mr Justice James Hyndman indicated that "as a Court of law it is incumbent upon us to decide the matter upon purely legal principles;" and Chief Justice Harvey declared that the Court "will endeavour in so far as lies in its power to furnish protection to persons who apply to it to be permitted to exercise their legal rights."[89]

The Chief Justice provided a profound personal demonstration of the Court's commitment to law through his own actions. He had dissented in *Lewis*. Yet he took leadership of the Court following the decision, defending its ruling—which, "so long as it remains unreversed...must be deemed to be the proper expression of law in this province"—against the military and the federal government.[90] Chief Justice Harvey was the face of the Court in the processes that led to the issuance of the writ of attachment and the Dominion government's ultimate capitulation.

Less obviously, the Court also expressed its independence from public opinion and private interest. Both conscription and the elimination of exemptions were extraordinarily unpopular with many segments of the Canadian public. The judges could not have escaped knowledge of the concerns of French Canada, and certainly the concerns of the Alberta farming, ranching, and industrial communities would have been well-known to the judges. They would have realized that reducing the number of workers in the province would adversely affect the province and the country. These matters, however, barely figure in the Court's decisions. Only Justice Beck referred to these external concerns, in a most fleeting and oblique manner, when he described the passage of the Military Service Act, 1917 as having been "the occasion of such fierce antagonisms both within and without Parliament" and as having "so stirred the whole people of Canada."[91]

The Court could be understood to have anticipated in practice a view articulated in theory in recent years. Judicial independence requires not only independence from the other branches of government, but independence from public and private influences. Mr Justice Charles Gonthier of the Supreme Court of Canada discussed this point in the *Mackin* case:

> Generally speaking, the expanded role of the judge as an adjudicator of disputes, interpreter of the law and guardian of the Constitution requires that he or she be completely independent of any other entity in the performance of his or her judicial functions. Such a view of the concept of independence may be found in art. 2.02 of the Universal Declaration on the Independence of Justice...which states:
>
> > Judges individually shall be free, and it shall be their duty, to decide matters before them impartially, in accordance with their assessment of the facts and their understanding of the law without any restrictions, influences, inducements, pressures, threats or interferences, direct or indirect, from any quarter or for any reason...

The adoption of a broad definition of judicial independence by this Court was confirmed, moreover, in *Provincial Court Judges Reference...* where Lamer C.J., for the majority, stated the following:

> Finally...I do not wish to overlook the fact that judicial independence also operates to insulate the courts from interference by parties to litigation and the public generally....[92]

Third, the Court did not suggest that judicial independence is good in itself; it is a means to an end. Judicial independence derives its constitutional value from protecting legal norms. In the words of Mr Justice John C. Major of the Supreme Court of Canada, "[j]udicial independence serves not as an end in itself, but as a means to safeguard our constitutional order and to maintain public confidence in the administration of justice...The principle exists for the benefit of the judged, not the judges."[93] Or, as Chief Justice Harvey argued in 1918, the Court bears its duties "for the purpose of guarding the rights of the subjects."[94]

Again, the Court's approach to its role may be interpreted to prefigure a modern conception of judicial independence. The commitment to law and an understanding that judicial independence draws its worth from protecting the rule of law could be interpreted in a "neutralist" fashion. Essentially, this view suggests that the Court's job would be to vindicate the law, regardless of the parties before it. The Court, like Justice, is blindfolded. Mr Justice Anglin of the Canadian Supreme Court seems to have adopted this sort of neutralist position in the *Gray* case: "[a]t all events all we, as a court of justice, are concerned with is to satisfy ourselves what powers Parliament intended to confer and that it possessed the legislative jurisdiction requisite to confer them."[95] In contrast, political scientist Peter McCormick describes the modern approach as one in which the "courts are not just the resolvers of disputes, or the referees of federalism...Instead, the courts are the 'protectors of the constitution' and the rights of citizens within the constitutional framework."[96] In that sense, courts raise the blindfold enough to see whether the rights of individuals are threatened. So while Justice Anglin preferred the neutralist stance, the Alberta judges adopted this more protective role. They tilted in favour of individual rights and against the expansion of State interference with individual rights. Justice Stuart referred to the Court's special duty to protect individual liberty against State encroachment:

"As [Mr Justice Frederick] Low, J., said in *Rex v. Superintendent of Vine Street Police Station*...'This court is specially charged as between the Crown and the subject to exercise the greatest care in safeguarding the subject's liberty.'"[97] Along similar lines, Justice Beck referred to Parliamentary procedural safeguards that exist for "the protection of the lives, liberties and property of the subjects of the Crown."[98] Chief Justice Harvey stated that the Court is "duly and legally constituted for the purposes of protecting the legal rights of all persons who may come before it" and referred to the Court's "duties with which it is entrusted for the purpose of guarding the rights of the subjects;" and to the Court's duty to provide "protection to persons who apply to it to be permitted to exercise their legal rights."[99] The Alberta judges of 1918 would have concurred with Mr Justice Major of the Supreme Court of Canada, who stated in 2003 that "[c]ourts also ensure that the power of the state is exercised in accordance with the rule of law and the provisions of our Constitution. In this capacity, courts act as a shield against unwarranted deprivations by the state of the rights and freedoms of individuals."[100]

(IV)

Despite the points of convergence with the modern conception of judicial independence, the Alberta Court's conception bore its own distinguishing features. Through its commitment to the law, the Court held itself independent from governmental, public, and private influences. In *Lewis*, the judges did refer briefly to the commencement of the war and the passing of the War Measures Act, 1914 and acknowledged the debates surrounding the Military Service Act, 1917. Further, it is true that in *Lewis* the wisdom of P.C. 919 was not in question. The judges also laboured under constraints respecting the types of evidence and information that could be considered in the course of statutory interpretation.[101] Hence, the judges did not mention the controversies of the election or the series of habeas corpus applications being heard across the country, or even delve overmuch into the debates around the Military Service Act, 1917. They focused on the bare words of statutes.

To modern eyes, the Court's abstraction from the *Lewis* case's practical matrix is remarkable. If a contemporary court heard *Lewis*, it would not likely refrain from reference to and analysis of the controversies around conscription and the promises to provide exemptions. A contemporary court would be driven to these issues by the

Charter.[102] After all, habeas corpus is a Charter-protected remedy.[103] Sending a man to the trenches certainly threatens his life, liberty, and security, protected by s. 7 of the Charter. The legislative means would be assessed in terms of whether they were consistent with the "principles of fundamental justice." If a limitation of Charter rights were to be found, the court would assess (among other things) the objectives pursued by the government in limiting the individual's interests. Even without the Charter, as McCormick has argued, the modern Supreme Court, and hence all other courts, have adopted a "contextual" approach to the interpretation of statutes, as opposed to the old "formalist" approach.[104] Mr Justice Franck Iacobucci of the Supreme Court of Canada described the contextual approach to statutory interpretation in this way:

> Elmer Driedger in *Construction of Statutes* (2nd ed., 1983) best encapsulates the approach upon which I prefer to rely. He recognizes that statutory interpretation cannot be founded on the wording of the legislation alone. At p. 87 he states:
>
>> Today there is only one principle or approach, namely, the words of an Act are to be read in their entire context and in their grammatical and ordinary sense harmoniously with the scheme of the Act, the object of the Act, and the intention of Parliament.[105]

A member of the Alberta Court in 1918 might have thought that the consideration of "contextual" elements could undermine its independence for, by considering what is not law, a court potentially makes political and not legal determinations. And if a court becomes a political entity, it has no special claims to protections beyond those enjoyed by any other political entity. A modern judge might reply that the courts need not fear considering "contextual" elements. The courts, like philosophers of language, have realized that meaning is not inherent in bits of text alone. Meaning can only be understood in context.[106] The job of the courts is, in part, to make authoritative determinations of meaning. Considering context only entails that the interpretation is accomplished with an awareness of relevant information. Context informs and does not subvert the task of judicial interpretation.

An argument might be made that the "formalist" approach to interpretation was never truly context-free. Instead, context was considered silently or without full acknowledgment. This reflection leads to a second distinguishing aspect of the Court's judicial independence. Although "formalistic," the Court's decision in *Lewis* may not have been free from contextual assessment. There is the possibility, for example, that the Court's rejection of the government's attempt to eliminate conscription exemptions was based on a policy assessment that this attempt would damage the country, or at least Alberta farmers, ranchers, and industrial workers. This possibility, however, involves sheer speculation. No textual evidence supports this point. Some evidence, however, supports the view that at least Justice Stuart conceived the independent Court not only as protecting individuals' legal rights, but as protecting a way of life secured by those rights.

Justice Stuart made the following remarkable observation in *Lewis*: "Fortunately, we were not, at the beginning of the war, living in a country where our actions and lives were regulated in great detail by laws. We were a free people and the field given to individual liberty of action by the absence of detailed legislation and regulation was enormous."[107] The language is revealing: "we were not, at the beginning of the war" [as opposed to now]; "we were [past tense] a free people." The *Lewis* case may teeter at the cusp of a change in Canadians' relationship with government.

The "field given to individual liberty" before the war should not be exaggerated. Alberta in 1914 was not in a state of nature; neither was it the Wild West. The Alberta statute books established a healthy number of governmental departments. Provincial legislation regulated (for example) provincial taxes and duties, public works, telephones, education, public health, agriculture and animals; statutes governed commercial sales and secured financing, companies, some labour issues, and established standards for varieties of technologies. Federal legislation regulated (for example) banks, combines investigation, companies, customs, railways, electrical standards, food standards, weights and measures, the post office, federal policing, the federal judiciary, criminal law, evidence, and penitentiaries. The war, however, propelled the federal government into private affairs in new ways.

The imposition of federal personal and corporate income tax, introduced as a "temporary measure" in 1917 through the Income War Tax Act, might be taken as a symbol of this new federal incursion. Changes as or more far-reaching, though, were accomplished through the War Measures Act, 1914. Under this Act, the federal government took over the production of artillery shells, becoming the nation's largest employer. The government created the National Employment Service, the federal Department of Health, and laid the foundations for health and employment insurance. It imposed a variety of economic controls, through such measures as food and fuel controllers who prevented hoarding by merchants, and Cost of Living Commissioners. In June 1917, the Board of Grain Supervisors (which became the Canada Wheat Board) took over the exclusive marketing of that crop. The result was an increased centralization of power.[108] Government intervention, like federal income tax, tends to be sticky. Once introduced, it seldom retreats on its own. Craig has commented that "[i]t is not too much to say that no country was entirely exempt from this drift toward totalitarian political methods."[109] Furthermore, the War Measures Act, 1914 permitted and encouraged non-parliamentary, executive interventions. Craig comments that for all of the belligerents, there was a "growth of executive authority and expansion of government powers in areas formerly considered private."[110] While these developments did not proceed as far or with such ill effects in the West as in Eastern Europe, these developments in the West were, nonetheless, marked.

Justice Stuart's words may be a window into the Court's deeper commitments in *Lewis*. Relying on its independence, the Court may have been fighting a rear-guard action against the interventionist executive State. Consistent with this interpretation, we find Mr Justice John Idington, who dissented in the Supreme Court of Canada, appealing to high principle: "The delegation of legislation in way of regulations may be very well resorted to in such a way as to be clearly understood as such, but a wholesale surrender of the will of the people to any autocratic power is exactly what we are fighting against."[111] Along with Justice Idington, Justices Beck, Simmons, and Hyndman came close to recognizing an "unwritten" constitutional principle that the rights of subjects can be eliminated only through statutes—that is, only in accordance with the "due process" protections established in parliamentary procedure for the production of Acts of Parliament. The more expeditious process for generating orders-in-council, even if buttressed by parliamentary resolutions, provides insufficient procedural protections for eliminating rights established by statute.

The final distinguishing aspect of the Court's conception of judicial independence is perhaps the strangest to the modern observer. The conflict between the Court and the State played out on the level of physical force. In theoretical terms, the political technology of governmentality involved physical measures—violence. The military and governmental response to the *Lewis/Norton* circumstances was certainly physical. The military refused to produce Lt. Col. Moore or the draftees as required by the Court. When the Court issued the writ of attachment for contempt, the military responded with a serious threat of severe violence. Chief Justice Harvey stated that "without doubt there is enough might though not right behind the military authorities to prevent the Court's officers from performing their duty, and even to destroy both the members of the Court and its officers...."[112] This threat of force was, in Chief Justice Harvey's apt phrasing, "astounding." To be sure, armed resistance to court process may occur today. Such resistance, however, would be by individuals or groups not forming part of government. It would be unthinkable now for a branch of the executive to meet an adverse judicial decision with armed resistance. Today, the sheriff would be met not by soldiers but by lawyers. Intergovernmental interactions take place through discourse, not physical coercion.

But even more astounding and more important to the Court's conception of judicial independence was its response to the threat of violence. The Court understood itself to be overmatched and physically vulnerable, yet it met force with force—the force of the Court against the force of the military. The Chief Justice confirmed that the Courts have had to exercise their powers "in the face of hostile opposition and even against hostile force."[113] If an order to produce individuals is disobeyed, "unless the Court is to confess impotence it must send someone to obtain and produce them."[114] Chief Justice Harvey even referred to the Court's "machinery" for dealing with hostile forces:

> It would be surprising then if machinery did not exist for such an emergency. Such machinery does exist. The Court's officers in carrying out the decrees of the Court have the legal right and authority to call upon all able-bodied men within their jurisdiction to assist in the execution of the Court's orders and it is not merely the right, but the duty of everyone so called to furnish such assistance and what he does in giving such assistance is legal and justifiable while any opposition to the Court's officers and those assisting is illegal and punishable, no matter from whom it comes.[115]

The Court participated in the political technology of force. Judicial independence was conceived to involve a measure of violence so as to maintain independence.

Chief Justice Harvey did have a machinery of violence to deploy, and this machinery was deployed. On point was the sheriff. Sheriffs were appointed by the lieutenant-governor under The Sheriff's Act.[116] This Act did not specify their duties. Under s. 37 of the Supreme Court Act, sheriffs (among others) "shall aid, assist and obey the court and the judges thereof respectively in the exercise of the jurisdiction conferred by this Act." Statute confirmed the historical duty of sheriffs to courts. All orders of the English Supreme Court were directed to the sheriff, and the sheriff was obligated to execute them.[117] In theory, the sheriff was the "chief executive officer for the execution of criminal process."[118] To apprehend offenders and arrest those who opposed the execution of process, the sheriff had the unique right to raise the *posse comitatus*.[119] Under the law of the day, "[l]egally every person in a county is still bound to be ready at the command of the sheriff and at the cry of the country to arrest a felon...."[120] Failure to assist a sheriff in the execution of his duties of arrest was an offence.[121] The sheriff and the *posse comitatus* were the physical arm of judicial independence.

This physical conceptualization of judicial independence has, however, disappeared. The old political technology of violence is no longer a tool of intergovernmentality. The mechanism has all but vanished, although some vestiges of the *posse comitatus* remain.[122] The sheriff's role as law enforcer has been entirely eclipsed by the development of policing (evidently, in 1918, the young Provincial Police Force had not reached this stage), and the civil functions of the sheriff have been privatized.[123] More importantly, the will to use violence—the assumption that independence must carry with it physical means of asserting independence—has also vanished.[124] It is now true that the judiciary is the "least dangerous" branch.[125] McCormick can now properly observe that "the courts have no enforcement or follow-up mechanisms under their control; their decisions are always entirely dependent upon the actions of other parties or other actors within the system."[126] It is true that judicial determinations may have physical consequences—sentences of imprisonment provide an obvious example. The sentence, however, is not carried out by the courts, but by the correctional authorities, a separate organ of the State. One might argue that physical force was never properly part of judicial independence. The court's role is founded on the law, not on the monopolization of means of violence. The modern court works with a self-conception refined by 100 years of experience. It has become, in both idea and reality, an institution based on law and not on physicality. To protect itself, it has no need of sheriffs or posses, with six-guns or swords. It can be physically helpless, because its strength lies in the authority of law.

The world of 1918 is, to our eyes, both similar to our own and very different. The conception of judicial independence of 1918, too, is both similar to our own and very different. In 1918, Chief Justice Harvey and his brother judges were faced with extraordinary challenges. Their commitment to judicial independence helped to preserve the Court we have inherited. We can only hope that we are not similarly tested—but if we are, we can only pray that we can display the backbone that Chief Justice Harvey and the Supreme Court of Alberta did, in that summer long ago.

NOTES

1 *Provincial Court Judges' Association of New Brunswick v. New Brunswick (Minister of Justice)*, Supreme Court Reports [citer hereafter SCR] 2 (2005): 286, *per curiam*, at 301-02; *Re Application under s. 83.28 of the Criminal Code*, SCR 2 (2004): 248, Iacobucci and Arbour JJ at paras. 80-83; *Ell v. Alberta*, SCR 1 (2003): 857, Major J; *Reference re Remuneration of Judges of the Provincial Court of Prince Edward Island*, SCR 3 (1997): 3, Lamer CJ ["*Provincial Court Judges Reference*"]; *Beauregard v. Canada*, SCR 2 (1986): 56; *Valente v. The Queen*, SCR 2 (1985): 673, Le Dain J. A battle may be shaping up over the independence of superior court judges. The Harper government may reject the recommendations of a 2004 Judicial Compensation and Benefits Commission report: J. Tibbetts, "Tories want judges' raise tied to the cost of living," *Edmonton Journal*, 27 May 2006, A6.
2 I find myself—again—following a trail blazed by Dean Wilbur Bowker. See "The Honourable Horace Harvey, Chief Justice of Alberta," *Canadian Bar Review* [cited hereafter CBR] 32 (1954): 932 and 1118. See also Dale Gibson, "The Supreme Court of Alberta Meets the Supreme Law of Canada," in this collection.
3 R.S.C. 1906, c. 41. It was eventually repealed under S.C. 1950, c. 43 (s. 250), which established the National Defence Act.
4 Britain entered the war on that date, and as part of the Empire, Canada did too: E.H. Armstrong, *The Crisis of Quebec, 1914-1918* (Toronto: McClelland and Stewart, 1974), 55. At this time, the Dominion of Canada was not a sovereign state distinct from Britain: P.W. Hogg, *Constitutional Law of Canada, Loose-leaf edition* (Scarborough, Ontario: Carswell, 1997), 3-1, 3-2. I am indebted to the editor of this collection, Professor Jonathan Swainger, for his assistance with some references in this section of my paper.
5 5 Geo. V. 1914. c. 2, 2nd session.
6 Quoting historian Jeffrey Keshen, Pierre Berton described press censorship in Canada "as among the most brazen affronts to democracy in the country's history." Pierre Berton, *Marching as to War: Canada's Turbulent Years, 1899-1953* (Toronto: Doubleday Canada, 2001), 162. See generally, Jeffrey A. Keshen, *Propaganda and Censorship During Canada's Great War* (Edmonton: University of Alberta Press, 1996).
7 See D. Morton, *A Military History of Canada* (Toronto: McClelland & Stewart, 1992), 130, 133; D. Morton, *A Short History of Canada*, 5th ed. (Toronto: McClelland & Stewart, 2001), 175; E. McInnis, *Canada: A Political and Social History* (Toronto: Holt, Rinehart and Winston of Canada, 1982), 484, 485; R. Cook, with J. Ricker and J. Saywell, *Canada: A Modern Study* (Toronto: Clarke, Irwin & Co., 1977), 185; Armstrong, *Crisis of Quebec*, 55; Berton, *Marching as to War*, 130-31, 192. This unity was not unique to Canada—"In all of the countries that participated in the war, the beginning of the fighting elicited a wave of patriotism and a closing of ranks," G.A. Craig, "Mobilizing the Home Front for Total War," in *World War I*, ed. D.J. Murphy (San Diego: Greenhaven Press, Inc., 2002), 162 at 163. For an examination of the meaning of World War I in Canadian society, see Jonathan F. Vance, *Death So Noble: Memory, Meaning, and the First World War* (Vancouver: UBC Press, 1997). Eventually, Alberta would have the provinces' highest casualty rate: Howard Palmer (with

Tamara Palmer), *Alberta: A New History* (Edmonton: Hurtig Publishers, 1990), 167.
8 Paul Stanway, *The Albertans: From Settlement to Super Province 1905–2005* (Edmonton: CanMedia Inc., 2005), 89. Also see J.G. MacGregor, *A History of Alberta* (Edmonton: Hurtig Publishers, 1981), 229–30, in which McGregor provides a more nuanced discussion, pointing out that several ethnic communities in Alberta, including Scandinavians and Germans, did not have unbridled enthusiasm for the British cause. For the most recent examination of Alberta during World War I, see Duff Crerar, "Enthusiasm Embattled: 1916 and the Great War," in *Alberta Formed, Alberta Transformed*, ed. Michael Payne, Donald Wetherell, and Catherine Cavanaugh (Edmonton: University of Alberta Press, 2006), 386–411.
9 *Calgary Daily Herald*, 5 August 1914, 1.
10 Ibid.
11 "The Germans would have to be taught a short, sharp lesson, but it would all be over by Christmas—in all likelihood before any Canadian troops saw action," Stanway, *The Albertans,* 88–89; Morton, *Military History of Canada*, 131; Morton, *Short History of Canada*, 176; Berton, *Marching as to War*, 132.
12 Palmer, *Alberta*, 168; Morton, *Short History of Canada*, 179; McInnis, *Canada*, 486; Armstrong, *Crisis of Quebec*, 81–82, 104.
13 McInnis, *Canada*, 478; Morton, *Short History of Canada*, 177; Berton, *Marching as to War*, 133.
14 See, respecting the matters referred to in this paragraph, Morton, *Military History of Canada*, 133, 136, 152; Morton, *Short History of Canada*, 179; Berton, *Marching as to War*, 158, 193, 194; McInnis, *Canada*, 486, 487; Armstrong, *Crisis of Quebec*, 83, 90, 130. On the Ontario Schools conflict, see Berton, *Marching as to War*, 193; Morton, *Short History of Canada*, 174; McInnis, *Canada*, 486; Cook, *Canada: A Modern Study*, 191; Armstrong, *Crisis of Quebec*, 91–98, 154–59. Ibid., 184. Palmer, *Alberta*, 171, 185; McGregor, *History of Alberta*, 232.
15 See, respecting the matters referred to in this paragraph, Morton, *Military History of Canada*, 151, 152, 162; Morton, *Short History of Canada*, 184; Armstrong, *Crisis of Quebec*, 173; Berton, *Marching to War*, 193.
16 Morton, *Military History of Canada*, 153; Armstrong, *Crisis of Quebec*, 173.
17 Conscription under the Military Service Act, 1917 was preceded by a system of National Service registration, "which was in reality an inventory of the man power of the country," Armstrong, *Crisis of Quebec*, 161. This system required men to complete and submit registration cards. The standard history of conscription in Canada is J.L. Granatstein and J.M. Hitsman, *Broken Promises: A History of Conscription in Canada* (Toronto: Copp Clark Pitman, 1985).
18 Paragraphs (a), (d), and (f).
19 For Justice Duff's role as central appeal judge for cases arising out of the Military Service Act, 1917, see David Ricardo Williams, *Duff—A Life in the Law* (Vancouver: UBC Press, 1984), 90–95.
20 See, respecting the matters referred to in this paragraph, Granatstein and Hitsman, *Broken Promises*, 68. The context of Borden's maneuverings in the lead-up to conscription and the formation of the Union coalition government are examined in John English, *The Decline of Politics: The Conservatives and the Party System, 1901–20* (Toronto: University of Toronto

Press, 1977), 121–85. The "long and heated" debate is recounted by Granatstein and Hitsman, *Broken Promises*, 68. See also Armstrong, *Crisis of Quebec*, 175–77, 182–83, and 200.
21 *Calgary Daily Herald*, 8 December 1917, 1.
22 Ibid.
23 Ibid. This attitude, it appears, was typical of the English newspapers: Armstrong, *Crisis of Quebec*, 207.
24 "Cheering Up Fritz's Drooping Spirits," *Calgary Daily Herald*, 8 December 1917, 1.
25 *Calgary Daily Herald*, 15 December 1917, 1.
26 Palmer, *Alberta*, 186.
27 Armstrong, *Crisis of Quebec*, 237, 241.
28 Ibid., 237–38.
29 *Canada Gazette* 51, no. 43 (27 April 1918): 3747.
30 Ibid.
31 See, for example, the resolution prepared by the Canadian Council of Agriculture: *Calgary Daily Herald*, 9 July 1918, 9; and see Armstrong, *Crisis of Quebec*, 227–30; Berton, *Marching as to War*, 200; Morton, *Military History of Canada*, 157–58; Morton, *Short History of Canada*, 188; McInnis, *Canada*, 489.
32 Morton, *Short History of Canada*, 188.
33 See Bowker, "The Honourable Horace Harvey," 935–36; L. Knafla and R. Klumpenhouwer, *Lords of the Western Bench: A Biographical History of the Supreme and District Courts of Alberta, 1876–1990* (The Legal Archives Society of Alberta, 1997), 2, 70; W.G. Morrow, "An Historical Examination of Alberta's Legal System—the First Seventy-Five Years," *Alberta Law Review* 19 (1981): 148 at 152.
34 *In re. Lewis*, Alberta Law Reports [cited hereafter ALR], (1918): 423 (SC).
35 *In re. Norton*, ALR (1918): 457 (SC). The ALR and Westlaw versions of *Lewis* and *Norton* indicate that the cases were heard by the "Appellate Division," but the Supreme Court Act did not then provide for an "Appellate Division": S.A. 1907, c. 3.
36 *In re Gray*, SCR, vol. 57 (1918): 150.
37 "Quebec Justice is Threatening to Arrest Officer," *Calgary Daily Herald*, 11 July 1918, 11; see also 12 and 13. An "avalanche of applications of writs for *habeas corpus*" was brought in Quebec: "Quebec Draftees Flock to Courts to Get Freedom," *Calgary Daily Herald*, 13 July 1918, 1; [*Edmonton*] *Morning Bulletin*, 10 July 1918, 1; 11 July 1918, 1; 12 July 1918, 3—where reference to a British Columbia application is also found.
38 *Lewis*, Beck J, 442.
39 The Court focused on P.C. 919. This order eliminated exemptions. P.C. 962 ordered draftees to report, under the authority of P.C. 919. If P.C. 919 fell, P.C. 962 would also.
40 Stuart J made the useful observation that circumstances of emergency should not alter the interpretive approach to the statutes. "But the *Militia Act* itself was not passed for peaceful times. It was passed for the emergency of war. Resort to its provisions was specially intended to take place in time of war as its terms declare," *Lewis*, 435.
41 Ibid., 444. See "William Charles Simmons," in *Lords of the Western Bench*, Knafla and Klumpenhouwer, 167–68.
42 Ibid., Stuart J, 436, 437.

43 Ibid., Beck J, 442.
44 Ibid., Stuart J, 437.
45 Ibid., Beck J, 443; see Hyndman, 455. "The debates on the Military Service Bill in the Dominion Parliament, which lasted for more than two months, were followed with a passionate interest throughout the country, but nowhere with closer attention than in Quebec," Armstrong, *Crisis of Quebec*, 182.
46 *Lewis*, Stuart J, 438; Simmons J, 444.
47 Ibid., Hyndman J, 446.
48 Ibid., 440–41.
49 *Lewis*, 429.
50 Ibid., 431.
51 *Norton*, 460; Bowker, "The Honourable Horace Harvey," 934.
52 Ibid., at 176. See "Habeas Corpus Motion is Made," *Toronto Globe*, 12 July 1918, 12.
53 For a discussion of the "delegation" doctrine, see Hogg, *Constitutional Law of Canada*, 14-3, 14-4; and D.J.M. Brown and J. Evans, *Judicial Review of Administrative Action in Canada* (Toronto: Canvasback Publishing, 2004), 13:3100 and 13:5433.
54 "Complaints Court Rule Not Obeyed," *Calgary Daily Herald*, 8 July 1918, 1 and 10. It appears that Lt. Col. Moore, rather than Col. Macdonald, was the main target of the allegations, because the affidavits in support stated that the draftees were in his custody: ibid. Dean Bowker correctly noted that the dates in the *ALR* headnote (reproduced in the Westlaw version of *Norton*) are inaccurate: Bowker, "The Honourable Horace Harvey," 936 n. 2.
55 "A writ of attachment commands the sheriff to attach a person and bring him before the court touching a contempt alleged...," *Halsbury's Laws of England* 7 (London: Butterworth & Co., 1909), "Contempt of Court, Attachment, and Committal," para. 651.
56 *Calgary Daily Herald*, 10 July 1918, 1.
57 There was even a rumour that Lt. Col. Moore had been spirited away by Katherine Stinson, one of North America's original female aviators, who had been in Calgary performing the first air mail flight in Western Canada. (For additional information respecting Ms Stinson, see Hargrave Aviation and Aeromodelling, Interdependent Evolutions and Histories—the Pioneers, http://www.ctie.monash.edu.au/hargrave/ stinson_bio.html (accessed 31 May 2006); and McGregor, *History of Alberta*, 237.
58 *Calgary Daily Herald*, 11 July 1918, 12. See also "Ottawa Says Resist Arrest," *Toronto Globe*, 12 July 1918, 1.
59 [*Edmonton*] *Morning Bulletin*, 11 July 1918), 1.
60 *Norton*, 461.
61 [*Edmonton*] *Morning Bulletin*, 11 July 1918, 1. See also "Must Settle Lewis' Case," in *Toronto Globe*, 11 July 1918, 3.
62 The Alberta Provincial Police were formed in 1917: The Alberta Provincial Police Act, S.A. 1917, c. 4 (until 1932, this police force was responsible for provincial policing, instead of the Royal Northwest Mounted Police), and *Norton*, 459.
63 [*Edmonton*] *Morning Bulletin*, 12 July 1918, 1.
64 Ibid.

65 *Calgary Daily Herald*, 11 July 1918, 1.
66 Ibid., at 13; also see Bowker, "The Honourable Horace Harvey," 933.
67 *Calgary Daily Herald*, 11 July 1918, 1.
68 Ibid.
69 Ibid.
70 *[Edmonton] Morning Bulletin*, 13 July 1918, 10.
71 "Martial Law in Province is Now Being Talked Of: Situation Now Believed to be Approaching Very Acute Point," *Calgary Daily Herald*, 11 July 1918, 1.
72 *[Edmonton] Morning Bulletin*, 13 July 1918, 1.
73 "Must Settle Lewis' Case," *Toronto Globe*, 11 July 1918, 3. For the play of events on the evening of 11 July, see "Ottawa Says Resist Arrest," *Toronto Globe*, 12 July 1918, 1.
74 The substance of the telegram was reprinted in "Ottawa Asks Proceedings at Calgary to be Stayed," *Toronto Globe*, 12 July 1918, 1 and 4.
75 "Judges will comply with New Request but want Colonel," *Calgary Daily Herald*, 11 July 1918, 1.
76 *Norton*, 462.
77 *[Edmonton] Morning Bulletin*, 13 July 1918, 1.
78 Ibid.
79 Col. Macdonald justified his initiative under military regulations (in the face of his superiors' intransigence and his apparently contrary orders) on the basis of his authority as the officer faced with a developing situation: *Calgary Daily Herald*, 13 July 1918, 1.
80 The Privy Council's "Guide to Canadian Ministries Since Confederation" indicates that the Hon. Sydney C. Mewburn was Minister of Militia and Defence and the Hon. Mr Martin Burrell was Secretary of State: http://www.pco-bcp.gc.ca/default.asp?Language=E&Page=Publications&doc=min//min_10_e.htm (accessed 31 May 2006).
81 Bowker, "The Honourable Horace Harvey," 936.
82 W.R. Lederman, "The Independence of the Judiciary," CBR, 34 (1956): 769 at 770-71; P.H. Russell, *The Judiciary in Canada: The Third Branch of Government* (Toronto: McGraw-Hill Ryerson Ltd., 1987), 75; P. McCormick, "Judicial Independence and Judicial Governance in the Provincial Courts" (Canadian Association of Provincial Court Judges, 2004), 1, 7; P. McCormick, "New Questions About an Old Concept: The Supreme Court of Canada's Judicial Independence Decisions," *Canadian Journal of Political Science* 37 (2004): 839 at 841-42; M. Friedland, *A Place Apart: Judicial Independence and Accountability in Canada* (Ottawa: Canadian Judicial Council, 1995), 3; H.G. Hanbury, *English Courts of Law*, 4th ed., by D.C.M. Yardley (London: Oxford University Press, 1967), 127; W. Renke, "Invoking Independence: Judicial Independence as a No-cut wage Guarantee," *Points of View/Points de vue*, no. 5 (Edmonton: Centre for Constitutional Studies, 1994): 12; *Provincial Court Judges Reference*, para. 83.
83 *Norton*, 459.
84 Bowker, "The Honourable Horace Harvey," 937. The outcome was different. The Chief Justice of the United States "acknowledged that the force of the military was greater than that of the writ [of *habeas corpus*]," ibid.
85 A challenge to judicial independence was raised with respect to the courts' role in the new anti-terrorism investigative detention procedures:

Re application under s. 83.28 of the Criminal Code, paras. 80–92; see LeBel J (dissenting).
86 *Norton*, para. 14.
87 *Gray*, 160. The Chief Justice's opinion echoes the past and is echoed now: "Lincoln's unconstitutional acts during the Civil War show that even legality must sometimes be sacrificed for other values. We are a nation under law, but first we are a nation," R.A. Posner, "Security versus civil liberties," *The Atlantic online* (December 2001), *http://www.theatlantic.com/doc/200112/posner* (accessed 2 June 2006).
88 *Lewis*, 435 and 444.
89 Ibid., 445, and *Norton*, 461.
90 *Norton*, 461.
91 *Lewis*, 443.
92 *Mackin v. New Brunswick (Minister of Finance)*, SCR 1 (2002): 405, para. 35.
93 *Ell v. Alberta*, para. 29; see *Provincial Court Judges Reference*, paras. 9, 88; Renke, "Invoking Independence," 2.
94 *Norton*, 460–61.
95 *Gray*, 182.
96 McCormick, "New Questions About an Old Concept," 848.
97 *Lewis*, 435, quoting King's Bench 1 (1916): 268 at 279. *Vine*, which followed the procedure for habeas corpus review, was a decision of a Divisional Court of the King's Bench Division of the High Court.
98 Ibid., 440.
99 *Norton*, 459, 460, 461.
100 *Ell v. Alberta*, para. 22.
101 R. Cross, *Statutory Interpretation* (London: Butterworths, 1976), 44.
102 Canadian Charter of Rights and Freedoms, being Part I of the Constitution Act, 1982, enacted by the Canada Act, 1982 (UK), c. 11.
103 Charter, s. 10(c).
104 McCormick, "Judicial Independence and Judicial Governance in the Provincial Courts," 11.
105 *Re Rizzo & Rizzo Shoes Ltd.*, SCR 1 (1998): 27, paras. 20, 21, 22; see *Manulife Bank of Canada v. Conlin*, SCR 3 (1996): 415; L'Heureux-Dubé J, dissenting, provides an interesting discussion of the "modern contextual approach," paras. 35–46.
106 See J.O. Urmson, *Philosophical Analysis: Its Development Between the Two World Wars* (London: Oxford University Press, 1956), chap. 11; J. Passmore, *A Hundred Years of Philosophy* (Baltimore: Penguin Books Inc., 1968), chap. 18.
107 *Lewis*, 436.
108 Morton, *Military History of Canada*, 133, 159; Morton, *Short History of Canada*, 177–78; Armstrong, *Crisis of Quebec*, 142; McInnis, *Canada*, 483; Cook, *Canada: A Modern Study*, 188.
109 Craig, "Mobilizing the Home Front," 166.
110 Ibid.
111 *Gray*, 165.
112 *Norton*, 462.
113 Ibid., 459.
114 Ibid., 461.
115 Ibid., 459.

116 S.A. 1906, c. 17, s. 2.
117 *Halsbury's Laws of England* 25 (London: Butterworth & Co., 1913), "Sheriffs and Bailiffs," para. 1409 [notes omitted].
118 A.W. Renton and M.A. Robertson, *Encyclopedia of the Laws of England*, 2nd ed., vol. 13 (London: Sweet & Maxwell, 1908), 378.
119 *Halsbury's Laws of England*, para. 1407 [notes omitted]; *Encyclopedia of the Laws of England*, 379.
120 *Halsbury's Laws of England*, para. 1408 [notes omitted]; *Encyclopedia of the Laws of England*, 378.
121 Criminal Code, R.S.C. 1906, c. 146, s. 142.
122 It is still an offence to fail, without reasonable excuse, to assist a "peace officer" (which includes a sheriff) in the execution of his duty in arresting a person, after reasonable notice requiring assistance: *Criminal Code*, R.S.C. 1985, c. C-46, s. 129(b).
123 Civil Enforcement Act, R.S.A. 2000, c. C-15, Part 2. On the public law side of the Court, the sheriff still plays a role in jury selection: Jury Act, R.S.A. 2000, c. J-3. Court security is not under the control of the courts; instead, it is a responsibility of the provincial Solicitor General and Public Security, Security Services branch. See Government of Alberta News release, 6 March 2006, http://www.gov.ab.ca/acn/ 200603/19564E5028250-B6C1-DF2B-54C9925752E48F98.html (accessed 1 June 2006).
124 The judiciary is now at a loss if parties refuse to abide by court orders. The modern response is to do more of the same—issue more orders. For example, Ontario Superior Court Justice David Marshall recently issued some orders to end an aboriginal occupation of a housing development at Caledonia, Ontario. The orders were not enforced. Justice Marshall "has taken the highly unusual step of ordering the provincial police, the Attorney General of Ontario, First Nations leaders, the developers and other parties to a special court session...to explain why his orders are being flouted." Professor Alan Young commented that "[j]udges usually assume their orders will be obeyed and maintain an 'out-of-sight, out-of-mind' attitude toward enforcement," *Edmonton Journal*, 30 May 2006, A5.
125 "[T]he judiciary...will always be the least dangerous to the political rights of the Constitution....The judiciary...has no influence over either the sword or the purse; no direction either of the strength or of the wealth of the society; and can take no active resolution whatsoever. It may truly be said to have neither force nor will, but merely judgment; and must ultimately depend upon the aid of the executive arm even for the efficacy of its judgments," A. Hamilton, "An Examination of the Judiciary Department," *The Federalist* (London: The Colonial Press, 1901), 427 at 428.
126 P. McCormick, *Canada's Courts* (Toronto: James Lorimer & Co., 1994), 127; see 168.

THREE

The Supreme Court of Alberta Meets the Supreme Law of Canada

DALE GIBSON

THIS ESSAY CONCERNS THE SUPREME COURT of Alberta's dealings with constitutional law. Constitutional law regulates the operations, and determines the rights and obligations, of all organs and levels of government in Canada. No law enacted by the Parliament of Canada, by a provincial legislature, or by a municipal institution is valid unless it complies with the Constitution. In recognition of the pre-eminence of constitutional law over all other laws, the Constitution Act, 1982 declares that the Constitution is the "supreme law of Canada."[1] This supremacy was not suddenly conferred in 1982, however; constitutional law has been supreme in Canada since at least 1867, when the Imperial British North America Act created Canada's basic constitutional structure.

To say that constitutional law supersedes all other law and is binding upon all courts is not to deny that its shape and content are determined, to no small degree, by the courts' own interpretations of constitutional text and sub-text. Judges are thus both subject to, and the oracles of, the supreme law of Canada.

The oracular role of the Alberta judiciary in relation to Canadian constitutional law has been considerably smaller than in most other areas of law. There are three reasons for this. In the first place, constitutional cases arise infrequently; they were especially rare in the first three-quarters of the Supreme Court of Alberta's first century. Second, provincial courts have seldom had the final word on constitutional matters, since their constitutional rulings can be appealed to higher tribunals: the Supreme Court of Canada and, or, until 1949, the Judicial Committee of the Privy Council. Finally, and with greater than average application to Alberta, most Canadian constitutional law has been determined without any prior input from provincial courts because the Government of Canada is able, by means of constitutional references, to direct important constitutional questions to the Supreme Court of Canada.[2] Alberta's two most celebrated constitutional decisions—the *Alberta Statutes Reference,* in which Premier William Aberhart's infamous Social Credit monetary legislation was struck down, and the "Persons" case in which women were held to be "persons" for the purpose of Senate appointments—involved such references.[3] A number of other important rulings, denying the province the jurisdiction to let provincial railway companies cross the lines of federal railway companies; rejecting the power of federal authorities to licence insurance companies operating in a province; confirming the extent of federal control over prairie natural resources prior to enactment of the Natural Resource Transfer Agreements; and denying Alberta the ability to legislate for the relief of depression-era debts, found their way to higher courts outside Alberta in a similar fashion.[4]

Alberta courts have nevertheless entertained considerable constitutional litigation since 1907, and in so doing have contributed significantly to the development of Canada's supreme law. It is hoped that the following sample will provide a reasonably representative overview of the constitutional work of the Supreme Court of Alberta. It consists of four chronological or topical cross-sections—Early Decisions, Social Credit Echoes, Natural Resources, and Rights and Freedoms. A question to bear in mind throughout is the extent to which the milestone decisions reviewed possess a distinctively Albertan flavour.

SECTION ONE: EARLY DECISIONS

The first cross-section—a chronological one—aims to demonstrate the sophistication and spunk of the five judges who, in the Court's earliest years, carried out its trial and appellate responsibilities: the redoubtable and long-lived Chief Justice Horace Harvey, the energetic, learned, and intellectually formidable Charles Stuart, and their competent colleagues Nicholas Beck, James Hyndman, and William Simmons.[5]

The judges of the Supreme Court of Alberta were committed from the beginning to the basic constitutional principles of judicial independence and the rule of law.[6] A dramatic illustration of this occurred in the final months of World War I, when the Court was involved in a David and Goliath confrontation with the Canadian Army.[7] Heavy casualty tolls in Flanders' trenches had created a desperate need for reinforcements. Although Parliament had authorized conscription by statute, there were so many exemptions that it was impossible to enlist as many troops as required.[8] The Government of Canada decided to eliminate some of the conscription exemptions, but rather than have Parliament amend the legislation, it chose to remove the exemptions through an executive order-in-council under the War Measures Act.[9] Albertans, like the majority of Canadians, were sharply divided by the measure. Most were patriotic supporters of the war effort, but many were concerned about the impact of conscription on agricultural production, since one of the exemptions applied to farm workers.

In the summer of 1918, the family of a young conscripted farmer named Norman Lewis retained Calgary lawyer and future Prime Minister R.B. Bennett to challenge the legality of the changes. He proceeded on the ground that statutory exemptions could only be amended by Parliament, not by order-in-council. Although Bennett generally supported Robert Borden's Conservative federal government, he did not hesitate to attack a process he said violated the fundamental constitutional principle of parliamentary supremacy. His arguments persuaded four of the five members of the Supreme Court, sitting *en banc:* Justices Stuart, Beck, Simmons, and Hyndman. Only Chief Justice Horace Harvey was of the opinion that the executive amendments were authorized by the War Measures Act. The majority of the Court granted Bennett a writ of habeas corpus ordering the military authorities to release Lewis.[10] A few days later, a group of twenty other conscripts were granted a similar order by Justice Stuart.

The Government of Canada's response was extraordinary. It promulgated an order-in-council stating that the cancellation of exemptions would remain in force "notwithstanding the judgment [of the Supreme Court of Alberta] and notwithstanding any judgment or any order that may be made by any court...."[11] On the date set by Stuart for the officer in charge of the conscripts, Lieutenant Colonel Phillip Moore, to produce them in court, another more junior officer showed up empty-handed, informed the Court that Moore had been instructed by Ottawa not to appear, and stated that some of the conscripts in question had already been removed from the province. Sheriff F.M. Graham was ordered to arrest Moore and bring him before the Court, and a scene unparalleled in Canadian legal history ensued.

A newspaper report described the scene the Sheriff and his officers encountered in Calgary:

> The Strathcona Horse has been brought in from Sarcee Camp to guard headquarters. Armed guards have been placed at every vantage point, and the Arts Building in which Col. Moore has his office is patrolled with a strong guard. Partitions have been torn down and two machine guns placed that will sweep the open space in front of the building.[12]

When the Sheriff reported the failure of his mission, Chief Justice Harvey found himself in an unenviable position. While he disagreed with his colleagues' decisions in the two cases, it was his responsibility as Chief Justice to ensure that the rule of law was respected. But how? As he may or may not have known, when Chief Justice Taney of the United States Supreme Court found himself in a similar confrontation with President Lincoln during the U.S. Civil War, he had quietly backed off.[13] Whether or not Harvey was aware of the American precedent, the Alberta Chief Justice was not prepared to retreat. After a couple of unproductive adjournments to facilitate possible compromise, he delivered an uncompromising pronouncement to a packed courtroom:

> This court is now confronted by a decision which is most astounding, arising as it does in this 20th century...[T]he military authorities and the executive government of Canada have set at defiance the highest court in this province... [T]he decisions of the courts of Canada are to be ignored and treated with contempt...
>
> [T]wo courses are open to this Court. It can either abdicate its authority and functions and advise applicants to it for redress of their wrongs and the protection of their legal rights that it is powerless, which of course means there is no power except that of force which can protect their rights, the consequence of which could scarcely mean anything less than anarchy, or it may continue to perform the duties with which it is entrusted...There can only be one answer...It will continue to perform its duties as it sees them...
>
> [T]his Court is not unmindful of the fact...that the need of Canada for soldiers is very great and urgent, but it is apparent that to allow such a consideration to be our guiding principle

would be to substitute expediency for law...It is also apparent to us that, without doubt, there is enough might, though not right, behind the military authorities to prevent the Court's officers performing their duty, and even to destroy both the members of the Court and its officers, but while the Court remains it must endeavour to perform its duty as it sees it.[14]

And so Sheriff Graham and his officers were directed to return to Col. Moore's barricaded headquarters and attempt "to obtain the persons of the applicants or such of them as may be within the jurisdiction."[15] Graham could not have been elated.

The tension in the courtroom was broken at that point by counsel for a very nervous Calgary City Council. He rose and asked the Court to stay the execution of its order until the following day in the hope that some mutually acceptable interim resolution could be found pending an appeal to the Supreme Court of Canada. The Court readily concurred and eventually agreed to stay the order temporarily in return for the Army's undertaking not to move any more conscripts out of the province without first notifying the Court. The Government of Canada had blinked under Chief Justice Horace Harvey's stern and courageous stare.

A week later, the Supreme Court of Canada brought the controversy to a close with a decision on the same issue in an Ontario case called *Re Gray*.[16] It ruled unanimously that the extensive delegation of emergency measure powers to the Cabinet under the War Measures Act was sufficient to justify even the amendment of an Act of Parliament by an order-in-council. Rejecting the argument that a delegation of Parliament's power to amend its own statutes would amount to an impermissible abdication of Parliament's constitutional supremacy, the Supreme Court of Canada held that under the circumstances the delegation of emergency powers under the War Measures Act did not constitute abdication. The dissenting reasoning of Chief Justice Harvey in *Lewis* was vindicated.

There are some who consider *Re Gray* to be a classic example of the hard case that makes bad law.[17] In the view of those observers, the Supreme Court of Canada yielded improperly to wartime expediency. Be that as it may, there can be no doubt that the Supreme Court of Alberta did itself proud. In a situation closely analogous to that in which the Chief Justice of the United States had given in to Abraham Lincoln, Chief Justice Harvey and his Alberta colleagues had managed to shame the Government of Canada into abiding by the rule of law.

The summer of 1918 was a busy time for the Supreme Court of Alberta. A few days after hearing the *Lewis* case, and before their decision appeared, the same panel of judges issued a judgment in *Board v. Board* that revolutionized divorce law in prairie Canada and, incidentally, clarified the status and authority of the Court.[18] William Board suspected his wife of infidelity and came to the Court with a petition for divorce. He faced a daunting legal hurdle. The Court had never before entertained such a claim because it was commonly supposed that the courts of most provinces, including Alberta, lacked the jurisdiction to dissolve marriage. Exclusive legislative competence over "marriage and divorce" had been bestowed upon the Parliament of Canada by s. 91(26) of the British North America Act, and no federal government since Confederation had been willing to provoke the possible wrath of Roman Catholic voters by enacting general divorce legislation.[19] Nor would any federal government do so for another half century. In the absence of such legislation, most lawyers assumed that divorce was impossible to obtain in Alberta except by private Act of Parliament. Indeed, one of the judges who sat on the *Board* case, Mr Justice Hyndman, had expressed that view in a decision about another matrimonial topic only a few months previously.[20]

On this occasion, however, the Court held, by a margin of 4 to 1, that it had jurisdiction to grant divorce. Even Justice Hyndman voted with the majority; the dissenter was once more Chief Justice Harvey. The basis for the majority's ruling was the English Matrimonial Causes Act of 1857, under which marriages could be dissolved. That statute formed part of the laws of England, as of 15 July 1870, that the three Prairie Provinces had inherited when they were created. Mrs Board's counsel contended that the English statute did not apply on the Canadian prairies because it referred to a special English matrimonial court, which had no counterpart here. The majority got around that difficulty by pointing out that the Supreme Court of Alberta possessed all the powers inherent to a superior court of record, one of which, according to the principle *"ubi jus, ibi remedium,"* was to provide a remedy wherever a right exists. If the Matrimonial Causes Act gave William Board the right to a divorce, it fell to the Supreme Court of Alberta to grant him that remedy.

An appeal to the Judicial Committee of the Privy Council, Canada's tribunal of last resort at the time, upheld the Alberta decision. While *Board* was not the only such case the Privy Council considered—a Manitoba decision to the same effect and an earlier Privy Council ruling relating to British Columbia were also reviewed—Viscount

Haldane, who wrote for the Privy Council, singled out the analysis of Alberta's Justice Stuart for particular comment, describing his reasons as "admirable."[21] As a consequence of *Board* and related cases, divorce was available in the courts of the four western provinces decades sooner than in central Canada.[22]

One member of the Alberta panel in *Board*, Justice Beck, was a devout and prominent Roman Catholic layman. Aware of the fact that some considered his support for the majority position to be inconsistent with his duties as a conscientious Catholic, he chose to address that issue at the conclusion of his reasons:

> ...[T]he opinion commonly prevails that, being a Catholic, I cannot with good conscience take part in any divorce proceedings arising in this Court....I cannot permit it to be supposed that in the event of my acting as Judge in a divorce case I shall be acting in any way with a bad or uneasy conscience. I accept absolutely without hesitation the doctrines of the Catholic Church with regard to faith and morals. I accept and fully recognize the obligations of conscience imposed upon me by the canon law of the Catholic Church. Yet, sitting as a Judge in a Court established by the authority of the State to administer the laws of the State, my duty is to find the true facts and to declare the civil law applicable to those facts.[23]

This passage became a *locus classicus* for Catholic lawyers. While it does not relate to constitutional law in the strict legal sense, some consider it to be an important explanation of a law whose supremacy, for them, transcends that of the supreme law of Canada.

The Canada that was created by the British North America Act in 1867 was by no means a constitutionally independent nation. It was fettered by numerous colonial bonds—legislative, executive, and judicial—that were gradually loosened as the country matured but were not fully removed for well over a century. The chief judicial constraint on autonomy was the appeal available to the Judicial Committee of the Privy Council, with leave, from all Canadian courts. Although civil appeals to the Privy Council were not abolished until 1949, a federal statute (prompted by public outrage that Louis Riel had—unsuccessfully—sought leave to appeal his conviction for treason to the Privy Council in 1885) had purported to end criminal appeals in 1888.[24] In 1925, however, the Appellate Division of the Supreme

Court of Alberta concluded that this embargo on appeals to the Privy Council in criminal cases was constitutionally defective. The decision would contribute indirectly but significantly to Canada's evolving constitutional autonomy.

These were Prohibition times, and the courts had their hands full of cases enforcing, challenging, and interpreting a complex web of federal and provincial temperance statutes. It was such a case that raised the issue of Privy Council appeals. Late at night on 29 September 1924, near Coleman, Alberta, the Alberta Provincial Police apprehended Frank Nadan at the wheel of a Cadillac loaded with liquor. Nadan was on his way from Fernie, British Columbia, where the liquor had been distilled, to Sweet Grass, Montana, where a thirsty market awaited. He was convicted of violating both federal and Alberta liquor legislation. His appeal to the Appellate Division, raising numerous complicated interpretational and constitutional questions, was dismissed by a 3-2 majority.[25] Perhaps because the legal issues were thorny and the majority was slim, the Appellate Division granted leave to appeal to the Privy Council. Although it does not seem to have given reasons concerning leave to appeal, the Appellate Division must have been of the view that the federal legislation purporting to abolish Privy Council appeals was invalid.

The Privy Council agreed, holding that the federal appeal abolition statute was not binding on the Privy Council itself, which therefore retained the power to hear Canadian appeals if it saw fit to do so.[26] On the merits, however, it ruled that because appeals should only be allowed in "exceptional cases," and since Nadan's appeal failed that test, it should be dismissed. Much more important than the outcome of the appeal was the ruling that the federal legislation abolishing Privy Council appeals was invalid. Two reasons were provided for that conclusion. First, a colony like Canada did not have the authority to make laws having effect beyond its own territory, and so the Criminal Code amendment could not be binding on the Privy Council. Second, the U.K. Colonial Laws Validity Act of 1865 invalidated any colonial legislation inconsistent with British legislation, and colonial appeals to the Privy Council were specifically authorized by a British statute.

Although the immediate impact of the *Nadan* decision was a blow to Canada's constitutional autonomy, it fuelled the long-term political demand that Canada, which had demonstrated its maturity and international significance as an Allied military power during World War I, should be granted formal legal independence. The eventual result of that demand and the negotiations it stimulated was the Statute of Westminster, 1931, Canada's first formal step toward independence.[27] The Statute of Westminster wiped out both of the constitutional obstacles to the Canadian abolition of Privy Council appeals. Section 3 bestowed the power to "make laws having extra-territorial operation," and section 2 exempted Canada from the operation of the Colonial Laws Validity Act. This paved the way for re-enactment of the legislation struck down in *Nadan* that, when challenged again a few years later, was held to be constitutionally valid.[28]

SECTION TWO: SOCIAL CREDIT ECHOES

The Supreme Court of Alberta was never provided an opportunity to rule on Premier William Aberhart's attempt in the late 1930s to institute a radical Social Credit monetary scheme and marginalize banks in the province. This was because the legislation in question was referred directly to the Supreme Court of Canada and was found to be unconstitutional by that Court and the Judicial Committee of the Privy Council.[29] In later years, however, Alberta courts did have occasion to consider the constitutional validity of two offshoots of the aborted Aberhart revolution—the Treasury Branches and the first Alberta Bill of Rights.

One component of the radical Social Credit economic system that survived judicial immolation was the Alberta Treasury Branch. At the heart of the Aberhart scheme was to be a network of bank-like institutions known as "State Credit Houses," which would deal in a proposed provincial quasi-currency known as "Alberta Credit" (critics called it "funny money") and would, like banks, accept deposits from and make loans to Albertans. They were linked to the provincial Treasury by a 1937 amendment to the Treasury Department Act, which expanded the breadth of the Department's mandate.[30]

Within months of the Supreme Court of Canada's decision striking down the rest of the Social Credit scheme, and even before the Privy Council could act, the Credit Houses were restructured, in modified form and with a different name, by a statute of the Alberta Legislature.[31] The new legislation established a body of provincially-owned community-sited financial institutions called Alberta Treasury Branches. Like the original State Credit Houses, they were empowered to accept and hold deposits, invest holdings, issue cheques, and, after 1940, make loans.[32] So keen was the provincial government to launch its Treasury Branches that, relying on orders-in-council issued under the authority of the 1937 amendment, it opened the first branch, in Rocky Mountain House, even before the legislation received royal assent.[33] William Aberhart had apparently decided that even if he could not drive federally chartered banks out of business in Alberta as he originally hoped, he could at least keep them in line through competition.[34]

Neither the chartered banks nor the Government of Canada challenged the creation of Treasury Branches, which gradually grew from six branches with an initial (and sole) government investment of $200,000 to become what the 2006 website of the organization, known today as ATB Financial, claims to be "the largest Alberta-based financial institution."[35] According to the same source, ATB now serves "over 600,000 Albertans in 245 communities through 150 branches [and] 135 agencies," has assets of $16.6 billion, deposits of $13.8 billion, loans of $13.1 billion, equity of $1.2 billion, and 2005 net earnings of $187 million.[36]

Remarkably, the constitutional validity of this financial behemoth has never been conclusively determined. The courts of Alberta have grappled with the question on two occasions, but never decisively, and the Supreme Court of Canada has been of little assistance. The nub of the question is that sections 15 and 16 of the Constitution Act, 1867 bestow "exclusive legislative authority" over "banking, incorporation of banks" and "savings banks" on the Parliament of Canada, and the operations of ATB are exceedingly difficult to distinguish functionally from those of an orthodox federally-chartered and regulated bank.

In a 1967 case called *Breckenridge Speedway Ltd. v. Alberta,* a defaulting ATB borrower attempted to rely on this constitutional uncertainty to avoid repayment obligations. The borrower and other associated parties initially sued ATB in the Alberta Supreme Court for rescission of the loan agreement, on the basis of certain steps taken by the lender; but when ATB counterclaimed for repayment, the plaintiffs responded by challenging the constitutionality of the provincial legislation under which the entire institution functioned. The trial judge, Mr Justice Neil Primrose, ruled that ATB was constitutionally sound because it was a product of the provincial Crown's royal prerogative, which he held to be unaffected by the Constitution Act's federal-provincial distribution of legislative powers.[37] Because he found no basis for rescission of the contract, and because the loan was clearly in default, he dismissed the action and granted the counterclaim.[38]

For the Appellate Division, the questions were not so clear-cut. Two of the five appellate judges, Mr Justice Marshall Porter and Mr Justice

Gordon Allen, were convinced that the ATB's legislative underpinnings were beyond the jurisdiction of the provincial legislature, and so held.[39] Justice Porter, "a probing judge and one of the best legal minds of the mid-century...some of [whose] most important judgments were in dissent," first disposed of the royal prerogative argument by showing that the authority of Treasury Branches is derived from statute, and that in any event "the prerogative of the Crown... is co-extensive with the division of the legislative powers...as between federal and provincial power."[40] Then, after a careful comparison of ATB and bank deposit and loan activities, he concluded that "the credit houses [sic] are engaged in the business of banking...and the statute therefore offends against [the Constitution]."[41] Justice Allen reached the same conclusion, finding that "the treasury branches do in fact carry on banking business in every sense of the word."[42] These views led Justices Porter and Allen to hold, in partial dissent, that because the loan was unauthorized, principles of restitution required the plaintiffs to repay the loan in full, and the ATB to return all property given as security.

Even the majority judges seemed to recognize, though they did not so rule, that the ATB's constitutional status is doubtful. Mr Justice Horace Johnson for example, stated baldly that "[t]he Alberta Government is carrying on a banking business through the treasury branches," and the reasons of Chief Justice Sidney Smith, with whom Mr Justice Edward Kane concurred, could be construed as agreeing with the dissenters that, as he put it, "the carrying on by the Province of the business of operating the treasury branch and the lending of money in that operation was beyond the powers of the Province..."[43] In the majority view, however, it was unnecessary to address the constitutional question at all, because, in the words of Chief Justice Smith, it did not "lie...in the plaintiffs' mouths" to challenge the authority of conduct from which they had benefited. The Chief Justice cited British and Canadian authorities to the effect that one cannot complain "of an act which is *ultra vires* if he himself has in his pocket at the time he brings the action some of the proceeds of that very *ultra vires* act."[44]

When the plaintiffs appealed to the Supreme Court of Canada, the Attorney General of Canada, who had not been previously involved in the litigation, intervened on the plaintiffs' side to the extent of submitting that the ATB legislation was unconstitutional. This did not bring about any change of result, however. Writing for seven of the nine members of the Supreme Court of Canada, Albertan

Mr Justice Ronald Martland upheld the Appellate Division for the reasons expressed by Chief Justice Smith and Mr Justice Johnson.[45] Supported by Mr Justice Wishart, Mr Justice Emmett Hall dissented, arguing that the Treasury Branches Act was unconstitutional, and then stated, "I do not think that I can usefully add anything to the reasons of Porter J.A....in this regard."[46]

The issue was litigated one more time, in 1973, in *Provincial Treasurer of Alberta v. Long*.[47] The dispute was similar: ATB sued a loan guarantor and was met by both a defence on the merits and a challenge to the constitutional validity of its legislative authority. Chief Justice James Milvain of the Trial Division disposed of the argument expeditiously.[48] In an oral ruling, the Chief Justice held that, in line with *Breckenridge*, "it is not open to a party to complain that a contract under which he has received substantial benefits was beyond the power of the party who made it."[49] He went on to state, "purely by way of *obiter*," that the provincial legislation was constitutionally valid since a Saskatchewan decision had held credit unions and similar financial institutions to be within the "overlapping" jurisdiction of the provinces, and that the federal Bank Act did not prohibit such provincial enterprises.[50]

The unwillingness of both the Alberta courts and the Supreme Court of Canada to face the substantive constitutional question raised by these cases must have been a relief to many. The reasons of Mr Justice Allen disclosed that by 1967 the original 6 branches had multiplied tenfold, the organization had more than 100,000 customers with assets in excess of $97 million, total deposits of some $66 million, loans of $49 million, and an annual profit of more than $500,000.[51] Upsetting so large a financial apple cart would have had very serious consequences for the province. Yet leaving the question dangling has meant that today Alberta's largest indigenous financial institution, vastly expanded since then, remains in a state of constitutional uncertainty.

The barbarities and repressions of World War II generated, in the immediate post-war period, a widespread desire, internationally and domestically, to enact legal guarantees of civil liberties. The United Nations began work on what would become the Universal Declaration of Human Rights, and in Canada there was much talk about putting bills of rights in place at both the federal and provincial levels.[52] The Legislature of Alberta led the way, enacting in 1946 a statute entitled the Alberta Bill of Rights Act.[53]

Although William Aberhart had been dead for three years, his protégé, Ernest Manning, who had succeeded him in the Premier's chair, still held the Social Credit torch aloft, and some provisions of the new rights enactment reflected its light. In fact, some thought that the legislation was enacted for the primary purpose of indirectly enacting yet another Social Credit economic scheme. The Alberta Bill of Rights Act had two Parts. The first Part was in a form generally similar to most classic guarantees of rights, embracing the fundamental freedoms of speech, conscience, and religion, but it concluded with general references to certain economic benefits—"gainful employment," "the necessities of life," "educational benefits," "medical benefits," and "a social security pension."[54] Part II expanded on those economic references by detailing the regulatory mechanisms that would establish a social credit monetary system through the licensing of banks, the regulation of bank deposits, and the issuance of Alberta Credit certificates.[55]

The statute stipulated that it would not come into force until its constitutionality had been considered by the courts.[56] Accordingly, the Manning Government presented a constitutional reference to the Appellate Division, with the Government of Canada intervening in opposition to the legislation. The Appellate Division held that Part II was void because it was essentially about "banking," a topic of exclusive federal jurisdiction. Part I, however, was found to be valid legislation on the provincial topic of "property and civil rights in the province" and, because the two Parts were sufficiently "severable" to stand alone in the Court's opinion, only Part II was struck down.[57] Both Alberta and Canada appealed directly to the Privy Council by a procedure that permitted the Supreme Court of Canada to be bypassed. The Privy Council agreed with the Alberta Court that Part II was impermissible banking legislation, but it went further, holding that Parts I and II were so closely linked as to be indivisible, and that the entire statute was therefore beyond provincial jurisdiction.[58] "[T]o all intents and purposes," one observer commented, "the [demise of] the 1946 Act wrote *finis* to attempts at social credit legislation in Alberta..."[59]

Since Part I was substantially about matters within provincial jurisdiction, and the references to economic matters had little or no operational significance, the Appellate Division's Solomon-like approach had much to recommend it. Had that approach prevailed, Albertans would have acquired Canada's first statutory bill of rights.

In the event, Saskatchewan achieved that distinction the following year, and the federal government of John Diefenbaker followed suit in 1960.[60] It was not until 1972 that Alberta re-enacted the Alberta Bill of Rights Act, stripped of all Social Credit trappings.[61]

SECTION THREE: NATURAL RESOURCES

Constitutional cases relating to the province's natural resources have loomed large. One of the first battles involved the obscure common law principle of "escheat," whereby the Crown is entitled to claim the land of owners who die without wills or heirs, and the twin principle of *"bona vacantia,"* which applies to property other than real estate. When Canada was created in 1867, no provinces existed west of Ontario. British Columbia was a separate colony and the land between it and Ontario belonged to the Hudson's Bay Company. When Britain acquired the Company's land and transferred its ownership to Canada, the area was granted territorial rather than provincial status. This meant that both the responsibility for the prairies and the right to benefit from their resources fell to Ottawa. When provincial status was conferred on Manitoba in 1870 and on Alberta and Saskatchewan in 1905, the federal government retained ownership of the natural resources. In all other provinces, resources were provincially owned.

Alberta's young government, understandably desirous of minimizing the extent of this federal land retention, adopted the position that once Crown land had been granted to private owners, the federal interest ended permanently. If an owner of such land died without successors and without devising the property to anyone, Alberta contended that it reverted to the province under the doctrine of escheat. Canada, on the other hand, argued that because it retained the ownership of all public land on the prairies, private land that became public belonged to it once more. When the issue first came before the courts in the Exchequer Court of Canada case *Trusts and Guarantee Co. v. Canada,* to which Alberta courts had no opportunity to contribute, both the trial court and a closely divided Supreme Court of Canada upheld the federal view.[62]

The province was not ready to give up. In 1921 the Alberta Legislature enacted an unusual statute entitled the Ultimate Heir Act, which stated that whenever anyone possessing land or personal property died without willing the property and without heirs, he or she would be deemed to have made a valid will leaving the property to the University of Alberta.⁶³ It was hoped that this would prevent escheat ever occurring, and ensure that ownerless property would benefit a worthy provincial institution. The constitutional validity of the Ultimate Heir Act was challenged, and several other escheat-related questions were raised, in three separate legal proceedings that were consolidated for purposes of an appeal to the Appellate Division.

The Appellate Division, with Mr Justice William Ives dissenting, ruled largely in favour of the province.⁶⁴ While acknowledging that the Exchequer Court of Canada's *Trusts and Guarantee* ruling meant land that belonged to the Crown in 1905 escheated to Canada, the Alberta court held that lands granted by the Crown to private owners *prior* to 1905 were entirely under provincial control because they were not "Crown lands" at the moment the province was born. As to property other than land, there was no basis for any federal interest whatsoever, so *bona vacantia* fell to the province. The Ultimate Heir Act was simply a legitimate exercise of the province's undeniable jurisdiction over inheritance law. The ruling, set out in well-crafted reasons by Mr Justice Alfred Clarke and Justice Hyndman, with the concurrence of Mr Justice William Walsh and Mr Justice Thomas Tweedie, drew heavily upon what Hyndman called "the spirit and scheme of confederation."⁶⁵ Hyndman's reasons pointed out that s. 3 of the Alberta Act, which is the province's Constitution, called for Alberta to be treated "as if...Alberta had been one of the provinces originally united..." except as varied by the Alberta Act itself.⁶⁶ Justice Clarke quoted from a Privy Council decision, concerning escheat and *bona vacantia* in the original provinces, to the effect that "royal territorial rights" were bestowed on the provinces for the "high political... purposes of revenue and government...," and said he thought "the same may be said" about the equivalent provisions of the Alberta Act.⁶⁷ These policy considerations persuaded the Appellate Division to adopt as generous and uniform an interpretation of provincial property rights as the constitutional text would permit.

The interpretive approach of Mr Justice Lyman Duff, who wrote the unanimous reasons of the Supreme Court of Canada overturning the Appellate Division's decision on all but the *bona vacantia* point, was not nourished by any such conceptual model of federalism.⁶⁸ Instead, Duff adopted a far-fetched interpretation of "Crown lands" that supported the federal claim, and cursorily rejected the Ultimate Heir Act as an "appropriation" by means of "a legal fiction" of land "belonging to the Dominion" rather than a genuine law about inheritance.[69] An appeal by the Province to the Privy Council was denied for reasons even more arid and distant from considerations of functional federalism than the Duff ruling.[70] While the immediate impact of the decision was hurtful to Alberta's interests, it ultimately had a major indirect contribution to the expansion of the province's autonomy—and that of the other prairie provinces—by helping to stimulate the national debate and federal-provincial negotiations that culminated in the ownership of natural resources being finally conveyed to the Prairie Provinces by the Natural Resources Transfer Agreements (NRTA), embodied in the Constitution Act, 1930.

When that historic step was finally taken, however, it was not possible to place the Prairie Provinces fully in the shoes of the other provinces in respect of their resources, because the federal Crown had, in the quarter century (60 years in Manitoba's case) between the birth of the provinces and the passage of the Constitution Act, 1930, conveyed large areas of public lands to private ownership, and the NRTA stipulated that the provinces must honour those transactions. In the early 1950s the courts were called upon in two important cases, argued at the same time, to determine the extent to which pre-1930 grants by federal authorities hampered Alberta's subsequent ability to benefit from its mineral resources. The province won one case and lost the other, but the victory was much more significant than the loss.

Western Canadian Collieries v. Alberta was a constitutional challenge to an attempt by the Alberta Legislature to impose new royalties on pre-1930 federal dispositions of coal deposits.[71] The royalties were stated in the legislation to apply "notwithstanding the terms of any...title, agreement...or lease..." Both the Trial Division and Appellate Division held that the new royalties were unconstitutional because the NRTA obligated the province to carry out the pre-1930 federal conveyances "in accordance with the terms thereof," and the Privy Council agreed. Although legislatures normally have the legal power to override such agreements by statute, that was not the case here because the NRTA, which bound the province to abide by the terms of the pre-1930 agreements, had been given constitutional status by the Constitution Act, 1930, and even legislatures are bound by the Constitution.

In the second case, *Huggard Assets v. Alberta*, the issue was whether the province was prevented by the NRTA from imposing new royalties on pre-1930 conveyances of oil and gas.[72] Here the province made no attempt to override existing agreements; instead, it relied on a provision *in the original conveyances* that permitted the Crown to assess royalties "from time to time." Both levels of the Supreme Court of Alberta, as well as the Supreme Court of Canada, held that the province was precluded from doing so for essentially the same reason as in the *Western Canadian Collieries* case. The Privy Council, however, in one of its final Canadian decisions, reversed the Canadian courts, pointing out that in the case of the pre-1930 mineral conveyances in question (which were apparently typical), the federal Crown had reserved "such royalty...from time to time prescribed by regulations."[73] Although the plaintiff company contended, and the Canadian courts agreed, that this did not permit the province to impose new royalties after 1930, the Privy Council held that "from time to time" extended beyond 1930. Had the Canadian courts been upheld, Alberta would likely have been much less prosperous now.

A constitutional shoot-out of great significance took place between the federal and Alberta governments in the early 1980s. It was set in the Alberta foothills immediately north of the Montana border, and editorial cartoonists pictured Alberta's Premier Peter Lougheed, six-shooter at the ready, white Stetson gleaming in the high noon sun, facing down the notorious, black-clad, eastern gunslinger Pierre Elliot Trudeau in front of a Wild-West saloon. For although the *Huggard* decision had brought a welcome improvement in Alberta's ability to profit from its mineral wealth, the Government of Canada remained in the constitutional driver's seat with respect to most areas of governmental activity. From World War II until the late 1970s, judicial interpretation of the Constitution had tended to favour the federal position. So far as resources were concerned, the apogee of federal power was reached in two widely criticized Supreme Court of Canada decisions striking down, on the basis of demonstrably flawed reasoning, Saskatchewan legislation regulating the sale of potash and taxing oil production.[74]

Perhaps emboldened by these judicial assurances of federal constitutional supremacy, the Trudeau government introduced in 1980 a National Energy Program (NEP), described by one writer as "one of the most sweeping government policies ever undertaken in Canada."[75] Ottawa sought to achieve three goals through the NEP: Canadian self-sufficiency in oil, greater Canadian ownership of the oil industry, and a greater federal slice of the oil wealth pie. The NEP made some brash assertions:

> Alberta, with 10% of the population, receives over 80% of the petroleum revenues gained by the provinces...and...

> The Government of Canada believes that the present system is inappropriate and unfair. It believes that more appropriate arrangements must be made, so that the national government, which is accountable to all Canadians, gains access to the funds it needs to support its response to national needs...[76]

The NEP provoked extreme hostility in the western provinces. Premier Lougheed was quick to strap on his side arms. Two days after the NEP was announced, he addressed Albertans on television, telling them "The Ottawa government has...simply walked into our home and occupied the living room."[77] He pledged determined resistance. Less than two weeks later, the Lougheed government announced that it would launch a test case in the Alberta Court of Appeal challenging the constitutional validity of a key component of the federal program.[78]

The test case questioned the extent of Ottawa's authority to tax Alberta's resources. The federal–provincial wrangling that preceded Alberta's decision to litigate may be illustrated by a fictitious conversation between the cowboy champions while they tossed back pre-duel drinks in the saloon of that imaginary frontier Alberta town:

TRUDEAU "Peter, my friend, why do you resist? You know how extensive our constitutional powers are: 'trade and commerce,' 'taxation,' 'peace, order, and good government.'"

LOUGHEED "You forget Pierre that we *own* the resources, and that s. 125 of the Constitution prevents you from taxing the property of provincial governments."

TRUDEAU "We in Ottawa would not be so stupid as to tax your property *directly*—we know that would not be permitted by the courts. Instead, we will just tax the *transaction of distributing* the gas and oil. You may keep them in the ground tax-free if you wish, but as soon as you try to profit by them we'll pounce on that transaction."

LOUGHEED "You'll never get away with it, Pierre."

TRUDEAU "Just watch me!"

LOUGHEED "I'll do more than just watch you—let's step outside."

The method employed by the Lougheed government to put the issue before the courts was imaginative. Choosing a parcel of Crown land close to the United States border, the Government of Alberta caused a provincially-owned gas well to be drilled there and connected to a pipeline capable of carrying the gas to the border for sale to American purchasers. The Alberta Court of Appeal was then asked whether the proposed federal transaction tax could lawfully be applied to such gas, conveyed in such a manner and destined for such a sale transaction. The Court of Appeal held unanimously that the proposed federal tax could not be imposed in those circumstances because the gas would be immune from taxation under s. 125 of the Constitution. It rejected the purported distinction between a tax on property and a tax on property transactions:

> [T]he practical effect of a tax on the transaction by which a Government disposes of its property...differs little from a tax on the property itself. We do not agree that the plain purpose of s. 125 can be avoided by so simple a device. The immunity extends not only to the property of a Province but also to a Province with respect to its property.[79]

The Supreme Court of Canada upheld the Court of Appeal. By a majority of 6 to 3, it dismissed Canada's appeal and held that the proposed tax would not apply to gas owned by the Crown in right of Alberta.[80] The federal hold on prairie resources had been loosened at last.

SECTION FOUR: RIGHTS AND FREEDOMS

If Alberta was not allowed to be the home of Canada's first Bill of Rights, it did become the site of some of the country's most significant early litigation under the Canadian Charter of Rights and Freedoms.[81] Despite their acceptance of the constitutionality of a provincial Bill of Rights in 1946, the superior courts of Alberta, especially the Court of Appeal, had displayed little enthusiasm for legally protecting rights and freedoms prior to the Charter's advent.[82] This remained largely true during many of the formative years of Charter interpretation. It was not initially so, however.

The first Alberta Charter case to reach the Supreme Court of Canada, and only the third Charter case from anywhere in Canada, *Hunter v. Southam*, exerted massive influence on subsequent Charter jurisprudence.[83] At issue was the validity of procedures for issuing search warrants under the federal Combines Investigation Act, a question on which the Alberta Court of Appeal saw eye-to-eye with the Supreme Court. Both courts held that the procedures did not meet the requirements of s. 8 of the Charter. If the Supreme Court's decision, with its call for "unremitting protection of individual rights and liberties" and its now classic exegesis of the "purposive" approach to Charter interpretation, went further than that of the Alberta Court, the two decisions were nevertheless entirely compatible.[84]

The same was true of Alberta's second landmark Charter case, *R. v. Big M. Drug Mart Ltd.*, in which a prohibition of certain business activities on Sundays under the senescent federal Lord's Day Act was struck down by an Alberta Provincial Court judge at trial, a divided Court of Appeal, and a unanimous Supreme Court of Canada, on the ground that it violated freedom of conscience and religion under s. 2(a) of the Charter.[85] The Supreme Court of Canada's explanation of the respective roles of "purpose" and "effect" in analysing legislation for constitutional purposes, which was probably the most important legacy of the case, had origins in the majority reasons of Mr Justice James Laycraft in the Alberta Court of Appeal.[86]

After the *Big M* case, however, Charter rulings of Alberta courts that were important enough to reach the Supreme Court of Canada were frequently at odds with those of the Supreme Court and tended to reject Charter claims. In fact, from the *Big M* case until the Alberta courts' centenary, the only major Charter cases in which the Ottawa Court agreed entirely with the Alberta Court of Appeal were two in which Charter claims were dismissed.[87] In three highly important cases during that period, on the other hand, the Supreme Court of Canada affirmed Charter rights that the provincial Court of Appeal had denied in whole or in part, and in a fourth case it rejected a Charter victory in the Alberta courts that many felt had ignored certain basic human rights values.

One of these cases, *Edmonton Journal v. Alberta*, resurrected ghosts of long-ago scandals that had helped to bring William Aberhart and his Social Credit regime to power in the 1930s.[88] On 3 August 1933, Alberta's Premier John E. Brownlee was packing his bags in preparation for a train trip to Ottawa for a three-month stint of hearings and meetings of the Royal Commission on Banking and Currency, to which he had been appointed by the Government of Canada.[89] Brownlee had reason to feel good about his position and prospects. A distinguished lawyer turned politician, he headed a stable United Farmers of Alberta (UFA) government that he had led successfully through two elections. It was true that the Great Depression had reached alarming severity, and that an extended drought had made matters much worse for prairie dwellers; nevertheless, there was hope that the Royal Commission Brownlee was about to join would come up with some solutions. His government had been damaged several months previously by revelations that a senior member of his cabinet, Tony McPherson, had participated in a spouse-swapping arrangement, resulting in a secret divorce granted at a hearing held out of the public eye in the judges' library in Edmonton; but he, Brownlee, had not been much stained by that scandal. Things were about to change.

That day Premier Brownlee received a "lawyer's letter" from counsel for a young woman, Vivian MacMillan, who had been Brownlee's secretary and protegé, and who claimed to have been seduced and debauched by the Premier over a two year period. The letter threatened legal action. Brownlee denied the accusations and subsequently fought the litigation all the way to the Privy Council.[90] He lost at every step. Although Brownlee resigned as Premier as soon as the trial jury found him liable in July 1934, his successor, Richard Reid, was unable to shake off the carnal odour that clung to his government as the *Brownlee* and *McPherson* cases lurched through the judicial gauntlet, pursued by a prurient press.[91] The notoriety of those proceedings, added to the economic desperation of the times and the allure of William Aberhart's Social Credit promises, assured the annihilation of Reid's UFA government and the unprecedented Social Credit electoral landslide the following year. In the spring of 1935, just before the electorate threw it out of office, the Reid government enacted legislation aimed at keeping such matrimonial litigation away from the prying eyes of the news media and general public in future. It prohibited the publication of any information about divorces and related proceedings, except for the names of the parties and their lawyers, a "concise statement" of the allegations on both sides, and the decision.[92]

That prohibition remained operative, and irksome to the news media, until 1986, when the *Edmonton Journal* sought a judicial declaration that the provincial statute offended freedom of expression and of the press under s. 2(b) of the Charter. At trial, Madam Justice Nina Foster held that the legislation, whose purpose she found to be "to prevent 'yellow journalism,'" did not infringe s. 2(b).[93] The Court of Appeal held that freedom of expression was violated by the restriction, but found it to be justified as a "reasonable limit" in a "free and democratic society" under s. 1 of the Charter. It was legitimately aimed, the Court said, at alleviating "the fear that the publicity might discourage litigants and witnesses from coming forward."[94] The Supreme Court of Canada confirmed that the legislation seriously contravened freedom of expression and restricted the openness of court proceedings, and it disagreed with the Court of Appeal about its justifiability under s. 1. The majority held that although a concern for the protection of privacy was a reasonably justifiable goal, the legislative provisions went further than necessary to achieve that goal. Even the three-judge minority, for whom Mr Justice Gérard La Forest authored a dissent, agreed that some parts of the legislation went too far.

It would be unfair to describe the next major Alberta Charter case, *Mahe v. Alberta,* as one in which the Alberta courts denied a right altogether and were fully reversed by the Supreme Court of Canada.[95] The case concerned the Charter's novel—and far from clearly expressed—guarantee in s. 23 of the right of French or English linguistic minorities in a province to have their children educated in that minority language. A group of Edmonton francophone parents sued for a declaration that the province was denying them certain rights to which they were entitled under s. 23. Both the trial judge and the Court of Appeal went a considerable distance, in largely unexplored constitutional territory, to support the rights claimed. The plaintiffs appealed both decisions, however, and in the end the Supreme Court of Canada went further than the Alberta courts, observing that the parent's appeal to it had been "substantially successful."[96]

The most important issue raised by the case was whether the guarantee of minority language educational "facilities" as outlined in s. 23(3) (b) included management and control by the minority language parents. The children of the plaintiff parents were being taught in two exclusively francophone schools operated by the Edmonton Roman Catholic Separate School Board, with the assistance of an advisory parental committee. The parents contended that they should have a greater management role: that there should, in effect, be an entirely separate francophone school system, under the exclusive control of francophone parents. The lower courts expressed the view that although parental management and control is constitutionally guaranteed, the parents' demands were excessive.

At trial Mr Justice Stuart Purvis held that in Edmonton francophone demographics did not support any change in the management status quo.[97] Speaking for the Court of Appeal, Mr Justice Roger Kerans felt that something better than an advisory committee was called for, but he declined to rule on the question because the school board was not a party to the litigation.[98] The Supreme Court of Canada was unwilling to order the creation of a separate francophone school system, or even to immediately strike down existing arrangements in Edmonton. It did declare, however, that the existing arrangement was in violation of s. 23(3)(b), and that francophone parents in Edmonton were entitled to proportional representation on the school board as full-fledged trustees with exclusive powers over key aspects of the francophone program.[99] The other major difference between the Supreme Court's ruling and that of the Alberta courts was that a provincial regulation requiring a minimum of about 20 per cent of class time to be spent on English language education, which the lower courts had found to be a "reasonable limit" permitted by s. 1 of the Charter, was struck down by the Supreme Court on the ground that there was no evidence that so much time for English was reasonably necessary.[100]

On most other matters, the views of the Supreme Court generally coincided with those expressed below, and it acknowledged at one point that it had "borrowed heavily from the statements of Purvis J. and Kerans J.A. in the Alberta courts...."[101] In light of this similarity of approach, coupled with the fact that the issues presented a moving target as they ascended the judicial ladder, due to a progressive sharpening of focus and shifting arrangements in the schools, it does not seem appropriate to brand this case as one in which the Supreme Court overturned Alberta decisions. It might be more accurately considered an illustration of a three-tier judicial system functioning as it should, with each successive court building upon and refining the work of the court below.

James Keegstra was a high school teacher in Eckville, Alberta. His teaching frequently included anti-Semitic content that Chief Justice Brian Dickson of the Supreme Court of Canada later described as follows:

> Mr Keegstra's teachings attributed various evil qualities to Jews. He thus described Jews to his pupils as "treacherous,"

"subversive," "sadistic," "money-loving," "power hungry" and "child killers." He taught his classes that Jewish people seek to destroy Christianity and are responsible for depressions, anarchy, chaos, wars and revolution. According to Mr Keegstra, Jews "created the Holocaust to gain sympathy" and, in contrast to the open and honest Christians, were said to be deceptive, secretive and inherently evil. Mr Keegstra expected his students to reproduce his teachings in class and on exams. If they failed to do so, their marks suffered.[102]

Charged with promoting hatred against Jews contrary to the "hate propaganda" provisions of the Criminal Code, Keegstra defended by attacking the constitutionality of those provisions. He complained in a pre-trial application that they infringed two Charter rights: freedom of expression (s. 2b), and the presumption of innocence (s. 116d). The latter objection was to a reverse onus section that allowed the truth of the statements to be a defence, but only if the accused proved it by a balance of probability. Mr Justice Francis Quigley dismissed the constitutional challenge, holding that freedom of expression does not protect the wilful promotion of hatred, and that even if it did the Criminal Code provisions were "reasonable limits" under s. 1 of the Charter.[103] He declined to consider the presumption of innocence point because the Crown had not been given timely notice of that objection. Keegstra was subsequently tried and convicted.

The Alberta Court of Appeal unanimously quashed the conviction, without considering the facts, on the ground that both Charter challenges to the legislation were justified. Justice Kerans's reasons on behalf of the Court were brilliant in analysis and eloquent in expression. [104] He made these observations:

> Telling the accused he must persuade the jury on the balance of probabilities is also telling the jury to ignore its doubts... [F]ree speech cannot be equated to polite speech...[I]f too many obstacles are placed in the way of the exchange of ideas, obstacles that too little heed human weakness, prudent people will never say a word....Shall there be no Hyde Park corner in Canada?...[A] well-informed people need not be protected from making the wrong choice....There is a risk that prosecutions under this law, which is designed to promote tolerance, might become a weapon of intolerance....

> The idea of democracy might well require a belief that the majority will never succumb [to hatred]...

Some of Kerans's remarks seemed, however, to suggest that in all but extreme situations the victims of hate propaganda must just grin and bear it:

> [A] distinction can be made between the pain suffered by the target of isolated abuse and the crushing effect of the systemic discrimination of which Shakepeare's Shylock accuses the larger society of his time. Nobody enjoys being the target of name-calling, but the sense of outrage and frustration may be bearable if that abuse is rejected by the community as a whole. Then the pain can be just a psychological pin-prick...[C]itizens in a democratic society must show a courage and stoicism in the face of abusive exercise of freedom of expression...Jews who would be offended by a provocative neo-Nazi march should simply not attend...

In light of these views it was perhaps not surprising that Justice Kerans and his colleagues held that neither the substantive prohibitions of hate propaganda nor the reverse onus clause was a "reasonable limit" on freedom of expression.

The Supreme Court reversed the Court of Appeal and reinstated Keegstra's conviction—though by a close margin. Chief Justice Dickson, writing for the four-person majority, disagreed with Justice Quigley's contention that hate propaganda could never qualify as "expression," but he found the legislation that was designed to combat discriminatory defamation to be a permissible s. 1 limit on Charter rights. Dickson noted that while the Court of Appeal's approach was "reasonably prevalent in America at present," the "Canadian conception of a free and democratic society" necessitated a "departure" from that view. The tone of Dickson's analysis differed sharply from that of Kerans. Its emphasis was on the "two sorts of injury caused by hate propaganda"—the "grave psychological and social consequence" of the "humiliation and degradation" suffered by members of the target group, and the "baleful and pernicious" "influence upon society at large"—rather than on freedom of expression as an abstraction.[105] That perspective led the majority to accord less weight in the s. 1 analysis to the expressive value of hate propaganda than to more socially desirable types of communication.[106] Three Supreme Court justices, Gérard La Forest, Charles Gonthier, and Beverley McLachlin, dissented for reasons similar to, though not as pungently stated as, those of Justice Kerans.

The Canadian Charter of Rights and Freedoms encompasses both the democratic rights of majority Canadians and the right of the members of Canada's many minorities to fair and equal treatment. As the *Keegstra* case demonstrated, interests, values, or attitudes of the majority can be at odds with those of some minorities. Another confrontation of majoritarian and minority considerations occurred in the final case to be considered here: *Vriend v. Alberta*.[107]

Delwin Vriend was employed as a laboratory coordinator at a religiously-oriented college in Edmonton. His work was well regarded by his employer, and he had received salary increases and promotions. But when it was learned that he was homosexual, he was fired for that reason. Vriend's complaint to the Alberta Human Rights Commission was dismissed on the ground that discrimination against sexual orientation was not prohibited by provincial statute at that time. He therefore applied to the Court of Queen's Bench for a declaration that the absence of that prohibited ground from the Individual Rights Protection Act, which proscribed other types of discrimination, violated his right under s. 15(1) of the Charter to equal protection of the law. At trial, Madam Justice Anne Russell upheld Vriend's claim, and ordered that "sexual orientation" be "read in" to the statute as an additional ground of discrimination. A majority of the Court of Appeal, led by the notoriously outspoken Justice John McClung, reversed.[108] The McClung reasons bristled with barbs against "the rights-euphoric, cost scoffing left" (606–607), "the validation of homosexual relations, including sodomy" (609), "the creeping barrage of the special-interest constituencies that now seem to have conscripted the *Charter*" (613), and "rights-restless judges [who] pitchfork their courts into the uncertain waters of political debate" (618). He concluded that because homosexuals and heterosexuals were equally entitled to protection against all types of discrimination that *were* prohibited by the statute, the Alberta Legislature had been "evenhanded" (602). He also held that a court should never read new provisions into legislation "where, after inspection of the background of the statute, it must be concluded that the 'omission' was a step that had been weighed and deliberately declined by the legislating body in whose jurisdiction it lay" (613). Mr Justice Willis O'Leary concurred and Madam Justice Constance Hunt dissented.

The Supreme Court of Canada overturned the Court of Appeal's ruling, agreeing with Justices Russell and Hunt that the statute's failure to prohibit discrimination on the basis of sexual orientation violated Vriend's Charter right to equality, and that the appropriate remedy was an immediate reading-in of sexual orientation. Mr Justice John Major, a former member of the Alberta Court of Appeal himself, agreed with the finding of discrimination, but dissented as to remedy, saying that it would be preferable to strike down the entire statute, subject to a delay of one year to permit the Legislature to take appropriate corrective measures.

§

It's time to return to the question asked at the beginning: Has there been a discernible Alberta approach to constitutional law that distinguishes the work of the Alberta superior courts from that of the Supreme Court of Canada and the Privy Council? With one possible exception, I think not. In three of the four cross-sections examined, the Supreme Court of Alberta and its successor Queen's Bench and Court of Appeal generally appeared to share the constitutional understandings of the courts of last resort. Their decisions were overturned from time to time, to be sure, but that is an inevitable feature of any hierarchical court structure. In terms of quality (admittedly a difficult criterion to apply, if only because the rulings of courts of final resort are automatically "correct" by virtue of their position on the judicial ladder), my assessment of the cases reviewed is that when the Alberta courts differed from the courts above them they "got it right" about as often as their superiors did.

In the fourth category—rights and freedoms—a case could be made that the Alberta decisions—in particular those of the Court of Appeal—exhibited a somewhat different character than those of the Supreme Court of Canada: less ardour for the Charter, and a tendency to favour majoritarian values and considerations over those of minorities. The sample presented here makes no claim to statistical significance, of course. It is much too small for that, and it was selected purely on the basis of the writer's unscientific sense of "importance." I nevertheless came away from the cases examined with a sense that the Alberta Court of Appeal generally showed less enthusiasm than the Supreme Court of Canada for the Canadian Charter of Rights and Freedoms; and that when it did uphold Charter rights, it tended to prefer those of a democratic or majoritarian character over those designed to protect or advance the well-being of minorities. It may also be noteworthy that the two most renowned Charter victories in Alberta courts, *Hunter v. Southam* and *Big M,* involved corporate plantiffs.

This is not to say that all Alberta superior courts justices have displayed this tendency; Queen's Bench judges seemed to show greater Charter sensitivity, and more sympathy for minorities, than did the Court of Appeal in the Charter cases reviewed. One distinguished member of the Court of Queen's Bench, Justice David C. McDonald, authored an important treatise on Charter rights.[109] Nor is it to suggest that Alberta courts have shown a different pattern than that of superior courts in other provinces; the situation in other provinces is beyond the scope of this essay.

One thing that does seem clear in all areas examined is that the Supreme Court of Alberta and its successor courts demonstrated from the beginning a high and generally consistent standard of competence, integrity, and courage. For every episode, such as the "public trial" in the judges' library, that causes one's eyebrows to rise, there are many more, such as Chief Justice Harvey's confrontation with the Army, that cause one's admiration to soar.

NOTES

1 Schedule B to the Canada Act 1982, (U.K.) 1982, c. 11, s. 52(1).
2 Currently Supreme Court Act, R.S.C. 1985, c. S-26, s. 53.
3 *Reference Re Alberta Statutes, Supreme Court Reports* [cited hereafter *SCR*], 100, (1938) (S.C.C.); *A.G. Alberta v. A.G. Canada, Appeal Cases* [cited hereafter *AC*] 117 (1939) (P.C.). See Dale Gibson, "Bible Bill and the Money Barons: The Social Credit Court References and Their Constitutional Consequences," in *Forging Alberta's Constitutional Framework*, ed. Richard Connors and John M. Law (Edmonton: University of Alberta Press, 2005), 191; and *Edwards v. Canada*, *AC*, 124 (1930) (P.C.).
4 *Alberta v. Canada & C.P.R.*, *AC*, 353 (1915) (P.C.); *Canada v. Alberta*, *AC*, 589 (1916) (P.C.); *Natural Resources Transfer Reference*, *AC*, 28 (1932) (P.C.); and *Alberta v. Canada*, *AC*, 356 (1943) (P.C.).
5 For an examination of the early court's personnel, see Louis A. Knafla, "The Supreme Court of Alberta: The Formative Years, 1905-1921," in this volume.
6 For the most recent examination of the conscription case crisis in 1918, see Wayne Renke, "The Power of Law: Judicial Independence and the Supreme Court of Alberta," in this volume. Also see James H. Gray, *Talk to My Lawyer* (Edmonton: Hurtig Publishers, 1987), 39-58; Wilbur F. Bowker, "The Honourable Horace Harvey, Chief Justice of Alberta," *Canadian Bar Review* [cited hereafter *CBR*] 32 (1954): 933.
7 See Wayne Renke, "The Power of Law: Judicial Independence and the Supreme Court of Alberta," in this volume.
8 *Military Service Act*, S.C. 1917, c. 19.
9 S.C. 1914, c. 2, P.C. 919, April 20, 1918. Supportive *resolutions* were, however, passed by both the Senate and the House of Commons.
10 *Re Lewis, Dominion Law Reports* [cited hereafter *DLR*] 41 (1918): 61.
11 P.C. 1697, July 5, 1918.
12 Bowker, "Horace Harvey," 61.
13 I am indebted to Dean Bowker's fine study of Chief Justice Harvey for this comparison: Bowker, "Horace Harvey," 62.
14 *Re Norton, et al., Alberta Law Reports* [cited hereafter *ALR*] 13 (1918): 457, paras. 4-14, paragraphing rearranged.
15 Ibid., at para. 13.
16 *SCR* 57 (1918): 150.
17 See Dale Gibson, "The Real Laws of the Constitution," *Alberta Law Review* [cited hereafter *ALR*] 28 (1990): 358.
18 *Board v. Board, Western Weekly Reports* [cited hereafter *WWR*] 2 (1918): 663 (S.C.A.-A.D.); affirmed *AC* (1919): 956 (P.C.). For an examination of the broader context of *Board v. Board* and family law in the Supreme Court of Alberta, see Marie Gordon, "The Marriage of Law and History: Family Law Cases in the Alberta Supreme Courts, 1907-2006," in this volume.
19 For the general historical context of divorce law in Canada prior to 1940, see James G. Snell, *In the Shadow of the Law: Divorce in Canada, 1900–1939* (Toronto: University of Toronto Press, 1991).
20 *Cox v. Cox*, *WWR* 2 (1918): 422.
21 *Walker v. Walker, Manitoba Law Reports* 28 (1917): 495 (Man. C.A.); affirmed *AC*

(1919): 947 (P.C.) and *Watts v. Watts*, AC (1908): 573 (P.C.).
22 The earliest such decision appears to be *M. v. S.*, *British Columbia Law Reports* 1 (1877): 25.
23 WWR 2 (1918): 633 at 662-63 (S.C.A.), passage abbreviated.
24 *R. v. Riel*, AC 10 (1885): 675 (P.C.). Also see M. MacGuigan, "Precedent and Policy in the Supreme Court," CBR 45 (1967): 627 at 628ff.; C.G. Pierson, *Canada and the Privy Council* (London: Stevens, 1960); Gordon Bale, *Chief Justice W.J. Ritchie* (Ottawa: Carleton University Press), 152-75.
25 *Nadan v. The King*, ALR 21 (1925): 231.
26 AC (1926): 482 (P.C.).
27 22 George V., c. 4 (U.K.). P.W. Hogg, *Constitutional Law of Canada* (Toronto: Carswell, looseleaf 2006), paras. 3.3 and 8.2 note the contribution of the *Nadan* case in bringing about the Imperial Conference of 1926, which led in turn to enactment of the Statute of Westminster.
28 *British Coal Corporation v. The King*, AC (1935): 500 (P.C.).
29 *Reference Re Alberta Statutes*, SCR (1938): 100
30 ATB Financial website, *http://www.atb.com/dev/aboutatb*
31 Treasury Branches Act, S.A. 1938, c. 3.
32 Ibid., sections 5 and 6 and S.A. 1940, c. 14, s. 2
33 O.C. 1069/38 and O.C. 1296/38; B.A. Powe, "The Social Credit Interim Program and the Alberta Treasury Branches" (MA thesis, University of Alberta, April 1951), 51.
34 A burdensome provincial bank taxation measure upon which the Privy Council had yet to rule would, if upheld (it was not), have placed the Treasury Branches in a favourable competitive position vis-à-vis banks. Although Alberta Social Credit "funny money" never re-surfaced after being judicially invalidated, there was a curious echo of it in an unusual "Transfer Voucher" account withdrawal practice followed by the Treasury Branches from 1938 to 1943. See Powe, "Social Credit Interim Program," 88ff.
35 ATB Financial website.
36 Ibid.
37 See "Neil Phillip Primrose," in *Lords of the Western Bench*, Knafla and Klumpenhouwer, 154.
38 *Breckenridge Speedway Ltd. et al. v. Alberta*, DLR, 2nd ser., 64 (1967): 488 (S.C.A a.d.). Trial decision unreported.
39 See "Gordon Hollis Allen" and "Marshall Menzies Porter," in *Lords of the Western Bench*, Knafla and Klumpenhouwer, 15-16 and 143-44, respectively.
40 DLR, 2nd ser., 64 (1967): 488 at 500. See Knafla and Klumpenhouwer, *Lords of the Western Bench*, 144.
41 DLR, 2nd ser., 64 (1967): 488 at 505
42 Ibid., at 525.
43 Ibid., at 513 and 496. See "Sidney Bruce Smith," "Edward William Scott Kane," and "Horace Gilchrist Johnson," in *Lords of the Western Bench*, Knafla and Klumpenhouwer, 172-73 and 78-80, respectively.
44 Ibid., at 490 and 494, quoting from *Towers v. African Tug Co.*, *Chancery* 1 (1904): 558 at 567.
45 Ibid., at 157.
46 DLR, 3rd ser., 9 (1969): 142 at 146 and 157 (S.C.C.).

47 *DLR*, 3rd ser., 49 (1973): 695 (S.C.A. T.D.).
48 See "James Valentine Hogarth Milvain," in *Lords of the Western Bench*, Knafla and Klumpenhouwer, 129–31
49 *DLR*, 3rd ser., 49 (1975): 700 (S.C.A. T.D.).
50 Ibid., at 700–701. The Saskatchewan case was *Caisse Populaire Notre Dame Ltee. v. Moyen*, *DLR*, 2nd ser., 61 (1967): 118 (Sask. Q.B.), a thorough analysis of the "near bank" question by Tucker J., Milvain C.J. also relied on *Re Dominion Trust Co.*, *WWR* 3 (1918): 1023 (B.C. S.C.).
51 *DLR*, 2nd ser., 64 (1967): 488 at 524.
52 See W.S. Tarnopolsky, *The Canadian Bill of Rights*, 2nd ed. (Toronto: Carleton Library, 1975), 3–7 and 11–12.
53 S.A. 1946, c. 11.
54 Ibid., s. 9–12. The Preamble also referred to "ordering [the] internal economy" and "control of policy with respect to the issue, use and withdrawal of credit."
55 Ibid., s. 15(2), 17(1), and 20(2).
56 Ibid., s. 20(2) and s. 24.
57 *Reference Re Alberta Bill of Rights Act*, *WWR* 3 (1946): 772 (S.C.A. A.D.).
58 *A.G. Alberta v. A.G. Canada*, *AC* (1947): 503 (P.C.).
59 Powe, "Social Credit Interim Program," 58. That sentence, written in 1951, concluded with the words "for the time being," but no further attempts have been made to date.
60 Saskatchewan Bill of Rights Act, S.S. 1947, c. 35 and Canadian Bill of Rights, 1960, S.C. 1960, c. 44. For an examination of the origins of the Canadian Bill of Rights, see Christopher MacLennan, *Toward the Charter: Canadians and the Demand for a National Bill of Rights, 1929–1960* (Montreal and Kingston: McGill-Queen's University Press, 2003).
61 Currently R.S.A. 2000, c. A-14. A QuickLaw computer search in May 2006 turned up 95 decisions of the Alberta Queen's Bench or Court of Appeal in which the Bill has been considered.
62 *Exchequer Court Reports* 15 (1915): 403, affirmed *SCR* 54 (1916): 107.
63 S.C. 1921, c. 11.
64 *Re Western Trust Company et al.*, *WWR* 1 (1926): 337 (S.C.A. a.d.). See "William Carlos Ives," in *Lords of the Western Bench*, Knafla and Klumpenhouwer, 76–77.
65 Ibid., at 340. See "Alfred Henry Clarks," "William Legh Walsh," "Thomas Mitchell March Tweedie," in *Lords of the Western Bench*, Knafla and Klumpenhouwer, 27–28, 187–89, and 183–84, respectively.
66 Ibid., at 342.
67 Ibid., at 347–348, quoting from *A.G. Ontario v. Mercer*, *AC* 8 (1882–83): 767 at 778 (P.C.).
68 See generally, David Ricardo Williams, *Duff—A Life in the Law* (Vancouver: UBC Press, 1984).
69 *Re Wudwud Estate*, *SCR* (1927): 136.
70 *AC* (1928): 475 (P.C.).
71 *WWR* 1 (1951): (N.S.) 622 (S.C.A. T.D.); affirmed *WWR* 3 (1951): (N.S.) 1 (S.C.A. T.D.); affirmed and varied *WWR* 8 (1953): (N.S.) 276 (P.C.).
72 *WWR* 2 (1949): 370 (S.C.A. T.D.); *WWR* 1 (1950): 69 (S.C.A. a.d.); *SCR* (1951): 427 (S.C.C.); *WWR* 8 (1953): (N.S.) 561 (P.C.). For a discussion of *Haggard Assets*

within the broader context of how the Supreme Court of Alberta approached oil and gas questions, see Alistair R. Lucas, "Energy Law: The Court and the Prosperity Bonus," in this volume.
73 Although Canadian appeals to the Privy Council were abolished in 1949, cases that were already under way by them continued to be appealable.
74 *Central Canada Potash Co. Ltd. v. Saskatchewan*, DLR, 3rd ser., 88 (1978): 609 (S.C.C.) and *Canadian Industrial Gas and Oil Ltd. v. Saskatchewan*, DLR, 3rd ser., 80 (1977): 449 (S.C.C.).
75 *The Canadian Encyclopedia* (Toronto: McCelland & Stewart, 2000), 1566.
76 *Reference re. Proposed Federal Tax on Exported Natural Gas*, DLR, 3rd ser., 136 (1982): 385 at 430 (S.C.C.), quoting from pages 15 and 16 of NEP.
77 *Globe and Mail*, Toronto, 1 November 1980, 14.
78 Ibid., 13 November 1980, 10.
79 DLR, 3rd ser., 122 (1981): 48 (Alta. C.A.).
80 DLR, 3rd ser., 136 (1982): 385 (S.C.C.).
81 Constitution Act, 1982, Schedule B to the Canada Act 1982, (U.K.) 1982, c. 11, Part I.
82 *Reference re. Alberta Bill of Rights Act*, WWR 3 (1946): 772 (S.C.A. a.d.). See for example, *Walter v. Alberta*, DLR, 2nd ser., 54 (1965): 750 (S.C.A. T.D.); affirmed DLR, 2nd ser., 60 (1966): 253 (S.C.A. a.d.), and DLR, 3rd ser., 3 (1969): 1 (S.C.C.), holding Alberta legislation restricting the number and size of Hutterite colonies to be constitutionally valid; and *Re Schmidt*, DLR, 3rd ser., 72 (1976): 330 (S.C.A. a.d.), reversing DLR, 3rd ser., 57 (1975): 746 (S.C.A. T.D.), denying Roman Catholic parents the right to send their children to Alberta public schools.
83 DLR, 4th ser., 11 (1984): 641 (S.C.C.), affirming DLR, 3rd ser., 147 (1983): 420 (C.A.), reversing DLR, 3rd ser., 136 (1982): 133 (Q.B.).
84 DLR, 4th ser., 11 (1984): 649 (S.C.C.).
85 DLR, 4th ser., 18 (1985): 321 (S.C.C.), affirming DLR, 4th ser., 5 (1984): 121 (C.A.) and WWR 4 (1983): 54 (P.C.A.).
86 See "James Herbert Laycraft," in *Lords of the Western Bench*, Knafla and Klumpenhouwer, 83-84.
87 *Jones v. The Queen*, DLR, 4th ser., 31 (1986): 569 (S.C.C.), affirming DLR 4th ser., 10 (1984): 765 (C.A.), reversing ALR, 2nd ser., 29 (1983): 349: holding that freedom of religion and liberty under ss. 2(a) and 7 of the Charter are not violated by a statutory requirement that every child be educated in accordance with statutory standards; and *Moysa v. Alberta*, DLR, 4th ser., 60 (1989): 1 (S.C.C.), affirming DLR, 4th ser., 43 (1987): 159 (C.A.), affirming DLR, 4th ser., 28 (1986): 140 (Q.B.), holding that freedom of the press under s. 2(b) of the Charter does not confer on journalists the right to resist lawful compulsion to disclose their sources.
88 DLR, 4th ser., 64 (1989): 577 (S.C.C.), reversing DLR, 4th ser., 41 (1987): 502 (C.A.), which affirmed ALR, 2nd ser., 40 (1986): 326 (Q.B.). See also Gray, *Talk to My Lawyer!*, 102ff.
89 See generally, Thomas Thorner and G.N. Reddekopp, "A Question of Seduction: The Case of MacMillan v Brownlee," *Alta LR* 20 (1982): 447-74.
90 See Patrick Brode, *Courted and Abandoned—Seduction in Canadian Law* (Toronto: The Osgoode Society for Canadian Legal History, 2002), 149-73.

91 *MacMillan v. Brownlee*, WWR 2 (1934): 511 (S.C.A. T.D.); WWR 1 (1935): 199 (S.C.A. a.d.); SCR (1937): 318 (S.C.C.); AC (1940): 802 (P.C.). Ewing J. of the S.C.A. T.D. held in an unreported trial decision that the judges' library divorce hearing had been held in "open court." The Appellate Division unanimously agreed: *McPherson v. McPherson*, WWR 1 (1933): 321 (S.C.A. a.d.). The Judicial Committee of the Privy Council disagreed, holding that the closed nature of the hearing rendered the divorce "voidable," although the fact that the appeal period had elapsed and some of the parties had remarried meant that it was too late to invalidate the divorce: AC (1936): 177 (P.C.).

92 At the time of the Charter challenge the version in effect was: Judicature Act, R.S.A. 1980, c. J-1, s. 30 and s. 31.

93 DLR, 4th ser., 22 (1985): 446 at 449 and 451 (Q.B.). See "Nina Leone Foster," in *Lords of the Western Bench*, Knafla and Klumpenhouwer, 46.

94 DLR, 4th ser., 41 (1987): 502 at 506 and 511. Kerans J.A., who wrote for a unanimous Court, concerned himself with what he saw as the modern usefulness of the legislation rather than its historical roots.

95 DLR, 4th ser., 8 (1990): 69 (S.C.C.), partly reversing DLR, 4th ser., 42 (1987): 514 (C.A.) and DLR, 4th ser., 22 (1985); (Q.B.).

96 DLR, 4th ser., 68 (1990): 69 at 109.

97 See "Stuart Somerville Purvis," in *Lords of the Western Bench*, Knafla and Klumpenhouwer, 156-57.

98 See "Roger Philip Kerans," in ibid., 80-81.

99 DLR, 4th ser., 68 (1990): 107-108.

100 Ibid., at 106-107.

101 Ibid., at 93.

102 *R. v. Keegstra*, SCR 3 (1990): 697 at 714, *per* Chief Justice Brian Dickson. See generally, Robert J. Sharpe and Kent Roach, *Brian Dickson: A Judge's Journey* (Toronto: The Osgoode Society for Canadian Legal History, 2003) and, for the Keegstra case specifically, see 407-10.

103 See "Francis Hugh Quigley," in *Lords of the Western Bench*, Knafla and Klumpenhouwer, 157.

104 DLR, 4th ser., 42 (1987): 514 (C.A.).

105 *R. v. Keegstra*, SCR 3 (1990): 697, at paras. 60-63.

106 Ibid., at paras. 91-94.

107 DLR, 4th ser., 156 (1998): 384 (S.C.C.), reversing DLR, 4th ser., 132 (1996): 595 (C.A.), which reversed ALR, 3rd ser., 18 (1994): 286 (Q.B.).

108 See: *R. v. Ewanchuk*, DLR, 4th ser. (1999): 193 at 225-27 (S.C.C.) for Madam Justice L'Heureux-Dubé's criticism of Justice McClung's sarcastic remarks about a victim of sexual assault. See "John Wesley McClung," in *Lords of the Western Bench*, Knafla and Klumpenhouwer, 115-16.

109 D.C. McDonald, *Legal Rights in the Canadian Charter of Rights and Freedoms*, 2nd ed. (Toronto: Carswell, 1989).

FOUR

The Supreme Court of Alberta and First Nations Treaty Hunting Rights
Federalism and Respect for "the Queen's Promises"

BRIAN CALLIOU

> It is satisfactory to be able to come to this conclusion and not have to decide that "the Queen's promises" have not been fulfilled. It is satisfactory to think that legislators have not so enacted but that the Indians may still be "convinced of our justice and determined resolution to remove all reasonable cause of discontent."
>
> JUSTICE ALEXANDER A. MCGILLIVRAY
> in *R. v. Wesley* (1932)

LEGAL HISTORICAL SCHOLARSHIP in the past two decades has made important strides in redressing the interpretative shortcomings and biases that have characterized the depiction of First Nations peoples and their histories. Part of this trend can be attributed to broader efforts centred on writing Aboriginal peoples into Canada's historical development and, specifically, into the nation's legal history. This latter development is mirrored in the appearance of numerous legal histories that consciously examine the experience of Aboriginal peoples across the nation.[1]

At the same time, Canada's legal system, and especially its courts, have been criticized for the way in which Aboriginal peoples have been treated.[2] Some critics suggest that the courts are at least discriminatory and, in some instances, racist.[3] Others argue that the traditional ways of Aboriginal life have been criminalized and that Canadian courts have shown an institutional bias.[4] Sidney Harring has pointed out, however, that the historic Canadian record is not so clear cut as these contemporary critics might claim. According to Harring, the Canadian courts historically gave "liberal treatment" to traditional Aboriginal laws and customs, but later became increasingly disrespectful of these traditions, Aboriginal law, and the treaty agreements negotiated between the Crown and First Nations.[5] As much as Harring's research is rooted in nineteenth-century jurisprudence, there are two cases from pre-Second World War Alberta that not only support his contention, but indicate that this liberalism survived into the twentieth century. In these two instances, Albertan judges sought a clear understanding of treaty hunting rights and did so through a broad interpretive approach, in contrast to a more literal reading of black letter law.[6] Although their efforts do not reflect the entirety of Alberta's approach to Aboriginal legal issues, these judges strove to uphold the honour of the Crown and keep "the Queen's promises"—made in the name of Victoria when the Dominion government negotiated treaties with the Aboriginals—and demonstrate that the all too simplistic expectation of a conservative Alberta fails to capture the subtleties of the province, its judges, and its legal heritage.

Framed by the explosion of historically informed scholarship addressing Canada's First Nations peoples in the past thirty years, this chapter highlights a small but notable piece of Alberta's legal history. These two cases, *R. v. Stoney Joe,* heard on appeal in 1910, and *R. v. Wesley,* heard on appeal in 1932, reveal empathetic judicial reasoning illustrating the seriousness with which three Albertan judges held the honour of the Crown and the equitable principles shaping its relationship with First Nations peoples. These decisions—and the fact that they failed to leave a discernable mark on the governmental and judicial approaches to First Nations peoples and their hunting rights—also reveal the persistence of provincial game laws in restricting First Nations peoples' traditional livelihood. Indeed, the modern Alberta Court of Queen's Bench and Court of Appeal, along with the Supreme Court of Canada, have adopted a view of First Nations hunting rights that is almost entirely contrary to the broad, liberal approach at the heart of *Stoney Joe* and *Wesley*. However, before turning to these two cases that would prove to be contrary to the emerging tenor of the times, we must first outline the context of federalism and game laws in what was the North-West Territories prior to the creation of Alberta and Saskatchewan in 1905.

FEDERALISM AND GAME LAWS IN THE NORTH-WEST

The British North America (BNA) Act, 1867, specified the jurisdictional divisions between the federal and provincial governments in sections 91 and 92. Included in section 91(24) was exclusive federal responsibility for "Indians and lands reserved for Indians." This supposedly clear indication of federal jurisdiction would be muddied by sections 109 and 117 that reserved to the *original provinces* the ownership and control over the lands and natural resources within their boundaries. For the North-West Territories, however, the federal government retained jurisdictional authority over all natural resources until the Natural Resources Transfer Agreement (NRTA) of 1930, although even then section 12 of the NRTA established constitutional protection for First Nations hunting and fishing rights. Therefore, while the jurisdictional clash over federally administered First Nations hunting rights in the original provinces was evident, no such conflict seemingly existed in the North-West Territories and, by extension, the prairie provinces of Saskatchewan and Alberta. For those familiar with Canadian constitutional history, however, such apparent certainty is often illusory. And as it turns out, federal jurisdiction over First Nations hunting rights was more complicated than it appeared.

In the decade after Confederation, the Dominion of Canada negotiated the acquisition of Rupert's Land from the Hudson's Bay Company and then turned to the task of entering into treaties with the First Nations peoples of Manitoba and the North-West Territories. The first treaty in what is now Alberta was signed in 1874 when a small area of southeastern Alberta was covered by Treaty No. 4.[7] Two years later Treaty No. 6 was negotiated to allow peaceful settlement of the prime farmland in the central part of the province, and in 1877 the powerful Blackfoot tribes of what is now southern Alberta entered into Treaty No. 7. Not until twenty years later, in 1899, in the aftermath of the Klondike gold rush and the discovery of minerals and other natural resources, did the Crown enter into Treaty No. 8 covering parts of northern Alberta, Saskatchewan, and British Columbia, and the southern part of the North-West Territories.[8] Lastly, in 1906, Treaty No. 10 was signed, covering the central northeast portion of Alberta.[9]

The treaty negotiations document that First Nations leaders sought out and obtained the protection of and respect for traditional livelihoods and, in particular, for the continuance of their hunting, fishing, trapping, gathering, and trading rights.[10] For his part, federal Indian Commissioner Alexander Morris consistently maintained that treaties were agreements between the First Nations and Her Majesty the Queen, whom he described as "a caring and benevolent Queen" whose generosity must be trusted.[11] Looking to the future, Morris saw a shared road where "I see Indians, gathering, I see gardens growing and houses building; I see them receiving money from the Queen's Commissioners to purchase clothing for their children; at the same time I see them enjoying their hunting and fishing as before, I see them retaining their mode of living with the Queen's gift in addition."[12] He indicated that the government did not want to maintain the First Nations but wished them to be self-supporting by relying upon traditional hunting and fishing and through agriculture. From the perspective of Treaty 6 First Nations, the treaty recognized that "much of the land was beyond the places where the white man would want to go... [and we] still had the rights to hunt, fish, and travel as freely as before."[13]

A year later, Indian Commissioner David Laird reported that in the course of negotiating Treaty 7, the First Nations "...were also assured that their liberty of hunting over the open prairie would not be interfered with, so long as they did not molest settlers and others in the country."[14] Consistent with Laird's statement, one Treaty 7 Elder of the Blood Tribe stated that free access to "wildlife [was] promised as well as the freedom to roam and get food and clothing."[15] Laird would also be a commissioner for Treaty 8 negotiations where First Nations leaders were assured that "they would be as free to hunt and fish after the treaty as if they never entered into it."[16] Specifically the treaty provided that

> Her Majesty the Queen HEREBY AGREES with the said Indians that they shall have the right to pursue their usual vocations of hunting, trapping and fishing throughout the tract surrendered as heretofore described, subject to such regulations as may from time to time be made by the Government of the country, acting under the authority of Her Majesty, and saving and excepting such tracts as may be required or taken up from time to time for settlement, mining, lumbering, trading or other purposes.[17]

Wanting to retain the proviso in the hunting clause regarding government regulations and taking up lands, Laird had to convince the

First Nations' negotiators that the condition was for their own benefit.[18] First Nations' persistence was such that Laird admitted that, "over and above the provision, we had to solemnly assure them that only such laws as to hunting as were in the interest of the Indians and were found necessary in order to protect the fish and fur-bearing animals would be made."[19]

To the extent that the language of s. 91(24) and the subsequent treaty negotiations demonstrated federal jurisdiction over Aboriginal peoples and the recognition of their traditional hunting rights, Manitoba nonetheless signalled its unwillingness to accept the exclusivity of federal authority. Specifically, in 1883 the province passed its first hunting regulations, and these, in their application, conflicted with federal authority over First Nations peoples.[20] In response, Dominion Department of Indian Affairs (DIA) officials requested that the province allow "certain indulgences in regard to the killing of game out of season to Indians."[21] Manitoba refused. In turn, the Dominion Department of Justice provided a legal opinion indicating that no restrictions "can be placed on Indians killing game at any time for their own use as they were assured by Treaties they would be allowed to do so."[22] But rather than disallow the legislation as an interference with federally protected First Nations hunting rights, the federal government preferred to negotiate with Manitoba.[23] The province refused to back down and First Nations hunters were soon charged with breaching provincial regulations. By October 1886 the matter had been appealed to the Manitoba Court of Queen's Bench in the form of *R. v. Robertson*. The Court determined that the regulation of hunting and trapping was entirely within provincial jurisdiction as defined in s. 92(13) and s. 92(16) as a matter of local concern along with civil and property rights.[24]

The case, and especially the federal disinclination to press the matter of federally recognized First Nations hunting rights despite s. 91(24), is intriguing. As suggested by Robert Irwin, the ambivalence of the DIA toward Aboriginal hunting and fishing rights proved to be the theme so far as Manitoba was concerned in the years after the flurry of treaty-making in the 1870s.[25] However, in the North-West Territories the situation was rather different, not the least because the federal government remained an active participant in framing the region's legislative makeup. Thus when in 1877 the Territorial Council passed regulations aimed at protecting the few remaining bison herds, the ordinance was aimed squarely at non-native hunters while recognizing the traditional rights of Aboriginal hunters and communities.²⁶ However, by 1889, and arguably influenced by the course of events in neighbouring Manitoba, the Territorial Council repealed any exemptions favouring Aboriginal peoples in the game ordinances. Unlike the response towards Manitoba's hunting regulations, the federal government did not hesitate to disallow the amendments as a violation of the treaty promises.²⁷ Perhaps the federal government had once hoped to woo Manitoba at a time when constitutional conflict with Ontario was on the horizon but, by the end of the decade, such attempts at winning over provincial allegiance to the federal cause had been abandoned.²⁸

Beyond whatever motivations may have shaped federal strategy in the course of the 1880s, the federal government's diminishing support and protection of First Nations' hunting and fishing rights was unmistakable, especially by 1890 when the federal Indian Act was amended to allow the Superintendent General to enact game regulations that would apply to Aboriginal hunters in Manitoba and the North-West Territories.²⁹ The shift in emphasis was important. Bennett McCardle has argued that in the 1880s the Dominion government based its definition of hunting rights on the treaties, whereas a decade later hunting rights were viewed in relation to the jurisdiction over Indians pursuant to s. 91(24) of the BNA Act.³⁰ This change signalled a reduction in the importance placed upon the treaty terms in determining the limits that could be placed on First Nations hunters. Consequently, "the control of Indian hunting practices moved gradually into provincial hands."³¹ To the extent that traditional Aboriginal hunting rights still existed on the Canadian prairies, they were to be subjected to regulation, regardless of how the treaty language of the 1870s might have been understood.

While both provincial and territorial pressure seemingly influenced the federal reappraisal of what constituted traditional hunting rights, these were not the only factors at play. The growing presence of sport hunters certainly played an important role in raising the stakes over these rights. Sport hunters lobbied the Superintendent General of Indian Affairs to have First Nations hunters, and especially the Stoney Indians in the foothills of the Rocky Mountains, made subject to local game laws.³² Early in 1893 a petition from the Calgary Rod and Gun Club, in concert with identical petitions from Lethbridge, Edmonton, Red Deer, McLeod, Maple Creek, and Moose Jaw, were received by the Minister of the Interior and the Superintendent General of Indian Affairs asking that local game laws apply to First Nations hunters.³³ Claiming to be motivated by the desire to encourage "sport with gun and rod" and to further "the protection of game," the petition singled out First Nations traditional hunting rights as contrary to game conservation, notions of equity, and a desire to eliminate the tensions created by the preferences given to Aboriginal hunters. This portrait of First Nations hunters as hunters like any others ignored their unique situation. First Nations hunters possessed existing claims to traditional hunting territories; hunting is an integral aspect of their "Indianness." They hunted for a living and entered into treaties in which "the Queen's promises" assured them that they could "hunt as before."

Nevertheless, this lobbying effort had the effect of prompting Lawrence Vankoughnet, Deputy Superintendent General of Indian Affairs, to raise the matter with T. Mayne Daly, the Superintendent General of Indian Affairs. Vankoughnet indicated that Hayter Reed, Indian Commissioner of the North-West Territories, had recommended that "a proclamation be issued under 53 Vic., Cap. 29, Sec. 10, being additional Sec. 133 of the Indian Act, placing the Indian Bands described in his letter under the provisions of existing Game Ordinances in the North-West Territories."[34] DIA officials believed that while they could breach "the Queen's promises" and restrict the First Nations hunters' treaty rights, provincial and local governments could not. Acting on a request from DIA, the Department of Justice provided Vankoughnet with a draft public notice on 28 February 1893 to be used in bringing specified First Nations under the North West Game Ordinance. The form indicated that

> Public Notice is hereby given in pursuance and by virtue of Section 133 of the Indian Act (as enacted by 53 Victoria, Chapter 29, Section 10) that on and after the day of _____ A.D., 1893, the Laws respecting game in force in the North West Territories shall apply to the following Indians, that is to say:
> (Here define the Indians whom the laws are to be extended.)
> Dated at the Department of Indian Affairs at Ottawa this day of February, A.D., 1893.
> Superintendent General of Indian Affairs[35]

Reed subsequently filled in the blanks and returned the completed form back to the DIA on 8 April 1893.[36]

This initial delegation of authority over Indian hunting included most of the bands in Treaties 4, 6, and 7—a total of 46 First Nations—

along with "stragglers at Medicine Hat, Maple Creek, Moose Jaw and Swift Current."[37] Indian Affairs delayed the coming into force of the proclamation until 31 December 1893 so as "to give [First Nations hunters] plenty of time before they are brought under the operation of the said laws" and "in order that the minds of the Indians may be prepared for the change."[38] Notably, and notwithstanding the animosity of sport hunters, the Department of Indian Affairs decided not to include the Stoney Indians, believing that they were not quite ready to be brought within the new game regulations.[39]

Word of the proclamation was greeted by immediate outcry and protest from First Nations leaders, who were quick to remind the government that the treaties had guaranteed the right to continue a traditional livelihood.[40] The DIA response articulated three points: protecting the game was in the best interests of Aboriginal peoples; the treaties had reserved for the federal government the right to make regulations to govern the Indians; and finally, exceptions could no longer be made for Aboriginal peoples and the provision of rations and aid was preferable to allowing year-round hunting.[41] The new policy signalled both an abandonment of "the Queen's promises" made during the treaty negotiations and a retreat from the notion that Aboriginal peoples ought to be self-sufficient. Further, the imposition of hunting regulations in concert with the disappearance of the bison from the prairies left affected First Nations communities compelled to take what was needed from local cattle herds, an action that did little to foster good relations with ranchers.[42]

Less than a year later, and acting upon information provided by sport hunters, Lieutenant Governor Charles H. Mackintosh of the NWT decided that legislation preventing "the destruction of Game within the limits of the Rocky Mountain Park by Stoney Indians" was needed.[43] Not only had a "gentleman of wide experience, and [an] ardent sportsman," provided valuable counsel to Mackintosh, but Mackintosh pointed to the establishment of a Rocky Mountain Park as a "domain of refuge" for the game to be free from "the intrusion of the slaughterer" as a prudent policy that would allow the animals to replenish unmolested so that the "sportsman [can] have his day."[44] The Lieutenant Governor's language was illustrative. Characterizing the Stoneys and other Indians as having been responsible for the "slaughter" of animals, sports hunters, businessmen, and government officials advocated the application of game laws to Indians so that sport hunting might flourish. Superintendent General T. Mayne Daly responded to Mackintosh six days later and indicated that while the Stoneys had been exempted from the 1893 proclamation, as of 1 January 1895 they would be brought under the game ordinances.[45] On the same day that Daly wrote Mackintosh, Indian Commissioner Hayter Reed instructed the Assistant Indian Commissioner A.E. Forget to issue an *immediate* order restricting all First Nations hunting within the Rocky Mountain Park. Reed also noted the complaints made about the Stoney Indian hunters and indicated that the "Police should be advised of the action taken, so that they may enforce that prohibition by driving out of the Park any Indian found hunting or trapping therein."[46] Acting on Reed's instructions, Forget issued a public notice under s.133 of the Indian Act, proclaiming that the NWT game laws were to be applicable to the Stoney Indians, effective 1 January 1895.[47]

The task of informing the Stoney Indians of the change fell to DIA farming instructor P.L. Grasse. After having been told of the new policy at a 17 May 1894 meeting that they were no longer exempt from territorial game regulations, the Stoneys raised many concerns. Grasse later reported that he convinced the Stoneys of the necessity of the regulations and had argued that the closed season would not affect them since they would be getting crops in, building and mending fences, tending to their cattle, and later haying and harvesting.[48] The message was unmistakable. The Stoneys were to become farmers and ranchers and, through the demands and routines of those occupations, they would be tied to the reserve and effectively prevented from pursuing their traditional livelihood.[49]

Beginning in the spring of 1900 a series of questions was raised about the new regulations. First, Indian Agent J.A. Mitchell, of the Muskowpetung Agency near Qu'Appelle, enquired as to whether amendments to the game laws after 1894 applied automatically to the First Nations named in the proclamation of 1894. The DIA indicated that "the Game Laws from time to time in force in the Territories apply to the Indians of the bands named in the Notice as the same laws are from time to time amended until the public notice is revoked."[50] Armed with this explanation, Secretary of Indian Affairs, J.D. McLean, informed Mitchell that the amendments were applicable to the First Nations named in 1894.[51] Three years later, Indian Commissioner David Laird recommended that "owing to the extension of the various railway systems and the rapid settlement of the country," a new proclamation should be issued to bring more bands under the game laws.[52] Accordingly, in a public notice dated 1 May 1903 and pursuant to s. 133 of the Indian Act, all those bands in the fertile belt that had been exempted were brought under the game regulations.[53] This final proclamation listed an additional 22 First Nations from the parklands coming under the game laws' ambit. Although this provision would undergo a number of minor changes, it "remained an integral element of the Indian Act until the 1951 revisions."[54] This erosion of traditional hunting rights at the turn of the century set the context for *R. v. Stoney Joe* in 1910 and how in that case Mr Justice Charles Stuart demonstrated that insofar as he was concerned, the Queen's promises remained an integral ingredient in the federal government's responsibilities to First Nations peoples into the early twentieth century.

R. v. Stoney Joe

Stoney Joe had been charged with selling the head of a mountain sheep contrary to the 1907 Alberta Game Act.[55] The accused was a member of the Stoney Indian tribe that occupied an area along the eastern foothills and slopes of the Rocky Mountains near Banff and had been hunters, fishers, and gatherers since "time immemorial." Magistrate Andrew Sibbald found Stoney Joe guilty. But on appeal to the Supreme Court of Alberta, the conviction was overturned. The ruling held that despite the Superintendent General of Indian Affairs proclaiming that the Stoney First Nation be subject to the territorial game laws pursuant to the 1894 public notice, subsequent amendments to the game laws had to be reviewed by the Department of Indian Affairs prior to implementation. Amendments did not apply to the First Nations hunters without a specific declaration from the DIA.

The presiding judge for the appeal was Mr Justice Charles Allen Stuart, who had practised law in Calgary until 1905 before being elected to represent Gleichen in the inaugural Legislative Assembly for Alberta.[56] Stuart's farm at Gleichen bordered on the Blackfoot Reserve (Siksika First Nation) where he most certainly would have had interaction with and knowledge of the local Blackfoot peoples. Described by Louis A. Knafla as a judicial activist who was unafraid to make new law, Stuart was keenly aware of the role that local custom ought to play in legal decision-making.[57] His ruling in *Stoney Joe* seemingly drew upon his own lived experience as a neighbour to the Blackfoot and, in equal measure, his own faith in a judge's responsibility to the law and to the community in which that law functions.

Although his approach in *Stoney Joe* centred on jurisdictional responsibility for Aboriginal peoples, he also placed considerable weight on the place of morality and honour in governmental choice and policy. His was not an interpretative world dominated by a literal reading of a statute so as to understand its intent. For Stuart the jurisdictional question began with the federal government's responsibility for Aboriginal peoples as framed by s. 91(14) of the BNA Act and the subsequent treaty process. The text of Treaty 7 indicated that the Stoney Indians had surrendered "all their rights, titles and privileges" and, in exchange, "Her Majesty agreed with the Indians that they should have the right to pursue their vocations of hunting throughout the tract surrendered 'subject to such regulations as may from time to time be made by the Government of the Country.'"[58] His respect for the solemnity of the treaty was clear in stating that "a treaty or contract between Her Majesty and them [the Aboriginal peoples] should be and I think always has been considered as being sacred and inviolable." Still, while he noted that the treaty negotiations had not addressed the possibility that the Indians might be subject to regulations restricting their right to hunt, Stuart did not consider whether this gap amounted to a misrepresentation on the part of the Queen's Commissioners. This possibility aside, the federal statute was nonetheless "valid and binding upon the Indians" and Justice Stuart chose to believe that Parliament had inadvertently violated the treaty promise concerning the continuation of traditional hunting.

Having established federal jurisdiction over Aboriginal peoples, Stuart then turned to the associated question of whether the provincial Game Act, by its own force, applied to treaty Indians residing in Alberta. Second, had the present provincial Game Act been made applicable by virtue of any Dominion enactment? Implicit in these questions was the understanding that regulating First Nations hunting was exclusively within federal jurisdiction. With respect to the first question, Justice Stuart held that provincial game laws did not apply of their own force to First Nations who entered into treaty. It was the federal Parliament's exclusive power under s. 91(24) to legislate in relation to "Indians and Lands reserved for Indians."[59] With respect to the second question, Stuart reviewed the wording of s. 133 of the Indian Act and the 1894 Public Notice bringing the Stoney Indians within the ambit of the local game laws and found "no further or other notice has ever been published or given up to the present time." He also noted that s. 11 of the Alberta Game Act, under which Stoney Joe was convicted at trial, did not appear in the 1894 Game Ordinance. Without a specific declaration from the DIA, the public notice of 1894 was insufficient to make s. 11 of the 1907 Alberta game regulations applicable to the Stoney Indians.

The point was crucial, for it raised "the much discussed question of the delegation of legislative powers."[60] Justice Stuart recited the principle that Parliament possessed the power to pass legislation that referred to provincial or territorial laws, an act that he termed "legislating by reference." His sources for this view were the 1882 case of *R. v. O'Rourke* and A.H.F. Lefroy's 1898 legal text, *The Law of Legislative Power in Canada*.[61] The judgment then cited the 1883 decision of *Hodge v. The Queen* as authority for Parliament to delegate its legislative power "to a particular official" who could then proclaim in a public notice that a territorial or provincial law was applicable to Indians.[62] Justice Stuart rejected the Crown's argument that the principle of delegation and sub-delegation allowed Parliament to transfer to a provincial government "the power in future to legislate upon a subject which the British North America Act has placed within the jurisdiction of the Dominion."[63] Reasoning that there was "a discretionary power" placed upon the Superintendent General of Indian Affairs "with respect to whether certain known and ascertained laws should be adopted," Stuart held that the Superintendent General did not have the discretion to hand over to a territorial or provincial legislature "the general power of making laws for the Indians."[64] The Public Notice in 1894, therefore, only had the effect of making the Stoney First Nations subject to the laws in force at that date.

The attempt to have the Stoney Indians governed by Alberta's game regulations had been undone by a technical error on the part of the DIA. It bears emphasis that had the DIA specifically indicated that the Stoney Indians were to be covered by s. 11 of the 1907 Alberta game regulations, then the technical requirements of the Superintendent General of Indian Affairs would have been fulfilled. But Justice Stuart was not prepared to let the matter rest on that point alone. While Parliament had delegated a discretionary power to the Superintendent General of Indian Affairs, this was not merely a policy decision. According to Stuart, the delegation carried a moral obligation to act in accordance with Crown sovereignty over the traditional hunting grounds as recognized by the Royal Proclamation of 1763 and to uphold the honour of the Crown in keeping the "Queen's promises." The special relationship between the Aboriginal peoples and Dominion government meant that the Crown was expected to protect the best interests of the First Nations. Further, while the concept of parliamentary supremacy meant that a right created by

Parliament could also be overridden by Parliament, such a decision did not absolve the government of its moral obligations.[65] Although Parliament possessed the authority to override treaty rights, Stuart thought it unconscionable to do so. Described by Douglas Sanders as the "honour of the Crown" argument, Stuart's ruling was a double-edged sword for the Stoney Indians and all of Canada's First Nations for, to the extent that they were protected by federal jurisdiction, the weight of that protection was ultimately founded on honour and morality.[66]

Despite the potential implications of Justice Stuart's ruling in *Stoney Joe*, the federal government seemingly took note only of the technical rationale and ignored the more challenging moral considerations. While it is plausible that the ruling was deliberately ignored "so as not to intensify Federal-Provincial tensions," it is equally true that Stuart's decision had provided an escape clause.[67] Still, Robert Irwin's characterization of the decision as one "filled with problems and contradictions" places blame at Stuart's feet, where it clearly does not belong.[68] For as much as Stuart had provided the opportunity to redress the administrative oversight, it was the government that chose to ignore what the judge evidently thought was just as relevant: the federal government's moral obligation to the First Nations. *Stoney Joe* "should have allowed Ottawa to reverse its policy and take a stand against local erosion of native hunting activities;" rather, the case was forgotten for over five decades until it was unearthed by a researcher working for the Indian Association of Alberta.[69] In the interim, the delegation of powers from the federal to the provincial governments continued apace and First Nations hunters and their traditional livelihood increasingly came under the aegis of provincial game laws.

Although the wilful ignorance of *Stoney Joe* suited Alberta's purpose in bringing the First Nations under provincial game regulations, a larger question still loomed in the background. Specifically, while the Manitoba Queen's Bench ruling in *R. v. Robertson* had indicated that regulation of hunting and trapping was within provincial jurisdiction as matters of local concern along with civil and property rights, federal control over natural resources in Manitoba, Saskatchewan, and Alberta seemingly left the door open if the federal government wanted to reassert its jurisdiction.[70] Motivated in large part by the provincial desire to secure resource revenue from natural resources, after nearly a decade of negotiations, the Dominion and the three prairie provinces signed the Natural Resources Transfer Act (NRTA), 1930.[71] As it pertained to First Nations' hunting rights, s. 12 of the

NRTA created an optical illusion suggesting that the traditional rights protected by the federal government were to be respected within provincially administered game regulations. Specifically,

> In order to secure to the Indians of the Province the continuance of the supply of game and fish for their support and subsistence, Canada agrees that the laws respecting game in force in the Province from time to time shall apply to the said Indians within the boundaries thereof, provided, however, that the said Indians shall have the right which the Province hereby assures to them, of hunting, trapping and fishing game and fish for food at all seasons of the year on all unoccupied lands and on any other lands to which the said Indians may have a right of access.[72]

To the extent that traditional hunting rights were to be respected by the provinces, the section left little room to question whether First Nations hunters would be subject to provincial hunting regulations. The scope of this new delegation was quickly challenged.

R. v. Wesley

Orchestrated by Norman Luxton, a trader who had dealings with the Stoney First Nations, M.B. Peacock, Calgary lawyer and activist, and William Wesley, a member of the Stoney First Nation, the 1932 case *R. v. Wesley* was a connivance intended to test s. 12 of the NRTA.[73] Wesley admitted the facts that he had killed a deer with horns smaller than specified by game laws, hunted without a licence, and hunted with dogs, but claimed that being an Indian with treaty rights to hunt, in accord with s. 12 of the NRTA, exempted him from provincial game regulations. After reserving the decision for one day, Police Magistrate Gilbert E. Sanders found Wesley guilty based upon a narrow approach to the case and literal readings of s. 12 of the NRTA and the official text of Treaty 7. At the hearing on 1 April 1932, Sanders refused to consider any extrinsic evidence. Indeed, when Peacock attempted to have Don Wildman Sr. and Hector Crawley, both of whom had been present at the signing of Treaty 7, testify to their understanding of the treaties, Sanders stated, "I will not hear what these Indians think they understand the Treaty to be, it speaks for itself."[74] The Police Magistrate added that the Stoney Indians ought to be able to make their living on the reserve and that the provincial game laws applied because they protected the animals for both Indians and Whites.

True to the intent of setting up the case in the first instance, Peacock quickly filed Wesley's appeal. Justices William Lunney, Alfred Clarke, Charles Mitchell, and Alexander McGillivray heard the appeal in the Supreme Court of Alberta.[75] Counsel for the Crown was H.J. Wilson, and Peacock continued as Wesley's lawyer.[76] The case produced two sets of written reasons: one authored by Justice Lunney for himself and the second for the Court's majority by Justice McGillivray. Lunney's shorter judgment rejected the Crown's argument that s. 12 of the NRTA altered the law applicable to Indians and found instead that s. 12 actually emphasized the right of Indians to hunt, trap, and fish. He also drew upon an 1890 report by then Minister of Justice, Sir John Thompson, who had recommended that a proposed Game Ordinance of the North-West Territories be disallowed for the following reasons:

i. Treaties promised continued hunting;

ii. Only the Dominion government could legislate hunting of Treaty Indians;

iii. The [game] Ordinance violates the [hunting] rights secured;

iv. The federal government must take the utmost care to see none of the treaty rights of the Indians are infringed without their concurrence;

v. The [Provincial] Legislature realized the difference in its special provisions for residents of the north between sportsman and food hunter;

vi. Only a competent body can legislate to curtail Indian hunting on unoccupied Crown lands

Relying upon Thompson's legal analysis of regulations of First Nations treaty hunting rights, Lunney concluded that s. 12 of the NRTA had not altered the Indians' traditional right to hunt, fish, and trap.

Writing for the majority, Mr Justice McGillivray, although he would conclude his judgment by denying any intention to author a treatise "as to the rights of Indians on the Indian Reserves," produced a "truly remarkable judgement" grounded in a legal historical survey of First Nations' rights going back to the conquest of

New France.[77] Adopting a broad and liberal interpretative approach, McGillivray echoed Justice Stuart's language of moral obligation in Stoney Joe, decided and then seemingly forgotten over two decades earlier. McGillivray wrote that it was "the duty and obligation of the Crown to carry out its promises contained in those treaties with the exactness which honour and good conscience dictate." Further, the decisions pointed out that Treaty Commissioner David Laird had acknowledged that the Chiefs were assured of their "privilege to hunt all over the prairies" and that the Queen's promises would be fulfilled. Thus to the extent that the treaty contemplated that the Indians would be subject to hunting regulations, Justice McGillivray doubted that this had meant that Indians were to be deprived of the right to hunt for subsistence.

Justice McGillivray then turned to the lawmakers' intent in drafting s.12 of the 1930 NRTA and there he found the section to be unambiguous and that the intent could be derived from the ordinary sense of the words. Therefore,

> Parliament assured to the Indians the supply of game in the future for their support and subsistence by requiring them to comply with the game laws of the Province, subject however to the express and dominant proviso that care for the future is not to deprive them of the right to satisfy their present need for food by hunting and trapping game...at all seasons on unoccupied Crown lands or to other land to which they might have a right of access.

Further, McGillivray rejected Crown counsel's claim that the word "game" did not include "animals whose destruction is prohibited" by the regulations, because such a view meant that a deer with antlers of a certain length was game while another with smaller antlers was not. Further, "in hunting for sport or for commerce the Indian like the white man should be subject to laws which make for preservation of game." However, when an Indian is "hunting wild animals for food necessary to his life, the Indian should be placed in a very different position from the white man who generally speaking does not hunt for food." Section 12 provided Indians "the continued enjoyment of a right [to hunt for subsistence] which he has enjoyed from time immemorial." Further, when the "Public Domain" was turned over to the Province of Alberta, the Dominion Government obtained assurances that when Indians were hunting for food, they "may kill all kinds of wild animals regardless of age or size wherever they may be found on unoccupied Crown lands...at all seasons of the year and can hunt with dogs or any other method and do not need a license."[78]

Ultimately, Justice McGillivray relied on a principle articulated in *Metropolitan Electric Supply Co.*: that we must look at what the law was before an Act was passed, determine what the mischief is that is intended to be addressed, and consider the remedy Parliament passed. In applying such a principle, McGillivray concluded that if s. 12, when taken as a whole, has any apparent inconsistency and two possible meanings, "in light of the external circumstances relative to Indian rights, that the law makers in 1930 were, in making the proviso, aiming at assurances to the Indians that they would have an unrestricted right to hunt for food in unsettled places." He believed that "It is satisfactory to be able to come to this conclusion and not have to decide that 'the Queen's promises' have not been fulfilled. It is satisfactory to think that legislators have not so enacted but that the Indians may still be 'convinced of our justice and determined resolution to remove all reasonable cause of discontent.'"

CONCLUSION

The subsequent legal history of First Nations' traditional hunting rights indicates that Mr Justice McGillivray had placed too much faith in the legislative and judicial will to answer these "causes of discontent."[79] Neither *Stoney Joe* nor *Wesley* enjoyed any immediate effect and, in terms of Alberta's legal history and that of the Supreme Court of Alberta, the cases catch our eye because they were ringing dissents within a less accommodating line of decisions. To suggest, however, that *Stoney Joe* and *Wesley* were lost opportunities privileges what might have occurred rather than considering what these cases teach us about the trajectory of traditional hunting rights, the Court, its history, and how these judges, at least, perceived their role in that history. For as much as Justices Stuart, Lunney, and McGillivray believed that the federal government had a moral obligation to fulfill the Queen's promises to protect traditional First Nations hunting, and that the courts were well-placed to remind the government of that obligation, the judges were silent on the question of whether this moral duty was justiciable. To the degree that the federal government acknowledged its obligations as detailed in the treaties, the BNA Act, and constitutional commitments extending back to the conquest of New France, it was another thing entirely to use the courts before the Second World War to compel the government to act upon the Queen's promises in a way that the First Nations thought best.

The improbability of Stuart, Lunney, or McGillivray framing the federal government's moral duty as a legal obligation reveals the dilemma of First Nations hunting rights or, indeed, any collective rights in the first half of the twentieth century in Canada. While prepared to emphasize the Crown's honour, and call upon the adventuresome spirit that sometimes characterized the Alberta Supreme Court, the three were still products of a perspective rooted in the rule of law, individual autonomy, parliamentary supremacy, and the ideal that judges extracted principles in casting their decisions.[80] The Queen's promises had been the principle (albeit not a legal one) that they could extract, but the remainder of their philosophical baggage prevented them from going further. Indeed, the very idea of collective rights collided with one of the truths of their nineteenth-century legal liberalism. And it is here that we return, once again, to legal historian Sidney Harring's assertion that, on balance, Canadian law gave "liberal treatment" to traditional Aboriginal laws.[81] For Harring adds that this treatment was a contradictory mixture of benevolence, paternalism, assimilationism, and individualism, leaving little room for an Aboriginal sense of identity. Ironically, the treatment had both too much and too little liberalism.

But the fact that these three Albertan judges were unable to move beyond the boundaries of the dominant legal perspectives of the late nineteenth and early twentieth centuries ought not to be characterized as their failing. Rather, we see in these judgments an adherence to the ideal that the courts ought to be a forum for seeking that which was just and right. Perhaps from the perspective of the Supreme Court of Alberta's centenary, such an expectation might seem overly optimistic or even painfully naïve. The fact that such notions were prized offers a glimmer of how those judges viewed their role in shaping the province and its history. Alberta could be a place where principle mattered, where judges could turn expectantly toward the honour of the Crown and the duty of keeping the Queen's promises. And while *Stoney Joe* and *Wesley* do not speak to the entire jurisprudence on First Nations hunting delivered by the Supreme Court of Alberta, the cases captured a moment in time when Aboriginal people turned to an imposed legal system to protect and to assert their unique position and *sui generis* rights.[82] Involved in a battle over the meaning of their own history, the Stoney First Nations encountered three Albertan judges who believed that a key element of that history—the "Queen's promises"—were very real and ought to be respected. And while it is true that the subsequent line of judicial decisions across the nation tended to misconstrue and devalue the Aboriginal sense of history, the prescience of Stuart, Lunney, and McGillivray suggests that these promises may still be kept.

NOTES

1 For example, see Constance Backhouse, *Petticoats and Prejudice: Women and the Law in Nineteenth-Century Canada* (Toronto: Osgoode Society, 1991); Constance Backhouse, *Colour-Coded: A Legal History of Racism in Canada, 1900–1950* (Toronto: Osgoode Society, 1999); Sidney L. Harring, *White Man's Law: Native People in Nineteenth-Century Canadian Jurisprudence* (Toronto: Osgoode Society and University of Toronto Press, 1998); Hamar Foster, "'The Queen's Law Is Better Than Yours': International Homicide in Early British Columbia," in *Essays in the History of Canadian Law*, vol. 5, *Crime and Criminal Justice*, ed. Jim Phillips, Tina Loo, and Susan Lewthwaite (Toronto: Osgoode Society, 1994), 41; Louis Knafla, ed., *Law and Justice in a New Land: Essays in Western Canadian Legal History* (Toronto: Carswell, 1986); and Louis Knafla and Jonathan Swainger, eds., *Laws and Societies in the Canadian Prairie West, 1670–1940* (Vancouver: University of British Columbia Press, 2005).

2 Alberta, *Justice on Trial: Report of the Task Force on the Criminal Justice System and its Impact on the Indian and Metis People of Alberta* (Edmonton: Solicitor General, 1991); Nova Scotia, *Royal Commission on the Donald Marshall Jr. Prosecution* (Halifax: Province of Nova Scotia, 1989); Manitoba, *Report of the Aboriginal Justice Inquiry of Manitoba* (Winnipeg: Queen's Printer, 1991); Canada, *Report of the Royal Commission on Aboriginal Peoples*, 6 vols. (Ottawa: Canada Communications Group, 1996).

3 Stephen Greymorning, "In the Absence of Justice: Aboriginal Case Law and the Ethnocentrism of the Courts," *Canadian Journal of Native Studies* 17 (1997): 1; Arthur J. Ray, "Creating the Image of the Savage in Defence of the Crown: The Ethnohistorian in Court," *Native Studies Review* 6, no. 2 (1990): 13; Dara Culhane, *The Pleasure of the Crown: Anthropology, Law and First Nations* (Burnaby: Talonbooks, 1998); John Borrows, "Frozen Rights in Canada: Constitutional Interpretation and the Trickster," *American Indian Law Review* 22, no. 1 (1998): 37; and see the critical reaction by diverse scholars to the *Delgamuukw* decision in the special issue of *BC Studies* (1992). For American examples, see Robert A. Williams Jr., "Documents of Barbarism: The Contemporary Legacy of European Racism and Colonialism in the Narrative Tradition of Federal Indian Law," *Arizona Law Review* 31, no. 2 (1989): 237; Karl J. Kramer, "The Most Dangerous Branch: An Institutional Approach to Understanding the Role of the Judiciary in American Indian Jurisdictional Determinations," *Wisconsin Law Review* (1986): 989; Rennard Strickland, "Genocide-at-Law: An Historic and Contemporary view of the Native American Experience," *Kansas Law Review* 34 (1986): 713.

4 Frank Tough, "Game Protection and the Criminalization of Indian Hunting in Ontario, 1892–1931" [unpublished research report for Ontario Native Affairs Secretariat, June 1994]; see also Katherine Pettipas, *Severing the Ties That Bind: Government Repression of Indigenous Religious Ceremonies on the Prairies* (Winnipeg: University of Manitoba Press, 1994); Joan Ryan and Bernard Ominayak, "The Cultural Effect of Judicial Bias," in *Equality and Judicial Neutrality*, ed. Sheila Martin and Kathleen Mahoney (Toronto: Carswell, 1987).

5 Harring, *White Man's Law: Native People in Nineteenth-Century Canadian Jurisprudence*.
6 For a discussion of the common law development of canons of interpretation regarding Aboriginal and treaty rights, see Leonard I. Rotman, "Taking Aim at the Canons of Treaty Interpretation in Canadian Aboriginal Rights Jurisprudence," *University of New Brunswick Law Journal* 46 (1997): 11; for an American discussion, see Jill de la Hunt, "The Canons of Indian Treaty and Statutory Construction: A Proposal for Codification," *University of Michigan Journal of Law Reform* 17 (1984): 681. For a recent critical inquiry into the development of the Court's principles of treaty interpretation, see Gordon Christie, "Justifying Principles of Treaty Interpretation," *Queen's Law Journal* 26 (2002): 143.
7 For an excellent overview of the numbered treaties, see Arthur J. Ray, Jim Miller, and Frank Tough, *Bounty and Benevolence: A History of Saskatchewan Treaties* (Montreal & Kingston: McGill-Queen's Press, 2000). Also see Richard Price, ed., *The Spirit of the Alberta Indian Treaties* (Edmonton: University of Alberta Press, 1999).
8 Brian Calliou, "1899 and the Political Economy of Canada's North-West: Treaty 8 as a Compact to Share and Peacefully Co-Exist," in *Alberta Formed Alberta Transformed*, ed. Michael Payne, Donald Wetherell, and Catherine Cavanaugh (Edmonton and Calgary: University of Alberta Press and University of Calgary Press, 2006), 300.
9 Debate continues over Treaty No. 8 and, in particular, whether those peoples overlooked or ignored by the Crown are obliged to negotiate an adhesion to treaty. Perhaps the most notable example concerns the Lubicon peoples of northeastern Alberta.
10 Treaty 8 Commissioners Report (Ottawa: Queen's Printer, 1966); also see the diary entry of the Catholic Mission at Fort Chipewyan on 13 July 1899 as quoted at p. 77 in Rene Fumoleau, *As Long As This Land Shall Last: A History of Treaty 8 and Treaty 11, 1870–1939* (Toronto: McClelland and Stewart, 1973) by an eyewitness who stated the Cree Chief said the following conditions had to be guaranteed before he would be willing to accept the treaty: "complete freedom to fish, complete freedom to hunt, complete freedom to trap, ..."
11 Alexander Morris, *The Treaties of Canada With the Indians* [originally 1880] (Toronto: Coles, 1971), at 200-211. Also see Jean Friesen, "Alexander Morris" in *Dictionary of Canadian Biography*, vol. 11 (Toronto: University of Toronto Press, 1982), 608-15 and the chapter on Morris as a judge in Dale Brawn, *The Court of Queen's Bench of Manitoba, 1870–1950: A Biographical History* (Toronto: The Osgoode Society for Canadian Legal History, 2006), 21-46.
12 Alexander Morris, *Treaties*, at p. 231.
13 Delia Opekokew, *The First Nations: Indian Government and the Canadian Confederation* (Saskatoon: Federation of Saskatchewan Indians, 1979), at 11.
14 Alexander Morris, *Treaties*, at 257-67. Also see Andrew Robb, "David Laird," *Dictionary of Canadian Biography*, vol. 14 (Toronto: University of Toronto Press, 1998), 786-81.
15 Ibid., at 120-21.
16 Treaty 8 Commissioners Report, at 6.
17 Treaty 8 Commissioners Report.

18 Treaty 8 Commissioners Report, at 6. Treaty 7 only mentions hunting, while Treaty 6 mentions hunting and fishing. Neither of the latter two hunting clauses mentions trapping.
19 Ibid.
20 Robert Irwin, "Not Like the Others: The Regulation of Indian Hunting and Fishing in Alberta," in *Forging Alberta's Constitutional Framework*, ed. Richard Connors and John Law (Edmonton: University of Alberta Press, 2005), 240.
21 Lawrence Vankoughnet, Superintendent General of Indian Affairs to John A. Macdonald, 30 September 1884, National Archives of Canada (cited hereafter NAC), RG 10, vol. 3692, file 14069.
22 Lawrence Vankoughnet, Superintendent General of Indian Affairs to Minister of Justice, 8 April 1885, in ibid.
23 Irwin, "Not Like the Others," at 241. For a discussion of the disallowance power, see L. Wilson, "Disallowance: The Threat to Western Canada," *Saskatchewan Law Review* 39 (1973-74): 180.
24 *R. v. Robertson* (1886) *Reports of Cases Argued and Determined in the Court of Queen's Bench, Manitoba With Tables of Cases and Principal Matters*, vol. III, ed. John S. Ewart (Winnipeg: Robert D. Richardson, 1886), 613.
25 Irwin, "Not Like the Others," 242-43.
26 Peter Cumming and Kevin Aalto, "Inuit Hunting Rights in the Northwest Territories," *Saskatchewan Law Review* 38 (1974): 267.
27 Ibid., 267-69.
28 The literature on the constitutional struggles of the post-Confederation era is substantial. For some of the most thoughtful discussions, see Paul Romney, *Mr Attorney: The Attorney General for Ontario in Court, Cabinet and Legislature, 1791-1899* (Toronto: The Osgoode Society, 1986), 240-81; Robert C. Vipond, *Liberty and Community: Canadian Federalism and the Failure of the Constitution* (Albany: State University of New York Press, 1991); Garth Stevenson, *Ex Uno Plures: Federal-Provincial Relations in Canada, 1867-1896* (Montreal and Kingston: McGill-Queen's University Press, 1993); John T. Saywell, *The Lawmakers: Judicial Power and the Shaping of Canadian Federalism* (Toronto: The Osgoode Society for Canadian Legal History, 2002), and, for a sampling of his considerable scholarship, see R.C.B. Risk, *A History of Canadian Legal Thought* (Toronto: The Osgoode Society for Canadian Legal History, 2006).
29 Ibid., p. 269 and Irwin, "Not Like the Others," p. 241.
30 Bennett McCardle, *The Rules of the Game: The Development of Government Controls Over Indian Hunting and Trapping in Treaty Eight (Alberta) to 1930* (unpublished Treaty and Aboriginal Rights Research report for the Indian Association of Alberta, Edmonton, 1976), 92.
31 Richard T. Price and Shirleen Smith, "Treaty 8 and Traditional Livelihoods: Historical and Contemporary Perspectives," *Native Studies Review* 9, no. 1 (1993-1994): 51, 63.
32 Brian Calliou, "Losing the Game: Wildlife Conservation and the Regulation of First Nations Hunting in Alberta, 1880-1930" (unpublished LLM thesis, Faculty of Law, University of Alberta, April 2000), 89-145. The campaign to remove the Stoneys from Banff National Park has been examined in Theodore Binnema and Melanie Niemi, "Let the Line Be Drawn Now:

Wilderness, Conservation, and the Exclusion of Aboriginal People from Banff National Park in Canada," *Environmental History* 11 (October 2006): 724–50. Thanks to Theodore Binnema for sharing this article prior to its publication.

33 The following description is based on "Petition from Calgary Rod and Gun Club," 3 February 1893, NAC, RG 10, vol. 6732, file 420-2. Each petition was identical but had separate lists of signatories.

34 Lawrence Vankoughnet, Deputy Superintendent General of Indian Affairs to The Honourable T. Mayne Daly, Superintendent General of Indian Affairs, 18 February 1893, NAC, RG 10, vol. 6732, file 420-2.

35 Acting Deputy Minister of Justice to Lawrence Vankoughnet, Deputy Superintendent General of Indian Affairs, 27 February 1893, NAC, RG 10, vol. 6732, file 420-2.

36 See correspondence to and from Indian Commissioner, 6 March 1893, NAC, RG 10, vol. 6732, file 420-2

37 Public Notice of s.133 application of game laws signed by T. Mayne Daly, June 1893, NAC, RG 10, vol. 6732, file 420-2.

38 L. Vankoughnet, Deputy Superintendent General of Indian Affairs to T. Mayne Daly, 13 April 1983, NAC, RG 10, vol. 6732, file 420-2.

39 T. Mayne Daly, Superintendent General of Indian Affairs to Lieutenant Governor Mackintosh at Regina, North-West Territories, 8 May 1894, NAC, RG 10, vol. 6732, file 420-2.

40 Indian Agent J.A. Markle of Birtle, Manitoba, to the Indian Commissioner, Regina, 2 November 1893, NAC, RG 10, vol. 6732, file 420-2.

41 Ibid. and Deputy Superintendent General of Indian Affairs to the Assistant Indian Commissioner at Regina, 13 November 1893, NAC, RG 10, vol. 6732, file 420-2.

42 See for example Vic Satzewich, "'Where's the Beef?': Cattle Killing, Rations Policy and First Nations 'Criminality' in Southern Alberta, 1892–1895," *Journal of Historical Sociology* 9, no. 2 (1996): 188; John Jennings, "Policemen and Poachers—Indian Relations on the Ranching Frontier," in *Frontier Calgary: Town, City, and Region, 1875–1945*, ed. A.W. Rasporich and Henry Klassen (Calgary: University of Calgary Press and McClelland and Stewart West, 1975), 87; and Warren Elofson, *Cowboys, Gentlemen, and Cattle Thieves—Ranching on the Western Frontier* (Montreal and Kingston: McGill-Queen's University Press, 2000), 113–14.

43 Lieutenant Governor Mackintosh to T. Mayne Daly, 2 May 1894, NAC, RG 10, vol. 6732, file 420-2.

44 Ibid.

45 T. Mayne Daly, Superintendent General to Lieutenant Governor Mackintosh, 8 May 1895, NAC, RG 10, vol. 6732, file 420-2.

46 Hayter Reed to A.E. Forget, Assistant Indian Commissioner, Region, NWT, 8 May 1894, NAC, RG 10, vol. 6732, file 420-2.

47 Public Notice from T. Mayne Daly, Superintendent General of Indian Affairs, 9 May 1894, NAC, RG 10, vol. 6732, file 420-2.

48 P.L. Grasse, farmer, Stoney Reserve, Morley, to the Assistant Commissioner, Regina, 17 May 1894, NAC, RG 10, vol. 6732, file 420-2.

49 Calliou, "Losing the Game," *supra* note 32, pp. 130–38.

50 "Game Laws, N.W.T." by Law Clerk, Department of Indian Affairs, 6 March 1900, NAC, RG 10, vol. 6732, file 420-2.
51 J.D. McLean, Secretary to J.A. Mitchell, Indian Agent, Muskowpetung's Agency, Qu'Appelle, 6 March 1900, NAC, RG 10, vol. 6732, file 420-2.
52 David Laird, Indian Commissioner to Secretary Department of Indian Affairs, 2 April 1903, NAC, RG 10, vol. 6732, file 420-2.
53 Public Notice under the hand of W. Mulock, Acting Superintendent General of Indian Affairs, 1 May 1903, NAC, RG 10, vol. 6732, file 420-2.
54 Robert Irwin, "Not Like the Others," see above note 20, at 261.
55 *Rex v. Stoney Joe, Judgement of Justice Stuart*, unreported decision contained in National Archives of Canada, RG 10, vol. 6732, file 420-2A. This judgment was eventually published by the Native Law Centre at the University of Saskatchewan in *CNLR* 1: 117.
56 See "Charles Allan Stuart," in *Lords of the Western Bench—A Biographical History of the Supreme and District Courts of Alberta, 1876–1990*, Louis A. Knafla and Richard Klumpenhouwer (Calgary: Legal Archives Society of Alberta, 1997), 176–78.
57 See Louis A. Knafla, "The Formative Years: The Supreme Court of Alberta, 1905–1921," in this volume.
58 The following description is taken from *R. v. Stoney Joe*, supra note 55, p. 118.
59 Ibid., p. 119.
60 Ibid., p. 120.
61 Ibid.; *Regina v. O'Rourke* (1882) U.C.C.P. 388, 1 O.R. 464; A.H.F. Lefroy, *The Law of Legislative Power in Canada* (Toronto: Toronto Law Book, 1898). For a discussion of Lefroy, see R.C.B. Rick, "A.H.F. Lefroy: Common Law Thought in Late-Nineteenth Century Canada—On Burying One's Grandfather," in R.C.B. Risk, *A History of Canadian Legal Thought*, see above note 28, 66–93.
62 *Hodge v. the Queen, Appeal Cases* 9 (1883): 117, where the JCPC rejected an argument that the Dominion Parliament was merely a delegate of the Imperial British Parliament that could not further delegate, that is, subdelegate its powers. Instead, the JCPC found the BNA Act, 1867 gave both the Dominion Parliament and the provincial legislatures powers "as plenary and ample" as the Imperial Parliament.
63 Ibid.
64 Ibid., at 121.
65 See generally J.R. Mallory, "The Courts and the Sovereignty of the Canadian Parliament," *Canadian Journal of Economics and Political Science* 10 (1994): 165; George Winterton, "The British Grundnorm: Parliamentary Supremacy Re-examined," *Law Quarterly Review* 92 (1976): 591.
66 Douglas Sanders, "The Queen's Promises," in *Law and Justice in a New Land: Essays in Western Canadian Legal History*, ed. Louis A. Knafla (Toronto: The Carswell Company, 1986), 103.
67 *R. v. Stoney Joe*, supra note 55.
68 Robert Irwin, "Not Like the Others," *supra note* 20, p. 250.
69 *R. v. Stoney Joe*, supra note 55.
70 *R. v. Robertson, Reports of Cases Argued and Determined in the Court of Queen's Bench, Manitoba With Tables of Cases and Principal Matters*, vol. III, ed. John

S. Ewart (Winnipeg: Robert D. Richardson, 1886), 613. Also see *R. v. Morely*, *Western Weekly Reports* 2 (1932): 193.
71 See Frank Tough, "The Forgotten Constitution: The Natural Resources Transfer Agreements and Indian Livelihood Rights, ca. 1925-1933," *Alberta Law Review* 41 (2004): 999; Thomas Flanagan and Mark Milke, "Alberta's Real Constitution: the Natural Resources Transfer Act," in *Forging Alberta's Constitutional Framework*, ed. Richard Connors and John M. Law (Edmonton: University of Alberta Press, 2005), 165-90; Robert Irwin, "A Clear Intention to Effect Such a Modification: The NRTA and Treaty Hunting and Fishing Rights," *Native Studies Review* 13, no. 2: 62.
72 Section 12, NRTA
73 *R. v. Wesley*, *Western Weekly Reports* 2 (1932): 337. For the context of the set-up, see Douglas Sanders, "The Queen's Promises," in *Law and Justice in a New Land*, Knafla, *supra*, at 104. Sanders incorrectly suggested that the *Calgary Herald* had not covered the case prior to the appeal; see "Indian Hunting Rights Basis of Important Case," *Calgary Herald*, 1 April 1932, 15.
74 Transcript of Trial, Appeal File 1986, Court of Appeal Registry, Calgary, Alberta as cited in Sanders, "The Queen's Promises," 105. Also see "Indian Hunting Rights Basis of Important Case," in ibid.
75 See "Alfred Henry Clarke," "Henry William Lunney," "Alexander Andrew McMcGillivray," and "Charles Richmond Mitchell," in Knafla and Klumpenhouwer, *supra note 56*, at 27-28, 87-88, 120-21, and 131-32, respectively.
76 Ibid.
77 This characterization is found in Sanders, "The Queen's Promises," 104.
78 *R. v. Wesley*, *supra note 73*, p. 552. The Wesley appeal was noted in "Stoney Indian Wins Case Against Alberta Govt," *Banff Crag and Canyon*, 10 June 1932, 1.
79 Kent McNeil, *Indian Hunting, Trapping and Fishing Rights in the Prairie Provinces of Canada* (Saskatoon: Native Law Centre, University of Saskatchewan, 1983), and D.E. Sanders, "Indian Hunting and Fishing Rights," *Saskatchewan Law Review* 38: 45.
80 The influence of rule of law in Canadian legal thought has been skillfully demonstrated by R.C.B. Risk. For a recent anthology of his writing on this and other themes, see R.C.B. Risk, *A History of Canadian Legal Thought*, *supra note 28*.
81 Harring, *White Man's Laws*, *supra note 1*.
82 See Brian Calliou, "The Imposition of State Laws and the Creation of Various Hunting Rights for Aboriginal Peoples of the Treaty 8 Territory," in *Treaty Eight Revisited Selected Papers on the 1999 Centennial Conference*, ed. Duff Crerar and Jaroslav Petryshyn, in *Lobstick: An Interdisciplinary Journal* 1, no. 1 (1999-2000): 151.

FIVE

Space for Religion
Regulation of Hutterite Expansion and the Superior Courts of Alberta

JONNETTE WATSON HAMILTON

THIS ESSAY FOCUSES ON TWO GROUPS OF CASES involving the Hutterian Brethren Church that were decided by Alberta's superior courts. The first group deals with Alberta legislation restricting the expansion of Hutterite colonies. Several times between 1935 and 1971, Social Credit governments responded to public pressure and hostility toward the Hutterites by enacting discriminatory legislation to curtail the expansion of existing Hutterite colonies and the establishment of new ones. The superior courts in the province heard four cases that involved this legislation. After the repeal of the legislation in 1973, provincial laws no longer singled out Hutterite land acquisitions, but the biased application of general land use controls did. The second group of cases, also four in number, concerned the discriminatory application of land use bylaws by the Municipal District of Starland No. 47 in the 1990s. All eight cases are concerned with "space" for the Hutterites in the literal sense, that is, with the physical space this communal agrarian sect needs to survive. These cases are not the only ones involving the Hutterites that were decided by the superior courts of Alberta. Nor are they necessarily the most significant for either the Hutterites or the rest of us; that distinction probably belongs to those cases concerned with more figurative space.[1] The eight cases reviewed in this essay are, however, relatively distinctive to Alberta. Most of the legislation considered in this essay is unique to this province.[2]

Most Albertans are aware that the Hutterian Brethren are a religious sect living in small colonies scattered throughout the province and that their values and beliefs are different from those of the majority. A thorough discussion of their religion and their history is beyond the scope of this essay and well covered by many authors.[3] Some points must be made, however, to understand why the Hutterian Brethren need more physical space than that provided by a building dedicated to religious worship.

Like other Anabaptists, such as the Mennonites and the Amish, the Hutterites' history can be traced back to Switzerland in 1525, when their ancestors attempted the restoration of the first-century Christian church. Thus, they began almost five centuries ago as an effort to separate from the institutions and values of the society in which they lived, and they continue these efforts today. Few other minority groups in Canada hold values and beliefs that differ more from those of the larger surrounding society than do the Hutterites. Like all Anabaptists, these beliefs include adult baptism, the rigid separation of church and state, and the establishment of the church as a Christian community that follows Jesus in all areas of life.[4] What distinguishes the Hutterian Brethren from other Anabaptist groups is the Hutterites' belief in communal property, based upon the description of the early Christian church in Acts 2:44: "And all that believed were together, and had all things in common." All property within a Hutterite colony is church property; there is no distinct church organization in a colony because the community is the congregation. Professor Esau's description of a colony is especially evocative: from the Hutterite perspective, a colony "may be thought of as a communal ark of salvation that leads to eternal life in heaven, while the rest of the world is drowning in the flood of temporary selfish pride and pleasure leading to death."[5]

The Hutterian Brethren have survived as a distinct religious and ethno-cultural group; of all Anabaptist groups, they have made the fewest adaptations to their host societies. Their viability over almost five centuries has been attributed to their very distinctiveness and to their creation and maintenance of literal and figurative boundaries between their communities and the larger surrounding society.[6] One of the most important boundary mechanisms used by the Hutterites to preserve their way of life is the geographic and social isolation of their individual colonies.[7] Geographically, each colony is established on a huge tract of land comprising thousands of acres, as isolated as possible from more highly populated centres. As agriculturalists, it is possible for the Hutterites to have more of the isolation that is necessary for survival and to maintain a much greater degree of unified, autonomous self-sufficiency than would be possible otherwise.[8] A certain level of economic independence prevents too much interaction with the larger surrounding society.[9] Socially, each Hutterite colony is virtually institutionally complete, with its own educational, political, economic, and legal institutions.[10] Each colony is highly coordinated and based on core Hutterite values that include co-operation, consensus, frugality, non-violence, self-discipline, and the deference of the will of the individual to the will of the community.

The legislation and cases concerning the regulation of Hutterite land acquisitions to facilitate expansion are important because the creation of new colonies is necessary to the sect's survival. The self-sufficiency of isolated colonies is dependent on the Hutterites' unique branching-out method of colony expansion.[11] When a colony becomes sufficiently large, it divides into two: a "mother" colony and a "daughter" colony. This occurs approximately every 15 to 20 years, when the mother colony reaches a population of between 140 to 175 members.[12] Branching out ensures the average colony consists of 90 to 100 persons.[13] A small, self-governing group such as the Hutterites depends on common worship, face-to-face interaction, and unspecialized law-making processes. If the group were to become too large, its law-making would have to become more specialized to adjudicate increasingly conflicting norms.[14] The decision to branch out is also based partially on economic viability, because daughter colonies must be subsidized initially.[15] The politics of colony management are also a factor. A colony with fewer than the average of 90 to 100 persons has a tendency to become clannish and dominated by one family. Any more, however, and the colony risks a manpower surplus; a surplus, coupled with the limited number of managerial positions available in a colony, means that young men become frustrated.[16] Thus, expansion is a proven method for ensuring the continual strength and viability of the Hutterian Brethren Church.

From their very beginnings, the Hutterites' religious beliefs and practices have challenged the values and authority of the established state. Their history of relations with their host nations has therefore been one of broken promises, persecution, and flight. Persecution in Switzerland forced them to flee to Moravia, and broken promises and persecution followed them from Moravia to Hungary, Romania, and then Russia. Broken promises and persecution in Russia brought the few remaining Hutterites to South Dakota in the 1870s. There, the Hutterites' pacifism, their use of the German language, and their communal lifestyle made them objects of hostility during the Spanish–American War in the late nineteenth century, and again during World

War I. Relying on Canadian government assurances that their communal land holding system, their culturally and religiously specific educational system, and their pacifism would be accommodated, the Hutterites fled to Canada in 1918.[17] Two of the three branches of the Hutterites—the Dariusleut and the Lehrerleut—fled to Alberta, and the third—the Schmiedleut—resettled in Manitoba. What awaited them in Canada, however, was the same pattern of broken promises and persecution.[18]

The movement of the Hutterites to Canada in 1918 met with a great deal of criticism. The First World War, as well as the upheavals in Russia following its revolution, impelled Canadians to become more concerned with social harmony and more demanding that immigrants assimilate to Anglo-American norms.[19] In 1919, in response to public and provincial government pressure, the federal government removed the Hutterites' exemption from military service and temporarily banned their immigration.[20] The ban was justified by a reference to a widespread feeling in western Canada that the Hutterites (as well as Mennonites and Doukhobors) were "undesirable owing to their peculiar customs, habits, modes of living and methods of holding property and because of their probable inability to become readily assimilated to or to assume the duties and responsibilities of Canadian citizens within a reasonable time after their entry."[21]

While attitudes toward the Hutterites in Alberta were more favourable for a brief period of time in the 1930s,[22] the outbreak of the Second World War saw the return of animosity. One of the main reasons for the 1942 legislated ban on Hutterite land acquisitions in Alberta was said to be that "[t]he Veterans of the last wars disapprove of their failing to join the fighting forces."[23] Many Alberta municipalities and veterans' organizations had passed resolutions asking the federal and provincial governments to legislate against the Hutterites. Some Alberta towns held mass protest meetings, with the agitation focused in the Raymond area.[24] The Raymond area, south of Lethbridge, was one of the two comparatively small areas in Alberta where the original Hutterite colonies had concentrated; the other was along the Rosebud River around Beiseker, northeast of Calgary.[25]

The Land Sales Prohibition Act of 1942 banned sales of land in Alberta to "any enemy alien or Hutterite."[26] Solon Low, the provincial treasurer for the Social Credit government and a former school teacher from Raymond, indicated the purpose of the Act was "to allay public feeling which has been aroused to the point of threatened violence in some instances."[27] The 1942 statute was disallowed by order of the Governor General in Council in the spring of 1943,[28] but it was re-enacted in 1944 to apply only to Hutterites.[29] Although originally set to expire at the end of the Second World War, the Act was twice extended so that it remained in effect until 1 May 1947.[30]

Before the Act was set to expire in January 1947, the first of three committees of the Alberta Legislative Assembly was appointed to report on the "Hutterite problem in the Province of Alberta."[31] Farm, municipal, school, and community organizations made arguments against the Hutterites; they focused on issues of assimilation, education, and pacifism, and on the fear that the Hutterites would come to control large amounts of Alberta farmland.[32] The Alberta Farmers' Union, for example, noted the Hutterites already owned one-sixth of the land in the municipal district of Warner and asserted that when "[c]oncentrated in large numbers they become a real menace to the Canadian way of life."[33] The Alberta Schools Trustee Association argued that "groups that oppose education and resist the laws of the province ought not to be allowed to expand."[34] A brief filed on behalf of the Raymond, Magrath, Taber, and New Dayton Legions and Boards of Trade advanced this argument:

> [The] expiration of the Act at this time will permit these Hutterites to invade the farmland market with all the savings they have accumulated during the war years which were so profitable to those who remained at home, and to purchase almost overnight at inflated prices those farms which should be available for veterans and other deserving residents.[35]

As the language of these three examples makes clear, antagonistic feelings were strongly held. It was futile to point to the facts, such as the Hutterites' relatively small land holdings—275 square miles of the 67,621 square miles of occupied farm land in Alberta—or their purchase of nearly half a million dollars worth of interest-free war bonds.[36]

Although the hostile atmosphere of the Second World War contributed to the animosity toward the Hutterites in Alberta, it endured long after the war's end and has been attributed to nativist concerns for Anglo-American institutions and social homogeneity.[37] The prevailing concept of Alberta was of an Anglo-Saxon society that required minority ethnic groups to submerge their differences.[38] It was therefore no surprise when the 1947 committee reported that the conditions that had prompted the passing of the Land Sales Prohibition Act still existed and that "the communal form of living will continue to be a matter of concern to the people of Alberta unless regulations can be applied which will, in the public interest, control the expansion or increase of communal groups."[39] Support for the recommendations of that committee was not, however, unanimous. During the four-and-one-half hour debate in the Assembly, committee member F.C. Colborne warned that the provisions recommended in the Report were "completely impractical and entirely unjust"; some, he said, would "annihilate the Hutterites."[40] Still, the new Communal Property Act was passed handily under the sponsorship of the Social Credit government and Premier Ernest C. Manning and came into force 1 May 1947.[41] The Act is a particularly apt example of a policy that has caused the Social Credit party to be perceived as the party of the "old" Alberta, comprised of farmers, fundamentalists, and small-town dwellers.[42]

The 1947 version of the Act prohibited colonies from attempting to increase their land holdings beyond those held on 1 March 1944, subject to one major exception. Even though the Act was passed for the sole objective of controlling Hutterite land acquisitions, it was drafted to appear to be of more general application by restricting the land to be acquired by a colony. A *colony* was defined as a number of persons who held land as communal property, a definition said to explicitly include "Hutterites or Hutterian Brethren and Doukhobors." The Doukhobors had been added only because of rumours they might be moving to Alberta from British Columbia.[43]

The major exception in the Act allowed a colony to acquire land to increase its holdings to a maximum of 6,400 acres under certain conditions. Farmers wanting to dispose of land to Hutterite colonies, and colonies desiring to acquire land, had to apply to the director of assessment, Department of Municipal Affairs, for leave to do so. On receipt of such applications, the director was required to hold a hearing and determine, as a matter of "fact," whether the applicant had the "right" to dispose of or acquire the land. If the land to be acquired would not increase the acreage held by the colony beyond 6,400 acres, if it was more than 64 kilometres away from another colony, and if no offer had been made under The Veterans Land Act of 1942, then the applicants had the "right" to dispose of or acquire the land.

Any person or colony not satisfied with the director's decision could appeal that decision to a judge of the District Court. The first appeal against a decision by the director, *Hatch v. East Cardston Colony,* was heard in 1949.⁴⁴ Thomas Hatch had applied for leave to sell his farm lands to the East Cardston Colony, and the director had refused leave. On the appeal, Hatch and the colony admitted their proposed transaction came within the Act's prohibitions. It was the statute's constitutionality they wanted to challenge. However, Judge Elmore B. Feir, of the District Court of Southern Alberta, held that he did not have jurisdiction to consider whether the Communal Property Act was *ultra vires*.

Established in 1907, at the same time as the Supreme Court of Alberta, the District Courts were courts with limited jurisdiction in minor cases.⁴⁵ It was not, however, the limited nature of the District Court's jurisdiction that was at issue in the *Hatch* case. Instead, Feir held he was not hearing the matter as a judge of the District Court of Alberta but was merely acting as *"persona designata* to review, on appeal, the determination of the director in regard to specific questions posed in s. 9(4)...."⁴⁶ The concept of a judge as *persona designata* describes a person as an individual rather than as a person described as a member of a class. The doctrine of *persona designate*, today, is primarily one of historical interest.⁴⁷ However, at the time of the decision in *Hatch*, it was frequently an issue. Like other justifications for declining to exercise jurisdiction, the doctrine of *persona designata* could be employed as a means to avoid dealing with difficult issues. While Feir was known for his concise style, his judgments usually did feature a few brief citations to authority.⁴⁸ The fact that Feir did not offer any reasons for his conclusion that he was not acting as a judge of the District Court on the appeal, even though the appeal provisions of the Communal Property Act had not been judicially considered before, might indicate that he seized upon the doctrine as a method to avoid the division of powers issue.

There were only two appeals to the District Court on the merits of decisions to grant or refuse leave to sell or purchase land during the 24-year span of the Communal Property Act. One unreported decision, located in the files of the Communal Property Control Board, is the only appeal under the early version of the Act, when the director of assessment was the decision-maker. The second was taken after 1960, when the Communal Property Control Board replaced the director as administrator of the Act. Even Ernest Frederick Breach, the long-term chairman of the Communal Property Control Board and the former director of assessment, noted it was "rather unfortunate that parties not agreeing with the Board do not more often make use of the right of appeal."⁴⁹

The first appeal was made in 1951 and was also heard by Judge Feir.[50] The director had granted leave to John Hofer and Joseph Kleinsasser to purchase land from Charles David Ronan for the purpose of establishing a new colony. A neighbour of the vendor, Frank Cooney, appealed under section 9(6) of Act, which provided that "any person dissatisfied" with the director's decision could appeal to the District Court. The issue was Cooney's standing to appeal as a "person dissatisfied."

Feir noted the Act allowed only the proposed seller and proposed buyer to apply to the director for leave and that the director was not required to hold a public hearing or inquiry. This appeal revealed that the director had allowed Cooney to attend the hearing and take part in the proceedings even though there was nothing in the Act to suggest the "hearings" were to be anything other than meetings between the director, the applicants, and the applicants' lawyers. Feir did not, however, give any weight to the director's practice of expanding access to the hearings. On the matter of standing before the Court, he adopted the then usual approach that saw the government as the sole protector of the public interest.[51] He held that the "dissatisfied" persons entitled to appeal were limited to "those with a substantial interest and the interest of an individual, distinct from the interest or welfare of the whole community."[52] It was the director, he said, who "stands as the guardian of whatever public interests are sought to be protected by the Act."[53]

Feir's decision limited the class of persons who could appeal the director's decisions, and this perhaps accounts, in part, for the limited number of appeals. As he noted, a very great number of people disagreed with each decision of the director. Had Feir held otherwise, dozens of disgruntled neighbours might have appealed each decision of the director that was favourable to Hutterite expansion.

However, if neighbours unhappy with the director's decisions could not appeal, they could contact their elected representatives to demand something be done. Public pressure on the Social Credit government can be inferred from the 1950 amendment to the Communal Property Act that required the consent of the provincial cabinet for the establishment of any new colony.[54] Decisions to approve or disapprove applications to add land to existing colonies were left with the director of assessment, with appeals available to the District Court. Decisions to set up new colonies, however, were subsumed by politics. Cabinet was to retain final say over this more controversial aspect of Hutterite expansion from 1950 to 1973, when the Act was repealed.

By the mid-1950s, the statutory requirement that there be a minimum of forty miles between colonies meant there could be no new colonies in Alberta except in the Peace River district. Established colonies faced overcrowding, and almost all had achieved their maximum allowable acreage.[55] Some Hutterites left the province; the first colonies in Saskatchewan, for example, were established in 1952. Although all land purchases in Alberta had been made in compliance with the Act prior to 1953, the Hutterites found ways to evade the restrictions when it became too difficult to acquire adequate land to sustain their way of life. Colonies would either farm land under hire-labour agreements after individual Hutterites leased or bought from their non-Hutterite neighbours, or they would take title in the name of a company.[56]

At the same time, and probably due in part to such unauthorized expansions, public hostility toward the Hutterites again reached the point that the Social Credit government deemed it necessary to act. A second legislative committee, the Hutterite Investigation Committee, was appointed in 1958.[57] Its terms of reference were broader than those of the 1947 committee, and they were explicitly assimilationist. The committee was directed "to determine whether or not the provisions of the Communal Property Act...are necessary and in the best interests of our agricultural industry"; it was also to study "any other matter relevant to the orderly and harmonious integration of the Hutterian Church into local communities."[58] As one lawyer who acted for a number of Hutterites colonies complained at the time, the goal of "harmonious integration" assumed it was necessary for his clients to change their religion.[59]

The 1958 committee again heard a variety of briefs, and Farmers' Union locals and others were again vocal in calling for greater restrictions. The Warner FUA, for example, charged that the Hutterites were "attempting to establish a country of their own within a country."[60] The second committee again concluded that some form of regulation governing the acquisition of land by Hutterites was necessary. They recommended changes to administrative procedures, including the replacement of the director of assessment by a board with discretionary power. E.F. Breach, then the director of assessment and soon to be the chair of the proposed board, noted that "in carrying out its inquiry the Committee found it very difficult to deal with the Hutterites as a whole."[61] Breach wrote of his respect for individual Hutterites and their peaceful nature, but he expressed concern that "in anything concerning their religious beliefs, they will have no consideration for their obligations as Canadian citizens or for the rights or privileges of anyone outside their own community."[62] In the committee's opinion, exercising control over the Hutterites' acquisition of land was therefore not enough. Their integration into the surrounding culture was required, and the committee recommended the proposed board's "paramount" consideration be a "long-range view looking toward assimilation of the Hutterites into our society."[63]

As a result, the 1947 statute was substantially amended in 1960.[64] The Communal Property Control Board was established with not more than three members appointed by and holding office at the pleasure of cabinet. Breach served as the board's chair from its inception in 1960 until its demise in 1971. Breach's report on his work with the 1958 Hutterite Investigation Committee suggested he held a fairly negative attitude toward the Hutterites; he was certainly in favour of their assimilation. However, by the mid-1960s, his official reports as chair of the board indicated more ambivalence toward the legislation he administered and his role. In a 1965 report to the then minister of municipal affairs, A.J. Hooke, Breach asserted that "[t]he Act itself is no more discriminatory than other planning regulations governing land use, but like all such regulation it may become discriminatory through the manner in which it is applied."[65] By 1971, at the end of his term, he acknowledged the Act was very restrictive: "unless care is taken in how it is administered, it can become an instrument of discrimination."[66] Breach also wrote of his experience of seventeen years of "being both oppressor and Santa Claus to the Colonies."[67]

Under the new version of the statute there were still two different land acquisition processes. If an application was for the acquisition of land to expand an existing colony's holdings, the board itself could make an order granting or refusing the application. These orders were based on two statutory criteria: whether the applicant had the right under the act to dispose of or purchase the land, and whether it was in the public interest that the application be granted. The "right under the act" referred to the Act's maximum acreage provisions.[68] As to the matter of "public interest," the board's policy favoured consolidation so that no individual farmer's holdings would be surrounded by Hutterite land.[69] Appeals of the board's orders, with respect to the expansion of existing colonies, remained available from the District Court.

If, however, an application was made to acquire land to establish a new colony, the board was required to hold public hearings to determine the public interest and submit its findings and recommendations to the minister of municipal affairs for consideration by cabinet. The board based its recommendations on three factors: first, there had to be a minimum of fifteen miles between colonies; second, there could not be more than two colonies in any average-sized municipal district; and third, not more than 5 per cent of assessed farm land in any one municipal district could be under communal ownership.[70] Cabinet could and did act irrespective of the board's recommendation. For example, in the late 1960s, cabinet sanctioned only 55 per cent of the board's recommendations to approve the establishment of new colonies.[71]

Hearings to determine the public interest were required for only two years, between 1960 to 1962. The Act was then amended to require that the board receive written evidence supporting or opposing the application, rather than hold hearings.[72] The hearings appeared to be unpopular with those regularly involved. The board's chairman complained that "opposing arguments mainly deal with the education of Hutterite children, their communal style of living, pacifism, etc., being matters of public interest outside the Board's jurisdiction"; he added that a public hearing "only serves to measure the degree of prejudice against Hutterites which prevails in the community."[73] Lawyers acting for Hutterite colonies also argued that the public hearings were a waste of time: "By this time everything that can be said against the Hutterites has been said by farmers, farm organizations, school trustees, etc. and, in Drumheller, the Baptist Church."[74] The Western Stock Growers' Association opposed public hearings because they saw them strengthening the Hutterites' position by emphasizing their differences and "arousing public sympathy for a minority group which is apparently being persecuted."[75]

The constitutional challenge that was not heard in *Hatch v. East Cardston Hutterian Colony* in 1949 was finally mounted in 1965, in *Walter v. Attorney-General of Alberta*.[76] Over the years, three different colonies had applied to either the director or the board to establish a new colony near the village of Brant, but all three applications were denied.[77] The land was finally bought by three individual members of the Rock Lake Colony from two vendors, Walter and Fletcher, without cabinet approval. The RCMP investigated the sale of Fletcher's land, and Fletcher, the individual Hutterite purchasers, and the Rock Lake Colony were all charged under the Communal Property Act. The prosecutions were stayed pending the outcome of litigation seeking to have the Act declared *ultra vires*.[78] The vendors and purchasers made three arguments: that the legislation related primarily to religion, which was not a matter of provincial jurisdiction; that the legislation was discriminatory and a breach of the assurances of the federal government, made when the Hutterites first immigrated to Canada; and that the legislation was contrary to the Canadian Bill of Rights.[79]

Mr Justice J.V.H. Milvain, then of the Trial Division of the Supreme Court of Alberta, gave short shrift to the latter two arguments. He held that, even if the Act was discriminatory, being discriminatory would not make it invalid and that the federal Bill of Rights was not relevant to a provincial statute. The superficial and general wording of the Communal Property Act came into play as Milvain noted that the definition of *colony* in the Act could describe any number of people, no matter their religion or the combination of religious faiths that might be included in the group of persons involved.[80] As for the assurances from the federal Department of the Interior given to the Hutterites before they immigrated, he held they had no binding effect on any legislative body acting within its constitutional field.

The main challenge, therefore, was the division of powers issue. With very little discussion, Milvain held that the Act, in its pith and substance, related to land tenure in the province and was therefore *intra vires*, coming within the provincial jurisdiction over property and civil rights. The fact that it might affect people of some religious faiths more than others was acknowledged but judged to be irrelevant. In a passage entirely typical of judicial attitudes in the days of parliamentary supremacy, Milvain cautioned:

> [W]e should remember we do not function in a land recognizing judicial review of legislation, as is the case in the United States. Such being the case we should not embark upon some of the metaphysical flights that are launched through policy considerations; that should be left to legislative bodies.[81]

The division of powers issue was more controversial when the *Walter* case was heard by the Appellate Division of the Alberta Supreme Court. The focus of the appellants' argument was that the Act was aimed at preventing the spread of Hutterite colonies in Alberta and, because the maintenance of these colonies was a cardinal tenet of the Hutterite faith, the Act in pith and substance was legislation in relation to religion, not land. Three of the five judges wrote separate opinions, but each judge reached the same result as Milvain.

Mr Justice Horace G. Johnson, with Mr Justice Edward W. Kane concurring, agreed the Act's "legislative history and the reports of legislative committees make it clear that it was aimed at controlling the expansion of Hutterite colonies in the Province."[82] Of the fifteen judges who heard the case at three different levels, Johnson was the only one to write an opinion stating that the Act constituted legislation in relation to religion. He noted that the Supreme Court of Canada had recently quashed the conviction of a Jehovah Witness who had been convicted of distributing pamphlets prepared by that sect without the permission of the chief of police as required by a Quebec City bylaw.[83] In a passage later disapproved of by the Supreme Court,[84] Johnson stated:

> If a by-law which prevents the distribution of religious tracts (the *Saumur* case) was an interference with religion, I find it difficult to say that legislation which is aimed at the restriction of new and existing colonies and the holding of land in common as practised by these colonies, when living in such colonies and holding lands in that manner are the principal tenets of Hutterian faith, does not also deal with religion.[85]

Johnson also discounted the artificially general wording of the Act. He said that widening the scope of the legislation to include "a non-resident sect [the Doukhobors] and other possible, but so far as we know, non-existent organizations" did not make the Act valid.[86] However, neither of these findings in favour of the Hutterites made any difference in the end. In Johnson's opinion, the power to legislate in relation to religion was possessed by the province. Even if it were an interference with a religion, he held there was "no binding authority which would prevent the Legislature enacting the Communal Property Act under its power to legislate in respect of property and civil rights within the Province."[87]

Mr Justice Neil D. McDermid held that the "true nature of the legislation was not to suppress the Hutterite religion but to prevent any group from acquiring land as communal property without consent."[88] Even assuming the Hutterites were the only group who held land as communal property and that the Act therefore adversely affected only one class of persons, he agreed with Milvain that the legislation in pith and substance related to land tenure within the Province and was therefore *intra vires*. McDermid dealt at some length with the propriety of admitting the 1947 and 1958 reports of the legislative committees charged with looking into the so-called Hutterite problem. Generally speaking, the Alberta courts at the time followed the British practice of not referring to the legislative history of a statute in interpreting it, and so the admission of these reports was unusual. McDermid considered it legitimate to look at the reports to see what mischief the Act was aimed at.

Mr Justice Marshall Porter stated that he agreed with both Johnson and McDermid that the Act was within the legislative competence of the Province of Alberta. Porter found the Act was aimed at discouraging settlement *en bloc* in order to produce a rural society with some amenities. Porter wrote a separate opinion because of what he called his "very real doubts about the adequacy of the scanty material on which a matter of this importance has been dealt with."[89] The case had proceeded on the basis of an agreed statement of facts and copies of the 1947 and 1958 legislative committee reports.

It is difficult to know what to make of Porter's decision. Porter was said to be "one of the best legal minds of the mid-century," and he was known for judgments that challenged received views.[90] In this case, however, Porter's judgment embodied, rather than challenged, those received views. His opposition to the Hutterian Brethren Church appeared to be based on matters within his personal knowledge. He wrote:

> It seems to me an anomaly that the Judges of this Court are placed in the position that they are required to adjudicate upon this matter in the absence of evidence on many essential matters which, although they may well be within the personal knowledge of most of us, are not matters of which we can take judicial notice.[91]

He discounted the legislative committee reports by noting that the legislature also had before it the personal knowledge of its members, many of whom came from areas with Hutterite colonies and that they "brought to their consideration in the Legislature a personal understanding of the consequences to the environment of the communal practices of these people."[92] Porter thought the admission that Hutterites owned 1 per cent of the patented land in Alberta might understate the significance of their holdings, and he listed the type of evidence he thought relevant to the division of powers issue:

> We should know something of the consequences of the development of these colonies on municipal government, on telephone communication, on transportation for school purposes, on snow clearance, and all of those other elements which go to make for better rural living. We should know what threat there is to the level of intelligence of our people who are struggling to improve the knowledge and education of our citizens in the environment of a sect whose practices may stultify the mental development of its members and unfit them for citizenship. We should know whether or not these people are prepared to undertake any responsibility for government, local, provincial or federal, and what the consequences of their failure to do so would be on our social order.[93]

Porter did not say, however, what difference it would have made to the conclusion that the Act was *intra vires* had the Appellate Division had that type of evidence before it. Would it have made the Act any more valid? Porter also lamented that there was no proof, but only an admission, that the communal holding of land was a fundamental principle of the Hutterite faith. He stated the validity of that principle was fundamental to testing the constitutionality of the Act. However, whether holding all property in common was an essential part of the Hutterites' religion or not would be relevant only if the Act was legislation in relation to religion and religion was not within the provinces' jurisdiction, or if discrimination on the basis of religion was enough to render the Act invalid. None of the other fourteen judges who heard the case thought either was possible.

In the Supreme Court of Canada, The Honourable Mr Justice Ronald Martland, writing on behalf of a unanimous Court, reached the same result as the Alberta courts, finding that the Communal Property Act was *intra vires*. Combining McDermid's focus on communal living and Porter's focus on settlement *en bloc*, Martland held that the scheme of the legislation indicated that the Legislature "considered the use of large areas of land in Alberta for the purposes of communal living was something which, in the public interest, required to be regulated and controlled."[94] He did not find the Act aimed at Hutterite religious belief or worship, but defined religion very narrowly: "Religion, as the subject-matter of legislation, wherever the jurisdiction may lie, must mean *religion in the sense that it is generally understood in Canada.*"[95]

This definition is an example of the narrow understanding of basic rights and liberties that Canadian courts adopted in the past. Even though serious interest in individual rights and freedoms appeared immediately after World War II, there is little in the *Walter* case, except in Johnson's opinion, to indicate that interest had undermined discrimination based on religious and ethnic differences.[96] Even Johnson's opinion illustrates the doctrine of the supremacy of Parliament that Canada inherited from Britain—the idea that the federal and provincial governments are supreme in their respective jurisdictions.

More generally, the legislation, the 1947 and 1958 committee reports, the Communal Property Control Board hearings, and Porter's perspective in the *Walter* case also illustrate the extent to which assimilation was demanded by the majority in mid-twentieth century Alberta. There is also some evidence in these sources of the populism that still prevails in the province. Alberta is a province with a strong populist tradition, which is partly a legacy of an American rural influence. The tradition has been especially evident in the organization of rural community structures and farmers' organizations.[97] Populism, at its simplest, is about the concerns, interests, and values of the so-called "little guy." The slogan of American populist William Jennings Bryan—"Equal Rights For All—Special Privileges For None"—was used by rural Albertans to criticize the Canadian Pacific Railway, eastern bankers, and the Hutterites.[98] While populism stressed formal equality and democratic practices, it also exercised a "rhetoric of exaggeration drawn from a susceptibility to conspiratorial fantasy."[99] In the case of the Hutterites, the alleged conspiracy was the domination of rural Alberta. For example, a letter protesting the establishment of a new colony near Rowley, submitted to the Communal Property Control Board in 1970, asserted, "if they are allowed to keep establishing colonies[,] in time they will take over the entire province."[100] Howard Palmer, the noted ethnic historian, categorized this statement as fitting within the "paranoid style," evincing a mind set that detects political, religious, and ethnic conspiracies threatening to destroy a specific way of life; the expression conveys the qualities of heated exaggeration, suspiciousness, and conspiracy fantasy.[101] According to Palmer, the paranoid style was deployed most often against French Canadians, Hutterites, and Jews in Alberta, and, in connection with the Hutterites, the triggering issue was land expansion.[102]

The final court case concerning the Communal Property Act was heard in 1967 by Chief Judge John Decore of the District Court for

Northern Alberta.[103] Unlike the other cases reviewed to date, the results and the reasons in *Re Communal Property Act* proved helpful to the Hutterites. They also caused consternation within the board.

The Hutterite Brethren at Castor appealed a refusal by the board to approve their purchase of 636 acres from Henry Watson. The only issue was whether or not it was in the public interest that the application be granted. The board referred to its policy of endeavouring to consolidate colony holdings and noted the Watson land was two miles from the colony's building site and one mile from its nearest holdings. The board concluded this "certain scattering" of holdings was not in compliance with its policy and therefore not in the public interest. The board also indicated it had received "a number of letters strongly opposing the proposed sale."[104] One of the three letters Decore quoted was from R. Kopfman, who protested that "[t]heir policy is to give high prices for a piece of land such as Section 35 and then try to buy the rest at their own price." Later in the same letter, Mr Kopfman complained, "[s]ince when do we have to do everything these black hated fellows want, we were here first."[105]

Decore acknowledged the tone of the letters indicated strong feeling in certain individuals who opposed the colony. Nevertheless, he found that there was no evidence that any individual's pecuniary interest or legal rights would be adversely affected if the application was approved, with the possible exception of the pecuniary interest of R. Kopfman. Mr Kopfmann had argued that because some of his land was adjacent to the Watson land, the approval of the application might adversely affect its sale value if he decided to sell in the future. Assuming that argument was true, did it follow that approval for the sale of Watson's land would be contrary to the public interest? Decore said it did not, holding that the "public interest" could not be interpreted "as meaning something so narrow and so limited in scope as the interests of an individual."[106] It must involve something more, he said, something in which "the community at large, has some right or some interest which may be adversely affected."[107]

The board interpreted Decore's decision—that permission to sell land to an existing Hutterite colony could not be refused merely because it would or might adversely affect one individual's pecuniary or legal interest—as disapproval of its policy in favour of consolidation. In an exchange of letters between the board's chairman and the County of Camrose No. 22 a few months after the decision, in *Re Communal Property Act,* Breach stated that the board's "compact unit" policy had been appealed and that the judge had allowed the appeal. He warned the county that this established a precedent affecting the board's future decisions and that the policy in favour of compact units might need to change.[108] This prompted the following response from the County: "Your statement that the Board considers the recent judgment of the District Court Judge as a precedent that will affect the Board's future decisions in matters is however exceedingly disturbing to this Council."[109] Breach reassured the county that the board would continue applying its policy, noting that while there might be future appeals, the policy was justified and the Act might be changed to reflect that.[110] The Act was not, however, amended, and it is not clear that the board ever pressed for such a change. A year after the exchange with the County of Camrose, Breach still complained that "[t]he efforts of the Board to maintain the holdings of a colony as a compact unit were frustrated by a judicial decision in 1967."[111]

Decore's 1967 decision was the last case decided under the statutory regime. In 1971, the Communal Property Control Board became such a significant political liability for the Alberta Government that its members were dismissed and the Act's operation suspended. The scandal—as it was referred to at the time—contributed to the establishment of the third legislative committee to investigate the Hutterites and to the repeal of the Communal Property Act in March 1973.[112] I will return to this scandal shortly, after a brief look at other more general reasons for the repeal of the discriminatory legislation.

The demise of the Communal Property Act was motivated by the election of a new government, Peter Lougheed's Conservatives, and that government's desire to enact an Alberta Bill of Rights. However, the reasons for reducing or eliminating restrictions on Hutterian Brethren Church expansion, as well as the reasons for the change in government and the attractiveness of human rights legislation, lay in broader social and economic trends that changed rural Alberta life in the 1950s and 1960s.

The conventional wisdom is that the long Social Credit reign ended due to urbanization, the expansion of the middle class, secularization, and increasing wealth in the province.[113] Half of prairie residents lived on farms in 1941; only 10 per cent did so by 1981.[114] The nature of the prairie economy changed considerably, too. Agriculture's share of the wealth produced on the Alberta prairies shrank from 50 per cent in 1941 to just 8 per cent in 1978.[115] Hutterites had been convenient targets to blame for the local effects of the economic upheaval and social disorganization of rural de-population.

The tension between restricting Hutterites' freedom to acquire land and the individual rights and liberties that gradually came to dominate political and legal thought after the Second World War was becoming less tolerable. By the 1970s, a growing number of Albertans began to attack the discriminatory features of the legislation. International pressure to move toward tolerance, which had been slowly mounting in the aftermath of Hitler's racism and the civil rights movement in the United States, had more impact in Alberta's urban areas and educated circles, but even in rural areas opposition to Hutterite colonies as neighbours had lessened by the late 1960s and early 1970s.[116] In his summary of the board's activity in 1970, Breach referred to a "noticeable change in the public attitude" when application was made to establish a new colony.[117] Whereas the early 1960s always brought a flood of opposing briefs and letters to the board, this was no longer the case.

All of these changes allowed the third legislative committee, appointed to "investigate the effects of the communal use of land on the economic and social climate of Alberta," to be more open to empirical evidence.[118] This Select Committee of the Assembly, established in May 1972, rejected the goal of assimilation that had guided the previous two committees. Nor did it hold public hearings; committee members did not want to "stir up emotionalism."[119] It did receive 126 briefs, 4 petitions endorsed by 118 people, and 1 brief endorsed by 13 municipal authorities. Seventy per cent of these submissions—and 84 per cent of the signatories—favoured maintenance of some type of restrictions on Hutterite expansion.[120] The Select Committee discounted the negative feelings of this majority, noting they relied upon information that, in the committee's opinion, was factually erroneous.[121] They recommended that the Communal Property Act be repealed and that the government establish a Hutterite liaison office to work with a Hutterite Committee of Elders to develop guidelines for Hutterite land acquisitions.[122] Both recommendations were implemented, and the Liaison Office within the Department of Municipal Affairs stills exists today.[123]

Despite—or perhaps because of—the repeal of legislated restrictions, many Albertans remained antagonistic to the Hutterites and to colony expansion.[124] The last four cases from the 1990s concern the efforts of the Starland Colony to establish a daughter colony in the Municipal District (MD) of Starland No. 47. The Starland Colony successfully challenged discretionary use zoning decisions by municipal officials and by development appeal boards three times before the

Alberta Court of Appeal, and in one further Queen's Bench action brought by the MD. The facts of these cases suggest that antipathy toward the Hutterites lasted many years after the legislation's repeal, at least in some areas of rural Alberta.

Starland, located north of Drumheller, is a very small MD, containing only 641,708 acres.[125] The history of interaction between the Hutterites and the other residents of the MD is a fairly long and complex one. The 1971 Communal Property Control Board scandal arose here with the establishment of the Starland Colony in 1970, the first Hutterite colony in the MD. The Lakeside Hutterian Brethren had applied to purchase 22 quarter sections near Rowley, and public notice was given of this application. According to the local MLA, the application was confusing because two different individuals had been taking listings or options as agents for two different colonies—one for the Lakeside Colony, and the other for the Handhills Colony.[126] Between them, the two agents had 80 quarter sections listed or optioned.[127] The two colonies were not acting in concert; the Lakeside Colony is a Dariuleut colony, and the Handhills Colony is within the Lehrerleut.

The Lakeside Colony's agent managed to assemble a sufficiently large block of land first, and this colony therefore applied to the board to establish a new colony. Their application was met by adamant opposition by the owners of farms near the proposed colony's location and by residents of nearby towns. The main themes of the letters were two: the need for assimilation of the Hutterites, and the value of formal equality—populism's "Equal Rights For All—Special Privileges For None." For example, one letter writer asserted, "If they were forced to live like the rest of us we would have no objections to them,"[128] and another demanded, "Let them live as we live abiding by all the laws, rules and regulations applying to other Canadian citizens."[129] Despite this opposition, the board recommended approval of the new colony in September 1970. It noted the application was for only 22 quarter-sections, that there was no other Hutterite colony in the MD, and that the nearest existing colony was 20 miles away.[130] Cabinet approved the establishment of the Starland Colony the next month.[131]

One month after cabinet approval, Lakeside Colony applied to the board for leave to exchange the lands that had been approved for the new Starland Colony. They asked to drop 10 of the 22 approved quarter-sections and add 52 new quarters, which would bring the new colony to the maximum of its permitted acres.[132] The land sought by the Lakeside Colony was most likely the land that had been optioned by the Handhills Colony; perhaps it was more productive land. The board treated their application as an application to expand an existing colony, rather than as a revised application to establish a new colony.[133] As an expansion, the responsibility fell within the board's decision-making authority. In December 1970, the board issued an order approving the purchase by "the colony to be known as the Hutterite Brethren of Starland" of the additional acres.[134]

The MD had not opposed the September application but was upset by the board's December order. It complained there was a big difference in the disruptive effect that the two different-sized blocks of land would produce, called the board's process "secretive and hurried," and objected that the methods of the realtors, "sanctioned by Board," were "unusual to say the least."[135] They copied their letter to Gordon Taylor, the Drumheller MLA and Minister of Highways in the Social Credit government. Breach immediately responded, asserting the Act had been followed and all proper procedures observed. He also observed that "a number of farmers lost the opportunity to sell at inflated prices for cash and are naturally quite unhappy."[136] He drew a sharp rebuke from Taylor, who called the whole episode "maneuvering of worst kind" and predicted it would "cost the government support."[137] Breach was apparently shaken by what he called "the Starland incident." In February 1971, he sent a letter to the secretary-treasurer of the MD, promising, "so far as the writer is concerned, there will be no more colonies in the Municipal District of Starland No. 47."[138] As events unfolded, it was the chairman's failure to honour this commitment that evolved into the scandal.

In the summer of 1971, rumours stared to circulate that the Handhills Colony was still interested in acquiring land in the MD of Starland, this time in Verdant Valley. Taylor contacted Breach and asked if there was any chance such an application would be approved; Breach assured him there was no reasonable chance because the MD was too small.[139] Much to everyone's surprise, the Social Credit government—after its defeat at the polls and within its last 48 hours in office—issued an order-in-council approving the new Verdant Valley Colony.[140] Whether the board itself had recommended the approval is unclear.[141]

The political debate over who was at fault remained heated but unresolved until 2 December 1971. On that date the lawyer retained by the MD of Starland, A.M. Harradence—later Mr Justice Harradence of the Alberta Court of Appeal—gave the new minister of municipal affairs, David Russell, a copy of Breach's February 1971 letter that assured the MD there would be no more colonies in Starland. The minister immediately fired Breach and the other board members. No new board members were appointed to replace them, and so no applications for Hutterite land purchases were accepted between December 1971 and March 1973, when the Act was finally repealed.[142]

Given this background, when the Starland Colony applied almost twenty years later for development permits to allow it to set up yet another new colony in the MD of Starland, opposition was not unexpected. Development permits were required because the new colony proposed to operate an intensive agriculture operation—a 450-sow farrow-to-finish, 50-milk cow, 5,000-chicken operation—which qualified as discretionary use under the MD land use bylaw.

The Starland Colony's application for the permits needed to establish the new colony was granted by the Municipal Planning Commission in June of 1990. However, neighbours of the proposed new colony appealed to the Development Appeal Board (DAB). It was later established that these neighbours' legal fees were paid for by the MD of Starland. At the first hearing before the DAB, the neighbours' appeal was allowed after the MD's engineer appeared and expressed the opinion that the Starland Colony had failed to provide sufficient information and it was therefore impossible for the MD to assess the adverse effects of the development.

The Starland Colony applied to the Court of Appeal for leave to appeal the DAB decision, which was granted. Both the motion for leave to appeal and the appeal itself were resisted by a joint factum filed by the MD's lawyer and the lawyer for the neighbours. In 1991, in a short *per curiam* judgment, the Court of Appeal allowed this first appeal and ordered a new hearing by the DAB.[143] It held that the DAB should have told the colony exactly what information it required and given them the opportunity to collect the information. In failing to do so, the DAB denied the colony a fair hearing. The Court of Appeal noted, "[O]ur concern is not minimized by the undercurrent of resentment against Hutterite expansion revealed in local correspondence to the Board."[144]

The main issue of the second appeal two years later, in 1993, was whether the MD's engineer and lawyer were too much aligned with the DAB and the neighbours who opposed the Starland Colony's application. At the second DAB hearing, the MD's engineer had assisted the DAB with the assessment of technical evidence even though the engineer had previously taken the position that the development posed excessive risks of pollution and danger to the water supply. The MD's solicitor had acted as the DAB's legal adviser, and when the Starland Colony produced a court reporter who proposed to use a shorthand machine, the MD's solicitor announced the reporter would be permitted to use a stenographic machine only if the colony's counsel undertook not to try to put the resulting transcript before the Court of Appeal. The DAB again denied permission for the establishment of the new colony with an intensive livestock operation, and the Starland Colony again sought and received leave from the Court of Appeal to appeal that decision. In the Court of Appeal, the MD's solicitor and the lawyer for the opposing neighbours again opposed both the motion for leave and the appeal and again filed a joint factum.

Mr Justice Jean E.L. Côté, writing for a unanimous Court of Appeal, held that these facts disclosed a clear case of operative bias and an error in law or jurisdiction.[145] A tribunal such as the District Appeal Board could not properly admit into its decision-making process one of the parties or someone too closely connected with one of the parties. Using a quintessentially Canadian metaphor, he found that neither the MD, nor its solicitor or engineer, were neutral:

> Counsel for the Municipality and the [DAB] now contends that the Municipality had not really been opposed to the Church, because at all previous proceedings its opposition had been on legal or procedural grounds, not on the merits of the development. I cannot see that that makes any difference. If the Municipality chose to don a uniform and sit on the neighbours' players' bench and to take the ice alongside the neighbours against the Church, it seems to me to matter little whether it played as goalie or forward. And that is quite apart from the question of whether it was paying the wages of the neighbours' team.[146]

The Court of Appeal allowed the colony's appeal from the DAB's decision and ordered a new, third hearing. Côté warned, however, "[i]f the Municipality really wants to get a decision on the merits, and have it stick without risking a third appeal to the Court of Appeal, it might want to see whether there is some legal way to have different more independent people sit on the [DAB] next time."[147]

The MD apparently took the Court of Appeal's advice when the neighbours lost at the subsequent DAB hearing. The third appeal to the Court of Appeal, in 1994, was an appeal by the MD from the DAB's decision, which had allowed the establishment of the daughter colony and its intensive livestock operation.[148] Four issues were raised by the MD of Starland, but the Court found only one to have any merit at all. That issue was whether any of the conditions attached to the permit by the DAB were illegal and, while the Court did find some of the conditions troubling, they held that none were illegal.

Five years and three Court of Appeal decisions later, the Hutterite Brethren of Starland had permission to establish the Blue Sky Colony and its intensive agricultural operation in the MD of Starland. However, that was not the end of the MD's attempts to thwart the establishment of this new colony, nor the end of the series of cases before the court. In 1996, Mr Justice Peter M. Clark of the Court of Queen's Bench dealt with an application by the MD for an injunction requiring the Starland Colony to cease operations and remove buildings from the new colony's land, and for an order to settle the terms of a development agreement covering that land.[149] The real problem was that the MD insisted on adding conditions to the development agreement beyond those imposed by the DAB. Clark denied the application, finding that the colony had complied with the MD's land use bylaw and had complied with the conditions attached to the development permit by the DAB. The only non-compliance by the colony was with conditions imposed by the MD, conditions it was not entitled to impose in the first place.

Clark also noted that no development agreements had been entered into by the MD that were similar in nature to the development agreement they proposed for the Blue Sky Colony. He concluded, "[i]t is quite obvious that the colony has been singled out for special treatment."[150] He agreed with the Colony that the Development Appeal Board could not have intended to give the right to determine the future of the Blue Sky Colony to its "most implacable opponent," noting the MD had resisted the development from the outset and had encouraged others to do so as well:

> It is apparent that the Municipal District is more concerned with its perceived duty to adjacent residents and its obligations and duties from an enforcement point of view than it is to the right of the Respondents to proceed with the

development in accordance with the Development Permit granted by the [DAB]. The Municipal District has taken an adversarial position with respect to the development and can hardly be described as having been even handed.[151]

The Starland cases illustrate a contemporary expression of local animosities and opposition to the establishment of new colonies that were seen in the days of the Communal Property Control Board. In these 1990s cases, the Alberta courts had little trouble recognizing that the Hutterites had been singled out for differential and discriminatory treatment and had put a stop to it. In many ways, however, the Starland cases were the proverbial easy cases: the MD's actions were blatantly biased against the Hutterite Brethren of Starland, and they violated even formal equality demands to treat everyone the same.

Has the Hutterian Brethren Church found space for their religious way of life in Alberta? When they first immigrated to Alberta in 1918, they established ten colonies of about fifteen families each, a number that had expanded to thirty-four by 1942, when Alberta legislation first prohibited further new colonies.[152] In 1970, after 23 years under the Communal Property Act regime, 78 colonies existed in Alberta with a population of about 7,000 souls.[153] At that time, the chairman of the Communal Property Control Board predicted that by the year 2010, Alberta might have a total Hutterite population of 15,000 scattered among 150 colonies with a total of 1.5 million acres of Alberta land under their control.[154] His prediction was not meant to be a measure of the Hutterites' success in Alberta; rather, it was intended as a warning of dire consequences for the province should this particular minority group continue to expand and continue to refuse to assimilate. We have not reached 2010 yet, but in 2005 there were 95 Dariusleut colonies in Alberta, with a further seven under construction, and 65 Lehrerleut colonies, with another three being built.[155] That is a total of 170 Hutterite colonies, more than Breach had predicted for 2010. It does seem relatively safe to conclude that the Hutterian Brethren Church has indeed found space for their religion and has thrived in Alberta, despite hostile attitudes and behaviours from the surrounding society, and despite discriminatory legislation in effect from 1942 to 1973.

The role of Alberta's superior courts in the successful expansion of the Hutterian Brethren Church has been, however, relatively minor. In the era of the discriminatory legislation, only the judgments of

Justice Johnson and Chief Judge Decore were out of step with prevailing anti-Hutterite opinion. By the time of the Starland case in the 1990s, government and popular opinion had changed for the most part, and the Courts' decisions were in line with the new attitude of increased tolerance for difference.

NOTES

1 Alberta cases concerned with the state's interference or non-interference in the internal disputes of the Hutterian Brethren Church include *Hofer v. Waldner, Western Weekly Reports* [cited hereafter WWR] 1 (1921): 177, where Mr Justice Walsh of the Trial Division of the Alberta Supreme Court refused to privatize the Wolf Creek Colony's property, and two cases concerning Jonathon J. Waldner's application for interim relief requiring him to be reinstated as a member of the Pondorosa Hutterite Colony: *Waldner v. Ponderosa Hutterian Brethren, Alberta Law Reports* [cited hereafter ALR], 4th ser., 12 (2003): 170 and *Waldner v. Ponderosa Hutterian Brethren,* ALR, 4th ser., 24 (2003): 203. These types of internal disputes were recently examined in-depth in Alvin J. Esau, *The Courts and the Colonies: The Litigation of Hutterite Church Disputes* (Vancouver: UBC Press, 2004). Professor Esau focuses on the protracted and complex dispute within the Lakeside Colony in Manitoba, resulting in litigation up to the Supreme Court of Canada in 1992, with a second round of litigation in 1994. See *Lakeside Colony v. Hofer, Supreme Court Reports* [cited hereafter SCR], 3(1992): 165, and *Lakeside Colony v. Hofer, Manitoba Reports*, 2nd ser., (1994): 161. Esau also deals with the schism in the Schmeideleut branch of the Hutterian Church, which split the group into two camps and resulted in considerable litigation involving a half dozen colonies.

2 There were numerous attempts to impose restrictions on the Hutterite expansion in Manitoba. Threats of legislation resulted in a so-called "gentleman's agreement" between the Union of Manitoba Municipalities and the Hutterites, in effect between 1957 and 1971. In Saskatchewan, a government committee worked with the Hutterites from 1958 to the late 1970s. See William Janzen, *Limits on Liberty: The Experience of Mennonite, Hutterite and Doukhobor Communities in Canada* (Toronto: University of Toronto Press, 1990), 61–65 and 75–82.

3 For this essay I have relied extensively on the following accounts with their focus on Canadian, Albertan, or legal events: Esau, *The Courts and the Colonies*; Janzen, *Limits on Liberty*; Robert Macdonald, "The Hutterites in Alberta," in *Peoples of Alberta: Portraits of Cultural Diversity*, ed. Howard Palmer and Tamara Palmer (Saskatoon, Saskatchewan: Western Producer Prairie Books, 1985), 348; Howard Palmer, *Land of the Second Chance: A History of Ethnic Groups in Southern Alberta* (Lethbridge: Lethbridge Herald, 1972); and Douglas Sanders, "The Hutterites: A Case Study in Minority Rights," *Canadian Bar Review* 42 (1964): 225.

4 Esau, *The Courts and the Colonies*, 3.

5 Ibid., x.

6 Evelyn Kallen, *Ethnicity and Human Rights in Canada*, 2nd ed. (Toronto: Oxford University Press, 1995), 91–102.

7 Simon M. Evans, "Some Developments in the Diffusion Patterns of Hutterite Colonies," *Canadian Geographer* 29 (1985): 4; William P. Thompson, "Hutterite Community: Its Reflex in Architectural and Settlement Patterns," *Canadian Ethnic Studies* 16 (1984): 53.

8 Karl A. Peter, "The Certainty of Salvation: Ritualization of Religion and

Economic Rationality among Hutterites," *Comparative Studies in Society and History* 25, no. 2 (1983): 222 at 223-24; Paul Diener, "Ecology or Evolution? The Hutterite Case," *American Ethnologist* 1, no. 4 (1974): 601.

9 Calvin Redekop and John A. Hostetler, "Minority-Majority Relations and Economic Interdependence," *Phylon* 27, no. 4 (1960): 367 at 372.

10 The institutional completeness of Hutterite colonies was recognized by Mr Justice Lambert of the British Columbia Court of Appeal in *Delgamuukw v. British Columbia*, WWR 5 (1993): 97 at para. 1016 (noting "the self-government and self-regulation practised by...a Hutterite community in relation to their own land and the resources on their land, and to the ordering of their internal affairs").

11 Kallen, *Ethnicity and Human Rights in Canada*, 98.

12 Carolyn L. Olsen, "The Demography of Colony Fission from 1878-1970 Among the Hutterites of North America," *American Anthropologist*, n.s., 89, no.4 (1987): 823 at 824.

13 John Andrew Hostetler, *Hutterite Life* (Scottdale, PA: Herald Press, 1983), 17.

14 Robert M. Cover, "The Supreme Court, 1982 Term, Foreword: *Nomos* and Narrative," *Harvard Law Review* 97 (1983): 4.

15 Donald B. Kraybill and Carl F. Bowman, *On the Backroad to Heaven: Old Order Hutterites, Mennonites, Amish, and Brethren* (Baltimore: Johns Hopkins University Press, 2001).

16 Macdonald, "The Hutterites in Alberta," 352.

17 For fuller treatments of the persecution and discrimination faced by the Hutterites in Canada, see Janzen, *Limits on Liberty*, and David Flint, *The Hutterites: A Study in Prejudice* (Toronto: Oxford University Press, 1975).

18 A.M. Willms, "The Brethren Known as Hutterians," *The Canadian Journal of Economics and Political Science* 24, no. 3 (1958): 391.

19 Ninette Kelly and Michael Trebilcock, *The Making of the Mosaic: A History of Canadian Immigration Policy* (Toronto: University of Toronto Press, 1998), 117.

20 Janzen, *Limits on Liberty*, at 15.

21 P.C. 1204, 2 June 1919. On the Doukhobor modes of living and methods of holding property, see J. McLaren, "The Failed Experiments: The Demise of Doukhobor Systems of Communal Property Landholding in Saskatchewan and British Columbia, 1899-1999," in *Despotic Dominion: Property Rights in British Settler Societies*, ed. John McLaren, A.R. Buck, and Nancy E. Wright (Vancouver: UBC Press, 2005), 222-47, and on the Mennonite communal customs, see A. Esau, "The Establishment, Preservation and Legality of Mennonite Semi-Communalism in Manitoba," *Manitoba Law Journal* 31 (2005): 81-110.

22 Macdonald, "The Hutterites in Alberta," 358.

23 A.J. Miller, Acting Director of Assessment, to Miss M.V. Ingram, 23 April 1954, Provincial Archives of Alberta [cited hereafter PAA], accession 80.111, box 1, file 10.

24 Howard Palmer, "Ethnic Relations and the Paranoid Style: Nativism, Nationalism and Populism in Alberta, 1945-50," *Canadian Ethnic Studies* 23, no.3 (1991): 7 at 15; Willms, "The Brethren Known as Hutterians," 402.

25 Simon Evans, "Spatial Bias in the Incidence of Nativism: Opposition to Hutterite Expansion in Alberta," *Canadian Ethnic Studies* 6, nos. 1-2 (1974): 1 at 7.

26 The Land Sales Prohibition Act, 1942 Statutes of Alberta, c. 16, s. 3, as amended by An Act to amend the Land Sales Prohibition Act, 1943 Statutes of Alberta, c. 30.
27 Janzen, *Limits on Liberty*, 68.
28 P.C. 2819, 7 April 1943. This Act was the last provincial statute to be disallowed. It was disallowed principally on the ground that it was an invasion of the field occupied by the federal Consolidated Regulations Respecting Trading with the Enemy. See Eugene Forsey, "Disallowance of Provincial Acts, Reservation of Provincial Bills, and Refusal of Assent by Lieutenant-Governors, 1937-47," *The Canadian Journal of Economics and Political Science* 14 (1948): 94-97, and G.V. La Forest *Disallowance and Reservation of Provincial Legislation* (Ottawa: Department of Justice, 1955).
29 The Land Sales Prohibition Act, 1944 Statutes of Alberta, c. 15.
30 An Act to amend The Land Sales Prohibition Act, 1945 Statutes of Alberta, c. 59, s. 1; An Act to amend The Land Sales Prohibition Act, 1946 Statutes of Alberta, c. 54, s. 1.
31 Select Committee of the Assembly, Report on Communal Property 1972 (Edmonton: Alberta Government, 1972), 6.
32 Ibid., summarizing the Report of the Legislative Committee regarding the Land Sales Prohibition Act, 1944 (Edmonton: Government of Alberta, 1947).
33 Submission of the Alberta Farmers Union on the Extension of The Land Sales Prohibition Act, PAA, accession PR1968.60, file 6, p. 2.
34 Brief submitted on behalf of the Alberta School Trustees Association, February 1947, PAA, accession PR1968.60, file 5, p. 11.
35 Brief submitted on behalf of the Raymond, Magrath, Taber, and New Dayton Legions and Boards of Trade, the Lions Club of Magrath, etc., 11 February 1947, PAA, accession PR1968.60, file 3, p. 8.
36 Brief submitted on behalf of The Hutterian Brethren living in Alberta, PAA, accession PR1968.60, file 2; Palmer, "Ethnic Relations and the Paranoid Style," 16.
37 Janzen, *Limits on Liberty*, 61.
38 Palmer, "Ethnic Relations and the Paranoid Style," 13.
39 Select Committee of the Assembly, Report on Communal Property 1972, 6-7, quoting Report of the Legislative Committee regarding The Land Sales Prohibition Act, 1944.
40 "Adopt Hutterite Committee Report," *Edmonton Journal*, 26 March 1947, 85; "Assembly Passes 'Hutterite' Bill," *Edmonton Journal*, 1 April 1947, 97, PAA, accession 80.111, box 2, file 52.
41 Communal Property Act, 1947 Statutes of Alberta, c. 16.
42 Howard Palmer and Tamara Palmer, "The 1971 Election and the Fall of the Social Credit in Alberta," *Prairie Forum* 1 (1976): 123; Howard Palmer and Tamara Palmer, *Alberta: A New History* (Edmonton: Hurtig, 1990), 325; Roger Gibbins, *Prairie Politics and Society: Regionalism in Decline* (Toronto: Butterworths, 1980), 137-39.
43 *Edmonton Bulletin*, 1 April 1947, 92, PAA, accession 80.111, box 2, file 52.
44 *Hatch v. East Cardston Hutterian Colony*, WWR 1 (1949): 900 (Alberta District Court), *sub nom. Hatch v. Alberta* (Director of Assessment).
45 District Courts Act, Statutes of Alberta, 1907, c. 4.

46 *Hatch v. East Cardston Hutterian Colony*, para. 5.
47 A unanimous Supreme Court of Canada effectively buried the *persona designata* doctrine—at least so far as judges were concerned and subject to any express statutory preservation—in *Herman v. Canada (Deputy Attorney General)*, SCR 1 (1979): 729 at 731–32.
48 Louis Knafla and Richard Klumpenhouwer, *Lords of the Western Bench: A Biographical History of the Supreme and District Courts of Alberta, 1876–1990* (The Legal Archives Society of Alberta, 1997), 43.
49 E.F. Breach, Chairman, Communal Property Control Board, to A.W. Morrison, Deputy Minister, Department of Municipal Affairs, 15 March 1971, PAA, accession 80.III, box 1, file 2.
50 In the Matter of the Application of John Hofer and Joseph Kleinsasser to purchase certain lands from Charles David Ronan of Medicine Hat, Judicial District of Medicine Hat, District Court, District of Southern Alberta, 17 December 1951, PAA, accession 80.III, box 1, file 7.
51 Historically, the standing rule restricted the right to use the courts to individuals seeking to protect a sufficiently direct, personal interest and to the government itself on the basis that the government was the sole protector of the public interest. See *Finlay v. Canada (Minister of Finance)*, SCR 2 (1986): 607.
52 Re Hofer and Kleinsasser, 6.
53 Ibid., 4.
54 An Act to amend the Communal Property Act, 1950 Statutes of Alberta, c. 10, s. 1.
55 E.F. Breach, Director of Assessment, to A.W. Morrison, Deputy Minister, Department of Municipal Affairs, 13 February 1956, PAA, accession 80.III, box 1, file 11.
56 Ibid.; Select Committee of the Assembly, Report on Communal Property 1972, 7.
57 Order-in-Council No. 1298/58.
58 Report of the Hutterite Investigation Committee (Edmonton: Alberta Legislative Assembly, 1959), available in the Leonard Halmrast fonds, PAA, accession PR1968.60.
59 H.D. Mann, to E.F. Breach, Chairman, Communal Property Control Board, 29 November 1960, PAA, accession 80.III, box 9, file 259.
60 Submission by Warner F.U.A. No. 1425, PAA, accession PR 1968.60, file 9, p. 2.
61 E.F. Breach, Chairman, Communal Property Control Board, to A.J. Hooke, Minister, Department of Municipal Affairs, 26 November 1959, PAA, accession 80.III, box 1, file 3.
62 Ibid.
63 Report of the Hutterite Investigation Committee, 20.
64 Communal Property Act, 1960 Statutes of Alberta, c. 16.
65 "1964 Report of the Communal Property Control Board," E.F. Breach, Chairman, to A.J. Hooke, Minister of Municipal Affairs, 21 January 1965, PAA, accession 80.III, box 2, file 42.
66 E.F. Breach, Chairman, Communal Property Control Board, to A.W. Morrison, Deputy Minister, Department of Municipal Affairs, 15 March 1971, PAA, accession 80.III, box 1, file 2.

67 "Administrative Report and Statistics for 1970," E.F. Breach, Chairman, Communal Property Control Board, to F.C. Colborne, Minister, Department of Municipal Affairs, 1 February 1971, PAA, accession 80.111, box 2, file 42.
68 An Act to amend the Communal Property Act, 1951 Statutes of Alberta, c. 13, s. 4, authorized dividing the province into zones based on the productivity of the land, and Order-in-Council 841/51 established three zones and designated the maximum number of acres the Hutterites could purchase in each zone.
69 Re. *Communal Property Act*, WWR 60 (1967), *sub. nom. Hofer v. Communal Property Control Board*.
70 E.F. Breach, Chairman, Communal Property Control Board, to Lorne Hurst, Liaison Officer, Department of Municipal Affairs, PAA accession 80.111, box 2, file 42.
71 E.F. Breach, Chairman, Communal Property Control Board, to E.H. Gerhart, Minister, Department of Municipal Affairs, 5 February 1969, PAA, accession 80.111, box 2, file 42.
72 An Act to amend the Communal Property Act, 1962 Statutes of Alberta, c. 8.
73 E.F. Breach, Chairman, Communal Property Control Board, to A.J. Hooke, Minister, Department of Municipal Affairs, 9 February 1962, PAA, accession 80.111, box 2, file 42.
74 Mann to Breach, see above, n. 59.
75 "The Hutterite problem in Alberta as Viewed by the Western Stock Growers' Association," brief submitted to L.C. Halmrast, Minister of Agriculture, 20 July 1961, PAA accession PR1968.60, file 18, p. 10.
76 *Walter v. Attorney-General of Alberta*, *Dominion Law Reports* [cited hereafter DLR] 54 (1965): 750 (Alberta Supreme Court, Trial Division); affirmed DLR 60 (1966): 253 (Alberta Supreme Court, Appellate Division); affirmed, SCR (1969): 383, *sub nom. Fletcher v. Alberta (Attorney-General)*.
77 Evans, "Spatial bias in the incidence of nativism," see above, n. 25, 1.
78 E.F. Breach, Chairman, Communal Property Control Board, to A.J. Hooke, Minister, Department of Municipal Affairs, 21 January 1965, PAA, accession 80.111, box 2, file 42.
79 The Canadian Bill of Rights, S.C. 1960, c. 44.
80 *Walter v. Attorney-General of Alberta* (Alberta Supreme Court, Trial Division), 756.
81 Ibid., 757.
82 *Walter v. Attorney-General of Alberta* (Alberta Supreme Court, Appellate Division), 263.
83 *Saumur v. City of Quebec and A.-G. Que.*, SCR 2 (1953): 299.
84 *Walter v. Attorney-General of Alberta* (Supreme Court of Canada), 390.
85 *Walter v. Attorney-General of Alberta* (Alberta Supreme Court, Appellate Division), 264.
86 Ibid., 264.
87 Ibid., 269.
88 Ibid., 273.
89 Ibid., 254.
90 Knafla and Klumpenhouwer, *Lords of the Western Bench*, see above, n, 48, 144.
91 *Walter v. Attorney-General of Alberta* (Alberta Supreme Court, Appellate Division), 257.

92 Ibid., 256.
93 *Walter v. Attorney-General of Alberta* (Alberta Supreme Court, Appellate Division), 255–56.
94 *Walter v. Attorney-General of Alberta* (Supreme Court of Canada), 389.
95 Ibid., 393.
96 Palmer and Palmer, *Alberta: A New History,* see above, n. 42, 295.
97 Palmer, "Canadian Immigration and Ethnic History," 486; David K. Stewart and Keith Archer, *Quasi-Democracy? Parties and Leadership Selection in Alberta* (Vancouver: University of British Columbia Press, 2001), 15.
98 Palmer, "Ethnic relations," see above, n. 24, 26.
99 Palmer and Palmer, *Alberta: A New History,* 291.
100 Mr and Mrs N.L. Hampton, Rowley, to J.I. Laferriere, Secretary, Communal Property Control Board, 27 September 1970, PAA, accession 80.III, box 9, file 264.
101 Palmer, "Ethnic Relations," at 7.
102 Ibid., at 8.
103 Re Communal Property Act, WWR 60 (1967): 559, *sub. nom. Hofer v. Communal Property Control Board.*
104 Ibid., at 561.
105 Ibid., at 563.
106 Ibid., at 564.
107 Ibid.
108 E.F. Breach, Chairman, Communal Property Control Board, to the County of Camrose No. 22, 7 June 1967, PAA, accession 80.III, box 4, file 108.
109 County of Camrose No. 22, to E.F. Breach, 27 July 1967, PAA, accession 80.III, box 4, file 108.
110 E.F. Breach, to the County of Camrose No. 22, 29 July 1967, PAA, accession 80.III, box 4, file 108.
111 "Recommendation re Lakeside Hutterite Brethren and M.D. Starland No. 47," E.F. Breach, to F.C. Colborne, Minister, Municipal Affairs, 17 September 1970, PAA, accession 80.III, box 9, file 264.
112 Select Committee of the Assembly, Report on Communal Property 1972, see above, n. 31, vii.
113 Palmer and Palmer, *Alberta: A New History*; Gibbins, *Prairie Politics and Society,* see above, n. 42; Bell, "The Rise of the Lougheed Conservatives and the Demise of Social Credit in Alberta," see above, n. 42.
114 Gerald Friesen, "The Prairie West Since 1945: An Historical Survey," in *Making of the Modern West: Western Canada since 1945,* ed. Anthony W. Rasporich (Calgary: University of Calgary Press, 1984), 1.
115 Ibid.
116 Palmer, *Land of the Second Chance,* see above, n. 3, 254.
117 "The Communal Property Control Board Summary of 1970 Activity," E.F. Breach, Chairman, to Lorne Hurst, Liaison Officer, Department of Municipal Affairs, PAA, accession 80.III, box 2, file 42.
118 Select Committee of the Assembly, Report on Communal Property 1972, 1.
119 Mr French, Select Committee member, *Alberta Hansard,* 17th Legislative Assembly, First Session, 16 November 1972, 77–7; Mr Buckwell, Select Committee member, *Alberta Hansard,* 17th Legislative Assembly, First Session, 16 November 1972, 77–12.

120 Select Committee of the Assembly, Report on Communal Property 1972, Appendix C.
121 Ibid., 15-17.
122 Ibid., at v.
123 The Communal Property Repeal Act, Statutes of Alberta, 1972, c. 103; Alberta Municipal Affairs, "2004-2005 Annual Report," retrieved from *http://www.municipalaffairs.gov.ab.ca/ma/pdf/ MAAnnualReport0405.pdf* (accessed 19 May 2006).
124 Howard Palmer, *Patterns of Prejudice: A History of Nativism in Alberta* (Toronto: McClelland and Stewart, 1982).
125 E.F. Breach, Chairman, Communal Property Control Board, to Secretary-Treasurer, MD of Starland No. 47, 17 August 1971, read into the record by MLA Gordon Taylor, *Alberta Hansard*, 17th Legislative Assembly, First Session, 20 April 1972, 33-62.
126 C.K. French, MLA, to F.C. Colborne, Minister of Municipal Affairs, 7 September 1970, PAA, accession 80.111, box 9, file 264.
127 Mrs James Montgomery, to Premier Harry Strom, 26 August 1970, PAA, accession 80.111, box 9, file 264
128 Mr and Mrs N.L. Hampton, to J.I. Laferriere, Secretary, Communal Property Control Board, 27 September 1970, PAA, accession 80.111, box 9, file 264.
129 Mrs N. Huskinson, to E.F. Breach, Chairman, Communal Property Control Board, 26 August 1970, PAA, accession 80.111, box 9, file 264.
130 E.F. Breach, Chairman, Communal Property Control Board, to F.C. Colborne, Minister of Municipal Affairs, 17 September 1970, PAA, accession 80.111, box 9, file 264.
131 O.C. No. 1905/70, PAA, accession 80.111, box 9, file 264.
132 Lakeside Colony, to E.F. Breach, Chairman, Communal Property Control Board, 5 November 1970, PAA, accession 80.111, box 9, file 264.
133 E.F. Breach, Chairman, Communal Property Control Board, to A.W. Morrison, Deputy Minister, Department of Municipal Affairs, 15 March 1971, PAA, accession 80.111, box 1, file 2.
134 Communal Property Control Board Order, 3 December 1971, PAA, accession 80.111, box 9, file 264.
135 D.J. Merritt, Secretary-Treasurer, MD of Starland No. 47, to E.F. Breach, Chairman, Communal Property Control Board, 10 February 1971, PAA, accession 80.111, box 9, file 264.
136 E.F. Breach, Chairman, Communal Property Control Board, to A.W. Morrison, Deputy Minister, Department of Municipal Affairs, 28 January 1971, PAA, accession 80.111, box 1, file 2.
137 Gordon Taylor, Minster of Highways, to E.F. Breach, Chairman, Communal Property Control Board, 18 February 1971, PAA, accession 80.111, box 9, file 264.
138 *Alberta Hansard*, 17th Legislative Assembly, First Session, 19 April 1972, 32-35.
139 Ibid., 32-35.
140 David Russell, Minister of Municipal Affairs, *Alberta Hansard*, 17th Legislative Assembly, First Session, 20 April 1972, 33-50, 33-51.
141 MLA Gordon Taylor said the board's chairman had admitted to him that the board had recommended approval: *Alberta Hansard*, 17th Legislative

Assembly, First Session, 19 April 1972, 32–35. The Minister of Municipal Affairs, David Russell, said that the board had strongly recommended against approval: *Alberta Hansard*, 17th Legislative Assembly, First Session, 19 April 1972, 33–50.
142 Evans, "Spatial Bias in the Incidence of Nativism," see above, n. 25, 14; *Alberta Hansard*, 7 March 1972, 4–14.
143 *Hutterian Brethren Church of Starland v. Starland No. 47 (Municipal District)*, (1991), *Municipal and Planning Law Reports*, 2nd ser., 6 (1991): 67 (Alberta Court of Appeal).
144 Ibid., para. 6.
145 *Hutterian Brethren Church of Starland v. Starland No. 47 (Municipal District)*, ALR, 3rd ser., 9 (1993): 1 (Court of Appeal).
146 Ibid., para. 26.
147 Ibid., para. 58.
148 *Hutterian Brethren Church of Starland v. Starland No. 47 (Municipal District)*, *Alberta Reports* 149 (1994): 288 (Court of Appeal).
149 *Starland No. 47 (Municipal District) v. Hutterian Brethren Church of Starland*, *Alberta Reports* 182 (1996): 373 (Court of Queen's Bench).
150 Ibid., para. 39.
151 Ibid., para. 39.
152 Select Committee of the Assembly, Report on Communal Property 1972, see above, n. 31, 3.
153 E.F. Breach, Chairman, Communal Property Control Board, to F.C. Colborne, Minister, Department of Municipal Affairs, 1 February 1971, PAA, accession 80.111, box 2, file 42.
154 Ibid.
155 *The 2005 Hutterite Directory*, Canadian ed. (Elie, Manitoba: James Valley Colony of Hutterian Brethren, 2005).

SIX

The Supreme Court of Alberta and Water Law

ARLENE J. KWASNIAK

WATER IS OUR MOST IMPORTANT NATURAL RESOURCE. Without it we have no farms, no industry, no development, no wilderness, and, ultimately, no life. Although government is the primary rule-maker for managing this resource, the role of Alberta courts in shaping water rights and management cannot be overstated. This essay examines how court rulings in Alberta have determined the superiority of private rights over Crown rights, have spoken to the hierarchy between common law and legislation, and have affected the actual hydrology of the province.

Although the Courts' rulings have had water-related impacts in myriad ways, out of necessity this essay considers but a few.[1] Part one provides an overview of water rights in Alberta. It begins with the settlement of the prairies, and in a general manner it describes the reception of English common law to the area that would become Alberta, as well as legislation altering the common law relating to water. Against this backdrop, part two focuses on the common law doctrine of accretion, a doctrine that challenges the heart of the Torrens registry system, held so dear by the province, and erodes Crown ownership of beds, shores of water bodies, and waterways. The discussion shows how Alberta courts have struggled, and continue to struggle, in pursuing a balance between this common law doctrine with Torrens legislation and Crown ownership. Part three then looks at how the Alberta Supreme Court defied common law purists by developing drainage rules tailored to the unique geography and hydrology of the province. Throughout, this essay highlights three themes evident in how the Alberta courts have managed water law within the contexts of the province's historic and contemporary settings. First, the courts attempted to reconcile government management of water resources with private riparian rights. Second, the courts endeavoured to reconcile various legislative initiatives not directly concerned with water and private riparian rights. Finally, given these efforts, it is hardly surprising that the Alberta Supreme Court has had, in the course of its first century, a significant role in shaping the provincial landscape. Part four provides closing comments.

Part One:
WATER LAW ARRIVES IN ALBERTA

In the late 1850s the British and Canadian governments began to contemplate seriously steps to develop western Canada. Prior to that decade, most observers viewed this area as a harsh wilderness with little value; tales of adventure and beauty, however, helped romanticize the West, and the pressure of the rapidly expanding United States prompted more interest in the region's potential and underscored the need to establish more effective control over it.[2] Indeed, as criticism of Hudson's Bay Company governance of the interior intensified, in concert with growing expansionist rhetoric in Canada (and especially the former Upper Canada), well-placed individuals and government officials came to envision an agrarian society that, in time, would provide the foundation of a new nation spanning from sea to sea.[3] Yet to realize this vision, both colonial and Canadian officials needed to put a number of processes in motion.

Of paramount importance was the need to clear the way for settlers. To do this the new Dominion exercised its constitutional authority over "Indians and Land Reserved for Indians"[4] by orchestrating the surrender of Aboriginal title to traditional lands, which facilitated settlement and development. This surrender was the object of numbered Treaties 1–8 and 10, entered into between 1871 and 1908, that pertained to the contemporary Prairie Provinces and to northeast British Columbia.[5] Second, the Dominion needed to establish a rail link with the West. The route proposed initially was considerably farther north than the eventual line. After negotiation of the railway contract, the CPR decided to move the line so that it ran across the southern part of the prairies—a strategic move aimed to prevent American railways from spreading northwards. The Dominion contracted with the Canadian Pacific Railway to realize this vision, and the railway was completed in late 1885.[6] Third, prospective settlers needed to be convinced that the land was suitable for farming. The key element for this was demonstrating that there was sufficient water available on the prairies. Following his famed expedition in the late 1850s, Captain John Palliser reported that the West held considerable potential for settlement. Yet at the same time he identified a large tract of semi-arid land, known as "Palliser's Triangle,"[7] that traversed southern areas of what are now Alberta, Saskatchewan, and Manitoba. About this area Palliser wrote: "This arid district, though there are many fertile spots throughout its extent, can never be of much advantage to us as a possession."[8] At the very least, if settlers were to be attracted to the West, the Dominion had to ensure the legal framework for obtaining water rights was appropriate to the geological and hydrological realities of the region.

The Dominion acquisition of Rupert's Land and the North-West Territory from the Hudson's Bay Company in 1870 included what is now Alberta within the new Northwest Territories.[9] Under the North-West Territories Act of 1870, this area received all English law pertaining to water except where such laws were deemed to be "inapplicable."[10] Included in this was arguably the most important area of English common law relating to water—the common law of riparian rights.[11] A riparian owner is a person whose land abuts the shore of a natural watercourse, such as a river or a creek, or a natural body of water, such as a lake. At common law, riparian owners or occupants possessed riparian rights. Although there are numerous riparian rights, the primary one is the right to use water. At common law, a riparian owner or occupier has the right to have the water continue to flow past the property in its natural state. For use for domestic purposes on the land itself, generally there is no limitation on how much a riparian could take. "Domestic purposes" meant household purposes such as water for drinking, cooking, fire control, and for watering domestic livestock. If a use was for what was called an "extraordinary" purpose, such as a commercial enterprise, the riparian use had to be reasonable, and water had to be returned to the watercourse substantially unaltered in quantity and quality.[12] As this essay demonstrates, the broad legal framework of English common law rights pertaining to water were not at the time of early settlement wholly appropriate for a new agrarian society. Indeed, one of the Supreme Court of Alberta's key tasks was to fashion a reconciliation of this law with the challenges of the Albertan environment and its developing economy.

The Dominion realized early on that water-use rights based on riparian ownership or occupancy would not be appropriate for settlers in this arid region. Given the lack of water in the prairies, early settlers could not expect that individual holdings would have a water source enabling them to exercise riparian rights. A key figure in the early history of water law on the prairies was William Pearce, a former surveyor for the Department of the Interior and, as of 1884, the Department's Superintendent of Mines.[13] In the days of early settlement in southern Alberta, Pearce, a staunch ranching advocate who questioned the viability of farming in southern Alberta, recognized the need for a water-rights framework that enabled irrigation from waters that might not be located on a homestead or ranch.[14] Pearce was determined that new legislation for the North-West Territories should completely abolish common law riparian rights. He believed that the Crown should control the diversion and use of all water, and that no water rights should stem from common law. Only with full government ownership and control of water could irrigation stimulate settlement and encourage investment in irrigation infrastructure.[15]

Pearce's vision was reflected in the original water-rights legislation in the North-West Territories, the North-west Irrigation Act of 1894.[16] The Act introduced a water-rights system based largely on the principle of 'first in time, first in right.' Priority to water was based on the date of completed application to the public authority. In times of shortage, junior licensees—those with a later-dated priority—had no right to water until all more senior rights were satisfied. The Act enabled licences to be issued for a variety of purposes, including domestic use. The Act required all current water users, including riparian users, to apply for a licence to validate their uses within one year of enactment.[17] This requirement was extremely unpopular because it applied to riparian rights for domestic use, and it had a short life as a result. In 1895 the Act was amended to exempt domestic users from the licensing requirement.[18] Accordingly, the Act abolished riparian rights in respect of extraordinary use, but it allowed riparian rights to domestic use to continue.

The Act did not deal with riparian rights other than use, such as quality, accretion, access, or the prevention of flooding.[19] In brief, the right to quality is often described as the right to the water flow "...without sensible alteration of its character or quality";[20] *accretion* means an increase in the size of land owned by riparians owing to the gradual, imperceptible retreat of waters, normally by virtue of natural processes; *access* is the common law riparian right of owners to access water through, for example, constructing works; and the riparian owners at common law have the right to prevent imminent flooding by, for example, building dikes or berms. Did these other riparian rights survive the legislation? Although in theory it was open to courts to find that these rights were "inapplicable" to the prairies, case law indicates that they persisted. Once it was determined or assumed that these riparian rights formed part of the local Canadian common law, the rights could only be altered by express legislation or necessary implication.[21] Nothing in the North-West Irrigation Act altered these common law rights explicitly or by necessary implication. However, other contemporary legislation did impact rights. Although this essay cannot cover all legislative alterations of common law riparian rights other than the right to use, part two of this article considers the extent to which the common law of accretion has survived legislation.

Another body of English common law that the Alberta courts had to consider was that of drainage. The key legal issue here was whether an owner of lower land is obliged at law to accept water that drains onto it from higher land, or whether the lower owner may block the water from coming on the land. Where the water flows from a river or a creek with a defined bed and shores, ordinary riparian-rights principles apply. Both the upper and the lower have right to the continued flow, and neither may interfere with that flow by blocking it and backing it up if that would interfere with the other's riparian rights.[22] However these rules do not automatically apply where the source of water is not an ordinary river or creek to which riparian rights apply. Part three of this article explores how the Alberta courts modified the English common law relating to drainage to meet the province's unique geography and hydrology.

The federal government retained ownership and legislative authority over prairie water, along with other natural resources and public lands until 1930, when public lands and natural resources were transferred to Manitoba, Saskatchewan, and Alberta pursuant to transfer of natural resources agreements.[23] Accordingly, federal legislation and the common law that survived it governed water rights in the prairies until the transfer. Following the transfer, the provincial transferees developed their own water-rights legislation, based on the federal Act. In 1931 the Alberta Legislature passed the Water Resources Act.[24] Although amended many times, this Act remained law in Alberta until 1 January 1999 when the Water Act came into effect and repealed and replaced its predecessor.[25] The Water Act retains the core principles of both predecessor Acts, notably the first in time, first in right principle. It also expressly confirms the continuance of any common law riparian rights, other than the right to the continued flow.[26] Hence, even today, the Alberta courts have a role in modelling the common law to suit the particular circumstances of this province.

Part Two:
ACCRETION IN ALBERTA

Issues concerning accretion first arose, although somewhat obliquely, in a 1921 decision of the Alberta Supreme Court, Appellate Division, in *Flewelling v. Johnston*.[27] The plaintiff, Flewelling, brought an action in trespass against the defendant, Johnston. Flewelling was a riparian owner. His land bordered the Pembina River about 60 kilometres northwest of Edmonton as the crow flies. Over time a strip of land was exposed between his land and the river. Johnston used this strip of land for his own purposes. Flewelling claimed that Johnston had no right to use this property on the grounds that it belonged to him. Had the English common law respecting ownership of bed and shores applied in Alberta, Flewelling's action would have succeeded for, at British common law, the property of a riparian owner included ownership of bed and shores. Where the property in the banks on each side of a watercourse were owned by different persons, *prima facie*, each owned the bed and shore up to the middle of the watercourse—the *medium filum aquae*.[28] If this law applied in Alberta, then Flewelling's property would have extended to the middle of the river, and so his action would have been successful. The Court concluded, however, that this English common law could not apply in Alberta. It based this on the claim of Crown ownership of the beds and shores of navigable and non-navigable waterways in The Irrigation Act.[29] This legislation ousted the British common law rule of riparian ownership over non-tidal beds. The Court refrained, however, from deciding ownership of the exposed strip. Flewelling had not claimed ownership to it, and the Crown was not represented in the proceedings. Accordingly, the Court found for Johnston, the defendant.[30] Although the Court dismissed the action, it identified a key issue that later courts would address: what principles apply in Alberta to determine ownership of accreted land?

The Court in *Flewelling* indicated that disputes over accretions concerned the Crown, as owner of the bed, and the riparian owner who sought to acquire title to exposed land. The question left for a future court to address was this: what principles apply to determine ownership? The 1928 seminal accretion case, *Clarke v. Edmonton (City)*,[31] provided the core of the answer. The dispute concerned an Edmonton riparian owner, Clarke, who claimed ownership over a one-and-one-half acre bench on the North Saskatchewan River that had formed over the previous 12 to 15 years. A bench is a level elevation of land along a shore or coast. At the western end of Clarke's property the bench was about 4 metres above water level, decreasing until it met the eastern edge of his property where it was 1.8–2.1 metres above water level. Evidence showed that the bench had formed, at least in part, because of the City's use of the area as an ash and general refuse dump.[32] Clarke sued the city of Edmonton for trespass in an attempt to stop it from depositing ash and refuse on the bench. The Court was faced with two issues. First, what principles of law applied to determine ownership of the bench? Second, in applying these principles, to whom did the bench belong?

Again, if this were an English case there likely would not have been an issue. As noted earlier, at English common law a riparian owner owned the bed and shores to the middle of a watercourse, and normally any accreted land would naturally belong to the riparian owner. Nevertheless, an accretion doctrine had arisen in England. The doctrine would be used, for example, to determine cases where the bed and shores did not belong to the riparian owner.[33] The Court reviewed the English accretion cases and noted that in England accretion occurs where the riparian land is slowly and imperceptibly added to, either by alluvion (detritus accumulation) or by the recession of the water of a river or lake. The new land formed belongs to the riparian owner in front of whose land it is formed. The process is deemed to be imperceptible where its effects are so gradual that it is not discernible from moment to moment, though it may be discernable from year to year or at shorter intervals. The question for the Court was: did these principles apply in Alberta?

One question addressed was whether the British accretion principles applied only in concert with the British doctrine of ownership to the *medium filum aquae,* or whether accretion principles could stand alone. Chief Justice Horace Harvey appeared to adopt the approach that "you can't have one without the other."[34] However, he did not have to decide this as he, for the majority, with Mr Justice N.D. Beck strongly dissenting, found that Clarke had not established accretion. Of note, the Court also made clear that if accretion principles applied in Alberta, the owner of the land had to be a riparian in the sense that the watercourse or water body formed the boundary of the property.

In Clarke's case, title to his land read: "Lot numbered Twenty-one in Edmonton Settlement aforesaid, as shown upon a map or plan of the said settlement, signed by Andrew Russell, for the Surveyor General of Dominion Lands, dated 25th May, 1883."[35] Although the plan for the area disclosed that "the north boundary appears to be the bank of the Saskatchewan River, without measurements,"[36] the Court found that because the original boundary was still physically visible there was some uncertainty over whether or not the river constituted the new boundary.[37] As well, the Court asserted that the formation of the bench was not gradual and imperceptible in the required sense. It considered the 12- to 15-year time frame over which the bench had arisen to be too short. It observed that the deposition was also due at least in part to the City's dumping, which constituted artificial and not natural means. It noted that true accretion was a natural occurrence.[38]

Thus, the Court of Appeal placed a heavy burden on riparian owners who sought to apply accretion principles. In doing so, it effectively buttressed Crown ownership of beds and shores. This approach accords with the original legislative intent behind claims of Crown ownership of bed and shores to ensure that Government, and not private land owners, possessed managerial powers over water courses and water bodies.[39]

The Court of Appeal's nod in favour of Crown ownership was short lived. Siding with the strong dissent at the Alberta Court of Appeal, the Supreme Court of Canada overturned the Appellate decision.[40] The Supreme Court made it clear that the English principles relating to accretion applied in Alberta even though legislation may have specifically altered the *medium filum aquae* principle.[41] Although the Supreme Court concurred with the Appellate Division in that for there to be riparian rights a property must have a water body or watercourse as a natural boundary, it disagreed that the physical presence of the earlier boundary indicated that the original boundary had not changed. The Court found that as long as the boundary was the river, and that accretion is otherwise established, it does not matter if the earlier bank is still visible.[42] The Court disagreed that the timeframe of 12 to 15 years was too narrow to establish accretion. What was critical, it pointed out, was that the deposition of alluvium had to have been gradual and imperceptible from moment to moment, in contrast to the overall time frame.[43] Finally, it found that "the fact that the increase is brought about in whole or in part by the water, as the result of the employment of artificial means, does not prevent it from being a true accretion, provided the artificial means are employed lawfully and not with the intention of producing an accretion, for the doctrine of accretion applies to the result and not to the manner of its production."[44] Thus, with this decision, the Supreme Court of Canada clearly confirmed that the English common law of accretion applied in Alberta.

Early accretion cases did not address whether accreted land could extend beyond a surface interest to encompass subsurface mineral interests. The issue is interesting because the Crown normally owns subsurface interests. This is because in 1887, by Order-in-Council made under the Dominion Lands Act[45] (the legislation governing Crown lands) the federal government reserved mineral rights from all Crown land grants west of the third meridian. Mines and minerals reserved by the federal Crown passed to Alberta by virtue of the Natural Resources Transfer Agreement of 1930.[46] Both the Provincial Lands Act and its successor, the Public Lands Act, carried forth the implied reservation.[47] Hence, since 1887, whenever the Crown disposes of an interest in land, unless the disposition specifically provides otherwise, the mines and minerals and the power to work them stay with the Crown. Consequently, in Alberta the provincial Crown owns over three-quarters of the mineral resources (such as oil, gas, coal, and metallic minerals) within the province, even though much of them are found under private land.[48] As well as owning the minerals in respect of private lands in the province, as owner of the fee simple, the Crown owns the minerals within public lands. Notwithstanding this reservation, some private landowners have acquired rights to mines and minerals, usually in one of two ways. First, the landowner could have acquired them from the Crown prior to 1887, or the landowner could have expressly acquired them after that time. Second, a landowner could acquire mineral title from the Hudson's Bay Company or the Canadian Pacific Railway, as both held considerable freehold land that included mineral title.[49]

Crown ownership of mines and minerals was critical to the Dominion and subsequently to the province of Alberta. It allowed for rational management of these resources in the public interest, and it ensured royalty income for the government. In 1980, the Court of Queen's Bench, in *Eliason v. Alberta*, was faced with the critical question regarding whether or not the ownership of mines and minerals could pass from the Crown to a private landowner by way of accretion.[50] Its answer affected not only common law but Crown control over mines and minerals. Eliason owned land just west of Wetaskiwin, in central Alberta. Eliason's application was for a court order declaring him to be the owner of accreted land, including mines and minerals except coal, and for an order directing the Registrar of Land Titles to accordingly amend his title. Eliason's certificate of title was to a quarter section of land, except for the area contained within the quarter section that was covered by a certain surveyed lake. All coal was reserved to the Crown. The lake subsequently dried up and Eliason claimed ownership of the entire quarter, including the mines and minerals, except coal, under the dried lake bed. The Court agreed that Eliason owned the mines and minerals under his own portion of the quarter section, and it determined that the lake bed had accreted to the larger parcel. The remaining issue was whether or not the mines and minerals under the lake bed, save coal, also accreted to the quarter section. Relying upon the maxim that an owner in fee of the surface *prima facie* owns the subsurface as well, the Court had little difficulty finding that the mines and the minerals went with the accretion of surface land.[51] Hence, in the absence of a statutory provision to the contrary or the existence of a separate title in another person granted by the Crown, the Court determined that where a person who owns both surface and mineral interests acquires the fee simple to the surface of further land by accretion, the person also acquires further title to the subsurface. The matter, however, was not yet resolved, because the Province of Alberta contended that there was indeed a statutory provision to the contrary. The Court considered section 20 of the Mines and Minerals Act[52] and subsections 4(1) and 34(1) of the Public Lands Act.[53] It dismissed the relevance of the Mines and Minerals Act because it prohibited sales of minerals without an authorizing Act of Legislature. There was no sale involved in the accretion. It dismissed the relevance of subsection 4(1) of the Public Lands Act because it sets out a Crown claim of ownership of beds and shores, but it does not mention mines and minerals. It dismissed the relevance of subsection 34(1) of that Act because although it specifically reserves mines and minerals to the Crown, it does so only in respect of "dispositions," and the Court could not find one. The Court awarded the rights to Eliason.

There is much to criticize in this decision. First, the Court overlooked the reasons for Crown ownership in the first place. Such information would illuminate the Legislative intent behind subsection 34(1) of the Public Lands Act and predecessor sections. Rational management of oil and gas resources and royalty incomes for public purposes would not be aided by piecemeal private ownership of accreted parcels of land. Second, the Court did not apprehend the fact that accretion rights are incidents of riparian ownership, and that riparian ownership rights do not concern subsurface resources. Third, the Court too easily dismissed the relevance of subsection 34(1) of the Public Lands Act. Recall that the section reserves mines and minerals from Crown dispositions. The Act's definition of *disposition* could well capture a transfer from the Crown to private ownership that occurs by way of accretion. This is because clause 2(5)(i) of the Public Lands Act defined *disposition* to mean "every instrument executed pursuant to this Act...whereby any estate, right or interest in any lands of the Crown is or has been granted to any person or by which the Crown divests or has divested itself in favour of any person of any estate, right or interest in any lands..." Although the Public Lands Act did not define *instrument,* subsection 2(9) of the then-applicable Land Titles Act[54] defined it to include "...any document in writing relating to or affecting the transfer of or other dealing with land or evidencing title thereto." It would have been easy for the Court to rely on these provisions to conclude that the Court's order that an accretion had occurred was an instrument and that, accordingly, it also served as a disposition from the Crown of an interest in land. This would have automatically triggered subsection 34(1) of the Mines and Minerals Act and would have reserved the mines and minerals from the disposition.

Arguably this decision did not properly appreciate the importance of Crown retention of mines and minerals in Alberta. The Dominion's reservation of mines and minerals in 1887 indicates a strong intent that the Crown withhold these resources from all dispositions of Crown land (unless expressly included), whether the disposition be by grant, sale, or court order. The Alberta Legislature's carrying forth of this reservation indicates a continuous intent to keep mines and minerals in Crown ownership. By failing to analyse the situation from a historical or a policy point of view, the Court laid a foundation for accretion claims to overstep riparian interests and affect completely unrelated mineral interests.

This section of the essay considers the roles of the survey grid, survey and subdivision plans, and the Alberta land titles system in relation to common law accretion. The cases show that although the Alberta Supreme Court has struggled to refine the roles of these legal instruments and approaches, it has not reconciled them.

In the late eighteenth century, Thomas Jefferson, the third president of the United States, had a vision for the new nation. Jefferson affirmed these aims: "I have indeed two measures at heart...That of general education to enable every man to judge for himself what will secure or endanger his freedom...[and]...To divide every county into hundreds."[55] Regardless of his success or lack thereof with his first goal, none could deny his success with the second.[56] He perceived that the survey grid was a democratic way of ensuring equitable settlement. Homesteaders would not be allowed to choose only the lushest landscapes and the most arable lands for themselves; instead, each would have to settle for an entire squared parcel: some good farmland, some slough, some lowland—the good, the bad, and the ugly. The Dominion of Canada saw wisdom in Jefferson's approach and, based on the U.S. system, developed a grid system for the North-West Territories known as the Dominion Land Survey, or DLS system, which was brought to bear in 1871.[57] Covering about 800,000 square miles of the Canadian prairies, the DLS divided the area into 36-square-mile townships. Each township was divided into 36 one-square-mile sections. A section was divided into four 160-acre quarter sections.[58] Homesteaders could acquire title to a quarter section of land under the Dominion Lands Act[59] for a $10 fee after cultivating one-fifth of the quarter and after building a house.

The survey system should be considered along side the Torrens system, which was devised in 1858 for South Australia by Sir Robert Torrens and introduced to the North-West Territories in 1887. The Torrens land registration system was made possible by the accuracy of the original township and settlement surveys and by the careful collection and preservation of survey plans in the territories.[60] To appreciate the simplicity and beauty of the Torrens system, one need only contrast it with deed registry systems used in parts of Canada, mainly in the East. Deed registry systems are based on the English common law, as modified by legislation. Under a deed registry system, documents affecting interests in land are submitted to the registrar of deeds. There may be many deed registry offices in a province (for example, each of Nova Scotia's 18 land districts has its own deed registry). Usually a deed registrar will maintain a document for each parcel of land, sometimes called an "abstract of title," that consists of a list of other documents ("deeds") and events that set out dealings with the land, such as transfers, mortgages, leases, easements, restrictive covenants, and so on, over time. Documents are typically registered by the name of the person claiming the interest. To ascertain state of title to a parcel, a person interested in a parcel of land must conduct or arrange an in-person search to gather information about the parcel. This may require examining decades' worth of papers, making additional inquiries, and piecing together how documents and other information relate to each other to establish the state of a title. Depending on legislation, the registration of deeds in a province may not be required to maintain an interest in land, and thus determining the actual state of title may be elusive even after a title investigation.

In contrast, a Torrens-based registry system records ownership and other property interests against a parcel of land rather than in the name of the interest holder. Although western Canadian provinces adopted the Torrens system early on, other provinces have only made the transition fairly recently. Under the Torrens system, there should be no need to search historic records to determine state of title. Subject to certain exceptions as set out in applicable legislation, any person interested in a parcel can rely on a single title document to determine ownership and outstanding interests in a parcel of land and determine which interests have priority over others. Copies of encumbrances and other interests normally noted on title may be obtained from the registry office.[61] It is easy to see how common law accretion principles could butt heads with the Torrens system. Accretion could potentially alter the boundaries that are set out in titles. The Registrar, however, could reconcile discrepancies by amending title on application by the owner where common law title increased through accretion.[62] Where the Registrar is uncertain whether an accretion has occurred or where the Crown objects, courts get involved. The resulting cases are of utmost importance to both riparian owners and to the Crown, each of whom has an interest in retaining exposed beds and shores. These cases are also important to those interested in retaining the integrity of the Torrens registration system, which virtually guarantees that prospective purchasers may rely on title to determine the property boundaries.

Land use plans are documents registered at the Land Titles Office where land is subdivided from a larger parcel, often in the form of a surveyed grid parcel. The depiction of a parcel on a survey or subdivision plan can be critically important in accretion cases. This is because accretion is only possible where there is riparian ownership. How a parcel boundary is drawn on a survey or plan may indicate whether or not the parcel actually borders on a water body or watercourse. The leading case on this matter is the Supreme Court of Canada decision *Chuckery v. the Queen*, a Manitoba case.[63] There the Supreme Court found that where the boundary line of a parcel of land as set out in a registered plan is related to a particular river bank, then the boundary line, and the quantity of land, will vary as the bank of the river advances or recedes.[64] The plan in question in this case was filed at the Land Titles Office in 1875 and, at the time of the decision, the office records still showed that boundary. Nevertheless, as land had accreted at common law, the Court found that the plaintiff, Chuckery, owned more land than was reflected on the registered plan. Although on the Chuckery facts it may have been clear that the plan in question made the river a boundary of the parcel, the next case I'll examine reveals this is not always apparent.

In the 1989 case *Nastajus v. North Alberta*, the plaintiff, Nastajus, owned a waterfront lot in the Summer Village of Edmonton Beach, a popular lake-resort town that about 500 people call home in the summer months. The name was changed in 1999 to the Village of Spring Lake, owing, no doubt, to the facts that the village is 40 kilometres west of Edmonton, and that it has a year-round population of about 400 people. Spring Lake is a lovely fishing and recreational lake 2.4 kilometres long by 2.2 kilometres wide, replete with a variety of shorebirds and waterfowl.[65] It is easy to see why lakefront owners, such as Nastajus, would seek to increase their holdings on this gem of lake by means of the doctrine of accretion.

Nastajus claimed title to lands that were exposed through the recession of Spring Lake.[66] His certificate of title gave him ownership over of Lots 2 and 3 in Block 8, Plan 4880 S, which was a subdivision of part of the southeast quarter of a certain section registered in the Land Titles Office at Edmonton in 1907. The Trial Division Court examined subdivision Plan 4880 S to determine whether Lots 2 and 3 were riparian lots. The Court noted inconsistencies between the demarcations of boundaries by the various surveyors of the lots under the plan. Some property lines were noted by a hand-drawn line that appeared to follow the water's edge; other property lines were drawn with a straight line to indicate the water's edge and boundary; and others had the property lines drawn a metre or more from the water's edge. Nastajus's parcels had boundary lines that were drawn with a straight line such that there was about 18 metres of land between his parcels and the original water's edge. The Court of Queen's Bench decided it would not be fair to allow some but not all lot owners to claim accreted land owing to what probably amounted to stylistic differences in drawing survey lines. Accordingly, the Court found for Nastajus.[67] When confronted with the argument that this decision could create a maze of overlapping titles if all of the lakefront owners claimed accretion, the judge stated, "I can only hope that my involvement with this decision will disqualify me from hearing any further cases pertaining to this area, for I fear that even the wisdom of Solomon, which I clearly do not possess, will be sorely tested to find solutions to the competing claims which must ultimately follow."[68]

In deciding as it did, the Queen's Bench supported enlargement of private owners' rights against those of the Crown, and it potentially increased uncertainty with respect to the Torrens system by casting doubt on whether land use plans registered at the Land Titles Office reflect actual land boundaries. The Court of Appeal quickly saw errors in the Queen's Bench decision. It found that where there is no cogent evidence in respect of a subdivision other than the registered plan, the plan "must be accepted as conclusively fixing the boundaries of the lands."[69] In the Appellate Court's view, the matter turned on whether the boundary to a lot in the plan was a straight line, or whether it followed the bank of the lake. In Nastajus's case, the lines were straight, and so the Court determined that his lands did not border the bank of the lake and so there was no accretion. Thus, in this limited fashion, the Court provided a rule for determining when a subdivision (and by extrapolation a survey) line in respect of river or lake lots on a plan or survey registered at the Land Titles Office mirrors actual boundary size and when one must go beyond title to determine parcel size. Interestingly, the Court did not address how it might deal with a situation where the bank itself was a straight line!

The 2000 case *Robertson v. Wallace*[70] dealt with an intriguing situation concerning boundaries and accretion in respect to the Highwood River. The 162-kilometre-long Highwood River originates in the Alberta Rocky Mountains, and from there it flows through the foothills and snakes through the prairies to eventually join the Bow River about 8 kilometres southeast of Calgary.[71] Like other fast flowing Alberta rivers, the Highwood has changed its course over time, and this has caused consternation for at least some of those whose property borders the river.

At the Court of Queen's Bench, Madame Justice Rosemary Nation aptly put the dispute in historical context:

> In 1890, a Dominion Land Surveyor, James MacMillan, surveyed the West bank of the High River in s. 7-19-28-W4M. As he stood in the Prairie sun, he could hardly have anticipated what a keen interest would be shown more than one hundred years later in his field notes and his work. His

survey was incorporated into the Township Plan of 1893. The West bank of the river was used in the N.E. 1/4 of s. 7 as the natural boundary to divide land owned by the Wallace family to the north and west, and the Robertson family to the southeast. A dispute arose over the true boundary between the lands, as the river changed its course.[72]

At its simplest level, this complex case concerned alleged overlapping "ownership" created by accretion. One of the applicants, Wallace, applied to have her title amended to add the accreted land based on a survey she obtained in 1994. The Registrar amended her title without first getting Robertson's consent, as required by the Land Titles Act.[73] Unfortunately, a portion of the added part was already included in Robertson's registered title. Wallace sold her land. The purchasers later objected to Robertson, who knew nothing about the change of title, using the added land, which led Robertson to take action to right things. The Court of Queen's Bench was thus asked to sort out a situation in which a portion of the land in the purchaser's title legally belonged to another. The significant question was how was its finding to square with the Land Titles Act, which virtually guarantees that purchasers can rely on the title descriptions? In deciding the matter, the Court supported the Torrens system in one respect over the common law: it rejected the applicability of the common law principle of "conventional boundaries" that stipulates that where there is a lack of clarity regarding a boundary but the parties have agreed where it lies, both parties are estopped from later denying the agreed upon boundary.[74] Although there was evidence that Robertson and Wallace had agreed upon a boundary, the Court found that any such unregistered agreement could not be enforced against a purchaser for value.[75]

In another respect, it could be said that the Court upheld the common law while still invoking Torrens system principles as incorporated into the Land Titles Act—a remarkable balancing act. By applying the common law, the Court determined that some of Robertson's titled property properly belonged to Wallace. However, according to the Torrens system, both titles as they stood reflected actual ownership notwithstanding the fact that titles overlapped. In the end, the Court ordered that the certificates of title be amended to reflect its findings of actual boundaries. It found negligence on the part of the surveyor of the Wallace property on the basis that he owed a common law duty to Mrs Robertson and Wallace's purchaser. It found that the Registrar made a mistake by not getting Robertson's consent to Wallace's application; this decision enabled the injured parties to invoke the Land Titles Act provisions and take action against the Registrar.[76]

The 2000 decision *Red Deer (City) v. Pitt*[77] concerned a riparian owner whose land was being expropriated by the municipality. Pitt had hoped for increased compensation by claiming accreted land. His certificate of title read as follows: "All that portion of the northeast quarter of section thirteen (13) township thirty eight (38) range twenty eight (28) west of the fourth meridian in the said Province, lying to the north of the left bank of the Red Deer River, as shown on a plan of survey of the said township signed at Ottawa on the 13th day of August A.D. 1884, containing one hundred and thirty two and thirty three hundredths (132.33) acres more or less. Reserving thereout all mines and minerals."[78] Over time the Red Deer River changed its course so much that land accreted to Pitt's property in the northeast quarter; however, all of the accreted land was in the northwest quarter, which Pitt never owned. The Court was thus faced with the question of whether or not a change in physical boundaries of the river could override the quarter section limitation set in a title. The Queen's Bench and Appellate Division agreed that Pitt's land was limited to the quarter section described on the certificate of title, and that common law accretion could not extend the land beyond.[79] The Court of Appeal in the *Pitt* case stated, "It seems clear to us that the change of the physical boundaries of the watercourse cannot create an expanded title overriding the boundaries of the title he received."[80]

The Court made these determinations without posing a fundamental question: Why should there be such a limit? By its nature, common law accretion increases land ownership beyond that set out in a certificate of title. Why should accretion stop at the limits of the quarter section? The Court might have called upon Alberta history for a justification, but it did not. Homestead grants, as mentioned earlier, were normally for one quarter section, and it makes some sense that land that exceeds the original grant should not be added to title. But what if the parcel in question was less than a quarter section? Would that have made a difference? In the end, the *Pitt* decision leaves more questions unanswered than answered. But as the next case shows, the Court's dilemma over Torrens principles and the common law was not solved by what seem like *ad hoc* principles formulated to deal with fact situations but lacking a clear theoretical basis.

Andriet v. Strathcona (County) No. 20[81] concerned multiple claims to lands exposed through the recession of Cooking Lake. Cooking Lake is a large, shallow lake located about 25 kilometres east of Edmonton. The Cree name for the lake is *opi-mi-now-wa-sioo*, meaning *a cooking place*.[82] Cooking Lake has been cottage country for well over one hundred years since Sheriff Robertson of Edmonton built the first cottage there in 1893.[83] The lake area was, and still is, a popular resort, especially for nearby Edmontonians, and the shorelines were rapidly subdivided following, for the most part, the First World War. Eventually three hamlets developed around the lakeshore—South Cooking Lake, North Cooking Lake, and Collingwood Cove. The hamlets were densely populated with cottage owners, many of whom, as this case shows, were interested in extending ownership through application of common law accretion.[84]

In its efforts to resolve ownership claims, the frustration of the Court of Queen's Bench is underscored by its statement that "[t]rying to adhere to the common law principles associated with riparian owners and accretion in this case would end up creating a maze of overlapping interests incapable of resolving to the point of registerability in land titles."[85] The only land description set out in the case was that of Andriet, whose certificate indicated the following: "All that portion of the north west quarter of section thirteen (13) township (51) range twenty-two (22) west of the fourth meridian, not covered by any of the waters of Cooking Lake, as shown on a plan of survey of the said township…containing 4.36 hectares (10.77 acres) more or less."[86] Notwithstanding the certificate's linguistic similarities with those of numerous earlier successful accretion cases, the Court did not find that the parcel, or other parcels under consideration, had a natural boundary. The Court looked at the plans filed at the Land Titles Office and determined that the boundaries were frozen when registered, even where they followed the then bank of the lake.[87] Since those boundaries were no longer at the bank of the lake because land had been exposed since completion of the plans, the Court found the owners were not riparian owners. Accordingly, it concluded there was no accretion.

Although the decision flies in the face of earlier cases, including jurisprudence from the Supreme Court of Canada in *Chuckery v. the Queen* described above, one can appreciate the difficulty of the Court's position. The Court found no rational way to deal with the situation and so, in effect, it refused to do so. In justifying the approach taken, the Court stated, "Invariably the context in the reported decisions involved several parties claiming the same land[;] however, either the common law rights of riparian land owners offered up an answer, or resorting to the integrity of the survey system coupled with the Torrens system of registering title offered up an answer, and occasionally disputes could be settled by having regard to various survey techniques. However, in the peculiar circumstances of this case none of the usual methods for determining disputed boundaries brought about a fair and equitable conclusion, hence my resort to giving significant weight to the various plans to establish boundaries."[88]

The Court did not assert its authority to fix parcel boundaries at the natural boundaries set in survey or subdivision plans. This approach no doubt has considerable potential to erode the rule of accretion established in Alberta law. In doing so, it stands to boost Crown ownership by allowing the Crown to add to its ownership of beds and shores those lands that otherwise would have been privately accreted. As well, it would support the Torrens system since certificates of title would reflect actual ownership.[89] It must be borne in mind, however, that the approach would topple a century of accretion law principles set by higher courts, including the Supreme Court of Canada. The decision has been appealed, leaving the quagmire of overlapping titles to the Court of Appeal to sort out.

The development of the right to claim accretion in Alberta has been marked by the Court's performance of a delicate balancing act as it seeks to reconcile the competing interests of common law riparian rights, Crown ownership of bed and shores, and the tenets of the Torrens registry system. The Court's struggle is exacerbated because there are no settled underlying principles to apply to the accretion rule. Geological, hydrological, and climatic realities in Alberta that cause rivers to shift and the recession of water bodies make the Court's task more difficult. Climate change will add to its burden. Perhaps it is time for the legislature to step in and relieve the Alberta courts of a decision that might prove impossible to reconcile or balance.

Part Three:
WATER DRAINAGE PATHS AND AGRICULTURE

In the early twentieth century, the Alberta Supreme Court legally recognized Alberta's geological, hydrological, and agricultural realities in a manner that probably stunned legal purists. In a line of cases, the Court articulated 'Alberta common law' water drainage principles that clearly departed from the British common law. The Court adopted 'civil' law drainage principles, which it plainly did to reflect and accommodate local conditions.

The saga began in early 1917 with *Makowecki v. Yachimyc*.[90] Makowecki, the plaintiff, owned the southwest quarter of section 32, township 56, range 21 west of the 4th meridian, and the defendant, Yachimyc, owned the southeast quarter. Both parcels of land were located in the Beaverhills–Cooking Lake Moraine, east of Edmonton. A *moraine* is a hilly landscape with depressions that collect water.[91] The Beaverhills–Cooking Lake Moraine is particularly large, covering five Alberta counties (Beaver Hills, Camrose, Leduc, Lamont, and Strathcona).[92]

A natural drainage depression path on the moraine ran from the northwest corner to the southeast corner of Makowecki's land and then continued onto Yachimyc's land; eventually it discharged into the Saskatchewan River, about 9 kilometres from the path's beginning. Only rainwater and runoff collected in the depression; there was no discernable groundwater or other surface water source. The depression had no identifiable banks and would not normally be called a river or a creek; it was merely a depression in the land that served as a drainage path. It was dry most of the year but typically carried water in the spring, after the snow melt, or when there were heavy rains. Yachimyc objected to the water coming onto his land and so he built, at the edge of his property, a 61-metre-long earthen dam, between one-half and three-quarters of a metre high to block it. He successfully blocked the water, but the water backed up and flooded Makowecki's land, which caused damage. The question to the Court was simple: did Yachimyc—the lower proprietor—have a right at common law to block the water from coming on his land, or did Makowecki—the upper proprietor—have a right to have the water follow the natural drainage path onto Yachimyc's land?

If the drainage path had been a proper river or creek, the Court could have easily addressed the question. It would have applied familiar riparian rights principles that would have prohibited either riparian owner to significantly interfere with the riparian rights of the other. However, this was not a simple riparian rights case. The depression and drainage path was not the kind of geological and hydrological construct to which riparian rights obviously applied. Alberta's geography is rampant with such constructs, and the Court was faced with a novel fact situation. Its decision would not only carve a new legal path, it would affect farmers and watersheds. If the Court denied the lower proprietor the right to block the water, the Court would respect the integrity of established natural drainage paths. If it granted the right to block the water, it would sanction interference with natural drainage paths and allow farmers to alter their local watersheds. The consequences could be enormous.

According to the majority judgement, the English common law on the matter was not completely clear. However, the majority noted that a number of American cases represent the "common law" view as imposing no obligation on the lower proprietor to accept water draining onto the owner's property and giving the lower owner the right to obstruct such water.[93] The civil law view was clearer. Under it, the lower owner had to accept the water that naturally drained onto the owner's property, whether or not the water flowed in a defined channel. It is significant that the law in Ontario had been established by the time of the *Makowecki v. Yachimyc* case (1917) and that the *Makowecki* court acknowledged this.[94] In 1897 the Ontario Court of Appeal in *Ostrom v. Sills* found for the owner of the lower land and accepted what is called the "common law" doctrine.[95] This judgment was later affirmed by the Supreme Court of Canada. The Ontario court characterized the common law doctrine as holding that where there is "mere surface water precipitated from the clouds in the form of rain or snow...no right of drainage exists *jure naturoe* and that as long as surface water is not found flowing in a defined channel with visible edges or banks approaching one another and confining the water therein, the lower proprietor owes no servitude to the upper to receive the natural drainage." The case characterized the civil law position as imposing such a servitude.[96]

The Alberta court, however, was not prepared to go the way of Ontario. It adopted the civil rule and thereby provided Makowecki, the upper owner, a remedy. In its words:

> I am...of the opinion that, if ever there existed a common law rule differing from that of the civil law, it never became part of the law of this province and should not now be adopted, inasmuch as it is wholly inapplicable to a country bounded upon one entire side by mountains and having within its limits large tracts of land broken by hills, valleys, ravines, swales and sloughs, through which streams of very considerable size and force of current formed from melting snows upon the higher lands and heavy rainfalls run at certain seasons of the year in quite definite channels

without breaking the soil, and yet are of such magnitude as to be incapable of being dealt with as mere surface water according to the so-called common law rule. To attempt to apply any other rule than that which I have put down as my understanding of the civil law rule...would often create an intolerable situation in this province, while the rule as I have stated it would meet our requirements fully, and in the course of time, by reason of more close settlement of the country and the construction of drains by Government and municipal authorities, the necessity for appealing to any rule would in the course of time disappear.[97]

Thus the Court custom tailored law fit for Alberta by adopting a civil law principle, not common law, as characterized by the Supreme Court of Canada. As we will see, however, the Court erred in its belief that human settlement and government drains would render the principle obsolete.

Canada's national symbol, the beaver, brought a refinement to the *Makowecki v. Yachimyc* principle. The beaver deserves its monumental place in Alberta history. As elsewhere in Canada, the beaver played a weighty role in the exploration, development, and history of the province. After the demand for beaver pelts subsided acutely in the middle of the nineteenth century, owing to Europe's shift in fashion from beaver hats to silk hats, beavers, by then close to extinction, began to proliferate. Their activities and impacts soon became commonplace across the Canadian prairies. The beaver impact relevant to the rule from *Makowecki v. Yachimyc* concerns the damming of drainage paths. *Farnell v. Parks*[98] followed on the heels of *Makowecki v. Yachimyc*. The plaintiff, Farnell, occupied the northwest quarter of section 4, township 38, range 28, west of the 4th meridian. The land was about 40 kilometres east of Red Deer. The defendant, Parks, owned the northeast quarter of the same section. The two quarters, along with the southwest quarter and land to the west, were dotted with sloughs. Sloughs are commonplace in the Canadian prairies. Today these are considered to be important wetland features that may serve critical hydrological and environmental functions by virtue of their connection to aquifers and their role in groundwater recharge, flood control, and biological diversity maintenance and enhancement. However, courts in the early twentieth century often referred to them under the generic and somewhat pejorative title "sloughs" whether they had little or critical hydrological and ecological value.

Indeed, until the last few decades, these prairie water bodies were considered but a nuisance to farming.[99]

The sloughs in the *Farnell v. Parks* case were situated along natural depressions in the land that, together with the sloughs, constituted a natural water drainage path.[100] Water accumulated on Farnell's land, the higher parcel, and would have drained into the depression and onto Parks's land through the sloughs except for the work of beavers that dammed the flow. Subsequently, and to the scorn of the beavers, Farnell opened the dam to relieve flooding on his farmland. This allowed water to pass through to Parks's land. In due course Parks sealed the opening and thus blocked the flow, which backed the water up onto Farnell's land. Farnell claimed his right to allow the water to flow off his land on the basis of the principles from *Makewecki v. Yachimyc,* and asked the Court to require, among other relief, that Parks re-open the dam. Parks argued that the beaver dam resulted in the natural flow of the drainage path changing, and he also relied upon principles from the same case. The question put to the Court boiled down to this: does a beaver dam alter the natural drainage path, or does the previous, undammed natural course of the path persist? If the beaver dam altered the natural water course and formed a new natural course, then Parks would win; if the natural course persisted as before the dam, Parks would lose.

The Court found that the beaver dam did not alter the natural drainage course. Hence, Farnell had a right to have the water flow off of his property. The Court's judgement reads as follows: "If the obstruction is a beaver dam, as I find it to be, it was an adventitious obstruction, which, it seems to me, like any other obstruction, coming upon the land and interfering with its natural conformation, however occasioned, could rightfully be removed by any one interested, so as to restore the land to its original natural conformation...."[101] Although the decision might have been a practical solution in the circumstances, it is not clear that it was the best possible decision, given the long-standing and almost universal impacts of beavers on the Alberta landscape. A more refined decision would have recognized that beaver obstructions are different in kind from human obstructions: the former are works of nature, the latter the works of humans. It would also recognize that over time beaver impacts can alter natural drainage paths. Mr Justice Charles Stuart dissented: "For all that appears in the evidence it [the dam] may have been there for 100 years. I think it constituted part of the natural condition of the soil."[102] Stuart continued by arguing that if beaver dams can be removed on the basis that they alter a natural drainage path, then "bars washed up by a stream in an earlier geological period or even more recently although now obviously forming part of the natural condition of the soil could also thus be removed by the neighbour. Indeed, any obstruction caused by...

> Streams which swift or slow
> Draw down Aeonian hills and sow
> The dust of continents to be"

could be so removed.[103]

Of course, Stuart's allusion to Lord Tennyson's lines might not, so to speak, hold much water. Although *Makowecki v. Yachimyc* spoke to the right of higher owners to remove human-made obstructions, it certainly did not enable higher owners to remove natural obstructions that resulted from natural changes in drainage paths. Nevertheless, *Farnell v. Parks* is a bit unsettling, for if the Court meant to create a general principle that the action of beavers does not naturally change drainage patterns, this is manifestly wrong. In the Alberta landscape, beavers are plentiful, and in many cases beaver action has changed natural drainage paths. Insofar as this case stands for this proposition, it does disservice to a province that abounds with the famous rodent, beavering away at the Alberta landscape.

Later cases clarified that where water projects such as dams, ditches, or dikes increased the natural flow of water, the lower owner was not obliged to accept the increased flow. For example, in *Molden v. Kirkeby*, defendant Kirkeby's construction of a drain from a coal mine increased the natural flow across Molden's land.[104] The Court found that the plaintiff owed no servitude to accept the excess water that resulted from the drain's construction. This refinement of the rule, though appropriate for the Alberta rural landscape, which is littered with drains, ditches, culverts, and dams, created a difficult burden of proof for the plaintiff, who had to demonstrate that an increase in flow resulted from an artificial work.

The cases discussed so far are curious in that the Courts did not raise the role of regulatory controls on private drainage. Drainage activities in Alberta have been subject to statutory controls since 1894 due to the federal North-West Irrigation Act. The Act required anyone who contemplated drainage to first obtain a licence.[105] Following the transfer of public lands and natural resources from the federal government to the province in 1930, the Alberta Water Resources Act carried forth this requirement, and the requirement persisted through to the current Water Act.[106] It was not until 1997 that an Alberta court raised the issue that a drainage activity was not approved under legislation.[107] In 1993, David Percy noted that at that time only one prairie case, from Manitoba, had considered the effect of water legislation on the common law of drainage.[108] Percy rightly suggested that it was likely the lack of court attention to the legislation, paired with the Alberta Government's failure to enforce it in respect of unauthorized drainage, that led the agricultural industry to believe that rural owners had the right to drain their property without statutory authorization.[109] Fortunately, the Alberta Government is now more willing to enforce these legislative provisions. Unfortunately, the province acted very late. The lack of awareness in the rural community and elsewhere that drainage is in fact regulated has produced effects that are not limited to incidents of unauthorized drainage between upper and lower owners; lack of awareness is evident in other drainage activities, including unauthorized drainage to increase farmlands or to enable urban development. An enormous number of Alberta wetlands have been lost. About 60 per cent of Alberta's pre-settlement wetlands are gone. Based on a 1996 inventory, there were originally about 35,500 square kilometres of wetlands. About 50 per cent—17,750 square kilometres—were gone by 1960. By 1996, 21,300 square kilometres were gone, and by 1999, 21,500 square kilometres were drained. Of what remains, much has been impacted by agriculture.[110] Although the government is the party most responsible for this development because it has not enforced its legislation, the Alberta courts, and counsel arguing in them, have played a role in this devastation. If Alberta courts had openly recognized that drainage activities required statutory authorization, the agricultural community, which no doubt has an interest in drainage cases, would have been made aware of this requirement.

Part Four:
CLOSING COMMENTS

The cases reviewed in this essay reveal three prevalent themes. One is the role of courts in their attempts to reconcile private riparian rights with government ownership and management of water resources and bed and shores. This role developed due to one simple act: the reception of English common law riparian rights into the North-West Territory. Early on, courts determined or presumed that many facets of English common law riparian rights applied even though it was open to them to find at least some riparian rights were "inapplicable" to the geological and hydrological conditions of the prairies.[111] Courts could have taken the strong hint evident in the North-West Irrigation Act that lawmakers were intent on severely limiting riparian rights. They could have emulated western United States courts independently developed state common law appropriate to local conditions.[112] One may speculate what would have happened if Alberta courts had found that riparian rights not addressed in the North-West Irrigation Act or later legislation were inapplicable in this province. Certainly, many private- vs. public-right water-related clashes would have been avoided. Perhaps William Pearce's vision would have been better realized.[113] The Crown, at least, would have been given greater opportunity to manage water itself, as well as watercourses and bodies of water, in the public interest. But then again, there has been consistent public support for a balance between private rights and public rights. This is what the Alberta Supreme Court strove to achieve.

The second theme centres on how the Alberta Supreme Court has tried to reconcile legislation—other than water legislation—with private riparian rights. This is particularly evident in the interface between common law accretion rights and a legislated Torrens registry system. Courts could have avoided the problem had they found that the English common law of accretion was inapplicable to Alberta. The Alberta Supreme Court might have vigorously held that English common law accretion doctrine could only apply where riparian ownership extends to the bed and shores. Perhaps then the Supreme Court of Canada might not have overruled, so easily, the Alberta Supreme Court Appellate decision in *Clarke v. The City of Edmonton*.[114] Courts hearing early accretion cases may have found that the accretion doctrine did not apply in Alberta on the grounds that it was inapplicable by virtue of its incompatibility with Torrens principles. These principles were first incorporated into Alberta legislation in 1906, years before the first important accretion cases.[115] If the Alberta Supreme Court had done this, Crown management of beds and shores would have been greatly facilitated. As well, the huge headache of overlapping titles would have been avoided.[116] But, once again, the Court saw fit to support private rights over public rights, no doubt to the gratification of riparian owners.

The third theme to emerge points to how Alberta Supreme Court approaches have impacted the Alberta landscape. A key example is the

Court's approach to drainage rights between upper and lower owners. Here the Court recognized that the geography and hydrology of the prairies called for drainage principles distinct from those of English common law.[117] This approach, no doubt, helped maintain natural drainage systems that are so important to Alberta's watersheds. However, courts were less sensitive to the role of beavers in forming and altering natural drainage paths within those watersheds.[118] Because the Alberta Supreme Court did not openly recognize that drainage has been regulated in Alberta since becoming a province and that drainage activities in what would become Alberta were regulated prior to Confederation, two themes are brought together: it indicates strong support of private interests over public interests and, though likely inadvertently, it allowed landscape impacts to occur as a consequence of unauthorized drainage.[119]

For the most part, these themes are apparent only in retrospect. When in action, the Supreme Court of Alberta consistently manifested the desire to make decisions that were supported by legal precedent, were consistent with legislation, and would be appropriate for Alberta and Albertans. It should be congratulated for its many successes.

AUTHOR'S NOTE: The author thanks David Burns, third year law student, for his excellent background research, and Richard Panton, graduating law student, for thoughtful comments and suggestions, and invaluable editing assistance. The author also thanks the Institute for Sustainable Energy, Environment and Economy (University of Calgary) for research funding assistance.

NOTES

1 For a broad survey of the history of prairie water law, see Tristan M. Goodman, "The Development of Prairie Canada's Water Law, 1870–1940," in *Laws and Societies in the Canadian Prairie West, 1670–1940*, ed. Louis A. Knafla and Jonathan Swainger (Vancouver: UBC Press, 2005), 266–79.
2 See, generally, Douglas Owram, *Promise of Eden: The Canadian Expansionist Movement and the Idea of the West, 1856–1900* (Toronto: University of Toronto Press, 1980).
3 Chester Martin, *"Dominion Lands" Policy* (Toronto: McClelland and Stewart, 1973), 9.
4 Section 91(24) of the Constitution Act, 1867, 30 & 31 Victoria, c. 3.
5 Richard Bartlett, *Resource Development and Aboriginal Land Rights* (Calgary: Canadian Institute of Resources Law, 1991), 41.
6 Harold Innis, *A History of the Canadian Pacific Railway* (Toronto: University of Toronto Press, 1971, first published, 1923), 111.
7 Annual precipitation for the area averages 30.5–40.5 cm. Today, water scarcity is aggravated by shrinking glaciers that feed major watercourses and water bodies in the area, and by climate change. For a discussion of water shortage in the prairie provinces and legislative and policy responses, see David Percy, "Responding to Water Scarcity in Western Canada," in *Texas Law Review* 83 (2005): 291–92. The subsequent settlement history of the Palliser Triangle has been documented in David C. Jones, *"We'll all be buried down here": The Prairie Dryland Disaster, 1917–1926* (Calgary: Alberta Records Publication Board, Historical Society of Alberta, 1986), and in *Empire of Dust: Settling and Abandoning the Prairie Dry Belt* (Edmonton: University of Alberta Press, 1987).
8 James MacGregor, *A History of Alberta* (Edmonton: Hurtig, 1972), 76.
9 Alberta consists of portions of what used to be Rupert's Land and the North-West Territory. The North-West Territory comprised what is today the Yukon Territory, most of the Northwest Territory, northern Alberta, and northern Saskatchewan. Rupert's Land comprised the hydrographic basin of Hudson's Bay (which today comprises northern Quebec and Ontario), the entire province of Manitoba, most of Saskatchewan, and part of Alberta. From 1868–1870, the Dominion purchased Rupert's Land from the Hudson's Bay Company and amalgamated it with the North-West Territory, renaming the aggregate lands the "Northwest Territories." See C. Martin, *"Dominion Lands" Policy*, 2–5 and *Canadian Encyclopaedia*, entry for "North-West Territories, 1870–1905," available online at http://www.thecanadianencyclopedia.com/PrinterFriendly.cfm?Params=A1ARTA0005805 (accessed 22 February 2006).

10 (Can.) 49 Victoria c. 25, s. 3. See also J.E. Cote, "The Introduction of English Law into Alberta," *Alberta Law Review* 3 (1964): 262-92, 263. Later this article explores how courts developed tests to determine inapplicability with respect to some aspects of common law that were not replaced by legislation.
11 For a detailed discussion of common law water rights and legislative alteration throughout Canada, see David Percy, *The Framework of Water Rights Legislation in Canada* (Calgary: The Canadian Institute of Resources Law, 1988).
12 See, for example, *Miner v. Gilmour* (1858), *12 Moore's Privy Council Cases*, P.C.
13 On Pearce see Jones, *Empire of Dust*, 9-12. David Breen has authored a biographical entry on Pearce that will appear in the forthcoming volume of the *Dictionary of Canadian Biography*.
14 Pearce was a great champion of the development of irrigation in southern Alberta and the driving force behind the *North-West Irrigation Act* of 1894, described in the text. See Alberta Irrigation Projects Association, *South Saskatchewan River Basin Irrigation in the 21st Century, Volume 1: Summary Report* (Lethbridge: Alberta Irrigation Products Association, 2002), 9.
15 Ibid.
16 The North-West Irrigation Act, 1894, 57-58 Victoria, 1894, c. 30.
17 Ibid., s.7.
18 An Act to Amend the North-West Irrigation Act, 1895, 58-59 Victoria, c. 33, s. 3 repealing and replacing s. 7.
19 See Arlene Kwasniak, *Alberta Wetlands: A Law and Policy Guide* (Edmonton: Environmental Law Centre and Ducks Unlimited Canada for the North American Waterfowl Management Plan, 2001), 49-58, for a discussion of all of the common law incidents of riparian ownership.
20 *John Young & Co. v. Bankier Distillery Company, Appeal Cases* (1893): 697 (House of Lords).
21 Applications of this legal presumption are noted in Ruth Sullivan, *Sullivan and Driedger on the Construction of Statutes*, 4th ed. (Markham and Vancouver: Butterworths, 2002), 395. For example, in 1956 the Supreme Court of Canada stated in *Goodyear Tire & Rubber Co. of Canada v. T. Eaton Co., Supreme Court Reports* [cited hereafter SCR] (1956): 610 at 614, that "...a Legislature is not presumed to depart from the general system of the law without expressing its intentions to do so with irresistible clearness, failing which the law remains undisturbed."
22 See generally, David Percy, *Wetlands and the Law in the Prairie Provinces* (Edmonton: The Environmental Law Centre, 1993), 11-34.
23 The agreements are attached as Schedules 1, 2, and 3 to the Constitution Act, 1930, Appendix II (formerly British North America Act (1930), 20-21- George V, c. 26 (U.K.)). For an examination of the Natural Resources Transfer Act and its role in Albertan history, see Thomas Flanagan and Mark Milke, "Alberta's Real Constitution: *The Natural Resources Transfer Act*," in *Forging Alberta's Constitutional Framework*, ed. Richard Connors and John M. Law (Edmonton: University of Alberta Press, 2005), 165-89.
24 S.A. 1931, c. 71.
25 S.A. 1996, c. W-3.5.
26 Ibid., s. 22(3).
27 *Flewelling v. Johnston, Western Weekly Reports* [cited hereafter WWR] 2 (1921): 374;

ALR 16 (1921): 409; *Dominion Law Reports* [cited hereafter *DLR*] 59 (1921): 419, (A.S.C., App. Div.).
28 *Bickett v. Morris* (1877) 2 *Appeal Cases* 839, at 853.
29 The Irrigation Act, R.S.C., 1906, ch. 61, sec. 7. In *Flewelling*, in *WWR*, p. 383, and *ALR*, p. 420, the court commented that "section 7 of the Act provid[es] that no grant shall be made by the Crown of any exclusive property or right in the land forming the bed or shore of any lake, river, stream or other body of water." The Crown first claimed ownership of bed and shores in the original 1894 North-West Irrigation Act, ss. 4–6. Although wording has altered through the years, the claim has persisted. Currently it is set out in s. 3 of the Public Lands Act, R.S.A., c. P-3. The Dominion originally viewed Crown ownership of bed and shores to be essential to rational water management in the North-West Territories. For example, in an 1894 official report of the debates of the House of Commons of the Dominion of Canada, Thomas Daly (a member from Manitoba) speaking in favour of the Bill stated that unless the principle of Crown ownership was firmly set in legislation, "...it would lead to interminable litigation,..." See *Official Report of the Debates of the House of Commons of the Dominion of Canada*: 4th session, 7th Parliament, 28 May–23 July, at 4951. Imprint: Ottawa: S.E. Dawson, 1894.
30 Ibid., at s. 5.
31 *Clarke v. Edmonton (City)*, *WWR* 1 (1928): 553; *ALR* 23 (1928): 233; *DLR* 2 (1928): 154, (A.S.C.App.Div.).
32 Ibid., ss. 10 and 11.
33 For example, *Hindson v. Ashby*, 1 Chancery 78 (1896) 78, on appeal 2 Chancery 165 (1896). In this case the owner of the bed and shores was the holder of fishing rights and not the riparian owner.
34 *Clarke v. Edmonton (City)*, at ss. 14–16.
35 Ibid., at s. 7.
36 Ibid., at s. 8.
37 Ibid., at ss. 22, 90, and 99.
38 Ibid., at ss. 17 and 21.
39 See n. 30.
40 *Clarke v. Edmonton (City)*, *SCR* (1930), 137; *DLR* 4 (1929): 1010, (S.C.C.); reversing: *WWR* 1 (1928): 553; *ALR* 23 (1928): 233; *DLR* 2 (1928): 154, (A.S.C.App. Div.), at s. 6.
41 Ibid., 150.
42 Ibid., 152–53.
43 Ibid., 147–48.
44 Ibid., 144.
45 S.C. 1872, c. 23. The Order-in-Council was dated 31 October 1887.
46 When Alberta became a province in 1905, the federal government retained ownership of its public lands and natural resources, just as it had done with Manitoba and Saskatchewan. As owner of these lands and resources, federal parliament retained legislative authority over them. In 1930, however, the federal government transferred most of the retained lands and resources to the respective provinces by way of three Natural Resources Transfer Agreements. These agreements form part of the Constitution Act and are attached as Schedules 1, 2, and 3. As a result of these agreements, each of

these provinces gained legislative authority over the transferred public lands and the natural resources within its borders.

47 Provincial Lands Act, S.A. 1931, c. 1931, s. 8. The current provision is the Public Lands Act, R.S.A. 1980, c. P-30, s. 34 (1).
48 Alberta Energy, Annual Report, 1989-90, at 10.
49 In exchange for Rupert's land, the Hudson Bay Company was paid £300,000 plus a quantity of land, of which more than 660,447 square kilometres were in Alberta. See MacGregor, *A History of Alberta,* at 82. The Canadian Pacific Railway was given considerable land grants in partial exchange for building the transcontinental railway. See Innis, *The Canadian Pacific Railway*, 108.
50 *Eliason v. Alberta (Registrar, North Alberta Land Registration District)*, WWR 6 (1980): 361; *Real Property Reports* 15 (1980): 232; DLR, 3rd ser., 115, 360 (Alta.Q.B.).
51 Ibid., at 363.
52 R.S.A. 1970, c. 238.
53 R.S.A. 1970, c. 297.
54 R.S.A. 1970, c. 198.
55 Andrew Lipscombe and Albert Bergh, eds. *The Writings of Thomas Jefferson* (Washington: The Thomas Jefferson Memorial Association, vol. XII, 1903), in *Letter to the Governor of Virginia.*
56 For a discussion of the effect of the grid on landscapes, see Arlene Kwasniak, "A Framework for How Laws and Legal Policies Affect Landscapes," *Landscape Journal* 15, no. 6 (1996): 154.
57 Martin, *"Dominion Lands" Policy*, 17.
58 See Robert McKercher and Bertram Wolfe, *Understanding Western Canada's Dominion Land Survey System* (Saskatoon: University of Saskatchewan, 1986), for a succinct overview of the DLS.
59 Dominion Lands Act, 60-61 Victoria, c. 29.
60 See the website, *http://www.alsa.ab.ca/system.htm* (accessed 22 February 2007).
61 Land Titles Act, R.S.A. 2000, c.4-1, s.62 states: "Every certificate of title granted under this Act (except in case of fraud in which the owner has participated or colluded), so long as it remains in force and uncancelled under this Act, is conclusive proof in all courts as against Her Majesty and all persons whomsoever that the person named in the certificate is entitled to the land included in the certificate for the estate or interest specified in the certificate, subject to the exceptions and reservations mentioned in section 61, except so far as regards any portion of land by wrong description of boundaries or parcels included in the certificate of title and except as against any person claiming under a prior certificate of title granted under this Act or granted under any law heretofore in force relating to titles to real property in respect of the same land." The current section is s. 66.
62 In 1985 the Land Titles Act was amended to set out a process for amendments. See S.A. 1985, c. 48, s. 93, adding s. 92.1 to the Land Titles Act, R.S.A. 1980, c. L-5.
63 SCR (1973): 694.
64 The Supreme Court of Canada adopted the reasoning of the dissent in the Manitoba Court of Appeal decision in *Manitoba Judgements*, no. 15.
65 Information from the website of the Village of Spring Lake is available at *http://www.springlake-ab.com/main.html* (accessed 22 February 2007).

66 *Nastajus v. North Alberta* (Land Registration District), ALR 64, 2nd ser.: 300; *Alberta Reports* 92: 363, (Alta. C.A.); reversing *Nastajus v. North Alberta* (Land Registration District) (1987), ALR 49: 2nd ser., 206, (sub nom. *Nastajus v. Edmonton Beach (Summer Village)*); *Alberta Reports* 76 (1987): 87, (Alta. Q.B.).
67 Ibid., Q.B., at s. 22.
68 Ibid., at s. 24.
69 *Nastajus v. North Alberta* (Land Registration District). C.A., at s. 7.
70 *Robertson v. Wallace*, ABQB (2000): 1020; *Alberta Reports* 276 (2001): 201; *WWR* 9 (2000): 141; 81 *ALR*, 3rd ser., 84; 33 *Real Property Reports*, 3rd ser., 264, (Alta. Q.B.).
71 Bow River Basin Council, A Report on the State of the Bow River Basin (Calgary: B.R.B.C., 2005), chap. 8 at 135.
72 *Robertson v. Wallace*, Alta. Q.B., s. 1.
73 Land Titles Act, R.S.A. 2000, c. L-4, s. 89(3)(3) requires the consent of any registered owners of parcels that may be adversely affected by an amendment to title to change natural boundaries.
74 *Robertson v. Wallace*, C.A., s. 18.
75 Ibid., s. 18.
76 Ibid., ss. 124–26.
77 *Red Deer (City) v. Pitt, Alberta Judgments* (2000), No. 1198; *Land Compensation Reports* 71: 166; *Western Appeal Cases* 234: 160; *Alberta Reports* 271 (2001): 160; 2000 Carswell Alta 1107; ABCA (2000): 281 (Alta. C.A.) affirming *Alberta Judgments* (1998), no. 965; *Alberta Reports* 230: 396; 65 *Land Compensation Reports* 1; 1998 Carswell Alta 804 (Alta. Q.B.).
78 Ibid., at s. 2.
79 Ibid., ss. 2 and 3.
80 Ibid., C.A. s. 12.
81 *Andriet v. Strathcona (County)* No. 20, (2005), 2005 Carswell Alta 1748, 2005 ABQB 848 (Alta. Q.B.)
82 *Atlas of Alberta Lakes* (Edmonton: University of Alberta, 1990) entry for "Cooking Lake."
83 Ibid. The text refers to Touchings, D., *Heritage Resource Inventory of the Cooking Lake Study* (Edmonton: Alberta Environment, 1976), app.10, vol. V, "Economic base and heritage resources."
84 *Atlas of Alberta Lakes*, entry for "Cooking Lake."
85 *Andriet v. Strathcona (County)* No. 20, at s. 12.
86 Ibid., at s. 5.
87 E.g., see s. 16.
88 Ibid., at s. 39.
89 The Court relied on a statement from an earlier case (*Rockland Holdings v. 309458 Alberta Ltd., Alberta Judgments* (1987): 1349 (ABQB) at para. 4), where that Court stated: "In my opinion, the present whereabouts of the river has no bearing upon the defendant's south boundary or the plaintiff's north boundary. To preserve the indefeasible titles of the Torrens system the north boundary of the plaintiff's property and the south boundary of the defendant's property is set by a readily available filed plan." Rockland Holdings was not an accretion case. It concerned a situation where two parcels of land were divided by a river. The issue was whether the movement

of the river changed the size and boundaries of each parcel. The Court concluded that it did not and that the filed plan determined the size and boundaries. See *Johnson*, Ibid, at s. 20.

90 *Makowecki v. Yachimyc*, ALR 10 (1917): 366; WWR 1 (1917): 1279; DLR 34 (1917): 130 (A.S.C., App. Div.).

91 Spencer Environmental Management Services Ltd., *Assessment of Environmental Sensitivity and Sustainability in Support of the Strathcona County MDP Review Final Report, Prepared for: Strathcona County* (Edmonton: Spencer Environmental Services Ltd., 2005), 2–1.

92 A. Kwasniak, *Reconciling Ecosystem and Political Borders: A Legal Map* (Edmonton: Environmental Law Centre, 1997), 2–3.

93 At s. 52, ibid., the Court notes that a number of states, including Massachusetts and New Jersey, had adopted the "common law view," under which the lower owner could block water flowing onto the land in such circumstances.

94 Ibid., at ss. 12 and 13

95 *Ostrom v. Sills*, Appeal Reports 24 (1897): 526 (Ont.), affirmed SCR 98 (1898): 485.

96 Ibid., at 589.

97 *Makowecki v. Yachimyc*, at s. 67.

98 *Farnell v. Parks*, DLR 38 (1917): 17.

99 Today we recognize their many valuable functions and we would classify such water-bodies under a variety of titles depending on function. See *Wetland Management in the Settled Area of Alberta: An Interim Policy* (Edmonton: Alberta Water Resources Commission, 1993), 1–5. This Policy is currently under review and a new Wetland Policy should be developed by mid-2007. The author is on the Wetland Policy development committee.

100 *Farnell v. Parks*, at s.16.

101 Ibid., at s. 17. The Court expanded this by adding that if the lower owner relied on the obstruction and the upper owner acquiesced, then this might impact any right to remove the obstruction.

102 Ibid., s. 5.

103 Ibid., at s. 5. The dissent refers to Alfred Lord Tennyson's *In Memoriam*, stanza XXXV, lines 10–12.

104 *Molden v. Kirkeby*, WWR 3 (1918): 1014.

105 North-West Irrigation Act, S.C. 1894, c. 30, section 4.

106 *The Water Act* (R.S.A. 2000, c. W-35, s. 36 and para. 1(1)(b)(A)) make it an offence to carry out an activity without an approval. Drainage is an activity.

107 See *Lamont No. 30 (County) v. Smith*, Alberta Judgments No. 1128 (1997). In the case the Respondent, Mr Smith, asserted that the municipality, Lamont No. 30, had no right to complain when he went on municipal land to remove an adventitious structure that blocked the natural flow onto his land. He claimed this on the basis of *Farnell v. Parks* (discussed earlier in this essay). The Court responded that even if *Farnell* does stand for that proposition at common law, the case has "been over-ruled in Alberta by the passage of the Water Resources Act. That Act states that no person shall divert any water, including surface water, except under the authority of the Act, or of a licence or permit under the Act. It is clear from the material filed on this hearing that Mr Smith does not have any licence or permit under the Act, and that

his claimed right to divert water is, in fact, subject to the provisions of this Act." *Lamont No. 30 (County) v. Smith*, at s. 14.
108 Percy, *Wetlands and the Law in the Prairie Provinces*, 36.
109 Ibid.
110 See Sara Wilson et al., "The Alberta GPI Accounts: Wetlands and Peatlands" (Pembina Institute: Drayton Valley, 2001), Report #23, 2.
111 See discussion *circa* n. 11.
112 Western U.S. state courts shunned or strictly limited common law riparian rights and replaced them with a prior appropriation system of water rights more suitable to local conditions than riparian rights. According to the prior appropriation model, the earliest appropriator who put water to a beneficial use had priority for that use over later appropriators. See Joseph L. Sax et al., *Legal Controls of Water Resources,* 3rd ed. (West Group, American Casebook Series: St. Paul, 2000), 98. The prior allocation system of rights set forth in the North-West Irrigation Act is based partly on this U.S. common law.
113 See discussion *circa* n. 14.
114 See discussion *circa* n. 32.
115 The Land Titles Act, S.A. 1906, c. 24.
116 See discussion *circa* n. 70.
117 See discussion *circa* n. 95.
118 See discussion *circa* n. 102.
119 See discussion *circa* n. 111.

SEVEN

Energy Law
The Court and the Prosperity Bonus

ALASTAIR R. LUCAS

THE ALBERTA SUPREME COURT had nothing to do with the Alberta government's 2005 "Prosperity Bonus—$400 paid to each and every resident of the province." Nevertheless, the Court's decisions certainly played a role in the development of Alberta's energy sector, whose oil and natural gas royalties funded the government's largesse. The Court had a hand in shaping the legal landscape in which the energy sector flourished. Working within an environment charged by a deeply rooted suspicion concerning any federal regulatory presence in Alberta's economy, the Court sought to encourage a co-operative environment for private developers and the provincial government, while identifying oil reserves (and in time natural gas) as resources to be conserved, developed, and sustained for Albertans. This did not mean the Court invariably sided with perspectives that industry, government, and the public might have considered advantageous to the province; rather, the Court attempted to establish an environment in which the contours were knowable and in tune with broader jurisprudence. Not surprisingly, this approach invariably confronted the mercurial distinctions between the law and what interested participants considered just.

Broadly stated, the legal history of oil and gas in Alberta hangs on key events in several eras. In the first era, early history was inextricably linked to the federal government's retention of mineral rights from the time Alberta and Saskatchewan were granted provincial status, in 1905. Federal retention of these rights meant that when oil reserves were sought in Alberta prior to 1930, it was at the behest of the Canadian federal and British governments, acting in what historian David Breen has described as an "ad hoc and essentially reactive manner." Indeed, Breen suggests it was the ad hoc nature of this approach that prompted Alberta to seek control over the natural resources beneath its soil.[1]

The second era followed in the wake of the 1930 Natural Resources Transfer Agreement. From this point forward, Alberta's courts assumed a greater role in orchestrating the province's energy resources.[2] A key objective was to establish the provincial government's jurisdictional ability to regulate oil and gas development in the province. A crucial battle on this front would be waged in the *Spooner Oils* case of 1932. The courts rejected Alberta's attempts to regulate oil and gas production on lands granted by the federal government prior to the 1930 Natural Resources Transfer Agreement, but the courts confirmed Alberta's regulatory powers over oil and gas produced on Alberta government leases.

The onset of the third era, comprising the development of Alberta's modern constitutional oil and gas industry, was marked by the Leduc discoveries of 1947 and the novel questions that surfaced in the aftermath. The *Huggard Assets* case of 1949 centred on the province's ability to set royalties for contemporary and future production. The case served as a cornerstone for Alberta's energy-based prosperity; it is worth noting, though, that the provincial Supreme Court was sharply divided on the question. Close on the heels of *Huggard Assets* was *Borys v. Canadian Pacific Railway*, which required that the crucial question of split ownership of mineral rights be addressed. Both *Huggard Assets* and *Borys* were eventually settled by the Judicial Committee of the Privy Council. The unveiling of the National Energy Program, and the "perfect storm" it produced, heralded Canada's emergence as an Alberta-centred energy superpower and instigated the fourth era of Alberta's energy history, which saw the Court focus on the oil and gas control issue that had become the core of the province's identity.[3]

As much as these four eras outline a framework within which to understand the Supreme Court of Alberta's role in shaping the province's oil and gas history, it is equally true that these divisions were intersected by a variety of disputes. Some have been private—occurring between oil and gas companies and others involved in the energy industry—and some have been public—between the Alberta government and its agencies, on the one hand, and energy industry participants on the other, and sometimes between federal and provincial governments.

This chapter assesses the Court's role in these four eras in relation to three issues that have been central in shaping the present-day Alberta-centred Canadian energy sector. These are (1) public ownership and management of privately developed provincial energy resources, (2) development of the expertise and credibility of provincial energy regulators with corresponding deference by the Court, and (3) effective and efficient private development of energy resources. While not always successful in creating a co-operative environment, the Court has held to the proposition that the province as a whole would benefit from a locally controlled and regulated industry.

Section One
PUBLIC OWNERSHIP AND MANAGEMENT
—THE SPOONER OILS CASE

The decision to create the new prairie provinces of Alberta and Saskatchewan in 1905 was the product of a lengthy and often acrimonious debate.[4] One key issue was that of public lands and natural resources. While territorial leaders were adamant that the new provinces escape the Manitoban dilemma of being denied control over these resources, Wilfrid Laurier's federal government, and especially Clifford Sifton, the prominent and influential Interior Minister, was resolute that Ottawa retain control. Ultimately the federal government prevailed, and both Alberta and Saskatchewan were ushered into existence without control over mineral rights. Consequently, when early efforts to develop the province's oil and natural gas reserves were initiated in the quarter century after 1905, the federal government occupied centre stage while Alberta fumed. When the rights finally devolved to the province under the 1930 Natural Resources Transfer Agreement, the Alberta government essentially continued the federally established system of oil, gas, and coal leases to private developers.[5] Yet despite this continuity, the Supreme Court was soon presented with the question of whether Alberta conservation regulation of oil and gas operators was, in fact, constitutional.[6] This was to be the first of a series of constitutional conflicts that have arisen in relation to provincial ownership and management of energy resources.

Alberta's oil and gas rights tenure system has developed in stages.[7] Small area prospecting permits were issued in the early 1930s. Larger area petroleum and natural gas reservations (up to 40,000 hectare) were introduced in the 1930s. In 1962, a two-stage system of reservations potentially convertible to leases was implemented to promote shallow gas development in southeastern Alberta. The current system of shorter-term natural gas licences and five-year oil and gas leases dates from 1976. Crucial for the oil and gas industry was security of title under the Crown mineral dispositions so that the necessary exploration and development financing could be obtained. The Alberta Courts' decisions in *Spooner Oils v. Turner Valley Gas Conservation Board* provided that assurance early in the development of Alberta's Crown oil and gas leases and like contracts.[8] Crown leases were characterized as more than mere statutory permission to explore for, produce, and market hydrocarbons. In fact, they were contractual instruments by which the Crown, as owner, granted property rights to leasees. Crown leases continue to be drafted using contractual language such as "grant" and "consideration" to confirm their contractual character. The trial judge in the *Spooner Oils* case reasoned that the leases created a relationship akin to that of landlord and tenant, and the Alberta Court of Appeal did not disagree, noting that the lessee, under the terms of the lease, has the right during the currency of the term to pursue "mining and operating for petroleum and natural gas...."[9]

Prior to 1930, there was a federal system for granting public land and resource rights and for regulating oil and gas production. When the resources transfer occurred in 1930, prior federal land grants remained valid. Early federal grants included oil and gas rights, and this was the case in the Turner Valley Field. There was no industry regulation until 1928, when the federal government promulgated regulations that required producers to minimize "waste" of natural gas. These regulations did not apply to previously acquired rights, however, including those of Spooner Oils. In these circumstances, Alberta's Turner Valley Gas Conservation Board was adamant about the necessity to restrict loss of the natural gas resource.

Spooner Oils disputed the Alberta government's legal authority to limit production of naphtha (a liquid petroleum substance) from its Turner Valley wells, which would reduce waste of concurrently produced natural gas. The oil company had obtained the land (including mineral rights) on which the wells were situated from the federal government prior to 1930, when public lands and their natural resources were transferred to Alberta.

David Breen has chronicled the events that led up to the *Spooner Oils* case.[10] Ultimately, as Breen shows, the result was the failure of Alberta's first proration program that aimed to curb wasteful flaring of Turner Valley natural gas and maximize the field's petroleum production. But in the longer term, confirmation by the Court, in this case, of Alberta's constitutional authority to regulate natural gas production proved crucial for provincial regulation of the industry. The Supreme Court of Canada reversed the Alberta Courts, concluding that the Turner Valley Gas Conservation Board's prorating order, issued under the Alberta Turner Valley Natural Gas Conservation Act,[11] was invalid because it "affect[ed] or alter[ed]" the terms of the Spooner lease,[12] contrary to Article 2 of the Natural Resources Transfer Agreement, as confirmed by the British North American Act, 1930.[13] However, the Supreme Court of Canada judges did not address the Alberta Appellate Division's conclusion that the Act as a whole was within the constitutional authority of the Alberta legislature. This constitutional jurisdiction to regulate development and management of energy resources, which was to prove critical for Alberta's later development, was confirmed in subsequent Alberta Supreme Court and Supreme Court of Canada decisions.

The result of the *Spooner Oils* case was a serious setback for the conservation objectives embodied in the Turner Valley Gas Conservation Act. Conservation regulations could not be applied to oil and gas rights acquired under the 1910 and 1911 federal regulations. This constituted a major portion of the Turner Valley oilfield.[14] But enactment of the Turner Valley Gas Conservation Act by the government of Premier J.E. Brownlee proved not to be in vain. William Aberhart's Social Credit regime adopted a "hands off" policy that responded in particular to the concerns of small, independent companies that held a significant number of the Turner Valley producing properties.[15] However, by 1938, with wellhead oil prices dropping, the government recognized the need to maximize Turner Valley oil reserves over the longer term while pursuing Eastern markets.[16] This ultimately led to the Oil and Gas Conservation Act of 1938, which provided oil and gas conservation authority broadly similar to that defined under the Turner Valley Act and vested powers in a new Petroleum and Natural Gas Conservation Board.[17]

The board made orders establishing proration schedules that set overall field quotas and production allowables for individual oil and gas wells. Legal challenge by affected companies was swift. Several companies, including Mercury Oils Ltd., applied to the Alberta Supreme Court Trial Division to quash the board's orders on decision-making jurisdiction and constitutional grounds. Mr Justice William Ives dismissed the Mercury Oils application.[18] He accepted argument by counsel for the board that the highly technical issues before the Court required a complete factual basis that was not available in an application for a writ of *certiorari* to quash the decision. Such an application would, under the Rules of Court, be based only on a paper record of affidavit evidence and legal argument by counsel. Issues so important to the future of the Alberta oil and gas industry could not be decided in such a narrow legalistic manner.

The result was oilfield "rebellion," particularly by gas producers who felt that crude oil producers had received favourable treatment under the orders. A significant number of producers simply refused to comply.[19] This led to the appointment of a royal commission, stormy commission proceedings, government-industry agreement, and amendment of the Oil and Gas Conservation Act, 1938.[20] The Amending Act included provisions for producer compensation, but there was also a section that purported to prevent judicial challenge of decisions or orders of the board.[21] This type of provision, later characterized as a *privative clause* in legal terms, would prove important but not decisive in protecting board decisions from judicial review.[22]

The *Spooner Oils* case was fundamental in confirming the regulatory powers of the board—now known as the Alberta Energy and Utilities Board—to conserve and manage oil and gas resources.[23] Since this initial skirmish in 1930, the scope and content of the board's statutory powers, as well as its fairness in exercising those powers in the public interest, have been tested in the Alberta Supreme Court on numerous occasions.[24] Through these decisions, the Court has, in broad terms, upheld the conservation scheme and, more importantly, has explicitly recognized and deferred to the experience and expertise of the board in its policy role and in its application of statutory requirements to oil and gas operators in the province. Further, while the nature and structure of the oil and gas industry has promoted risk-sharing through co-operative exploration, development, and transportation initiatives, it has also produced its share of disputes.[25] The Supreme Court's resolution of these disputes, using pragmatic approaches with due regard for the practices and expectations of the industry, has facilitated industry co-operation while ensuring relative security of oil and gas property rights.

Section Two

THE LEDUC FALLOUT
— HUGGARD ASSETS AND BORYS

Perhaps the most important judicial decisions in the evolution of Alberta's system of the private development of public energy resources were initiated in 1949, when Huggard Assets Ltd. sought a declaration before Mr Justice Boyd McBride in the Alberta Supreme Court Trial Division. Huggard Assets owned oil and gas rights in 1,320.5 acres, located in the McMurray District of Northern Alberta.[26] It is not extravagant to suggest that this case laid the groundwork for the petroleum royalty riches that fuel the economic boom within which the Court celebrates its centenary. The problem concerned the obligation to pay royalties to the Provincial Crown on hydrocarbons produced from the property. Though no production had yet occurred, the province had made it clear that under the terms of the original patent for the land, issued by federal order-in-council in 1913, and, under the National Resources Transfer Agreement devolved to Alberta, it was entitled to production royalty. Moreover, said the government, it was entitled to fix a royalty if and when there was production from the property. For Huggard Assets, its mineral rights asset was considerably more valuable without a royalty obligation—so much so that it invested in the legal action and claimed a declaration that no royalty was payable.

Justice McBride characterized the matter at issue as a property rights dispute that turned on the language of the original Crown grant. It was thus a matter of contract interpretation. The key was the meaning of the "reddendum," or payment clause, which provided for "...such royalty upon the said petroleum and natural gas, if any, *from time to time prescribed by regulations of our Governor in Council...*"[27] (emphasis added). The issue was whether these words were intended to authorize the Crown to prescribe royalties in the future. At the time of the hearing, no royalties had yet been prescribed. Relying on the 1941 *Majestic Mines* case, in which an Alberta government royalty claim was denied, McBride applied what he considered to be "well-established law."[28] The principle was that if a grantor of land intends to reserve any rights over the land granted, this must be done expressly by clear and unambiguous language. Here the judge found the language neither clear nor unambiguous. He said he could "...see nothing in the words 'from time to time'...when added either to the royalty clause in *Majestic Mines,* or to the patent before him that would 'add a prospective outlook.'"[29] Thus, the petroleum industry prevailed in the initial Crown royalty skirmish.

On appeal to the Appellate Division, the battle intensified. Two of the four sitting judges held in favour of the respondent Huggard Assets Ltd. The Court being equally divided, the appeal was therefore dismissed. Mr Justice George O'Connor and Mr Justice William A. MacDonald, who ruled for Huggard Assets, directed their attention to the federal Petroleum Regulations and the individualized orders-in-council that approved the grant to one Bennetto and a related company, Huggard Assets' predecessor in title.[30] The recital to the 31 May 1911 order-in-council stated:

> Under the circumstances it is not felt that the Department of the Interior would be justified in continuing the reservation of the tract originally set aside in Mr Bennetto's favour, but in view of the large expenditure which has been incurred in boring for oil by Mr Bennetto and the company, the Minister recommends the reservation of another area of petroleum and natural gas rights and if oil or natural gas be discovered in paying quantities that the Minister be authorized to sell the lands to the company.

This was reiterated in the Special Order-in-Council of 21 March 1913, which authorized the grant of petroleum and natural gas rights. The judges noted the "large sums of money expended" ($75,000) by Bennetto and the company in drilling an unsuccessful exploratory well.[31] Both judges concluded that in these circumstances there was an outright sale of petroleum and natural gas rights under the Special Order-in-Council, and not a lease with reserved royalty. The 1906 Dominion Petroleum Regulations provided for a sale subject to royalty (though no royalty had been prescribed) if oil in paying quantities were discovered, at a price of $1 per acre for the first 640 acres.[32] Here, there was no oil discovery, and the price was $3 per acre for the entire 1,920 acre property.

As to the language of the grant, the two judges interpreted the words "if any" to modify "royalty" and not "petroleum and natural gas."[33] The system was to encourage exploration and sell the rights to the explorer if a discovery were made, the Crown retaining a royalty. Thus, because no petroleum and natural gas was found by Huggard Assets, there was no royalty. Both judges adopted this reasoning from the judgment of Justice Clarke in the *Majestic Mines* case.[34]

Mr Justice Harold Parlee, with whom Mr Justice Frank Ford concurred, delivered a dissenting opinion.[35] Though he too noted "the large expenditure made...in active boring operations...," he concluded that the language of the Crown patent was critical in determining whether a royalty was reserved.[36] In his opinion, the royalty provision "looks to the future and has a prospective outlook."[37] The patent made the grant subject to the regulations in force in 1909, which included provision for a royalty "at such rate as may from time to time be specified."[38] His approach was to scrutinize the patent within its legislative framework to decide whether or not the grant gave the Governor in Council authority to impose a royalty in the future. The remainder of Justice Parlee's analysis removed a large part of the basis for the authority of the *Majestic Mines* case, relied upon by his majority colleagues. He noted that *Majestic Mines* concerned a patent that did not contain the words "from time to time prescribed" after the words "if any," that it was not made subject to the petroleum and natural gas regulations in force in 1909, and that it reserved a royalty only on coal.[39] It was not surprising that Mr Justice Albert Hudson, in *Majestic Mines*, spoke of a requirement for the "clearest and most definite authority from a competent legislative body" to impose a royalty on petroleum and natural gas.[40] When the *Huggard Assets* case reached the Supreme Court of Canada, Mr Justice Patrick Kerwin, who dissented, was in agreement with Justice Parlee on this point. So was the Judicial Committee of the Privy Council, which allowed the ultimate appeal by Huggard Assets.

The Supreme Court of Canada was unanimously of the opinion that the Alberta Courts were in error.[41] It concluded that there was statutory authority for the patent and that the grant must be interpreted to authorize the Crown in Right of Alberta to impose royalties on petroleum and natural gas by regulation after the date of the grant. But the Supreme Court of Canada was not done. It proceeded, by a 4–3 majority, to dismiss the appeal for a reason not raised before it or before any of the Alberta courts. The majority analyzed the royalty to determine its legal character—that is, how it should be characterized in terms of the historical common law categories of real property interests. They noted that a royalty is akin to a rent derived from the historic knight service tenure.[42] But by the English Statute of 1660, c. 24, which applied to Rupert's Land, and by the North-West Territories Act of 1875, which applied to Alberta, this was converted to "free and common socage" tenure, which required that the "service" be certain.[43] Because the variable royalty was not certain, it was void, and the legislature had not established a new statutory tenure.[44] It took the Judicial Committee of the Privy Council, on further appeal, to bring the issue back to the legislation and the grant. The board's opinion, expressed in the speech of Lord Asquith, doubted that the Act of 1660, which addressed complex and oppressive elements of feudal military tenure, was intended to apply beyond England and Wales "to a vast tract of country thousands of miles away which was only inhabited at the time by a few Indians and half-castes."[45] They also discussed the "learned disagreement" about the nature of the certainty required for "free and common socage" tenure.[46]

The board did not decide the historical tenure issue, but proceeded on the assumption that "free and common socage" tenure was inconsistent with the 1913 grant. They assessed the legislative context to determine whether the Dominion Parliament had provided for the grant. In particular, the judges carefully analyzed the Dominion Lands Act to decide whether it authorized the two orders-in-council that approved the grant. Their conclusion was that it did.[47] The Governor in Council could sell or lease mineral lands. Further, the Governor in Council could make orders to deal with special cases not specifically provided for by the Act. This included the unusual circumstances in which Bennetto and his company made a large exploration expenditure but were forced by squatters from the original land authorized for grant. In making these orders, there was nothing to prevent the Governor in Council from stipulating that the grant be made according to the terms of superseded regulations that had contemplated a variable royalty.[48]

Finally, the Judicial Committee confirmed the conclusion reached by Justices O'Connor and Parlee in the Alberta Appellate Division, that the mineral rights had been transferred to Alberta under the Natural Resources Transfer Agreement and its implementing statutes. In administering these resources, the Privy Council concluded that Alberta had authority to legislate for their disposition, including reserving a variable royalty. Confirmation of this power by the Government of Alberta to levy a variable royalty was to prove critical for Alberta's share of oil and gas revenues. Royalties could be tied to production volumes and could be adjusted by regulation to ensure, in periods of rapidly rising market prices, that an equitable share of excess "rent" was captured for the public benefit. This is precisely the royalty regime that has emerged and that has generated the surplus revenue from which the 2005 "Prosperity Bonus" was paid to residents of the province. The *Huggard Assets* case also presents the intriguing coincidence that the mineral rights in question were located on the edge of the McMurray Settlement, what is now the heart of the Athabasca Oil Sands, the petroleum resources that are the subject of unprecedented development and that seem likely to become, in time, the main source of provincial natural resource royalties.

A year after *Huggard Assets* began working its way through the courts on the way to the Judicial Committee of the Privy Council (JCPC), a second dispute, rooted in the heart of the Leduc discoveries, was launched. Among the decisions rendered by the Alberta Supreme Court on private energy sector disputes, none is more significant than *Borys v. Canadian Pacific Railway*.[49] The case involved respective owners of oil and natural gas rights in the same parcel of land, located in the Leduc area, when the Alberta oil industry was in the earliest stage of its development. The problem was that oil and natural gas are associated hydrocarbon substances. If the ownership is separate—and if the oil owner cannot avoid producing incidentally natural gas with its oil but can be enjoined by the Court from doing so—the fledgling oil industry would be in grave difficulty.

Though the land in question had been in the family since Michael Bory's father, Simon, purchased it from the Canadian Pacific Railway in 1906, it was only after Imperial Oil Ltd.'s nearby 1947 oil discovery that Michael Borys realized he might be the owner of valuable mineral rights. In 1918, when Simon Borys had paid out and performed all conditions under his installment purchase contract, the CPR executed a transfer of the land to him "...reserving all coal, petroleum and valuable stone on or under the land."[50] There was no specific reservation of a right to work—that is, to drill for and produce the substances. The land with its interest acquired from the CPR passed to Michael Borys. Meanwhile, the CPR had granted a petroleum lease to Imperial Oil Ltd., and the company was anxious to exploit the petroleum reservoir that previous drilling strongly suggested extended under Borys' land. It began to drill a well on the Borys land. The Imperial lease conveyed the "petroleum" rights that the CPR had reserved in the original Borys conveyance. In these circumstances, Michael Borys applied to the Alberta Supreme Court Trial Division for an interim injunction to stop the drilling. The injunction was granted. At the same time, Borys commenced an action claiming a declaration that he was the owner of natural gas under the land, and an injunction restraining Imperial Oil from using, removing, or interfering with that natural gas.

The action was heard by Chief Justice William Howson.[51] A great deal of scientific and technical evidence was presented by witnesses for both sides.[52] Some concerned geology and reservoir mechanics, which described what was known at the time about the behaviour and function of gas in petroleum production; other evidence dealt with the meaning of the word *petroleum* as it was understood in the oil and gas industry and by land owners at the time of the land transfer by the CPR to Simon Borys. The reason such evidence was advanced was that case law had already established that the "vernacular" meaning at the time of transaction was the appropriate standard to apply.[53] There was evidence that Simon Borys neither read nor wrote English, and Justice Howson noted that there was no word in the Ukrainian language for *petroleum,* the nearest word being *Olivha—oil,* in English—and concluded that it was "manifest" that Borys understood petroleum in the sense of oil.[54] Similarly, the evidence suggested that in the oil and gas industry, natural gas was commonly understood to be a different product than petroleum. Thus, Chief Justice Howson found that natural gas and petroleum were separate substances "whether dry, or wet or held in solution with mineral oil..."—the former was held by Borys, and the latter by Imperial Oil Ltd.[55] He went on to conclude that Borys was entitled to a permanent injunction against Imperial Oil Ltd.

Writing for the Court of Appeal in a 4-1 decision, Mr Justice Parlee agreed with the trial judge that petroleum and natural gas are two different substances.[56] But his conclusion on the interpretation to be given to *petroleum* in the reservation differed. Instead of natural gas including all gas in its different states and phases, the Court of Appeal majority was of the opinion that Imperial Oil Ltd.'s petroleum included gas in solution as it exists under pressure in the reservoir, even though this may be in gaseous form when produced at the surface. Other free gas belonged to Borys. But a problem remained: it is necessary in petroleum production to use and incidentally produce some of the free gas in the reservoir gas cap overlying the petroleum-bearing strata. The Court considered the analogy of mineral owners' rights to use the surface for mining, subject to maintaining surface support, in carrying out mining operations. Mineral owners are also entitled to use and remove ground water that they encounter in mining. The result, according to the Court, is that the owner of the petroleum is entitled to produce the oil even if there is interference with and incidental production of gas, provided reasonable and modern production practices are used.⁵⁷ The appeal by the CPR and Imperial Oil Ltd. was thus allowed.

In what has become (at least for oil and gas lawyers) a famous judgment, the Judicial Committee of the Privy Council dismissed a further appeal by Michael Borys. The board accepted the findings of the Alberta Courts that—though each is composed of the same elements—petroleum and natural gas are separate substances. It agreed with the Court of Appeal's conclusion that what is included in the respective substances should be determined at reservoir pressure rather than at the surface when produced.⁵⁸ The Judicial Committee also agreed with the Appellate Division that the oil could be produced even though this interfered with and incidentally produced some of the Borys gas.⁵⁹ Lord Porter quoted with approval from the judgment of Justice Parlee in the Court of Appeal; however, in summarizing the conclusions of Justice Hewson at trial and the majority of the Court of Appeal, he said "...the Court of Appeal adopted a compromise [on the question of whether petroleum includes gas in solution], *viz., the condition of the substance as it emerges from time to time from the reservoir.*"⁶⁰ This statement proved contentious when split-title ownership issues came before the Alberta courts in subsequent cases.

The petroleum and natural gas ownership issues many thought had been decided in *Borys* were back before the Alberta courts in the 1990s, notably in *Anderson v. Amoco Canada Oil and Gas.*⁶¹ The problem was that though the *Borys* case decided that petroleum and gas ownership was based on the phase of the particular hydrocarbon in the ground, neither the Alberta courts nor the Privy Council decided *when* the determination of whether a hydrocarbon substance was petroleum or gas should be made. This is important because production decreases pressure in a reservoir, with the consequence that some liquid hydrocarbons "evolve" into a gas phase and become indistinguishable from hydrocarbons originally in a gas phase.

In *Prism Petroleum Ltd. v. Omega Hydrocarbons Ltd.*, the issue was ownership under a unit agreement of solution gas produced from land near Provost, Alberta.⁶² At trial, Mr Justice William G.N. Egbert interpreted the unit agreement, particularly the definition of *oil*, and concluded that the solution gas belonged not to Omega, owner of the oil, but to Prism, owner of the natural gas—the "unitized substances" defined in the Gas Unit Agreement.⁶³ However, the Court of Appeal ruled that the trial judge had erred by interpreting the definition of *oil* as relating to surface rather than reservoir conditions.⁶⁴ Thus the decision was mainly based on interpretation of the particular agreement. But the Court of Appeal also denied emphatically that the Privy Council in the *Borys* case had focused on the surface rather than the underground reservoir as being the point of recovery of the oil.[65]

Anderson v. Amoco Canada Oil and Gas was a series of test cases that dealt with split mineral titles, not interpretation of development agreements, as in *Prism v. Omega*. These test cases are the modern extension of the *Borys* case, presenting the question of ownership of solution gas—not initially, prior to penetration of a reservoir, as in *Borys*—but later in the course of hydrocarbon production from the reservoir. Madam Justice Adelle Fruman's trial judgment was lengthy and comprehensive, even reviewing relevant American case authorities. She wrestled with an argument by the plaintiff landowners based on the statement by Lord Porter in the *Borys* case quoted above. The idea was that the *Borys* decision spoke to conditions in the reservoir at the time the hydrocarbon substances enter the bottom of the well bore. Solution gas emerging at that point, they said, belongs to the natural gas owner.

However, Justice Fruman firmly rejected this argument, noting that the quoted statement from *Borys* was an inaccurate description of Justice Parlee's Court of Appeal majority judgment.[66] The statement was also inconsistent with the Privy Council's references to initial reservoir conditions. She also rejected textual arguments based on the specific verb tenses used by Mr Justice Parlee in the Alberta Court of Appeal and by Lord Porter in the Privy Council. Justice Fruman concluded thus:

> *Borys,* as confirmed by *Prism,* stands for three propositions: (1) solution gas belongs to the petroleum owner; (2) free gas or primary gas cap gas belongs to the non-petroleum owner; and (3) gas that emerges from solution in the reservoir, at the bottom of the well or, at the surface, or anywhere in-between, belongs to the petroleum owner...The meaning of *Borys* is clear and uncontroversial. Fifteen *obiter* and inaccurate words by Lord Porter do not make it less so.

In a unanimous judgment, the Alberta Court of Appeal agreed with Justice Fruman's analysis of the plaintiff's argument based on the extract from Lord Porter's judgment. "Borys," the Court said, "is a complete answer to the appellant [landowner's] position."[67] The *Borys* decision, it emphasized, dealt with interpretation of the reservation of petroleum at the time of the grant when the hydrocarbons were at initial reservoir conditions. In its decision on a further appeal, the Supreme Court of Canada had little to add to the analysis of the Alberta Courts. Mr Justice John C. Major, writing the judgment of the Court, stated that the Alberta Courts were correct to find that *Borys* decided that the mineral reservation "included all hydrocarbons which were in liquid phase in the ground at the time of transaction."[68] It is this rule that must be applied in the *Anderson v. Amoco* test cases. This may make it difficult for natural gas and petroleum owners to quantify their respective interests at any particular point during production from a reservoir. But as Justice Major noted, Justice Fruman answered this concern about uncertainty by pointing out that the industry is accustomed to relying on reserves estimates, and these will have to suffice for determining ownership.[69] The Alberta courts, with the approval of senior courts, had given the oil and gas industry guidance on the fundamental question of hydrocarbon substance ownership in the common split-title situation. But the issue is by no means dead. Already industry strategy is being directed to the undecided question of dividing up ownership of coal and coal bed methane from the large number of split coal–natural gas mineral titles that exist in the province.[70]

Section Three
THE NATIONAL ENERGY PROGRAM AND THE MATURATION OF ALBERTA'S ENERGY SECTOR

The suggestion that the launch of the National Energy Program (NEP) in late 1980 stands as a key moment in Alberta's history and the province's identity is both accurate and understated. Indeed, in his recent examination of the NEP, historian Douglas Owram described the fallout in federal provincial relations as "the perfect storm" that ultimately catapulted the program to the status of mythology in Alberta.[71] And as mythology, one needs to be vigilant to recognize that the distinctions between credible and incredible are often blurred, especially with an event that looms so large in a community's identity and subsequent history. What was essentially a program "to maintain Canadian prices below the world market, provide direct incentives for certain types of oil exploration and production, and enhance Canadian ownership and control of oil and natural gas" became a lightning rod for Albertan dissatisfaction with the nation's economic and political environment.[72] This concern was voiced in many ways, including bumper stickers suggesting that Albertans should "Let Those Eastern Bastards Freeze in the Dark," and sabre-rattling rhetoric over the possibilities of secession. A major part of the province's response to the NEP was, however, a strategic constitutional reference to the Alberta Court of Appeal. This opportunity was presented by a federal Notice of Ways and Means Motion to amend the Excise Tax Act by levying a tax on exported natural gas.[73] The amendment was subsequently introduced as Bill C-57, 1980.[74] Under the Bill, a tax would be imposed on "the receipt of marketable pipeline gas by a distributor." A gas exporter that had not paid the tax was deemed to be the distributor and to have received the gas at the time of export.

The specific reference questions crafted by the Alberta government were twofold:

(a) If the tax on exported natural gas imposed under the said legislation is *intra vires* the Parliament of Canada, is the said natural gas that is exported from Canada for use outside Canada liable to taxation under the tax on exported natural gas having regard to the British North America Acts, 1867 to 1975, and in particular section 117, 125 or 126 of those Acts or any combination of those sections? and

(b) Is the tax on exported natural gas imposed under the said legislation, with respect to the said natural gas that is exported from Canada for use outside Canada, *ultra vires* the Parliament of Canada either in whole or in part, and, if so, in what particular or particulars and to what extent?[75]

Attached to these questions was a statement of facts describing a natural gas drilling, production, transportation, and export scenario that formed the basis for the reference. Within this scenario the province caused a well to be drilled at a specified southern Alberta location that resulted in production of natural gas in commercial quantities. Under agreements with private corporations, Alberta had the gas gathered, compressed and processed the gas, and transported it by a dedicated pipeline to a purchaser in the United States. The province maintained ownership of the gas until it was delivered to the purchaser on the Montana side of the Canada–U.S. border. Revenue from the sale was to be paid into the provincial General Revenue

Fund. The federal excise tax, as proposed, was assumed to be levied and paid on the exported gas.

While representing a plausible scenario, it was not one familiar to the Alberta oil and gas sector. For while the Alberta government managed and sold oil and gas rights and collected rents and production royalties, it was not and never had been in the business of drilling, producing, and transporting natural gas. The province had no plans to nationalize the industry or to compete with private operators through a public oil and gas company. Its scenario was strategic, designed to permit reliance on the strongest constitutional basis for provincial jurisdiction over natural resources that might be subjected to federal export taxes. The constitutional provision invoked was not one of fundamental provincial jurisdiction over property and civil rights in the province, or the management and sale of public lands.[76] Rather, the key provision was section 125 of the Constitutional Act, 1867, which established a reciprocal immunity protecting the lands and property of a government from taxation by another level of government.

Presented with this scenario, the Alberta Court of Appeal concluded that the proposed export tax was *ultra vires* the government of Canada as contrary to section 125.[77] The Court assessed and rejected federal arguments based on the clever and unusual manner in which the tax was framed and the specific language used. The argument was that it was not a tax on provincial resources or property, but rather on the export transaction, on the movement of gas, or on the consumption of gas. Thus the tax was levied on the "distributor," and the exporter (including, in the scenario, the provincial Crown) was deemed by the legislation to be a "distributor." According to the Court of Appeal, this deeming provision "created an artificial and non-existent situation, applied it to the property of a province and [the federal government] has purported to base its tax on the result."[78] The "real bite" of the tax, it concluded, was on the province in relation to its property, an act prohibited by section 125.

A further federal argument was that the province, by acting in the same manner as a private operator, "applies industry" to the gas so that the tax immunity is lost. The Court responded that the activity in question was merely primary production—production and sale of a resource.[79] It concluded grandly, invoking the "living tree" constitutional analogy, and rejected the argument that this kind of commercial activity by a government was never contemplated by the Constitution Act division of powers.[80] The Court wisely refrained from addressing an argument by the Attorney General of Alberta that the National Resources Transfer Agreement and its implementing legislation placed Alberta—as resource owner—in a position superior to that of the older provinces in relation to the property provisions of the Constitution Act, 1867.[81] On appeal, the Supreme Court of Canada minority judges characterized provincial superiority as "a far-fetched submission."[82]

A majority of the Supreme Court of Canada dismissed the federal government appeal.[83] Their reasoning was similar to that of the Court of Appeal. The Supreme Court devoted more analysis to the question of whether the proposed tax was really a regulatory device, justifiable as a matter of federal Regulation of Trade and Commerce, and explicitly concluded that under the scenario the province would not be an ordinary commercial trader outside the section 125 immunity. The dissenting minority quoted copiously from the National Energy Program document and viewed the proposed tax as a transaction tax, collected in this case by the provincial Crown, but not a tax on provincial property or resources contrary to section 125. Though narrow and based on unrealistic hypothetical facts, the Gas Tax Reference nevertheless played a role in halting the National Energy Program. The gas export tax was never implemented. Meanwhile, constitutional amendment came to dominate the national political agenda. One element of the resulting Constitutional Act, 1982, apart from its central amending formula and the Canadian Charter of Rights and Freedoms, was the Resources Amendment, adding s. 92A to the Constitution Act, 1867. Consistent with the provincial policy behind the Reference, and its result, this amendment confirmed exclusive provincial jurisdiction over exploration, development, conservation, management, and sale of non-renewable natural resources. Provinces may legislate in relation to export from the province to another part of Canada in terms of the "primary production" of non-renewable resources; however, there must be no discrimination in price or supply. *Primary production* is defined as the resource in its form upon recovery or severance without refining or processing.[84]

The Alberta Court of Appeal's role in turning back the NEP demonstrated its confidence in managing the complex and often politicized issues arising from the province's energy sector. This confidence manifested itself in a willingness to confront the issues at stake and in the Court's willingness to make way for provincial regulation in the form of the Energy and Utilities Board (EUB), successor to the original Turner Valley Natural Gas Conservation Board. But it has also made it clear that not all issues require deference to the board. In particular, questions of law—either general law questions (such as matters of contract interpretation, issues of "pure" statutory interpretation), and legal principles, or "tests," based on the exercise of broad statutory powers—may be reviewed by courts using an intrusive "correctness" standard.[85]

Under the modern law, judicial conclusions about the standard of review for each discrete issue involved in board decisions are by no means a matter of intuitive characterization. A pragmatic and functional analysis is used to determine whether the appropriate standard is correctness (most intrusive), reasonableness (somewhat deferential), or patent unreasonableness (most deferential).[86] The latter requires a reviewing court to determine whether a decision is "clearly irrational," "evidently not in accordance with reason," or "so patently unreasonable that...[it] cannot be rationally supported and demands intervention by the court upon review."[87] Reasonableness requires an assessment to determine whether a tribunal decision is sufficiently rational to stand up to a "somewhat probing analysis."[88] Correctness permits the court to go beyond the tribunal's reasons and apply its own legal principles and analysis to decide an essentially legal issue.[89]

Early judgments in actions challenging the scope and correctness of Conservation Board decisions contain implicit recognition of the board's expertise. In the *Mercury Oils* case, Mr Justice William Ives accepted that the geological and reservoir mechanics issues before the board were highly technical and should not be, in effect, recharacterized as technical legal issues.[90] Thus, the Court deferred to the technical expertise of the board. A further implication was that the economic and political issues underlying the board's prorating order were to be sorted out by the parties—the oil companies, the board, and the government.

The Alberta Court, particularly the Court of Appeal, has developed this deferential approach to both major types of EUB decisions—energy decisions concerning approvals and compliance in relation to energy facilities (including single wells and massive oil sands mines and upgraders), and utility decisions concerning public interest regulation of the rates and service of oil and gas pipelines and electricity transmission facilities.[91] Public utility regulation is a discrete area of law and regulatory policy designed to protect the public from the monopolistic behaviour of utility operators.[92] Following *Mercury Oils*, the Alberta Court continued this deferential approach to

Conservation Board decisions while recognizing that essentially legal matters, such as the constitutional jurisdiction issue raised in *Spooner Oils*, were within its own expertise and required little deference to the board. In the late 1970s, in a decision that echoed *Mercury Oils*, the Appellate Division in *Rozander v. Alberta (Energy Resources Conservation Board (No. 1)*, blocked the more direct judicial review route via *certiorari* to the Trial Division unless an applicant could demonstrate "exceptional circumstances."[93] Persons challenging board decisions had to proceed directly to the Court of Appeal via the statutory appeal route, which included a preliminary application for leave to appeal. These leave applications were then, as now, heard by a single judge of the Appellate Court.

The Supreme Court of Canada's pragmatic and functional analysis, which addresses the uncertainty and potential incoherence resulting from reliance on the concept of jurisdiction for determining relative judicial deference to board decisions, has been embraced by the Alberta Court. This approach, used to decide which standard of review applies, involves consideration of four factors: (1) the existence of a privative clause or a statutory appeal; (2) the expertise of the tribunal on the particular issue, relative to that of the Court; (3) the purpose of the legislation and the empowering provision in particular; and (4) the nature of the question—that is, whether it is essentially one of law or fact.[94]

With respect to the EUB, the Alberta Court of Appeal has noted the importance of the statutory discretion and the wide range of specific powers given by the legislature to regulate the energy sector.[95] This, along with the board's undoubted technical expertise, supports a deferential standard. There is a "privative" provision that excludes judicial review of board decisions. And the statutory right of appeal to the Court of Appeal, with leave of that Court on application filed within 30 days of the decision, has, itself, a privative quality.[96] It speeds and structures appeals by limiting them to questions of law or jurisdiction—classic matters on which little deference is appropriate. The result is that the fourth factor, the nature of the question, is particularly important when applying the pragmatic and functional analysis.[97] If the question is one of fact finding, then the board's expertise and experience, and its close engagement with the evidence and its sources, support a deferential approach. On the other hand, a question of general law or a question of statutory interpretation, particularly one that is non-technical and involves a matter of relatively general application, is a question of law that attracts little deference.

The difficulty arises when questions are matters of mixed fact and law involving the application of a legal standard to a set of facts. This has been described as drawing inferences, a process analogous to but distinct from fact finding, which involves drawing factual inferences from a set of facts. These two decision processes are often confused, as the Supreme Court of Canada noted in *Housen v. Nikolaisen*,[98] a motor vehicle negligence case. In *Housen* the Supreme Court noted, however, that once a court has decided that the question is a question of mixed fact and law that involves application of a legal standard to facts, the court must then determine and apply the appropriate standard of review. It then quoted, as follows, from *Canada (Director of Investigation and Research) v. Southam Inc.*, one of its judicial review cases:

> ...if a decision-maker says that the correct test requires him or her to consider A, B, C, and D, but in fact the decision-maker considers only A, B, and C, then the outcome is as if he or she had applied a law that required consideration of only A, B, and C. If the correct test requires him or her to consider D as well, then the decision-maker has in effect applied the wrong law, and so has made an error of law...Therefore, what appears to be a question of mixed fact and law, upon further reflection, can actually be an error of pure law.[99]

On the other hand, some errors of mixed fact and law involve a correct application of legal principle to the relevant facts. This requires a more deferential standard. There is a spectrum of application, so that some cases are so factually unique that decisions about whether they satisfy the appropriate legal tests or not have no particular precedential value. These attract a deferential standard. But where application of legal principles to relevant facts produces a general principle capable of application in future cases, this is evidentially more a matter of law requiring a correctness standard. Applying this approach to the motor vehicle negligence matter in *Housen*, the Supreme Court summarized the proper approach as follows:

> To summarize, a finding of negligence by a trial judge involves applying a legal standard to a set of facts, and thus is a question of mixed fact and law. Matters of mixed fact and law lie along a spectrum. Where, for instance, an error with respect to a finding of negligence can be attributed to the application of an incorrect standard, a failure to consider a

required element of a legal test, or similar error in principle, such an error can be characterized as an error of law, subject to a standard of correctness. Appellate courts must be cautious, however, in finding that a trial judge erred in law in his or her determination of negligence, as it *is often difficult to extricate the legal questions from the factual.* It is for this reason that these matters are referred to as questions of "mixed law and fact." *Where the legal principle is not readily extricable,* then the matter is one of "mixed law and fact" and is subject to a more stringent standard.[100] (Emphasis added.)

This idea of an "extricable" legal principle that requires an intrusive judicial standard of review has been applied by the Alberta courts in judicial review of Energy and Utilities Board decisions. The Alberta Court of Appeal did this explicitly in ATCO *Gas and Pipelines Ltd. v. Alberta (Energy and Utilities Board)* [ATCO *Gas 2005*] and at least implicitly in ATCO *Electric Limited v. Alberta (Energy and Utilities Board)* and ATCO *Gas and Pipelines Ltd. v. Alberta (Energy and Utilities Board)* [ATCO *Gas 2004*]. ATCO *Gas* 2005 concerned an appeal to the Alberta Court of Appeal by ATCO, a gas distribution utility, of a decision by the Alberta Energy and Utilities Board that certain ATCO natural gas supply management decisions were not "prudent." The issue was ATCO's decision to withdraw natural gas from its Carbon, Alberta, storage facility on a "flat" rate basis, rather than at flexible rates in response to price fluctuations during the winter of 2000–2001. Evidence before the board included an expert report, introduced by the City of Calgary, which concluded that had ATCO used flexible instead of flat-rate withdrawal during the relevant period, gas customers would have saved as much as $8.9 million. ATCO, of course, presented its own expert evidence in response. To this the board applied the following test: "[T]he utility would be found prudent if it exercises good judgment and makes decisions which are reasonable at the time they are made, based on information that the owner of the utility knew or ought to have known at the time the decision was made. In making a decision, a utility must take into account the best interests of its customers, while still being entitled to a fair return." The board concluded that ATCO's decision to use a flat withdrawal strategy during the period was imprudent.[101] It should have taken action to mitigate the high cost of gas during the winter of 2000–2001. This decision was ultimately based on the EUB power under the Gas Utilities Act to fix "just and reasonable rates."[102] The board ordered ATCO to refund the potential savings, estimated at $4 million, to customers through future rates.

The Court's analysis determined the appropriate standard of review by applying the Supreme Court of Canada's pragmatic and functional analysis with its four functional criteria.[103] First, the Court noted that there was no privative clause, but rather a statutory appeal on questions of law or jurisdiction. It commented that the fact that leave to appeal a question of law or jurisdiction had been granted did not mean that the standard is necessarily correctness. The Court stated that matters within the board's jurisdiction require deference notwithstanding the statutory right of appeal. This factor thus pointed to "limited deference."[104] Second, the Court's assessment of expertise related closely to the precise nature of the question that the board decided. However, this question was not perfectly clear: the Court concluded that the question was whether the board adopted the proper test of prudence, not whether the board had jurisdiction to establish and apply such a test.[105] It formulated its prudence test in the course of setting "just and reasonable" rates—a matter "squarely within the board's expertise."[106] This is a "polycentric" issue that affects ATCO and other utilities and their customers in the public. Consequently, on this issue the board's expertise exceeded that of the Court and deference was required.[107] Third, considering legislative purpose, the Court looked at the statutory scheme as a whole.[108] It considered that the board's general mandate was regulating public utilities to protect the public interest. It also looked for the statutory power that the board actually exercised and concluded it was the broad discretionary power to set "just and reasonable" rates by using accepted public utility practice. In this case, the matter in issue was ATCO's gas cost management strategy, "including the execution and management of a hedging plan."[109] The board had to assess these management decisions in determining just and reasonable rates. To do this it had to determine and apply an appropriate test that would balance consumer interests and those of the utility. In its conclusion, the Court came back to the discretionary nature of the rate setting powers. This factor, it said, suggests deference.[110] Fourth, in considering the nature of the question, the Court began with the related factor of relative expertise.[111] It characterized the board's determination and application of the prudence test as one of mixed fact and law. According to *Housen v. Nikolaisen*,[112] the Court can deal with this kind of question only where there is an "extricable" legal issue. Here, the Court concluded that the question of whether the board's prudence test was correct (as opposed to its application) was such an extricable question of law.[113] Nevertheless, it is still a question that falls within the board's wide statutory discretion. Therefore, "some deference" must be given.

The Court's balancing of the factors involved two main considerations: only one of the four factors pointed to a less deferential standard, and the "import of the prudence test to the utility industry."[114] This led to the conclusion that the appropriate standard is reasonableness—the intermediate, somewhat deferential standard. This requires the Court to ask whether there is a "rational basis for the decision."[115]

In applying this standard, the Court of Appeal considered that the only issues before it were whether the board properly acknowledged a presumption of prudence and properly articulated the prudence test in reviewing the decisions by ATCO's management. It concluded that the board's articulation of the test was consistent with its previous decisions and with authorities on the concept of prudence in public utility law. There was thus a rational basis for the board's decision.[116] However, the issue of application of the prudence test involves questions of fact and is therefore for the board and not the court to determine. In the result, the Court of Appeal found no error and dismissed the appeal.

ATCO Electric involved appeals by ATCO of EUB decisions on its proposed electricity rates for 1999 and 2000.[117] These decisions concerned negotiated settlements on rates by ATCO, its customers, and other interested parties, which were approved by the board under a process alternative to the board's traditional quasi-judicial hearing process. Specific issues included these: whether ATCO was entitled to 2000 carrying costs on "deferral accounts" established to permit a utility to document variances between approved electricity rates based on forecasted costs and the utility's actual costs for a particular period; whether the board erred in approving or failing to vary the negotiated settlements; and whether the board erred in the methodology it used to calculate ATCO's 2001 and 2002 carrying costs on the deferral accounts.[118] The context for these issues was the complex process implemented by the Alberta government to deregulate or restructure elements of the provincial electricity industry.[119]

Applying the same pragmatic and functional analysis as in *ATCO Gas 2005*, the Court of Appeal concluded that for the core issue of ATCO's entitlement to 2000 carrying costs, it should apply the mid-range reasonableness standard. The board's regulatory role and its statutory discretion suggested a more deferential standard, but the nature of the question before the board, and its expertise in contract interpretation (concerning the second issue about the negotiated settlements) relative to that of the Court, pointed to a correctness standard. However, the Court considered that the importance to the utility industry of the negotiated settlements and their approval by the board pointed to less deference.[120] As to the third question concerning methodology, this issue, because it engages the board's expertise in economics, financial markets, and the operation of regulated utilities, requires maximum deference—a patent unreasonableness standard.[121] In the result, the Court answered all three questions in the negative and dismissed the appeal.

In ATCO Gas 2004, the issue was whether the Energy and Utilities Board had jurisdiction to allocate the proceeds of a sale of property by ATCO to ATCO customers and company shareholders.[122] This jurisdiction (or legal authority) question fell, relatively clearly, within the expertise of the Court rather than the board, so that a correctness standard applied.[123] But the Court of Appeal considered that related issues, concerning retroactive ratemaking and even application of relevant case law precedents required a more deferential standard.[124] Applying this correctness standard to the core issue, the Court concluded that the board lacked legal authority to allocate the proceeds of the land sale. The majority of the Supreme Court of Canada was in general agreement with the Court of Appeal, both on standard of review and result.[125] Nonetheless, Justice Michel Bastarache, for the majority, pointedly noted that, as the Alberta Court stated, though the board's authorizing statutory provisions may in a sense suggest "polycentric" decisions that required balancing between constituencies, the fundamental issue was one of interpretation—a legal, not a polycentric, question.[126]

In 1996, a coalition of local citizens challenged the EUB's decision to permit Shell Canada Limited to expand its Caroline area sour (high sulphur content) gas processing plant. The citizens group was disappointed by the result of an intensive public consultation process and extensive public involvement in the board's public hearing. A majority of the Court of Appeal made clear that legal issues—issues "genuinely jurisdictional in nature"—would be analyzed using an intrusive correctness standard.[127] On these legal questions, the court is the expert. But the majority did recognize the relative incoherence of this concept of jurisdiction and the potential for judicial usurpation of board authority. In this vein, the Court simply took the position that in discharging its statutory duty to consider the public interest, the scope of evidence heard was at the discretion of the board. Thus, the board made no jurisdictional error in declining to consider evidence of the potential effects of increased SO_2 emission levels on cattle in the vicinity of the proposed expanded gas processing plant.[128] This, the Court ruled, had already been taken into account by the board when it granted the original gas plant approval following full public hearings.[129] The Court went on to find that if the board had erred in law in this way, its decision was not unreasonable in the circumstances.[130]

We have already seen that the Alberta Courts adopted a "vernacular" approach to interpret the language of mineral reservations in grants of land.[131] This helped balance the interests of the energy industry and landowners in the province. The Court also relied on a pragmatic approach to the interpretation of oil and gas industry agreements that facilitated commercial arrangements in an industry that required co-operation to spread risk and that often worked against time limits within agreements and against the forces of nature in instances of remote exploration and development operations.

Alberta judges have been sensitive to the history and practices of the industry. They have confirmed the validity of informal letter agreements for joint exploration and development of oil and gas rights, common in the industry, even though subsequent formal agreements were contemplated by the parties.[132] Oral agreements, such as an agreement to pool oil and gas rights to make up a spacing unit necessary to obtain an Energy and Utilities Board licence to drill a well, have also been upheld.[133] Another example includes the group of decisions that addresses whether overriding royalties on gross oil and gas production constitute interests in land that bind purchasers of oil and gas working interests and not merely contractual rights enforceable against only the original grantor. In these decisions, Alberta courts have emphasized industry practices and expectations and have given less weight to conceptual common law property categories. A number of courts have been guided by the following observations of Justice Constance Hunt in *Scurry-Rainbow Oil Ltd. v. Galloway Estate:*[134]

> [I]n trying to come to grips with some of the novel legal problems created by the industry's presence in our country, Canadian courts have often drawn upon English common law concepts, especially those of real property law. That this should be the case is hardly surprising, given our legal

traditions. Moreover, these traditional concepts have often proven helpful in sorting out complex problems. On the other hand, too rigid a reliance on common law principles that have developed in vastly different circumstances can lead to results that are out of touch with the realities of the industry and that deviate from the sorts of solutions needed by the affected parties....[A] related point is that judicial resolutions of industry-related problems have typically occurred long after the fact, for example, long after a contract was entered into. Thus, the courts may have interpreted the language of a document two or three decades after it was drafted. These judicial views are often argued to be binding in the interpretation of other agreements entered into long before the jurisprudence was in existence, and of course, long before the parties could possibly have known how the courts might construe the language they have chosen.... While these authorities should not be disregarded simply because they were later in time and thus could not have been in the contemplation of the drafters of the Agreements before me, the discrepancy in time is a factor to be weighed in considering the persuasiveness of such authorities in the context of the issues raised here.[135]

Madam Justice Hunt also commented on the use of American authorities as follows:

[S]ince the development of the oil and gas industry in Alberta and other parts of western Canada, Canadian courts have been called upon to make many decisions relating to the industry's activities. Due to the early dearth of jurisprudence and the fact that many industry practices in Canada were modelled upon those in the United States, Canadian courts have at times relied upon American decisions. Although such decisions can be of assistance, in my view they must be used cautiously because of the fact that different American jurisdictions have adopted varied approaches to basic concepts of oil and gas law, approaches that at times are in distinct contrast to those of Canadian courts....[136]

Justice Hunt's views on American authorities have been quoted with approval by a number of Alberta judges.

In *Bank of Montreal v. Dynex Petroleum Ltd.*, the Court of Appeal was faced with a technical argument: an overriding royalty based on an oil and gas lease cannot be an interest in land because a royalty is essentially a rent. In English law, a rent cannot be based on an "incorporeal" right. The Court of Appeal stated:

> The longstanding dichotomy between corporeal and incorporeal rights, described by A.H. Oosterhoff and W.B. Rayner, *Anger and Honsberger Law of Real Property* (Toronto: Canada Law Book, 1985) at pp. 10-11 as "meaningless and confusing," and which underlies the old rule that rent cannot issue out of an incorporeal hereditament, should not be an obstacle to a reasonable result in the case of overriding royalties.[137]

The functional criteria for determining whether a royalty is an interest in land developed by the Alberta Court of Appeal in the *Dynex* case were approved by the Supreme Court of Canada;[138] they were then applied by Mr Justice Ged Hawco in the Alberta Queen's Bench when the matter was remitted by the Supreme Court for decision on the evidence.[139] The same approach was used by the Alberta courts to determine the validity of royalty trust certificates issued by trustees on the basis of trust agreements made by lessors under oil and gas leases. If the interest conveyed to the trustee is an interest in land, the royalty trust certificates remain valid even if the original oil and gas lease has expired. Key decisions confirmed that the lessor's royalty was normally an interest in land and that, depending on contextual interpretation of royalty trust agreements, lessors could assign property interests that continued beyond the expiry of the original lease. These include the so-called "Gross Royalty Trust Test Cases": *Scurry-Rainbow Oil Ltd. v. Galloway Estate*;[140] *Guaranty Trust Co. v. Hetherington*;[141] and *Scurry-Rainbow Oil Ltd. v. Kasha*.[142] These decisions supported the gross royalty trust system that was commonly used by landowner-lessors in the early years of the Alberta oil and gas industry to create marketable interests.

CONCLUSION

Cases involving disputes about energy resources have kept the Alberta Supreme Court busy for the greater part of its 100 years. This legal activity had been sporadic but has gradually increased as the oil and gas industry has come to dominate Alberta's economy.

Though not the only critical decisions, the cases discussed in this chapter are landmarks in the development of the energy industry. They illustrate the Court's role in creating a positive and co-operative legal environment for the industry. The Court's decisions supported Alberta's government system that features private development of provincially owned natural resources. Its decisions, though by no means satisfying all interests, recognized and enhanced the credibility of the regulatory regime administered by the Energy and Utilities Board, which intended to promote rational development of oil and gas resources in the interest of Albertans.

Alberta's control of its energy resources was confirmed by the Court in the 1930s in the landmark *Spooner Oil* and *Huggard Assets* cases. Later, in the 1980s, the Court's Natural Gas Tax Reference judgement gave Alberta timely support in its epic Natural Energy Program battle with the federal government. In 2007, as the Court marks 100 years, courtrooms buzz with new energy sector litigation. The outcomes of these cases, which include challenges to the regulatory powers of the Energy and Utilities Board over oil sands development, and resource ownership disputes among private energy companies, will affect the future of Canada's vibrant Alberta-based energy sector.

NOTES

1. See David H. Breen, "Anglo-American Rivalry and the Evolution of Canadian Petroleum Policy to 1930," in *Canadian Historical Review* 62, no. 3 (1981): 302. Also see Breen, "Turner Valley 'Waste' Gas and the Early Conservation Movement," in his *Alberta's Petroleum Industry and the Conservation Board* (Edmonton: University of Alberta Press, 1993), 3-76.
2. See the Agreement between the Dominion and the Province of Alberta respecting transfer to the Province of public lands, confirmed by British North America (BNA) Act 1930. For the relation between water law and the Natural Resources Transfer Agreement (NRTA), see Arelene J. Kwasniak "The Supreme Court of Alberta and Water Law," in this volume. On the NRTA, see Thomas Flanagan and Mark Milke, "Alberta's Real Constitution: The Natural Resources Transfer Agreement," in *Forging Alberta's Constitutional Framework*, ed. Richard Connors and John M. Law (Edmonton: University of Alberta Press, 2005), 165-90.
3. The perfect storm label is historian Douglas Owram's, see "The Perfect Storm: The National Energy Program and the Failure of Federal-Provincial Relations," in *Forging Alberta's Constitutional Framework*, ed. Richard Connors and John M. Law (Edmonton: University of Alberta Press, 2005), 391-410.
4. See generally David Hall, "1904-1905—Alberta Proclaimed," in *Alberta Formed—Alberta Transformed*, vol. 1, ed. Michael Payne, Donald Wetherell, and Catherine Cavanaugh (Edmonton: University of Alberta Press, 2005), 333-55.
5. Alberta Natural Resources Act, S.A. 1930, c. 21; Peter Hogg, *Constitutional Law of Canada* (Toronto: Carswell, 4th ed.), para. 28.1.
6. See Canadian Oil and Gas Order No. 1 under the Turner Valley Gas Conservation Act, S.A. 1932, c. 6.
7. See Bankes and Bennett Jones Verchere, *Canadian Oil and Gas* (Toronto: Butterworths, continuing service) vol. 1, paras. 3.177-3.186; Constance Hunt and Alastair Lucas, *Oil and Gas Law in Canada* (Toronto: Carswell, 1990), 14-16.
8. *Spooner Oils Ltd. v. Turner Valley Gas Conservation Board*, Dominion Law Reports [cited hereafter DLR] 4 (1932) (Alta. App. Div.), varying DLR 4 (1932): 729 (Alta. T.D.), rev'd. DLR 4 (1933): 545 (S.C.C.).
9. *Spooner Oils*—Appellate Division, 15.
10. David Breen, *Alberta's Petroleum Industry and the Conservation Board* (Edmonton: University of Alberta Press, 1993).
11. 1932 (Alta.), c.6.
12. *Spooner Oils*—Supreme Court of Canada, 562.
13. *Supra*, n. 1.
14. Breen *supra*, n. 10, 94.
15. Ibid.
16. Ibid., 117.
17. S.A. 1938 (2nd sess.), c. 1.
18. *Mercury Oils Ltd. v. A. G. Alberta*, 1938.
19. Breen *supra*, n. 10, 139.
20. Ibid., 140-47.
21. Oil and Gas Conservation Act, 1938, *supra*, n. 17, Part 1.
22. See section three *infra*.

23 *Supra*, n. 8.
24 See Steven Kennett, ed., *Canadian Energy Law Service—Alberta* (Toronto: Thompson-Carswell, continuing service), Alberta Energy and Utilities Board Commentary.
25 See generally, *Canadian Oil and Gas*, vol. 1, commentary.
26 See "James Boyd McBride" in *Lords of the Western Bench: A Biographical History of the Supreme and District Courts of Alberta, 1876–1990* [cited hereafter *Lords of the Western Bench*], Louis A. Knafla and Richard Klumpenhouwer (Calgary: The Legal Archives Society of Alberta, 1997), 113-14.
27 *Huggard Assets Ltd. v. Attorney General at Alberta*, DLR 4 (1949): 211 at 214. (Alta. Trial Division).
28 *Majestic Mines Ltd. v. Attorney General of Alberta*, Western Weekly Reports [cited hereafter WWR] 2 (1941): 353 (Alta. T.D.), aff'd. DLR 1 (1942): 474 (Alta. A.D.), aff'd. DLR 4 (1942): 593 (Supreme Court of Canada); *Huggard Assets*—Trial Division, 215.
29 *Huggard Assets*—Trial Division, 216.
30 See "George Bligh O'Connor" and "William Alexander MacDonald," in *Lords of the Western Bench*, Knafla and Klumpenhouwer, 139 and 90-91, respectively.
31 *Huggard Assets Ltd. v. Attorney General of Alberta*, DLR 1 (1950): 823 at 826 (Justice O'Connor), 828 (Justice MacDonald) [*Huggard Assets*—Appellate Division]
32 Regulations consolidated in 1906 and repealed in March 1911. See *Huggard Assets*—Supreme Court of Canada, 310 (Justice Kerwin), and 317 (Justice Rand).
33 *Huggard Assets*—Appellate Division, 827 (Justice O'Connor), 829-30 (Justice MacDonald).
34 *Majestic Mines*—Appellate Division, 479.
35 See "Harold Hayward Parlee," "William Alexander MacDonald," and "Frank Ford," in *Lords of the Western Bench*, Knafla and Klumpenhouwer, 140-41 and 45, respectively.
36 *Huggard Assets*—Appellate Division, 832.
37 Ibid., at 833.
38 Ibid.
39 Ibid., at 834.
40 *Majestic Mines*—Supreme Court of Canada, 596.
41 *Huggard Assets Ltd. v. Attorney General of Alberta*, DLR 2 (1951): 306 (Supreme Court of Canada).
42 Ibid., 319 (Justice Rand), 322 (Justice Kellock).
43 S.C. 1875, c. 49, as amended, S.C. 1886, c. 25.
44 *Huggard Assets*—Supreme Court of Canada, 319 (Justice Rand), 324 (Justice Kellock).
45 *Attorney General of Alberta v. Huggard Assets Ltd.*, DLR 3 (1953): 225 (Judicial Committee of the Privy Council), 234.
46 Ibid., 235.
47 Ibid., 239.
48 Ibid., 242-43.
49 *Borys v. Canadian Pacific Railway and Imperial Oil Ltd.*, DLR 4 (1951): 427 Alta. Trial Division, rev'd., DLR 3 (1952): 218 (Alta. A.D.), aff'd, DLR 2 (1953): 65 (Judicial Committee of the Privy Council).

50 Quoted in *Borys*—Trial Division, 428.
51 See "William Robinson Howson," in *Lords of the Western Bench*, Knafla and Klumpenhouwer, 72–74.
52 *Borys*—Trial Division, 432–41.
53 *Barnard-Argue-Roth Stearns Oil & Gas Co. v. Farquharson, Appeal Cases* [cited hereafter AC] (1912): 864, 869 (Judicial Committee of the Privy Council).
54 *Borys*—Trial Division, 431.
55 Ibid., 442.
56 *Borys*—Appellate Division.
57 Ibid., 237.
58 *Borys*—Privy Council, 73–74.
59 Ibid., 77–78.
60 Ibid., 72, emphasis added.
61 ABQB (1998): 620 (Can LII) (Alta. Q.B.), aff'd. in part, WWR 1 (2003): 174ii (Alta. C.A.), aff'd. *Supreme Court Reports* [cited hereafter SCR] (2004), 3 (Supreme Court of Canada).
62 *Prism Petroleum Ltd. v. Omega Hydrocarbons Ltd., Alberta Law Reports* [cited hereafter ALR], 3rd ser., 4, (1992): 332 (Alta. Q.B.), rev'd., ALR, 3rd ser., 18 (1994): 225 (Alta. C.A.).
63 *Prism*—Queen's Bench, 339. See "William Gordon Neil Egbert," in *Lords of the Western Bench*, Knafla and Klumpenhouwer, 39–40.
64 *Prism*—Court of Appeal, 232–34.
65 Ibid., 235.
66 *Anderson*—Queen's Bench, 29 (ABQB).
67 *Anderson*—Court of Appeal, *supra*, at 190 (WWR).
68 *Anderson*—Supreme Court of Canada, 30.
69 Ibid., at para. 40.
70 Janice Buckingham and Patricia Steele, "Coalbed Methane: Conventional Rules for an Unconventional Resource," ALR 42 (2004): 2–5.
71 Owram, "The Perfect Storm," 391–410.
72 Ibid., 407.
73 Sessional Paper No. 321-1/310E, 1980.
74 "An Act to Amend the Excise Tax Act and to Provide For a Revenue Tax in Respect of Petroleum and Gas."
75 Quoted in *Reference Re Proposed Federal Tax on Exported Natural Gas*, WWR 3 (1981): 408 at 411 [*Gas Tax Reference*—Court of Appeal].
76 Constitution Act 1867, s. 92(3) and (5).
77 *Gas Tax Reference*—Court of Appeal.
78 Ibid., 426.
79 Ibid., 432.
80 Ibid., 431, quoting Lord Sankey in *Edwards v. A G Canada*, AC 124 (1930): 136.
81 Section 1 of the British North America Act 1930 provides that the Agreement is "confirmed and shall have the force of law notwithstanding anything in the British North America Act, 1867..." But the Preamble of the Agreement clearly refers to "equality with the other provinces...," as Chief Justice Laskin noted in the Supreme Court of Canada: *Reference Re Proposed Federal Tax on Exported Natural Gas*, SCR 1 (1982): 1004 at 1029–1030 [*Gas Tax Reference*—Supreme Court of Canada].

82 Ibid., 1030.
83 Ibid.
84 Constitution Act 1867, Sixth Schedule added by Constitution Act, 1982.
85 *Alberta Energy Company Ltd. v. Goodwell Petroleum Corporation Ltd.*, Alberta Court of Appeal [cited hereafter ABCA] (2003): 277; *ATCO Gas and Pipelines Ltd. v. Alberta (Energy and Utilities Board)*, ABCA (2005): 122; *ATCO Gas and Pipelines Ltd. v. Alberta (Energy and Utilities Board)*, ABCA (2004): 3 (Alberta Court of Appeal), affirmed with a variation, 2006 S.C.C. 4 at para. 30; *ATCO Electric Limited v. Alberta (Energy and Utilities Board)*, ABCA (2004): 215 (Alberta Court of Appeal).
86 *Pushpanathan v. Canada (Minister of Citizenship and Immigration)*, SCR 1 (1998): 982 (Supreme Court of Canada); *Canada (Director of Investigation and Research) v. Southam Inc.*, SCR (1997): 748.
87 *Canada (Attorney General) v. Public Service Alliance of Canada*, SCR 1 (1993): 941 at 963–64, and *Canadian Union of Public Employers Local 963 v. New Brunswick Liquor Corp.*, SCR 2 (1979): 227.
88 *Southam*, at para. 56.
89 *Construction and General Workers Union v. Voice Construction Ltd.*, 2004 S.C.C. 23 at para. 15.
90 See "William Carlos Ives," in *Lords of the Western Bench*, Knafla and Klumpenhouwer, 76–77.
91 The board classifies its decisions as energy or utility decisions, see http://www.eub.ca
92 *ATCO Gas*—2004—Supreme Court of Canada, para. 3.
93 *ALR*, 2nd ser., 203 (1978): 219.
94 *Pushpanathan*, *supra*.
95 *ATCO Gas*—2005, para. 46; *ATCO Electric*, para. 56.
96 *ATCO Gas*—2005, para. 35.
97 See *ATCO Electric*; *ATCO Gas*—2004 and 2005; *Goodwell*.
98 SCR 2 (2002): 235, para. 26.
99 Ibid., para. 27.
100 Ibid.
101 Alberta, Energy and Utilities Board Decision 2001-110, 13 December 2001, 10.
102 RSA 2000, c. G-5, ss. 16, 25, 28 and 32.
103 *ATCO Gas*—2005, para. 30.
104 Ibid., para. 36.
105 The court pointed out that ATCO was not granted leave on the jurisdiction issue, but rather on the question framed as one of law: Ibid., para. 42.
106 Ibid., para. 43.
107 Ibid., para. 44.
108 Ibid., para. 45.
109 Ibid., para. 52.
110 Ibid., para. 53.
111 Ibid., para. 54, citing *Voice Construction Ltd. v. Construction and General Workers' Union, Local 92*, supra, n. 89, para. 29.
112 *Supra*, n. 98.
113 *ATCO Gas*—2005, para. 55.
114 Ibid., para. 58.

115 Ibid.
116 Ibid., para. 74.
117 *ATCO Electric.*
118 Ibid., para. 48.
119 Ibid., Background Information, paras. 11–24. See S.A. 1995 c. E. 5.5, as amended by S.A. 1998 c. 13, now ss. 121(2)(a)(b) of the Electric Utilities Act, S.A. 2003 c. E. 5.1.
120 Ibid., para. 59.
121 Ibid., paras. 62-64.
122 *ATCO Gas*—2004, Court of Appeal, para 31.
123 Ibid., para. 38.
124 Ibid., para. 39.
125 *ATCO Gas*—2004, Supreme Court of Canada.
126 Ibid., para. 30.
127 *Coalition of Citizens Impacted by the Caroline Shell Gas Plant v. Alberta (Energy and Utilities Board)*, AJ No. 745 (1996) (Alberta Court of Appeal).
128 Ibid., para. 19.
129 Ibid., para. 5.
130 Ibid., para. 25.
131 *Huggard Assets, supra.*
132 *Home Oil Company Limited v. Page Petroleum Ltd.*, WWR 4 (1976): 598 (Alberta Trial Division).
133 *Paddon Hughes Development Co. v. Pancontinental Oil Ltd.*, ALR, 3rd ser., (1992), 343 (Alberta Queen's Bench).
134 WWR 4 (1993): 454 at 465-66 (Alta. Q.B.), aff'd., WWR 1 (1995): 316 (Alta. C.A.), leave to appeal denied, ALR, 3rd ser., 26 (1995): n. (Supreme Court of Canada).
135 Quoted in *Bank of Montreal v. Dynex Petroleum Ltd.*, WWR (2000): 693 at 699 (Alta. C.A.).
136 Ibid.
137 Ibid., 708.
138 *Bank of Montreal v. Dynex Petroleum Ltd.*, SCR 1, (2002): 146 (Supreme Court of Canada).
139 *Bank of Montreal v. Dynex Petroleum Ltd.*, ABQB (2003): 243 (Alta. Q.B.).
140 WWR (1993): 454 (Alta. Q.B.), aff'd., WWR 1 (1995): 316 (Alta C.A.), leave to appeal to Supreme Court of Canada refused, ALR, 3rd ser., 26, in.
141 WWR 3 (1987): 316 (Alta. Q.B.), varied, WWR 5 (1989): 340 (Albta C.A.).
142 DLR, 4th ser., 135 (1996): 1 (Alta. C.A.), leave to appeal to Supreme Court of Canada denied 1 May 1997.

EIGHT

The Marriage of Law and History
Family Law Cases in the Alberta Supreme Court, 1907–2006

MARIE L. GORDON

SOUTHERN ALBERTAN RANCH WOMAN Irene Murdoch became, quite unexpectedly, a heroine for countless Canadian women in the early 1970s. Having provided meals for the work crews on the cattle ranch she shared with her husband and then later contributing chores, hay raking, swathing, mowing, truck and tractor driving, along with dehorning, vaccinating, and branding cattle, Murdoch had also shouldered the responsibilities of overseeing the entire ranch operation while her husband Alex was absent on Stock Association business for five months of every year. After 25 years of marriage, Murdoch separated from her husband in 1968 and turned to the Supreme Court of Alberta to uphold her claim for a declaration of partnership or joint ownership of the land they had worked together.[1] The Court found that despite Irene Murdoch's labours, she had not made any direct financial contribution to the ranch. Mr Justice David MacDonald of the Trial Division stated:

> As I have said, I have no evidence that I feel would justify me in making a declaration of a partnership or joint ownership and, although this has nothing to do with the decision I am required to make, I must say that under the circumstances I would find it almost impossible to understand how Mr. Murdoch will be able to continue his farming and ranching operations if the declaration request were possible to grant. It would involve, presumably, the disposition of all of his farm assets, and would likely involve reliance for income on the net value of the investment alone. What I am saying, in

effect, is this, that Mrs. Murdoch may be far better protected in the long run by an Order for alimony and continuation of her dower interest than by an effort to destroy and disrupt, perhaps, the going interest in the ranching undertaking.[2]

Justice MacDonald's *obiter* comments seem primarily concerned with the future of the family farm in Alberta and thus suggest that support and dower should suffice as remedies available to a farm wife. Although partly rooted in Albertan concerns over the farm economy, MacDonald's views also reflected broader sentiments opposing the introduction of matrimonial property legislation.

MacDonald's trial decision was upheld by the Alberta Supreme Court, Appeal Division on 1 February 1972 and subsequently by the Supreme Court of Canada.[3] In the end Irene Murdoch had been denied a property entitlement and instead was awarded $200 per month support for her efforts. But it was Mr Justice Bora Laskin's spirited call for an expansion of the trust remedy to meet the need to value a wife's labour exceeding "mere household duties" that ignited a nationwide movement for law reform that, in turn, produced the 1979 proclamation of the Alberta Matrimonial Property Act.[4] While *Murdoch* was certainly not the only incentive for legislative action, it reverberated for decades across Canada and even in 2006 it yields an immediate reaction, especially for women over 50. Symbolizing the unfairness that seemingly could not be remedied in the courts, it cried out for modern legislative reform that resulted in a wave of matrimonial property legislation passed across the nation between 1978 and 1980.

Although no court was ever prepared to recognize Irene Murdoch's property interest, she achieved partial success by returning to the Alberta Supreme Court Trial Division before Mr Justice Donald H. Bowen in 1976.[5] Murdoch had made an application to set aside a conveyance of real property made by her former husband to his son, which she alleged was done earlier in order to thwart her claim to property. In applying the Statute of Elizabeth, Justice Bowen set aside the conveyance, restored the property to Alex Murdoch, ordered a $65,000 lump sum of support to Irene Murdoch, and terminated the periodic payment of $200 per month. In the end, Irene Murdoch ended up with about one-third of the value of her ex-husband's property but, in the process, she had managed to make history. And to the extent that it illuminated but one aspect of family law in the history of the Supreme Court of Alberta, the decision captures how the

Court played a role in the province's history despite the fact that the consequences were not always those intended.

Family law cases in Alberta have been a steady part of the judicial diet over the past century, and while the flavour of the cases has changed dramatically over the years, there is little doubt that the court has had a significant impact on a broad cross-section of individuals and families. Generally the cases from the first half of the twentieth century often involved questions centred on the formal validity of marriage, the earliest divorces, the bars to those divorces, and a variety of cases involving archaic actions for domestic torts such as loss of consortium and enticement. Beginning in the 1960s, concomitant with liberalization of Canada's divorce laws, issues such as the custody of children, property claims, and child and spousal support grew in importance while the historic preoccupation with the formal status of marriage or divorce declined. During this same period we witness the emergence of modern matrimonial property legislation across Canada in the aftermath of the *Murdoch* case. And finally, in the post-Charter era, Albertan judges played a leading role in developing modern Canadian jurisprudence in areas such as support for children and spouses, as well as custody of children while, at the same time, making the courts "family-law friendly" to litigants and family lawyers.

However, to the degree that these trends are discernable, they do not capture the entirety of family law in Alberta or, more specifically, the manner in which the province's Supreme Court has addressed the myriad issues circling around family law. Thus in an attempt to capture a sense of how these questions were addressed by the Supreme Court in Alberta and offer some insight into how the Court mirrored the province, this paper addresses some of the earliest family law cases dealing with divorce, domestic torts, and validity of marriage and the later emergence of post-Charter issues where Alberta's courts were called upon to expand the family circle to include unmarried co-habitees, children born of unmarried parents, as well as gays and lesbians. These cases were some of the most interesting decided in the last two decades.

Discerning the degree to which the Court consciously attempted to render decisions with a particular Albertan flavour is an unwieldy task. But it is equally certain that while contemporary observers might question a ruling or the apparent rationale, the expectation that some sort of "cowboy" or "redneck" jurisprudence was the typical result of the Court's work is simply unfounded. Indeed on most counts Albertan trial and appellate judges have been responsible for some of the most purposive and principled findings in the nation and have, through these judgments, been responsible for contributing numerous landmark decisions to the body of Canadian family law.

I: EARLY FAMILY LAW

As with all courts across Canada, a large part of the Supreme Court of Alberta's family law caseload prior to the 1960s and 1970s examined fundamental questions concerning the formal validity of marriage and the nature of, and relative access to, early divorce.[6] Exclusive jurisdiction over divorce was granted to the federal government under s. 91(26) of the British North America Act, 1867. However, it was not until 1968 that the federal government actually exercised its legislative powers to pass comprehensive legislation dealing with divorce. As a result of this 101-year legislative gap, Canadians had to process their requests for divorce in extremely cumbersome ways. In the early years, not only were there huge procedural obstacles, but Canadians were forced to rely on the English law of divorce and annulment in force as of 15 July 1870 as the substantive law governing their affairs.

In 2007 it is difficult for us to imagine the procedural difficulties (and no doubt the concomitant expenses) faced by a spouse seeking a divorce in the pre-1918 period. Prior to that date, any Albertan seeking a divorce was required to commence proceedings in Parliament by way of a petition, preceded by the publication of a notice of intention to petition in *The Canada Gazette*. Each petition had to be presented by a senator and was then forwarded to a hearing and inquiry before the Divorce Committee, which functioned as a quasi-court. Following the recommendation of the Divorce Committee of the Senate, a formal private bill needed to be passed by both the Senate and the House of Commons (accompanied by all the evidence heard by the committee).[7] It took the passage of a bill by Parliament to terminate a marriage by way of a divorce in the early days of Alberta's history.

Even though s. 92(14) of the British North America Act, 1987 gave the provinces authority over the "administration of justice in the province, including the constitution, maintenance and organization of provincial courts, both of civil and criminal jurisdiction, and including procedure in civil matters in those courts," no divorces were heard in the Alberta courts until 1918. In fact it was the Alberta decision in *Board v. Board*, initiated by William Board who, on the grounds of his wife's adultery, brought a Petition for Divorce before

Mr Justice William Legh Walsh in 1918, that proved to be a legal landmark.[8] The Appeal Division of the Alberta Supreme Court determined that it possessed the jurisdiction to hear the matter and grant a divorce, using the English Divorce and Matrimonial Causes Act of 1857. Because Alberta, Saskatchewan, and Manitoba had inherited the laws of England as they existed on 15 July 1870, those provinces already possessed the legislation allowing for the granting of a divorce petition. Along with the statutory right to divorce, the Alberta Supreme Court Appeal Division applied the remedy, without which the right would have been meaningless. Board was granted his divorce and Alberta judges started dealing almost immediately with the divorces of a number of other Alberta couples. The Appeal Division ruling was eventually confirmed by the Judicial Committee of the Privy Council in 1919 and thus solidified the right to divorce in Alberta.[9] Although only a procedural change, it radically altered the way in which Albertans were able to apply for divorces. Rather than having to petition Parliament, Albertans were able to turn to the provincial courts to dissolve a marriage. The grounds warranting such an action were, however, strictly limited and biased in favour of the husband.[10]

Although signalling only a procedural change, the effects of *Board* were immediate. In May 1919 a Mrs Coleman commenced an action for divorce, her husband having left her in 1914 while "carrying on an intrigue with a dissolute woman of the town."[11] The first in a series of cases addressing the issue of domicile as it pertained to divorce, the *Coleman* case was rooted in the changing realities of Albertan society during and after the First World War. Increasing mobility and the dislocations of wartime had placed enormous strains on countless marriages, and adhering to the notion that a couple would have but one domicile—that of the husband—stood in stark contrast to these new circumstances. As such, despite the traditional view that the wife's domicile was that of the husband, the court held that Mrs Coleman could initiate the action based on his domicile of origin because he had since moved to the United States, deserting both his wife and children. An even more forceful statement of this Albertan innovation is in *McCormack v. McCormack,* where an English war bride had joined her husband in Lethbridge and she learned that in his job with the railway he had taken up residence with a war widow. Adding insult to injury, her husband had suggested that all three of them take up residence together before he deserted his wife and moved to Montreal with the widow. In hearing the case, Mr Justice Charles

Stuart felt there was no reason to deny jurisdiction because the Court ought "to lay down a rule to fit the justice of the case..."[12] Three years later Stuart once again took the lead in *Cook v. Cook and the Attorney General of Alberta* by ruling that, having gained a judicial separation in 1921, a wife could obtain a divorce although her husband resided in Ontario. Writing for a 4-1 majority, Stuart indicated that the judicial separation had created a separate domicile for the wife and thus she was no longer bound by her husband's domicile.[13]

The gains made in the suite of cases beginning with *Board* were in the area of divorce entitlement and marital status rather than in the substantive areas of support, custody of children, and property distribution. While the Albertan courts had taken important steps establishing their own jurisdiction over divorce, this advance was not matched by similar progress respecting grounds for divorce. For example, both Board and Coleman had successfully cited adultery in their divorce petitions—a rationale that was consistent with established practice in Canada and England. But in *B. v. B.*, which came forward in the same year as Board and Coleman, the wife requested a divorce because her husband had come home drunk and called her terrible names in front of a number of people. Her petition was turned back as not being sufficient in law to warrant a divorce.[14] Indeed, as Terry Chapman has pointed out, physical violence (let alone verbal violence) was not, in and of itself, grounds for divorce. Apparently, a sitting member of the House of Commons was sought out to forward a divorce petition by another young woman who reported, "My husband kicked and pounded me so hard I had to leave him three times." Although the Member of Parliament sounded sympathetic and assured the woman that her husband's behaviour was "improper," it was not a ground for divorce.[15] As B. learned in her case, cruelty alone was not enough to warrant a divorce; her marriage subsisted, unhappy as it was.

Essentially, while the Supreme Court of Alberta was prepared to shoulder the responsibility of hearing divorce petitions, it, like its fellow courts across the nation, was less than enthusiastic about expanding the grounds on which a divorce might be sought. The result was that while access improved, it nonetheless remained limited and overtly biased in favour of husbands. Under the English Divorce and Matrimonial Causes Act of 1857, a husband could successfully sue for divorce if his wife had committed adultery while a wife could sue if her husband had "...been guilty of incestuous adultery, or bigamy with rape, or of sodomy, or bestiality, or of adultery coupled with such cruelty as without adultery would have entitled her to a divorce *a mensa et thoro,* or of adultery coupled with desertion without reasonable excuse for two years or upward."[16] As historian James Snell has written, legislative discussions in Canada during and after the First World War that broached the topic of expanding the grounds for divorce were tentative in the extreme and almost invariably entangled in moralistic rhetoric.[17] Lacking clear legislative direction from Parliament, judges were left to find their own way and, not surprisingly, the bench in Alberta and beyond did not stray far from well-worn paths. Yet the judges did not hesitate to pronounce on the character and morality of those appearing before them. Not surprisingly, early divorce cases in Alberta were a venue for punishing moral turpitude and rewarding proper marital behaviour. In 1922, Mr Walkden became suspicious of his wife's adultery and carefully managed to secure evidence of her wrongdoing while continuing to live with her for two months. His wife's suggestion that such condonation would bar the granting of a divorce was rejected by the Court, and he was granted his divorce, custody of the children, and considerable damages of $5,000 against the offending co-respondent.[18] Similarly, in the 1926 case of *Spring v. Spring,* desertion for over two years by a spouse could revive an old adultery, and effectively "cancel" the husband's forgiveness and thereby allow him a divorce on the ground of his wife's adultery.[19] Two years later in *Wright v. Wright,*[20] Justice John Boyle of the Alberta Supreme Court granted a husband's divorce because the wife lived "in open adultery with a negro." In noting the Court's characterization of the wife's behaviour as "particularly inexcusable and thoroughly disgusting to a sense of decency," Snell wondered whether the sexual or racial character of the case was the greater concern.[21] Given the attitudes toward Blacks in Alberta and the nation as a whole, it is likely that race was not an insignificant factor.[22] The point was clear. While Alberta's judiciary was uneasy with divorce actions and the threat they posed to society writ large, they rarely shied away from recognizing the circumstances that all too often led to marital breakdown.

Since adultery was effectively the only ground for a divorce, the very nature of the adultery informed settling of affairs in the aftermath of a divorce. Suing her husband in an action for alimony in 1914, Mrs Lloyd learned that despite her husband's conviction for an assault, she was viewed by Justice David Scott as having "provoked her husband unreasonably."[23] Consistent with the predominant notions of the age, Scott indicated that since Mrs Lloyd's life was not in danger, she was not justified in leaving her husband and therefore was not entitled to either alimony or to the custody of her two infant sons.[24] Scott wrote that

> ...the Plaintiff has not shown that she is entitled to a judgment for alimony. In view of my having so held, I must also hold that the Plaintiff is not entitled to a declaration that she is entitled to the custody of the children of the marriage. It is shown that the Defendant is fond of the children, that he has a proper home for them, and that he is a man of steady habits, and he states that he has a young couple ready to come and take charge of them until he can get his niece from the Old Country for the purpose. Such being the case, I see no reason why he should not have the custody of them.[25]

On appeal the Court set aside the award for custody, largely because Mr Lloyd had not even asked for such relief.

Clearly, while the Albertan judiciary took steps to expand access to divorce, they did so with their preconceptions and reservations intact and in this they were hardly exceptional. Indeed, their sober and solemn consideration of divorce actions reflected a generalized social ambivalence about the whole issue. Divorce was still considered an affront to the absolute sanctity of marriage, and it is certain that members of the court were troubled by the idea of granting a divorce. For example, Mr Justice Nicholas D. Beck of the Supreme Court Appellate Division was clearly torn in considering the matter of *Board v. Board* in 1918.[26] Beck wrote:

> Now, as is well and generally known, I am a Catholic...[T]he opinion commonly prevails that, being a Catholic, I cannot with good conscience take part in any divorce proceedings arising in this court...I cannot permit it to be supposed that in the event of my acting as Judge in a divorce case I shall be acting in any way with a bad or uneasy conscience. I accept absolutely without hesitation the doctrines of the Catholic Church with regard to faith and morals. I accept and fully recognise the obligations of conscience imposed upon me by the Canon Law of the Catholic Church. Yet, sitting as a Judge in a Court established by the authority of the State to administer the laws of the State, my duty is to find the true facts and to declare the civil law applicable to those facts.[27]

For judges Catholic or Protestant alike, the balancing act described by Beck was all too familiar. In this instance at least, Beck was certain of the path he was obliged to follow.

That the issues coming to light in petitions for divorce troubled some of the early judges and offered increasingly subtle challenges for later members of the bench in Alberta is certain. Equally true, some members of the bench may have preferred to have handled these matters as quietly as possible. Yet at the same time, divorce cases had to be held in open court despite the efforts of at least one member of the Alberta Supreme Court. In what would prove to be the first of two trials scandalizing the United Farmers of Alberta government as it faced the rising Social Credit movement in 1934, an undefended divorce action was brought by O.L. McPherson, then Minister for Public Works in Alberta, before Mr Justice Thomas Tweedie, who convened the hearing in the judges' library of the Edmonton Courthouse on 22 April 1931.[28] While public access to the library was not prohibited per se, there was a "private" sign on one side of the entrance swinging doors leading to the judges' library, off a public corridor. The issue of the propriety of the divorce case being heard in a private venue as opposed to a public courtroom was raised on appeal by the former Mrs McPherson, who had been granted special leave to present and prosecute her appeal before the Privy Council *in forma pauperis*. She argued that the exclusion—intentional or not—of the public would effectively nullify the decree nisi granted to her husband as well as the order giving him custody of the four children. The Privy Council refused to set aside the divorce as a nullity, but nonetheless held that even undefended divorce cases as a matter of principle must be heard in a court accessible to the public. O.L. McPherson's new marriage (interestingly enough to the wife of the former Mrs McPherson's adulterous partner) survived, but so did a clear understanding of what "open court" would need to mean in the future for the hearing of all cases, including family cases.

Concerned with questions of character, morality, and the sanctity of marriage, early Alberta judges saw very little "law" in the awarding of support. In this the bench was very much in accord with fellow courts across the nation. Support was ordered to keep dependents off the public purse or to meet the most basic of social obligations; it was not considered a vehicle for achieving social or familial justice. Nor were the courts enthusiastic about adopting such a role. Consistent with the tangle of interests shaping access to divorce in Alberta, pre-Second World War cases treated support as both a reward for the socially appropriate conduct of one party and a punishment for immoral or inappropriate behaviour by the other. In the 1932 case of *Olynyk v. Olynyk*, the wife was found guilty of adultery and accordingly her support was to be followed by a *dum sola et casta vixerit*[29] provision operating as a reminder to her and other family law litigants that the right to support was conditional upon remaining single and chaste.[30] Further, the early cases are replete with cautions about "over-awarding" support and concerns about impeding the ability of the payer to arrange his affairs as he saw fit. Indeed, in *Olynyk*, the Court concluded that although it did have the right to secure the wife's obligation to support against the husband's assets, it declined to do so, stating, "There is no authority to deprive the husband of his property and transfer it to the wife."[31]

Yet by the end of the Second World War, the times and judicial attitudes had begun to change. In 1946, Mr Olsen and his lawyer opposed Mrs Olsen's application for a decree of judicial separation and alimony by pointing to a 1926 written agreement whereby she had agreed to child support of $15 per month per child and no money for herself.[32] In answer to her request for alimony after the children had grown up, Mr Justice Clinton Ford noted the husband's position that "she had left him of her own accord without just cause and that she can return to him or otherwise maintain herself."[33] However, Mr Olsen's "tough love" approach was rejected by the Court, and Mrs Olsen was granted her decree and alimony of $35 per month. The Court noted that one of the obligations inherent in the sanctity of marriage itself was the obligation of maintaining a dependent wife. The 1958 case of *Rudiak v. The Public Trustee* over a decade later added a new layer to such obligations.[34] Mr Rudiak's desertion of his wife and two children on a debt-ridden farm left Mrs Rudiak with no means of support and led to her living with another man and her subsequent adultery. The attempt by the husband's estate to disentitle her to any support or dower rights was unsuccessful, given Mr Justice Harold Riley's treatment of the law of condonation on the rather compelling facts of the case.[35] Riley seems to have implicitly recognized that in some cases, for financially vulnerable women, adultery and reliance on a new male partner was a matter of basic survival. In this instance the power to forgive rested with the court and not the spouse.

The arc from *Olynyk*, where the court declined the opportunity to step into the financial relations between a husband and wife, to *Rudiak*, where the court adopted a far more active role in recognizing the harsh realities of some women in the aftermath a divorce, traces the enormous difference between the Alberta of the early 1930s and the late 1950s. Although many of the early twentieth-century notions about marriage and women's roles in society were still very much in evidence, the verities of the pre-Second World War years were increasingly difficult to uphold. At the very least, the court was compelled to accept the possibility that maintaining a marriage at all costs was not necessarily the best policy and that all interested parties deserved a reasonable standard of living in the aftermath of divorce. The 1959 case of *Cipperly v. Cipperly* provides one of the earliest imputations of income for a self-employed husband. Represented by J.H. Laycraft and J.C. Major, Mrs Cipperley was portrayed as living in a small and "inadequate" suite in Calgary and was "not in too good health."[36] The Court found that "She has been spending very little, and has been quite penurious."[37] In endeavouring to establish a remedy, the challenge facing the Court was to determine the husband's income, which, despite his ownership of a farm, a vehicle dealership, and a number of rental houses, was reported to be only $4,000 a year. Mr Justice R.M. Cairns rejected that figure and ruled that "I feel that I should look at his income position on the basis of estimating what his income could easily be rather than what he chooses to restrict it to."[38] Cairns concluded that the husband's assets amounted to $200,000 with an annual income of approximately $12,000. Given these estimates, the judge determined that the former Mrs Cipperly should be provided $275 per month.

Still, to the degree that legislative and judicial opinion about the legal relationship of wife and husband had shown signs of change in the quarter century after 1930, established law and the perspectives that nurtured it changed slowly. For example, the claim for loss of consortium was originally an action at common law allowing a husband to sue another man for enticing and persuading his wife to leave him, without the husband's consent, and in so doing, depriving the husband of society, comfort, and other benefits of the marital relationship. As Stella Bailey noted in her 1979 examination of consortium in the Alberta courts, one of the peculiarities of the claim was that wronged wives had, at first, no access to the claim and then, in the course of the twentieth century, uneven access.[39] The elements of a successful claim for loss of consortium were examined in the 1958 case of *Fediuk v. Lastiwka*. Mr Justice Neil Primrose held that since the common-law claim of loss of consortium had been codified in ss.31–33 of the Alberta Domestic Relations Act[40] so as to require that a husband must lose both the comfort and society of his wife in order to have a cause of action, a loss of sexual relations or housekeeping alone would not found a claim.[41] The husband in this case was unsuccessful because his wife had never actually left him; she had admitted to adulterous romps with the defendant in the Alberta rural landscape (once picking mushrooms and once picking berries) but, after being confronted and leaving for a few days to see her mother, she had returned to try to save her marriage. Given Mr Justice Primrose's conditions, the claim therefore was not made out; Mr Fediuk lost his case, but gained back his wife. And in *Wener v. Davidson*, which reads like an early Alberta sexual equality case, Mr Justice William Kirby determined in 1970 that in Alberta a wife was able to sue another woman for loss of consortium, even though the original cause of action and the provisions of the Domestic Relations Act only referenced a husband's right to sue for the loss of a wife's consortium.[42] The original writ, *de uxore abducta cum bonus viri*,[43] was historically grounded in a wife's status at law as a possession of the husband. Traditionally this of course meant that no claim was maintainable by a wife against another woman, just as a servant had no cause of action against another servant for enticing away his master. But Kirby, citing a number of Ontario and English decisions to support his ruling, determined that the statute had not removed the wife's original common-law right, and "that the conjugal consortium is mutual in kind and quality"[44] and that there should be equality between the sexes.

Thanks to the mounting rights awareness of the post-Second World War era, Albertans, like all Canadians, were participants in what has become half a century of debate, discussion, and reflection on the nature and meaning of human rights.[45] Not surprisingly the environment directly affected family law as Albertans and their courts wrestled with the implications of this heightened awareness. While during the first half-century much of the Supreme Court of Alberta's involvement with family law concerned framing jurisdictional boundaries, the second half-century would be increasingly occupied with the expansion and elaboration of those boundaries in light of new realities. Existing at the heart of how Albertans have come to view family law, questions related to the meaning of family in Alberta, the nature of support in the aftermath of a relationship's breakdown, and the nature and meaning of custody provide insight into how the Supreme Court navigated in areas unimagined by its earlier brethren.

11: THE MEANING OF FAMILY IN ALBERTA

Section 15 of the Canadian Charter of Rights and Freedoms ignited an energetic debate over the question of equality in the family. After decades of defining family by the status of its participants (married versus unmarried), the ranking of its children (legitimate versus illegitimate), and the gender of its spouses (one man and one woman versus same-sex couples), Alberta society and courts were confronted with the challenge of how to define a family unit and its members in a more functional, equality-based fashion. The coming into force of the Charter's equality provisions in 1985 placed Alberta judges, like judges across the country, in a position of having to deal with challenges to the validity of statutes in a way that they had seldom been required to do before. Yet notwithstanding Alberta's "redneck" reputation, for the most part the province's bench has assumed a modern, thoughtful, and forward-thinking approach toward the application of the Charter to family law cases.

From a historical vantage point, one of the most important changes in the definition of "family" has been the accordance of equal status to children born out of wedlock to those born of marriage. Admittedly, the changes in the province's legislative landscape were late in coming, and for much of the post-Second World War era, Alberta judges operated in what might be described as a legislative backwater. Indeed, until the proclamation of the Family Law Act in 2005, "legitimate" and "illegitimate" children were treated quite differently within Albertan family and divorce law.[46] Still, the existence of discriminatory provincial legislation did not prevent the Supreme Court of Alberta from using the Charter to craft a more even-handed judicial environment. In the relatively early Charter case of *Milne (Doherty) v. Alberta (Attorney General)*, Mr Justice David Mason tackled the differential treatment, for child support purposes, of children who were born in and out of wedlock. Specifically, the case involved a challenge to section 23(1)(b) of the Alberta Maintenance and Recovery Act, which directed that maintenance for a child born out of wedlock would end automatically with the marriage of the mother.[47] No such harsh treatments applied to children of married parents and accordingly, Mr Justice Mason struck down the section as inconsistent with section 15 of the Charter. This case marked the earliest judicial opportunity to use the Charter in order to treat children in Alberta the same, regardless of their status as "legitimate" or "illegitimate." On another front, even though the Federal Child

Support Guidelines for unmarried couples had existed since 1997, there were no Alberta Child Support Guidelines in place until the October 2005 proclamation of the provincial Family Law Act. Despite the eight-year lacuna, Alberta judges had no trouble ensuring that the Federal Child Support Guidelines were applied to cases involving children of *unmarried* parents, using the approach outlined by Justice Brian Burrows in *M. (T.C.) v. U. (L.)*:

> Since the parties were never married the Divorce Act has no application. Accordingly I am not bound by the Federal Child Support Guidelines in this matter. However the practice has developed of using the Guidelines in the context of the provincial Parentage and Maintenance Act to set the level of maintenance on the reasonable theory that it would be illogical and unjust to apply different regimes in determining the level of child support payable depending on whether or not the parents were married to each other.[48]

Alberta's Court of Appeal later confirmed this decision in *Cavanaugh v. Ziegler*.[49]

In tune with the tone set by the Supreme Court of Alberta in the 1990s, Madam Justice Joanne Veit rejected differential treatment in the payment of child support in the 1995 case of *C.M. v. C.M.*[50] In that case, a father had proposed a different level of support for his single "legitimate" versus single "illegitimate" offspring, an approach soundly rejected by the Court. Veit wrote:

> There may indeed have been a time when the law recognized that a distinction should be made between "legitimate" families and other families. It was believed that social policy should support legitimate families. The mother who agreed to have children with a man she knew had a legitimate family was assumed to be accepting, on behalf of the children born of that union, a lower level of financial and other commitment for those children. The law does not currently maintain that point of view.[51]

Four years later in *Janfield v. Foote*, Veit was asked by court administrators whether or not her written decision under the Parentage and Maintenance Act should remain unpublished.[52] The historical shame associated with illegitimate children found its way into section 23(3) of the Act, which provided for restriction on publication of decisions related to children of unmarried parents. In her delightfully balanced decision, Justice Veit decried the "lingering whiff of disapproval of such family structures" and wrote of the importance of treating all parents and children equally, regardless of parental marital status.[53] She directed that her decision be published in the same fashion as any other family law decision, notwithstanding the statute.

One of the last Alberta cases dealing with the differential treatment of children born of married versus unmarried parents is that of the Alberta Court of Appeal in *T.(P.) v. B.(R.)*.[54] Rather than simply declaring the Parentage and Maintenance Act unconstitutional, Mr Justice Jack Watson decided to read a right of support into the old Maintenance Order Act for adult children of unmarried parents. The rather tortuous and convoluted reasoning at both the Chambers level and on appeal in order to comply with Charter values while not striking down offensive legislation is worthy of note. Still, despite the efforts at circumnavigation, it was certain that the historic environment for Alberta family law legislation left a great deal to be desired. As the late Jay McLeod noted in his annotation to *T.(P.) v. B.(R.)*,

> Historically, Alberta family law legislation has been among the most reactionary legislation in the country. Alberta appears to be the last Canadian province to move away from illegitimacy legislation and to recognise that a man should not have reduced responsibility towards his children merely because he was not married to the mother. Maintaining a distinction between support rights for children born inside and outside marriage suggests that there is something almost illegal about extramarital sexual relations. Any idea that punishing an unwed mother by denying her the money she needs to care for her child will somehow discourage other women from engaging in extramarital sex ignores reality. The historical and religious values used to justify illegitimacy laws have long since been rejected in a spousal support context, so that it seemed inconceivable that anyone would suggest that they continue to apply to limit a child's right to support from a biological parent.[55]

Fortunately, the 2005 proclamation of the Alberta Family Law Act brought most of this discussion to a close.

A. *Cohabitational and Same-Sex Relationships in Alberta*

While unmarried parents have had the right to apply for child support since the 1969 passage of the Maintenance and Recovery Act, there was no entitlement to spousal support for common-law spouses in Alberta until Mr Justice Peter Power of the Court of Queen's Bench of Alberta decided to read such a right into the Alberta Domestic Relations Act in the 1996 case of *Taylor v. Rossu*.[56] This case involved a couple who had started cohabiting in 1964 and lived together in a common-law relationship for 30 years before separating. Justice Power drew on *Armstrong v. McLaughlin Estate*, the only prior Alberta case extending equal rights to unmarried spouses under the Family Relief Act, in support of his reasoning.[57] The decision in *Taylor v. Rossu* was upheld by the Alberta Court of Appeal, which offered a lengthy and in-depth analysis of equality rights in the family law context.[58] Adopting a modern trend, the Court relied upon statistical studies on the growing number of cohabiting partners affected by the lack of legislation in Alberta, and engaged in a rigorous equality analysis. Several years passed before the Alberta legislature amended the Domestic Relations Act to include a right of support for common-law couples, but the Alberta courts had forced these reforms, ending decades of second-class treatment for common-law couples in this area of the law.

Gays and lesbians across Canada have used the Charter's equality provisions in court to define, enlarge, and enforce their individual rights. Frequently, these challenges have taken place in the family law context. And as much as some might characterize Alberta as a bulwark of legal conservatism, Alberta judges have not, for the most part, shied away from the use of the Charter when necessary to uphold the equality rights of gays and lesbians in the family context.[59]

In 1999, in one of the first prominent cases involving a same-sex couple in Alberta courts, *Re C.*, Mr Justice Peter Martin found that it was reasonable and just that children of same-sex couples have the same legal rights associated with private adoptions as would children of heterosexual couples.[60] He also found that there was a significant emotional benefit to both the child and adoptive parent in having legal recognition of their relationship and that that benefit should be available to a child of a same-sex couple. This decision put the end to an era when heterosexual couples in Alberta were the only ones capable of adopting children. Two years later, in *Johnson v. Sand*, Justice Delmar Perras found that sections 1, 3(3), and 4 of the Intestate

Succession Act violated section 15(1) of the Charter by excluding both opposite and same-sex common-law partners from recovery from the estate of a deceased partner.[61] Justice Perras ordered a temporary suspension of the declaration of invalidity of the Act's impugned provisions for a period of nine months. The decision gained substantial coverage in the press, painting the picture of a rather normal couple who were deprived of rights of intestacy by virtue only of their sexual orientation and the lack of a formal marriage binding them. *Johnson v. Sand* was part of a growing wave of same-sex/Charter litigation building across the country on this and other issues.

In the most recent case involving a same-sex couple, *Fraess v. Alberta*, Justice C. Phillip Clarke of the Alberta Court of Queen's Bench reviewed the provisions of the newly passed Family Law Act.[62] In this case, a lesbian married couple purchased sperm from an anonymous donor and one of them underwent artificial insemination, resulting in a child born in 2005. Section 13(2)(b) of the Family Law Act defines parental status where parents have used artificial insemination with gender-specific language ("mother" and "father"). Accordingly, the only way the female Petitioner could obtain parental status was to go through a step-parent adoption. On application for an Order declaring section 13(2)(b) of the Act in violation of section 15 of the Charter, Justice Clarke struck down the offending sections, and read into the section the words necessary to make it conform to the Charter, replacing "male person" and "father" with "parent." These cases individually and cumulatively have changed the landscape for Albertan same-sex couples. The Alberta courts have certainly not been trailblazers in this area, but when the cases have made their way to court, Alberta judges have been more than willing to use the equality provisions of the Charter to expand the definition of "family" in Alberta. Alberta judges were relieved of the obligation to deal with the issue of same-sex marriage by the Alberta government's change of heart in 2005, when it reluctantly agreed to allow same-sex marriages to take place under the existing Alberta Marriage Act.[63] While that political decision "closed the circle," it had been preceded by these key judicial decisions directing equal treatment for gays and lesbians.

B. *The Question of Child and Spousal Support*

What difference have the Alberta courts made in terms of child and spousal support? Once again, despite the province's reputation, Alberta judges have played a crucial role in the development of the modern support landscape in Canada. In some ways, they have helped set the national standard for the modern child and spousal support obligation. This happened only recently; in the early years of Alberta's legal history, Alberta judges frequently made relatively parsimonious awards without articulating their reasons for quantum or duration, or critically evaluating the impact of their decision on payors, recipients, and children.[64] Still, a number of Alberta judgments in the area of spousal support have iconic status. For example, in the 1970 case of *Feldman v. Feldman,* the wife was granted both lump sum and periodic support, something expressly allowed for in the 1968 federal Divorce Act but seldom ordered.[65] The award of $500 per month and $85,000 lump sum to Mrs Feldman was left undisturbed on appeal. Mr Feldman, who enjoyed a net worth of approximately $1.75 million, was ultimately unsuccessful in his bid to deny any support to his wife because of her conduct. Within several months of *Feldman,* Mr Justice André Dechene presided over *Wener v. Wener,* where the husband, represented by Arnold F. Moir, Q.C., had a net worth of between $1 and $2 million.[66] Mrs Wener and her husband had lived a luxurious lifestyle, but at the end of the marriage she had $8,000, a Buick vehicle, and "a large quantity of furs and jewels which have high intrinsic value, but which are not capable of attracting income."[67] Like Mrs Feldman, Mrs Wener was awarded a lump sum of $85,000 and monthly support of $500. Both these cases probably appeared generous at the time; in retrospect, they demonstrate the huge unfairness of the law to wives, who ended up with very little compared with their husbands after long-term marriages.

In the 1976 decision in *Kraus v. Kraus,* however, the Court cautioned against allowing lump sum spousal support to be awarded as a way of redistributing assets.[68] Alberta judges in this pre-matrimonial property legislation era were probably straining to achieve some measure of economic fairness, wanting to see wives have some access to something more than a monthly allowance. The decision in *Kraus,* however, was a stern and oft-repeated reminder to judges across the country of their obligation not to go beyond the jurisdiction granted to them in the Divorce Act to award "maintenance." Some of the same concerns about spousal support were echoed in 1991 in *Stricker v. Stricker,* which reminded judges that future changes of circumstance could not be anticipated by lump sum awards.[69]

A more modern tone emerged in the late 1980s when Alberta judges began to consider the post-separation economic consequences of the roles adopted by spouses during a marriage. In the 1987 decision of *Brookes v. Strohschein,* Mr Justice John MacKenzie held that a wife who had contributed to her husband's career development, or a wife whose earning potential had been eroded, restricted, or deferred by reason of homemaking duties, was entitled to have those circumstances taken into account in the determination of the right to, amount, and duration of spousal support.[70] This case represents an early Alberta articulation of the purposive and quite progressive sections of the (then new) 1985 Divorce Act. The decision may also have signalled a turning point in how the Court viewed questions of support and, within the decade that followed, Alberta judges began to demonstrate an appetite for making new law. Thus the Alberta Court of Appeal broke through a glass ceiling in spousal support with its 1991 decision in *Rosario v. Rosario,* concluding that a wife who had remarried would still be eligible for spousal support, if the original award was founded on a compensatory rationale.[71] Rosario was one of the first cases to openly reject the *dum sola et casta* dictates from centuries of earlier support law.

Since her appointment in 1981, Madam Justice Joanne Veit has been one of the most prodigious writers on family law topics. Her 1991 decision in *Row v. Row* exemplified a new approach to the consideration of entitlement to spousal support.[72] On an interim application, she recognized the need for more than a mere subsistence amount of spousal support and awarded the wife $5,000 per month. She engaged in a broad analysis of the factors and objectives of spousal support under the Divorce Act well before the landmark decision of the Supreme Court of Canada in *Moge v. Moge.*[73] Veit's decision in *Row* became a sign of things to come, and a signal that the quantum of support had to be considered in the overall context of the parties' standard of living, rather than merely a modest allowance—new thinking indeed. Post-*Moge* decisions such as *Wooldridge v. Wooldridge* established the willingness of Alberta judges to expand upon the more modern theories of spousal support entitlement coming out of *Moge.*[74] Instead of cutting off support on a three-year "review," the Court considered the impact of a 24-year marriage and continued the support in an increased sum for an indefinite period.

Judges in Alberta have also been responsible for ensuring an adherence to the modern child support obligation. Two decisions in 1992, *Eddy v. Eddy* and *Dumas v. Dumas,* both written by Madam Justice Marguerite Trussler, involved the staying of divorce applications until such time as appropriate child support arrangements had been made under section 11(1)(b) of the Divorce Act.[75] Justice Trussler wrote, "The materials before the court raise the suspicion that the Respondent deliberately left his employment to avoid providing child support. Such conduct, if true, can only be described as irresponsible and deplorable. A parent has a legal and moral obligation to support a child. Faced with this obligation, a parent should not voluntarily leave his or her employment without other equivalent employment already secured."[76] These cases sent out important signals to the Bar and to the public about the primacy of the child-support obligation and the Court's unwillingness to allow individuals to flout that obligation.

The issue of support for adult children has generated a great deal of judicial writing across the country, and a number of Alberta decisions have had enduring value. Justice Veit's decisions in the 1994 case of *N.(P.F.) v. N.(A.)* determined that a child could move from being a "child of the marriage" to outside that category and back in again for support purposes.[77] In the same year, Justice Ronald Berger heard *Baker v. Baker* and held that children who cannot obtain employment because of the economic climate should not be distinguished from children who cannot provide for themselves because they are in school; both may be entitled to support under section 2 of the Divorce Act.[78] And in 1999 and 2000, the late Madam Justice Cecilia Johnstone authored two thoughtful decisions contributing to law in this area: *Sherlow v. Zubko* and *Wahl v. Wahl*.[79] In *Sherlow v. Zubko,* she confirmed that the onus of establishing entitlement to support for adult children lies on the person claiming the support, but that the status "child of the marriage" is a question of dependency, not age. *Wahl* is frequently cited as one of the best decisions on this topic, and includes a discussion of the legal status of an adult child, student loans, the obligations of adult children, and the thorny area of parental rejection. Madam Justice Johnstone died in April 2006, but during her too few years on the bench, she was viewed by many family law practitioners as one of the best judges before whom to appear because of her energy, her aptitude for family law matters, and her willingness to tackle tough issues with intelligence and compassion.

Probably one of the most important child-support decisions authored by Alberta judges is the decision of the Alberta Court of Appeal in *Levesque v. Levesque*.[80] Child support determinations prior to *Levesque* were characterized by uncertainty, intuitive reasoning, inconsistency, and lack of rationale. *Levesque* emerged as a made-in-Alberta guide to the calculation of child support for the three years leading to the implementation of the Federal Child Support Guidelines in 1997. Its impact was felt across the country, and it is a high-water mark in thinking about child support awards.[81] The decision directed judges to determine the child-related portion of the parents' budgets, to apportion those expenses in proportion to their respective incomes, and to adjust the non-custodial parent's share for the pre-1997 taxability/deductibility of same. The case is truly noteworthy for a number of reasons:

1. The Alberta Court of Appeal articulates the principle that, to the greatest possible extent, children should not be financially disadvantaged because of marriage breakdown.

2. There is not only reference to, but reliance upon a host of studies, reports, and discussion papers about the economics of family spending patterns and the cost of raising children in the modern era.

3. Judges are given a "litmus test" in assessing the reasonableness of amounts needed to properly support children; while the court makes it clear that such figures are estimates only, its willingness to adopt a formulaic approach reflects judicial concern about the inadequacy of awards in the past and a desire to bring some consistency and predictability to this area of the law.[82]

4. There is a rather pointed admonition to "out-of-touch" judges to "get with the program." Family law has hit the modern age, and the old ways of randomly dealing with family law cases (each judge differently exercising his or her own unfettered discretion) are simply not going to pass muster any further.

Levesque was a bridge between the older era of intuitive decision-making about child support and the modern era of guidelines, formulas, and presumptions. Alberta courts led the way in the sort of thinking that produced the highly successful Federal Child Support Guidelines by 1997.

Linked to the Court's determination of the quantum of ongoing child support is the issue of retroactive support. Specifically, to what extent should judges award support for the period predating a formal court hearing? In the pre-Guideline era and before the decision in *Haismann v. Haismann*, retroactive awards under section 17 of the Divorce Act were frequently granted to vacate court-ordered arrears of support.[83] But in 1995, with the decision of the Alberta Court of

Appeal in *MacMinn v. MacMinn*, the scales of justice tipped slightly, and payees acquired the right to seek retroactive support.[84] And thus developed a line of cases from both the Alberta Court of Queen's Bench and the Alberta Court of Appeal between 1991 and 2005 leading to the issuance of a series of groundbreaking decisions known as the "Alberta Trilogy"[85] in February 2005. These consolidated decisions directed Chambers and trial judges to grant retroactive child support, regardless of notice, request, need, or blameworthy conduct, based on presumptive entitlement under the Child Support Guidelines. A fourth decision (*Hiemstra*) was joined on appeal to the Supreme Court of Canada. Two of the decisions were upheld and two were set aside,[86] rejecting some of the Alberta Court of Appeal's reasoning. Nonetheless, this important area of family law was developed in large part as a result of the long line of decisions authored by Alberta courts.

c. Custody: Moving from Parental Rights to "Best Interests" of Children

In 100 years of Alberta legal history, we have seen an extraordinary shift in the ways in which judges thought about the needs of children when their parents have separated or divorced. From an earlier Victorian era when children were viewed as little more than chattels, appendages, or rewards in their parents' divorces, we have moved to a child-centred approach in which parental interests are secondary to the well-being of their offspring. As early as 1923, in *O'Leary v. O'Leary*, we start to see an example of a more progressive approach toward the issue of custody.[87] In that case Mr Justice Beck ruled:

> The paramount consideration is the welfare of the children; subsidiary to this and as a means of arriving at the best answer to that question are the conduct of the respective parents, the wishes of the mother as well as the father, the ages and sexes of the children, the proposals of each parent for the maintenance and education of the children; their station and aptitudes and prospects in life; the pecuniary circumstances of the father and the mother—not for the purpose of giving the custody to the parent in the better financial position to maintain and educate the children, but for the purpose of fixing an amount to be paid by one or both parents for the maintenance of the children.[88]

This thoughtful analysis was years ahead of its time and anticipated the development of the "best interests" test fifty years later.

There are a number of factors that have contributed to this huge paradigm shift, not only in Alberta but in all Canadian provinces. First, in society generally, there is an acknowledgment of the rights of children as individual human beings rather than lesser beings under the control and essentially the ownership of adults within their families. The unanimous adoption of the Convention on the Rights of the Child on 20 November 1989 by the United Nations General Assembly and its subsequent ratification by member states formalized this growing awareness of the importance of children in their own right.[89] The principles guiding the Convention were the primacy of children's best interests in decision-making concerning them, the entitlement of children to protection, and the need to take into account the views of children in matters affecting them. These principles have infused the modern judicial outlook in dealing with child custody disputes. Second, judges no longer assume that they are intuitive repositories of wisdom in decisions about custody of children. Modern judges acknowledge the importance of drawing on the vast stores of expertise in literature on child development, family dynamics, parental pathology, and children's needs. Since the 1970s, the modern judge has been prepared to inform herself and strengthen her decision-making in this area through judicial education, the use of expert witnesses, and at times the appointment of *amicus curiae*. Judicial knowledge has been strengthened as well by an increasingly specialized and skilled matrimonial bar. Third, there has been a significant increase in the number of women judges sitting on our bench since the 1970s. This development has brought a level of experience, knowledge, and interest in family law matters generally that did not characterize the male-dominated bench in the earlier part of the century. This occurred at the same time as family law began to gain respect as an important and worthwhile branch of law.

Finally, we have seen a degree of judicial activism in Alberta to improve ways in which child custody cases have been resolved, either extrajudicially or in the court. Madam Justice Marguerite Trussler was appointed to the Alberta Court of Queen's Bench in November 1986 and, in addition to offering leadership on family matters generally, she has spearheaded initiatives dealing with children (mandatory parental education seminars, specialized family law chambers, the introduction of practice notes concerning allegations of sexual abuse, high-conflict custody and access cases, as well as case management initiatives). The late Chief Justice Tevie H. Miller was responsible for holding the first informal family law "mini-trials," which have developed into institutionalized Judicial Dispute Resolution processes held by members of the Court of Queen's Bench.[90] This pragmatic activism on the part of a number of members of our Court is in stark contrast to the traditional judicial rule, which was limited to formal adjudication of child custody disputes. Alberta has been a leader in implementing court-based initiatives that have been adopted by many other provinces.

A survey of Alberta cases reveals that there were relatively few reported cases on custody in the early part of the twentieth century. Where the early cases are reported, we see a judicial emphasis on conduct as paramount in determining who should "win" custody of children. "Good" marital conduct is rewarded; "bad" marital conduct can mean you "lose" the care of your children. Only in the mid-1970s did Alberta judges start adopting a more modern tone in their decision-making by concentrating less on parental rights and more on a genuine exploration of what a child's best interests might require. Not surprisingly, as the court began this undertaking, the rulings did not necessarily follow a singular or consistent course. In a relatively conservative 1978 finding, Justice J.W.H. Milvain, Chief Justice of the Trial Division of the Alberta Supreme Court, held in *Barber v. Barber* that children have a natural right to be brought up in a two-parent home.[91] Accordingly, he found that when a parent broke up the home by his or her wilful misconduct, such a parent was in breach of an important duty of parenthood. Such selfish conduct indicated to Justice Milvain that the actor had put gratification of his or her desires or passions before the welfare of the children. In this case, Mrs Barber had made her bed and was probably going to have to lie in it. She would not succeed in her claim for custody of her child for, as Milvain reasoned, "Her course indicates that at least on occasion she was prepared to follow her more selfish desires, her more personal interests than of sacrificing [sic] her interests to those of her child. I therefore feel that this child can receive the greatest contribution that she may receive from her more dedicated father by being in the father's custody and still at the same time receiving the contribution that can be made by her mother through access."[92]

A year later in *Mullen v. Mullen,* custody of two children was given to the father primarily because the mother had a new male companion.[93] Mr Justice Kirby indicated that "I find it most natural that the father, Mr Mullen, should react in the way he did to the fact that his wife was having an intimate association with another man and I find it most natural that Tim, a 13-year old boy, should react in the same way in which he did to that association."[94] In so doing the court rejected an expert's report that expressed a concern that the father was "accelerating and accentuating Tim's resentment by disparaging the boyfriend and the mother's moral character to Tim directly or indirectly." The judge relied in part upon his brief meeting with the children in the retiring room, and in his decision expressed the grave weight on his shoulders: "I, as a parent myself and as a judge, am deeply sensitive to the claims and to the profoundly held feelings of the parents."[95] Mr Mullen's deeply held feelings about his wife's new companion had found a most receptive audience. And as late as 1988 in *Davidovich v. Davidovich*, MacKenzie J. awarded custody of the two-year-old and the five-year-old to the father, who had come home unexpectedly from Fort McMurray and had found his wife involved with another man.[96] Notwithstanding the father's lack of involvement in parenting prior to the separation, he was granted custody. As Karen M. Munroe points out:

> Interestingly, MacKenzie J also refers to the fact that immediately before and at the time of the separation, the housekeeping care by the mother left a great deal to be desired. This lack of cleanliness was referred to no less than three times in this short judgment; the fact that the father forcibly removed the children from their home was mentioned once.[97]

This line of cases underlines the great importance of parental conduct "in the kitchen or in the bedroom."

Yet during the 1970s, the Court also provided evidence of moving toward a broader view of the interests at play in custody cases. Thus in the 1972 case of *Barka v. Barka*, Mr Justice Alan Joseph Cullen of the Alberta Supreme Court Trial Division held that the happiness of a child was not of primary importance in custody cases, but rather it was the welfare of the child that was the key issue.[98] Three years later Mr Justice D.C. MacDonald of the Alberta Supreme Court Trial Division held that a child's wishes were to be taken into account in custody determinations where the child was of an age to appreciate the issues involved. He also expressed the Court's sentiment that it was inexcusable when a custodial parent put the children in a difficult position by treating access with the other parent negatively. Access rights also began to be seen not just as a parental right but as part of a child's right to have a meaningful relationship with both parents, and this principle was articulated in the 1974 case of *Csicsiri v. Csicsiri*, where the Court held that access to a parent should only be denied in extreme cases.[99] And the 1978 case of *Adams v. McLeod* is a frequently cited authority for the proposition that the best interests of the children is the sole criterion for any judicial disposition respecting custody and access.[100] The case also reaffirmed that it is the trial judge who is the best one to make that determination. It would not be until 1990, however, that Madam Justice Ellen Picard, in the case of *Starko v. Starko*, would articulate exactly what was meant by a child's best interests.[101] These objective criteria now form the basis of most counsel's arguments on issues of primary care and have been frequently cited by many other courts.

Not surprisingly, as the Court navigated through the evolving custody environment of the 1970s and 1980s and, in the process, adopted notions such as "a child's best interests," assumptions about which parent was best situated to protect and further those interests was opened for examination. One of the key notions revisited during this period was that of the "tender years doctrine." Defined by Karen M. Munroe, the tender year doctrine meant that "...older, employable, male children stayed in the custody of the father. Thus, the statutory right to apply later became a preference in favour of mother-custody for a child of 'tender years,' that is, for a child under the age of seven."[102] Emerging in the middle of the nineteenth century, the tender years doctrine had signalled an important departure from the older notion that fathers ought to be granted custody as a matter of right.[103] But as the Court examined the breadth and depth of custody, the tender years doctrine was criticized in the 1983 case of *R. v. R.* heard in the Court of Appeal. Speaking for the Court, Mr Justice Roger Kerans wrote that the doctrine "...confuses cultural traditions with human nature; it also traps women in a social role not necessarily of their choosing, while at the same time freeing men: if only a mother can nurture a child of tender years, then it is the clear duty of the mother to do so; because the father cannot do it, he is neither obliged nor entitled even to try."[104] Further, "Taken in this context, the remarks made by judges in the past about 'tender years principle' do not come to much. All that can be said in this age of changing attitudes is that judges must decide each case on its own merits, with due regard to the capacities and attitudes of each parent...and we must remember that our role is not to reform society; our role is to make the best of a bad deal for the child who comes before us for help."[105] Following *R. v. R.*, and with no presumptions about gender to guide them, Alberta judges were left to deal with custody adjudication purely on a case-by-case basis. It was therefore noteworthy when the Alberta Court of Appeal issued its 1990 decision in *K.(M.M.) v. K.(U.)*.[106] Justices Milton Harradence, Joseph Stratton, and Allen Sulatycky placed emphasis on the primary caregiver role in determining the child's best interests.[107] While the Court did not enunciate a presumption in favour of the primary caregiver, this case signals an important recognition that the work done by primary caregivers, most of whom were mothers, was deserving of recognition and weight in a supposedly de-gendered parenting environment.[108]

One of the other innovations of the 1970s was that of awarding joint custody, which, at minimum, required parents to co-operate and consult on major decisions concerning their children. This also provided a means whereby the children could maintain a relationship with both parents. While sole custody orders were historically the norm until the late 1970s, joint custody orders seemed to appeal to many judges in Alberta and across the country as a way to ease the divisiveness of the divorce process on children. Orchestrating such arrangements while attempting to convince divorced parents to act civilly was, however, another matter. With the introduction of the Divorce Act of 1985, judges were provided some useful leverage in encouraging parents. Specifically, section 16(10) provided that "the Court shall give effect to the principle that a child of the marriage should have as much contact with each spouse as is consistent with the best interests of the child and, for that purpose, shall take into consideration the willingness of the person for whom custody is sought to facilitate such contact." Dubbed the "friendly parent rule," section 16(10) was applied swiftly and energetically by Justice Marguerite Trussler in *Tremblay v. Tremblay*, where she removed custody from a recalcitrant and unco-operative mother and reposed it in the father as a way of ensuring that the parent who was most willing to facilitate access would get custody.[109] Similarly, in *Burwash v. Mirosh*, Justice Trussler held that even when there was a restraining order against the father, joint custody was still preferable and appropriate as long as the order was properly structured.[110] She expresses cynicism about the view that joint custody cannot be awarded where parents cannot co-operate, reasoning that a failure to award joint custody frequently rewards bad behaviour on the part of one of the parents. And in another instance, the same judge awarded an order for parallel parenting[111] in *Broder v. Broder.*[112] Notwithstanding the outrageous behaviour of the father, Justice Trussler imposed an order for parallel parenting to "bring out the best" in both parents while minimizing contact between them, expecting no flexibility or negotiation, but nonetheless maximizing time between parent and child. This case is but one in a long line of Justice Trussler's ongoing attempts to make parents "behave better." These cases signalled that the Court would use its ultimate powers to implement the friendly parent rule.

And in what is perhaps the final Alberta case on the issue of joint versus sole custody, Madam Justice Anne Russell in *L.(V.) v. L.(D.)* discussed the interface between the federal Divorce Act and the Alberta Domestic Relations Act and logically concluded that the rights of joint guardianship enjoyed by married parents cannot and should not be easily curtailed by an order of sole custody under the Divorce Act.[113] Her thoughtful writing on this complicated and difficult topic is a closing bookend to a long-standing debate in the courts over when courts should award joint custody versus sole custody:

> Such judicial and legislative efforts to negate assumptions that custody is an all or nothing proposition underscore the import of the concept of residual guardianship and reaffirm the enduring rights of non-custodial parents beyond that of day to day physical custody of the child. Even authors who do not view the concept of joint custody as the solution to the problem of maintaining the involvement of divorced fathers, "cautiously support a presumption of joint legal custody largely on symbolic grounds."[114]

This is indeed a bookend, given that use of the word "custody" is now considered archaic and old-fashioned, especially with the introduction of the term "parenting orders" in Alberta's new Family Law Act.[115]

CONCLUSION

The history of family law in Alberta between 1907 and 2006 tracks the enormous changes in family form and function during that period. Reading the cases offers rare insights into general societal attitudes and assumptions about gender, morality, economics, religion, power, and the role of the individual within the family unit. As with the debates openly held in the provincial legislature and the federal Parliament over legislative reform, the voices of judges in these cases reflect a constantly changing familial landscape. Powerful shifts in the roles held by women and men, both inside and outside the family, have propelled many of the changes in judicial thinking about topics such as care of children, economic fairness, entitlement to property, and divorce. While operating within the constraints of the provincial and federal family law legislation in force at the time, Alberta judges have engaged in a wide-ranging process of examination and interpretation of the law related to family matters.

What, if anything, is unique about the work of the Alberta courts? On the one hand, judges across the country have moved with the times and have participated in the creation of a modern body of Canadian family law to fit the realities of the contemporary family. In the early years, judges in all jurisdictions were focussed almost exclusively on the formalities of marriage, the arcane remedies derived from British law, fault-finding, condonation, connivance, and collusion. Judges did more than simply adjudicate cases involving individual husbands and wives; they articulated the views of their class and their time on moral issues and appropriate social and familial behaviour. Clearly, the granting or withholding of remedies such as divorce, alimony, or the custody of children was but one way of reaffirming certain core values operating in society at the time. In this way, Alberta judges were no different from their brethren across the country. But on the other hand, the Alberta courts have consistently "punched above their weight." Leading decisions on divorce, custody of children, and child and spousal support have been authored by Alberta judges at all levels, disproportionately so to the population of the province.

Whereas the earlier part of the century was dominated by procedural issues and the formal marital status of litigants, the cases in the last 30 years have been heavy on substance and have attempted to focus on the practical needs of spouses and children going through difficult transitions. Rather than passive adjudications, a number of Alberta decisions reflect a forward-looking, progressive judicial temperament in the field of family law, and at times a bold appetite for breaking new ground: legal sodbusting, perhaps. This chapter has only touched on some family law cases from the Alberta Supreme Court, Court of Queen's Bench, and Court of Appeal; there are many other cases and issues deserving of discussion and review. This is a challenge that might be taken up by those with an eye not only on where the court has been, but where it might travel as it moves into its second century.

NOTES

1. The term *Supreme Court of Alberta* is used in this chapter as a shorthand reference that encompasses Alberta's Court of Appeal and Alberta's Queen's Bench, but the *Court of Appeal* and the *Court of Queen's Bench* are used for cases that occurred after the organizational reforms of 1978. For events prior to these reforms, references are made to the Supreme Court of Alberta, Trial or Supreme Court of Alberta, Appeal. See Jonathan Swainger's comments on these changes in his introduction to this volume, "History and Authority: The Past and Present in the Supreme Court of Alberta."
2. *Murdoch v. Murdoch, Alberta Reports* [cited hereafter AR] 95 (1989): 119. Although this decision was issued on 24 February 1971, it was not actually reported until 1989.
3. *Western Weekly Reports* [cited hereafter WWR] 1 (1974): 361.
4. Laskin's dissent is recorded in WWR 1 (1974): 361 (Supreme Court of Canada). It was only with the passage of Alberta's Matrimonial Property Act of 1979 that "mere household duties were recognised as having as much value as paid employment." See Philip Girard, *Bora Laskin: Bringing Law to Life* (Toronto: Osgoode Society for Canadian Legal History, 2005), 399-402 for a discussion of the *Murdoch* case and Laskin's dissent. Also see Carol Rogerson, "From Murdoch to Leatherdale: The Uneven Course of Bora Laskin's Family Law Decisions," in *University of Toronto Law Journal* 35 (1985): 499-505.
5. *Alberta Law Reports* [cited hereafter ALR], 2nd ser., 1: 135; WWR 1 (1977): 16; AR 1: 378.
6. Divorce in early twentieth-century Canada is examined in James G. Snell, *In the Shadow of the Law: Divorce in Canada, 1900-1939* (Toronto: University of Toronto Press, 1991).
7. Power, W. Kent, *The Law and Practice Relating to Divorce and Other Matrimonial Causes in Canada* (Calgary: Burroughs & Co., 1948).
8. See "William Legh Walsh," in *Lords of the Western Bench: A Biographical History of the Supreme and District Courts of Alberta, 1876-1990*, Louis A. Knafla and Richard Klumpenhouwer [citer hereafter *Lords of the Western Bench*, Knafla and Klumpenhouwer] (Calgary: The Legal Archives Society of Alberta, 1997), 187-89.
9. *Board v. Board*, WWR 2 (1918): 633, Alberta Supreme Court, Appeal Division; *Appeal Cases* (1919): 956.
10. Snell, *In the Shadow of the Law*, 54-63, discussed the national context and debate over divorce during these years.
11. *Coleman v. Coleman*, WWR 3 (1919): 490, para. 2.
12. As cited in Snell, *In the Shadow of the Law*, 80.
13. As cited in Snell, *In the Shadow of the Law*, 80-81. Also see Wilbur Bowker, "Procedure in Divorce Actions in Alberta," *Alberta Law Quarterly* 3 (1938-39): 54.
14. *B. v. B.*, WWR 3 (1919): 894.
15. Terry L. Chapman, "Problems in Researching Western Canadian Legal History: Wife Beating in Alberta, 1905-1920," in *Papers Presented at the 1987 Canadian Law in History Conference* (Ottawa: Carleton University Press, 1987), 187.

16 Christine Davies, *Power on Divorce and Other Matrimonial Causes*, 3rd ed., vol. 1: *Divorce* (Toronto: Carswell, 1976), 2. Also see Bowker, "Procedure in Divorce Actions in Alberta," 54.
17 Snell, *In the Shadow of the Law*, 54-65.
18 *Walkden v. Walkden*, WWR 1 (1922): 238.
19 *Spring v. Spring*, WWR 2 (1926): 78. And in the 1938 case of *Peters v. Peters*, the offending husband had slept with one of the wife's sisters and had a child with her, but he was taken back by his wife and forgiven. However, when he was subsequently charged with having carnal knowledge of the wife's other young sister, aged fourteen years, her forgiveness was wiped out and she was granted her divorce; see *Peters v. Peters*, WWR 3 (1938): 303. And while judges usually need evidence of adultery, the fact that a husband had syphilis while his wife was free of any venereal disease was sufficient evidence of his adultery for the divorce in *L. v. L.* to be granted in 1943; see *L. v. L.*, WWR 2 (1943): 136.
20 WWR 1 (1928): 383; *Dominion Law Reports* [cited hereafter DLR] 1 (1928): 934.
21 Snell, *In the Shadow of the Law*, 96.
22 See generally, Howard and Tamara Palmer, "The Black Experience in Alberta," in *Peoples of Alberta—Portraits of Cultural Diversity*, ed. Howard and Tamara Palmer (Saskatoon: Western Producer Prairie Books, 1985), 365-93.
23 *Lloyd v. Lloyd*, *Western Law Reporter* [cited hereafter WLR] 26 (1914): 772 (Supreme Court of Alberta, Trial Division); var'd WWR 6 (1914): 1387, DLR 19: 502 (Supreme Court of Alberta, Appeal Division). See "David Lynch Scott," in *Lords of the Western Bench*, Knafla and Klumpenhouwer, 163-64.
24 As in many of these older cases, the names and ages of the children are never mentioned.
25 *Lloyd v. Lloyd*, WLR 26 (1914): 772.
26 See "Nicholas Du Bois Dominic Beck," in *Lords of the Western Bench*, Knafla and Klumpenhouwer, 17-18.
27 *Board v. Board*, WWR 2 (1918): 662.
28 *McPherson v. McPherson*, WWR 1 (1933): 321 (Alta SC, AD); WWR 1 (1936); alt citation *Appeal Cases* 1 (1936): 177 (PC). The *McPherson* case has not attracted sustained attention, in part because it was followed closely by the *Brownlee* case. For a brief note, see Carl F. Betke, "The United Farmers of Alberta, 1921-1935," in *Society and Politics in Alberta—Research Papers*, ed. Carlo Caldarola (Toronto: Methuen, 1979), 28. The *Brownlee* case concerned allegations of seduction aimed at Premier J.E. Brownlee in 1934, see Thomas Thorner and J.E. Reddekoff, "A Question of Seduction: The Case of MacMillan v Brownlee," in *Alberta Law Review* [cited hereafter Alta LR] 20 (1982): 447-74 and Patrick Brode, *Courted and Abandoned—Seduction in Canadian Law* (Toronto: The Osgoode Society for Canadian Legal History, 2002), 149-73. Also see Dale Gibson, "The Supreme Court of Alberta meets the Supreme Law of Canada," in this volume.
29 "while she lives single and chaste"
30 *Olynyk v. Olynyk*, AR 26 (1932): 485 and WWR 1 (1932): 825.
31 Ibid., at 487.
32 *Olsen v. Olsen*, WWR 3 (1946): 389.
33 See "Clinton James Ford," in *Lords of the Western Bench*, Knafla and Klumpenhouwer, 43-44.

34 *Rudiak v. The Public Trustee*, WWR 25 (1958): 38.
35 See "Mr. Justice Harold William Riley," in *Lords of the Western Bench*, Knafla and Klumpenhouwer, 159-60.
36 *Cipperly v. Cipperly*, WWR 30 (1959): 226.
37 Ibid., 227.
38 Ibid., 229.
39 Stella Bailey, "A Married Woman's Right of Action for Loss of Consortium in Alberta" [cited hereafter Bailey, "A Married Woman's Right of Action"], in ALR 17 (1979): 513-31.
40 Statutes of Alberta 1942 c.300.
41 *Fediak v. Lastiwka*, DLR, 2nd ser., 12 (1958): 421; aff'd WWR 24 (1958): 481, DLR, 2nd ser., 12 (1958): 421 (Alta. C.A.); rev'd on other grounds *Supreme Court Reports* (1959): 262. Also see Bailey, "A Married Woman's Right of Action," 519-20. See "Neil Phillip Primrose," in *Lords of the Western Bench*, Knafla and Klumpenhouwer, 154.
42 *Wener v. Davidson*, WWR 75 (1970): 693. Also see Bailey, "A Married Woman's Right of Action," 520-21. See "William John Cameron Kirby," in *Lords of the Western Bench*, Knafla and Klumpenhouwer, 82-3.
43 "the husband shall recover damages for the taking away of his wife"
44 *Wener v. Davidson*, WWR (1970), para. 28.
45 See, for example, the establishment of the United Nations in 1945, its issuance of the Universal Declaration of Human Rights in 1948, the aborted creation of Alberta's Bill of Rights in 1946, the prolonged campaign for a national bill of rights culminating in the Diefenbaker Bill of Rights in 1960, and, finally, the establishment of the Canadian Charter of Rights and Freedoms in 1982 as indications of the rising rights consciousness.
46 Amazingly enough, residual differences still exist, for under s. 46(b) of the Family Law Act, adult children of unmarried parents do not have the same rights to support as adult children of married parents. The Divorce Act of 1985 allows a judge to characterize a child over the age of majority as dependent if the child is unable by reason of illness, disability, or other cause to withdraw from parental charge or to obtain the necessaries of life. However, the Alberta Family Law Act restricts support to children under 22 who are full-time students.
47 AR 107 (1990): 152.
48 AR 234 (1998): 398.
49 AR 228 (1998): 283.
50 *Reports of Family Law* [cited hereafter RFL], 4th ser., 18 (1995): 337.
51 Ibid., paras. 31 and 32.
52 ALR, 3rd ser., 74 (1999): 338. See "Joanne Barbara Veit," in *Lords of the Western Bench*, Knafla and Klumpenhouwer, 184.
53 At para. 2.
54 2004 Carswell Alberta, 906; RFL, 5th ser., 50 (2004): 206.
55 RFL, 5th ser., 50 (2004): 206.
56 Statutes of Alberta [cited hereafter SA], 1969 c.67 and *Alta LR*, 3rd ser., 44 (1996): 338; WWR 1 (1997): 672. See "Peter Charles Garneau Power," in *Lords of the Western Bench*, Knafla and Klumpenhouwer, 144 and 153.

57 See *DLR*, 4th ser., 112 (1994): 745 and *Revised Statutes of Alberta* [cited hereafter *RSA*] (1980), C.f-2.
58 *RFL*, 4th ser., 39 (1998): 242.
59 However, the 1996 decision of the Alberta Court of Appeal in *Vriend v. Alberta*, *DLR*, 4th ser., 132 (1994): 595; *WWR* 5 (1996): 617 (rev'd *DLR*, 4th ser., 156: 385 (SCC)), in the human rights context did not support such a characterization.
60 *DLR*, 4th ser., 181 (1999): 300; *RFL*, 5th ser., 2: 358.
61 *AR* 287 (2001): 290. See "Delmar Walter Joseph Perras," in *Lords of the Western Bench*, Knafla and Klumpenhouwer, 141–42.
62 See *RFL*, 6th ser., 23 (2005): 101 and *SA* 2003, c.F-4.5.
63 *RSA*, 2000, c.M-5.
64 This was in no way limited to Alberta judges. See Carol Rogerson, "Judicial Interpretation of the Spousal and Child Support Provisions of the Divorce Act 1985 (Part I and Part II)." *Canadian Family Law Quarterly* [cited hereafter *CFLQ*] 7 (1991): 271; E. Diane Pask and M.L. McCall, "How Much and Why? An Overview," *CFLQ* 5 (1989): 129; *Moge v. Moge*, *RFL*, 3rd ser., 43 (1992): 345 (S.C.C.).
65 *WWR* 75 (1970): 715; *RFL* 2: 173 (Alta. S.C.a.d.).
66 *WWR* 75 (1970): 721 (Alta. S.C.T.D.). See "André Miville Dechene," in *Lords of the Western Bench*, Knafla and Klumpenhouwer, 34–35.
67 *WWR* 75 (1970): 721 (Alta. S.C.T.D.) at para. 13.
68 *RFL* 33 (1991): 367; *AR* 118: 138.
69 Justice Veit's decision in *Stricker v. Stricker* actually presaged the landmark decision of the Ontario Court of Appeal in *Elliot v. Elliot*, *RFL*, 3rd ser., 48 (1993): 237, which came to the same conclusion two years later.
70 *AR* 84 (1987): 321; *RFL*, 3rd ser., 11: 163. See "John Horace MacKenzie," in *Lords of the Western Bench*, Knafla and Klumpenhouwer, 91.
71 *RFL*, 3rd ser., 37 (1991): 24; *AR* 120: 331.
72 *Alta LR*, 2nd ser., 82 (1991): 173; *RFL*, 3rd ser., 35: 127.
73 *RFL*, 3rd ser., 43 (1992): 345 (S.C.C.).
74 *RFL*, 4th ser., 45 (1999): 308; *DLR*, 4th ser., 172: 308; *DLR*, 4th ser., 172: 637.
75 *RFL*, 3rd ser., 39 (1992): 329 and *RFL*, 3rd ser., 43 (1992), 260; *AR* 134: 311. See "Marguerite Jean Trussler," in *Lords of the Western Bench*, Knafla and Klumpenhouwer, 181.
76 *RFL*, 3rd ser., 39 (1992), para. 9.
77 *AR* 160 (1994): 1.
78 *AR* 147 (1994): 227. See "Ronald Leon Berger," in *Lords of the Western Bench*, Knafla and Klumpenhouwer, 19.
79 *AR* 147 (1999): 66 and *RFL*, 5th ser., 2 (2000): 307; *AR* 257: 212.
80 *Alta LR*, 3rd ser., 20 (1994): 429 and *RFL*, 4th ser., 4 (1994): 375 (Alta C.A.).
81 Along with the earlier decision of the Ontario Court of Appeal in *Paras v. Paras*, *Ontario Reports* 1 (1971): 130; *RFL* 2: 323.
82 At para. 52, the Court said, "We think that the judge could apply a 'litmus test' for reasonableness. The mark against which we suggest that any sum proposed by the parties should be tested is this: 20% of the gross income of the parties in the case of one child, and 32% in the case of a 2-child family."
83 *Haisman v. Haisman*, *RFL*, 4th ser., 7 (1994): 1, leave to appeal refused; *RFL*, 4th ser., 15 (1995): 51 (note) (S.C.C.).

84 *RFL*, 4th ser., 17 (1995): 88.
85 See *Hunt v. Smolis Hunt*, *RFL*, 5th ser., 20 (2001): 409 (Alta. C.A.); *Ennis v. Ennis*, *RFL*, 5th ser., 5 (2000): 302; *Whitton v. Sheppelt*, *RFL*, 5th ser., 23 (2001): 437; *Burke v. Burke*, *RFL*, 5th ser., 26 (2002): 1 and *S.(D.B.) v. G.(S.R.)*, *RFL*, 6th ser., 7 (2005): 373 (Alta. C.A.); *Henry v. Henry*, *RFL*, 6th ser., 7 (2005): 275 (Alta. C.A.); and *W.(L.J.) v. R.(T.A.)*, *RFL*, 6th ser., 9 (2005): 232 (Alta. C.A.).
86 *RFL*, 6th ser., 31 (2006): 1 (S.C.C.).
87 *O'Leary v. O'Leary*, *WWR* 1 (1923): 501 (Alta S.C.a.d.)
88 Ibid., para. 100.
89 Although Canada ratified the UN Convention on the Rights of the Child, the Alberta government expressed concern about the impact of Articles 13 and 15 on parental rights. See correspondence from Ralph Klein, Premier of Alberta, 13 January 1999 to Jean Chrétien, Prime Minister of Canada, and Mr Chrétien's 3 March 1999 response to the Premier; photocopy of document in author's possession.
90 See "Tevie Howard Miller," in *Lords of the Western Bench*, Knafla and Klumpenhouwer, 128-29.
91 *WWR* 4 (1978): 411. See "James Valentine Hogarth Milvain," in *Lords of the Western Bench*, Knafla and Klumpenhouwer, 129-30.
92 Ibid., para. 43.
93 *AR* 24 (1979): 154.
94 Ibid., para. 10.
95 Ibid., para. 2.
96 *AR* 89 (1988): 27.
97 Karen Munroe, "The Inapplicability of Rights Analysis in Post-Divorce Child Custody Decision Making," *ALR* 30 (1992): 875.
98 *RFL* 9 (1972): 78. See "Alan Joseph Cullen," in *Lords of the Western Bench*, Knafla and Klumpenhouwer, 33.
99 *RFL* 31 (1974) (Alta. S.C.T.D.).
100 *SCR* 2 (1978): 621; *RFL*, 2nd ser., 1 (1978): 330 (S.C.C.). (Interestingly enough, the two counsel who argued this case in the Supreme Court of Canada, on appeal from the Alberta Court of Appeal, were Adam Germain and Jacqueline Coutu, both now members of our Alberta Court of Queen's Bench.)
101 *Alta LR*, 2nd ser., 74 (1990): 168; *AR* 106 (1990): 62. Picard J. identified the following six criteria: (1) provision of the necessaries of life including proper physical and health care, (2) stable and consistent environment to foster good mental health and emotional well-being, (3) opportunity and resources to learn, (4) fair and consistent discipline, (5) opportunity to know and be loved by family, and (6) the opportunity and freedom to grow.
102 Munroe, "The Inapplicability of Rights Analysis in Post-Divorce Child Custody Decision Making," 854.
103 See Jean McBean, "The Myth of Maternal Preference in Child Custody Cases," in *Equality and Judicial Neutrality*, ed. Kathleen Mahoney and Sheilah Martin (Toronto: Carswell, 1987), 184.
104 See "Roger Philip Kerans," in *Lords of the Western Bench*, Knafla and Klumpenhouwer, 80-81.
105 *RFL*, 2nd ser., 34 (1983): 277.
106 *RFL*, 3rd ser., 28 (1990): 189; reversing (1990), *AR* 105: 102 (Q.B.).

107 See "Asa Milton Harradence," "Joseph John Walter Stratton," and "Allen Borislaw Zenoviy Sulatycky," in *Lords of the Western Bench*, Knafla and Klumpenhouwer, 67–68, 176, and 178–79, respectively.
108 See L.J. Weitzman and R.B. Dixon, "Child Custody Awards: Legal Standards and Empirical Patterns for Child Custody, Support and Visitation After Divorce," *University of California at Davis Law Review* 12 (1979): 471. See also E. Diane Pask and M.L. (Marnie) McCall, "K.(M.M.) v. K.(U.) and the Primary Care-Giver," RFL, 3rd ser., 33 (1991): 418.
109 *Alta LR*, 2nd ser., 54 (1987): 283; RFL, 3rd ser., 10 (1988): 166. See also *P.(T.M.A.) v. P.(F.A.)*, RFL, 4th ser., 14 (1995): 290.
110 AR 282 (2001): 399.
111 Parallel parenting divides areas of decision-making between parents rather than directing them to co-operate in making decisions. For example, one parent might be given exclusive authority to make decisions in the area of education, while the other might have control over health and medical decisions.
112 RFL, 4th ser., 42 (1998): 143.
113 AR 293 (2001): 104.
114 At para. 63.
115 SA 2003 c.F-4.5.

NINE

The Province of Persons
The Alberta Supreme Court and Women's Equality

JENNIFER KOSHAN &
ELIZABETH WHITSITT

ALBERTA WOMEN SECURED SEVERAL IMPORTANT rights during the early part of the twentieth century. From 1910 to 1930, women obtained relief as (ex)wives, mothers, and widows; gained the right to vote and run in provincial and municipal elections;[1] and lost formal impediments to their participation in professions.[2] These legislative developments occurred in tandem with two important court challenges involving Alberta women.[3] In the first case, *Rex v. Cyr*, a criminal defendant questioned the capacity of a woman, Alice J. Jamieson, to preside as a magistrate in her criminal trial for vagrancy. After an extensive review of the law, the Alberta Supreme Court, Appellate Division, dismissed the challenge in 1917, ruling that women were not legally disqualified from holding the position of magistrate.[4] In the second case, five Alberta women lobbied for a reference to the Supreme Court of Canada on the proper interpretation of the word *persons* under s. 24 of the British North America Act, 1867, a section governing Senate appointments.[5] In 1928, the Supreme Court of Canada determined that the word *persons* could not include females, holding that the British North America Act, 1867, should be interpreted in accordance with the era in which it had been drafted. Because women were under a legal incapacity to hold public office in 1867, the Supreme Court reasoned that female "persons" could not hold office in the Senate in 1928.[6] On appeal, the Privy Council rejected the Supreme Court's approach to statutory interpretation, and on 18 October 1929 unanimously determined that the word *persons* included women, finding that the exclusion of women from public office was "a relic of days more barbarous than ours."[7]

Undoubtedly, these decisions were catalysts for change in notions about women's equality and personhood.[8] Today, women have more opportunity to obtain an education, they are succeeding in professions, they operate at the highest levels in politics, and they can more easily affect societal change than in the not-so-distant past. However, despite such gains women continue to struggle for equality in Canadian society. Gwen Brodsky and Shelagh Day make this observation in their 1989 study of constitutional equality jurisprudence:

> The illusion that women have achieved equality is almost as pervasive as the reality of oppression. Women's inequality is invisible because it is so ordinary, so massive, and so accepted. The failure to see women's inequality is not, however, simply the result of socially induced blindness. Not seeing it is useful; it serves the interests of those who are dominant. Perpetuating the myth that women have already achieved equality justifies doing nothing.[9]

Almost two decades later, this is still the case, particularly for women who are disadvantaged by their race, culture, class, disabilities, and sexual orientation.[10]

This essay explores the Alberta Supreme Court's contribution to women's efforts to be recognized as equal persons in Canadian society. We take an explicitly feminist perspective here by "asking the woman question":[11] how have Alberta courts fared in taking women's circumstances, realities, and inequalities into account, and have they assisted or impeded women in making progress towards equality? In terms of methodology, we searched legal databases using various terms related to women's equality to uncover relevant Alberta Supreme Court decisions.[12] Two observations about this search are in order. First, the search failed to identify a number of key women's equality cases, indicating that the courts had not necessarily used language that allowed for a comprehensive survey of cases significant to women's equality. Second, the cases that were identified dated from the 1970s onward, showing that equality language has been adopted by the Alberta courts only recently. This is true of case law in other jurisdictions as well.

However, this is not to say that the Alberta Supreme Court decided no important cases related to women's equality before the 1970s. As noted earlier, Alberta's first "Persons case," *Rex v. Cyr*, held as early as 1917 that women were entitled to sit as magistrates. This case, and its implications for the direction of the Court's approach to women's equality, will be discussed below. Further, as Marie Gordon's essay in this volume makes clear, the Alberta Supreme Court rendered several key decisions in the area of family law before the 1970s, decisions that affected women's rights to obtain a divorce, share in matrimonial property, and receive spousal and child support.[13] Beyond the area of family law and the *Cyr* case, however, there appears to have been little consideration of women's equality and personhood by the Alberta courts before the 1970s. This is perhaps not surprising. In spite of the formal recognition of women's legal capacity to participate in public life in the early twentieth century, many Alberta women continued to be marginalized in the public realm and to focus their attention on "the politics of the private sphere."[14] This continued into the 1960s and 1970s, when the enactment of human rights laws and the release of the Report of the Royal Commission on the Status of Women inspired a new wave of feminist activism.[15]

As a result of the volume of cases from the 1970s onwards, the difficulties in framing a precise and comprehensive search, and the coverage of family law cases elsewhere in this collection, we decided to focus on the development of women's equality and personhood within four areas of law significant to women's lives: civil law, human rights law, constitutional law, and criminal law. We analyse decisions that have made important contributions in these areas, and we explore contrasts with cases in which women's equality was absent or undermined. Further, we situate these cases within their historical and social contexts and examine how they fit within Canadian law. In doing so, we attempt to grapple with the issue of whether courts can create systemic change, or whether their influence is necessarily limited to the individual cases they are deciding.

We employ the term *women's equality* rather than *gender* or *sex equality* to signify that gender is not the sole equality issue for women. Indeed the struggle for personhood has been particularly difficult for women disadvantaged by gender as well as other aspects of their identities, and our essay explores how all of these elements of women's marginalization and oppression have been accounted for by the Alberta courts. As for a definition of equality, we examine the Alberta courts' jurisprudence on the basis of their contributions in a substantive equality sense. Formal equality is achieved when sameness of treatment is realized—as in the Persons case itself, where women were found to be as entitled as men to hold seats in the Senate. In the early stages of women's legal activism, this model of equality was seen to be sufficient, because the goal was to secure for women those privileges to which men were already entitled—the capacity to vote, hold public office, work in professions, and so on. During the second wave of feminist activism, beginning in the 1960s and 1970s, it was argued that formal equality might be insufficient and indeed counter-productive where women could not show themselves to be the same as men. In contrast, substantive equality recognizes that differential treatment may be required to achieve equality, especially where women have particular needs, based on their childbearing capabilities, for example. Substantive equality focuses on counteracting historic and systemic disadvantage and the need for equality of results, and it was adopted by the Supreme Court of Canada in *Andrews v. Law Society of British Columbia* as the governing concept under the Canadian Charter of Rights and Freedoms (the Charter) in 1989, having been recognized earlier in the human rights realm.[16] As we will show, recognition of substantive equality comes late in the one hundred-year history of the Alberta Supreme Court.

Rex v. Cyr—Alberta's First Persons Case

In 1916 in Calgary, Alice J. Jamieson became the second woman in the British Empire to be appointed a police magistrate, second only to Emily Murphy, one of the "Famous Five" women behind the "Persons case" and who became a magistrate earlier that year in Edmonton. In upholding Jamieson's capacity to sit as a magistrate, Justice Charles Stuart of the Alberta Supreme Court, Appellate Division, blazed the trail for a unique approach to women's equality in Alberta with this assertion:

> the Courts of this Province are not in every case to be held strictly bound by the decision of English Courts as to the state of the common law...We are at liberty to take cognizance of the different conditions here, not merely physical conditions, but the general conditions of our public affairs and the general attitude of the community in regard to the particular matter in question....
>
> I therefore think that, applying the general principle upon which the common law rests, namely that of reason and good sense as applied to new conditions, this Court ought to declare that in this Province, and at this time in our presently existing conditions, there is at common law

no legal disqualification for holding public office...arising from any distinction of sex. And in doing this I am strongly of the opinion that we are returning to the more liberal and enlightened view of the middle ages in England and passing over the narrower and more hardened view which possibly by the middle of the nineteenth century had gained the ascendance in England.[17]

In her history of women and the law in Canada, Brettel Dawson chronicles a series of decisions reflective of the fact that many jurisdictions had their own "persons" cases.[18] Courts in the late nineteenth and early twentieth centuries were called upon to assess the capacity of women to attend medical school, work as lawyers, hold public office, and sit as judges. While the *Cyr* case was not unique in this respect, Dawson notes it "[departed] from the judicial tide" of other decisions, including the Supreme Court of Canada's opinion in the federal "Persons case" that followed.[19] Although *Cyr* recognized the equality of women in only a formal sense, it was nevertheless significant because it bucked the trend of strictly interpreting the common law and legislation governing women's legal capacity so as to exclude rather than include women in public life. At the same time, the person who bore the brunt of Jamieson's entitlement to judge was herself a woman, and Lizzie Cyr's rights were beyond the Court's concern.[20] In contrast to Alice Jamieson, who was a leader in the community and the wife of a former mayor,[21] Lizzie Cyr "had no money, no employment at all and in effect...had no means of maintaining herself except prostitution."[22] Justice Stuart's decision in *Cyr* thus anticipates other cases reviewed in this chapter in terms of its somewhat equivocal advancement of women's equality.

Civil Case Law

One of the most important steps on the path to personhood for Alberta women was grounded in the province's settlement history and emergent concerns over the character and fitness of residents and newcomers. Motivated in part by these factors, in 1928 the United Farmers of Alberta government enacted the Sexual Sterilization Act and created a Eugenics Board empowered to sterilize inmates of mental hospitals where it was perceived there was a danger that those individuals could transmit mental diseases or disabilities to their progeny.[23] Amendments in 1937 increased the board's powers to sterilize those who were at risk of mental injury to themselves or others through procreation; simultaneously, the requirement of consent of "mentally defective" persons was eliminated.[24]

Alberta was one of only two Canadian provinces to enact sexual sterilization legislation.[25] It is widely agreed that this legislation was informed by the ideology of eugenics, according to which persons perceived to possess inferior genetic attributes would be prevented from passing these attributes to progeny.[26] Legislative debates and popular media at the time note the "menace" thought to be present in persons with mental disabilities in terms of their presumed immorality and heightened propensity for criminal behaviour, and the fear that procreation by persons with such disabilities would propagate this menace.[27] As noted by commentators, the legislation "offered reassurance to the middle class that social peace and harmony could be restored,"[28] supported "existing political opposition to immigration of any but the protestant Anglo-Saxon" kind,[29] and was influenced by "pervasive...sexist attitudes and beliefs."[30] Ironically, sexual sterilization was supported by Alberta women who were champions of gender equality in other contexts, including three of the "Famous Five"—Emily Murphy, Nellie McClung, and Louise McKinney.[31] The National Council of Women and the United Farm Women of Alberta also campaigned for the sterilization policy.[32] Wahlsten concludes that it was likely that "the earnest efforts of relatively few people were able to triumph in Alberta while they failed elsewhere in Canada because of a slightly different alignment of forces or an array of local factors unique to Alberta."[33]

The gendered and racialized nature of Alberta's eugenics policy is reflected in the number of sexual sterilizations authorized and performed under the legislation.[34] Based on an analysis of the Eugenics Board's files, Timothy Christian concluded in a 1974 study that the government's sexual sterilization policy was disproportionately carried out against females, young persons, Aboriginal persons, immigrants (particularly Eastern European), and Catholics.[35] In a more recent study, Grekul et al. found women were presented to the Eugenics Board at a rate double that of males relative to their populations in the institutions feeding the process.[36] Women were also disproportionately subjected to sterilization: 64 per cent of women presented to the board were sterilized, compared to 54 per cent of men.[37] Interestingly, there are no reported cases from the Alberta courts reviewing the legislation or its implementation during the tenure of the Sexual Sterilization Act. However, Alberta's sterilization policy was not without controversy over the years.[38] Soon after their election, Peter Lougheed's Conservatives repealed the Sexual Sterilization Act in 1972, citing human rights concerns as a major motivation.

These concerns were brought to light by Lellani Muir in her claim for damages against the Alberta government.[39] Lellani Muir was institutionalized in the Provincial Training School for Mental Defectives (PTS) in Red Deer in 1955 when she was ten years old.[40] Muir's mother, a Polish Roman Catholic immigrant, had applied to have her daughter admitted to the school. The admission records showed that Muir and her parents were living in conditions of poverty, and her parents cited financial reasons as a basis for institutionalizing Muir.[41] Although the available information suggested that Muir's problems "were possibly emotional and not mental," she was not fully tested for "mental deficiency" until she had been in the PTS for two years.[42] Indeed, there was no evidence to indicate Muir was a greater risk for having mentally defective children than the general population, nor that she was incapable of intelligent personhood.[43] Muir's case was brought to the Eugenics Board in November 1957, where she was presented as a "Mental defective-moron" who "[had] shown a definite interest in the opposite sex" and was in "danger of...transmission to the progeny of Mental Deficiency or Disability, [and was] also incapable of Intelligent parenthood."[44] She was approved for sterilization, which was irreversibly performed in January 1959, and Muir was finally released from the PTS in 1965.[45] She began the process of discovering and coping with her infertility in 1966 and eventually brought suit against the Alberta government.

In 1996, Madam Justice Joanne Veit of the Alberta Court of Queen's Bench awarded total damages of $740,780 to Ms Muir.[46] Veit found that Muir's sterilization was performed "primarily to control sexual activity in the institution rather than for any of the purposes set out in the legislation."[47] It is important to note that this was the basis of the government's liability for wrongful sterilization and that the sexual sterilization policy itself was not being challenged—the policy was codified in legislation and was within the powers of the provincial legislature at the time. Noting that the sterilization had a "catastrophic impact" on Muir and had "changed, warped and haunted her life," Veit awarded the maximum amount legally permitted for pain and suffering, $250,280.[48] A further award of $250,000 was made for the pain and suffering related to Muir's wrongful confinement in the PTS, which was based on the stigma of being branded a mental defective, her loss of privacy and liberty, her loss of contact with family and friends, the imposition of institutional discipline, and the experimental administration of drugs.[49] Aggravated damages of $125,000 were awarded on the basis that the Alberta government ignored the criteria in its own legislation when it sterilized Muir and labelled her a mental defective.[50] Veit noted that she would also have granted punitive damages in the range of $250,000 to punish the government for its actions, but she was dissuaded from doing so because the government did not raise a limitations defence to Muir's action.[51] Further, no damages were awarded for "defective education and training." Although Muir was found to be in the normal intellectual range despite her diagnosis as a mental defective at PTS, it was held that she had not proved she "would have completed the education and maintained the employment levels" that were predicted by her expert at trial, and so she was denied damages for lost future wages.[52] Veit later ordered costs of $230,000 to Muir.[53]

Following the success of the *Muir* case, others who had been sexually sterilized pursuant to orders of the Eugenics Board brought similar claims against the Alberta government. In March 1998, the government introduced Bill 26, the Institutional Confinement and Sexual Sterilization Compensation Act. This bill sought to limit the government's liability for damages for sexual sterilization, and would have applied notwithstanding the Charter and the Alberta Bill of Rights.[54] Faced with massive opposition from the public, the government withdrew Bill 26 one day after its introduction in the legislature.[55] Hundreds of other victims of sexual sterilization subsequently received compensation through settlements with the Alberta government, and the Alberta courts have not decided any further cases of damages for forced sexual sterilization subsequent to *Muir*.[56]

In assessing the impact of the *Muir* case in terms of women's equality, two points must be noted at the outset. First, this case concerned one individual subjected to the Alberta government's sexual sterilization policy; it was not a case concerning the policy as a whole. Indeed, this limitation is articulated in Justice Veit's decision, wherein she notes that the overall objective of such a case is simply to compensate an individual for the wrong done to her.[57] This limited role of the courts arises in other areas as well and will be discussed below. Second, while females were disproportionately subjected to sexual sterilization, males were also sterilized in large numbers and were the victims of policies particular to their gender, such as experimentation on the testicular tissues of sterilized males with Down syndrome.[58]

Nevertheless, "asking the woman question" requires examination of the extent to which the decision accounts for the gendered nature of sexual sterilization and forced confinement, and the particular impact of these practices on women.

There was some analysis of gender, race, and religion in Justice Veit's decision. For example, she noted that the "systemic bias" of the sterilization policy against those from "sub-cultural backgrounds" was "a factor" in the case, given that Muir's mother was a Roman Catholic Polish woman.[59] Veit also cited evidence of the "systemic" gender bias in the operation of the sexual sterilization policy and noted that in some instances the board authorized sterilization in cases of female masturbation, "lesbian tendencies," and to eliminate menstruation.[60] These considerations were viewed as a basis for awarding punitive damages, although this award was ultimately not made.

There was little analysis of the particular impact of sterilization and institutionalization on women in the *Muir* decision. Justice Veit accepted the evidence of a medical-legal expert on the effects of sterilization at the "middle stage" of the female lifecycle, "when issues of childbearing become very prominent for some women...[and] childlessness can become [sic] significant traumatic psychological factor" and can impact "a young woman attempting to build her self-esteem and an image of herself as an independent competent adult."[61] However, this evidence was not explicitly referenced in the quantification of damages. In fact Veit cited the Supreme Court of Canada's decision in *Re Eve* as authority for the "importance to *human beings* of the potential for conception"[62] and noted that "[s]ome *women and some men* seek out and welcome sterilization."[63] These latter statements suggest that sterilization is the same for women and men and thus takes a formal equality approach to this issue.

The formal equality approach of *Muir* can be contrasted with other Alberta cases in which more attention was paid to the gendered impact of sterilization. In *Kelly v. Lundgard*, Justice Veit, again, considered a woman's claim for damages for sterilization caused by a car accident.[64] She rejected cases where damages for infertility were lower than those awarded in whiplash cases, noting that "[s]uch awards do not properly characterize the loss to many, if not most, women of an important aspect of their sense of themselves as women," and awarded $100,000 damages for this loss.[65] Similarly, in *Hagan v. Dalkon Shield Claimants Trust*, Justice Marina Paperny heard a case involving sterilization allegedly caused by an IUD.[66] Although it was ultimately held that causation was not proved, Paperny set out the damage award that would have been appropriate if the plaintiff had been successful, noting that sterilization "is a significant physical and emotional loss and cannot be underestimated. While its impact varies on each woman, inability to bear children is on its own worthy of an award of substantial damages."[67]

Justice Veit's discussion of damages for forced confinement also lacks analysis from a woman's equality perspective. The Law Commission of Canada has noted the disproportionate institutional confinement of children who were poor, disabled, and racialized, and highlights the vulnerability of young women and girls to abuse in institutions.[68] Reports on the sexual sterilization policy confirm these inequalities of confinement in the particular context of Alberta's institutions for "mentally defective" children.[69] In addition, the evidence in the *Muir* case established that Muir was forced to perform household labour and to diaper adults at the PTS—highly gendered forms of "institutional discipline" to which she was subjected.[70] Accordingly, one would have expected some analysis of the woman-particular harms of forced confinement generally, and in the case of Lellani Muir specifically.

It may be that these harms were seen as irrelevant to damages awarded for pain and suffering for sterilization and forced confinement, because the maximum awards were made by Justice Veit in any event. Moreover, it must be acknowledged that this is a complex issue for women's equality advocates, as analysis of the gendered impact of sterilization might lead to or reinforce assumptions about women's role as bearers of children.[71] Nevertheless, the *Muir* case may have served as a bolder step towards women's personhood if a more nuanced, substantive equality analysis of Muir's forced sterilization and confinement had been undertaken. Further, the decision would have advanced the interests of women with disabilities more resoundingly if the sexual sterilization policy itself had been rebuked. These limitations are, at least in part, a reflection of the shortcomings of civil cases and of reliance upon the courts to institute systemic social change more broadly.[72]

Despite its limitations, the *Muir* case is an important precedent for damages for women subjected to violations of their person and has been cited by other courts in this context.[73] Moreover, Veit's decision is an affirmation of the sexual sterilization policy's "catastrophic" impact on women like Lellani Muir—those who were labelled "mentally defective," often because they were poor or "sub-cultural." To the extent that the policy "was a factor in the development of Alberta's image as a backward, authoritarian Province," then the *Muir* case can be seen as a challenge to the continuation of that image.[74]

Human Rights Case Law

As noted in the introduction, several legislative initiatives furthered the interests of Alberta women during the early twentieth century. Outside the realm of family law, however, these legislative reforms did not result in much litigation. Women's equality interests only became a central issue for the courts once Alberta explicitly recognized gender equality in its human rights legislation.[75]

Alberta enacted its first human rights statute in 1966.[76] Recognizing that "all persons are equal in dignity and human rights without regard to race, religious beliefs, colour, ancestry or place of origin," the Human Rights Act was a meaningful step toward the protection of certain fundamental freedoms. Interestingly, however, the statute did not prohibit discrimination on the basis of sex or gender. This protection was not extended until the early 1970s, when the Lougheed Conservatives defeated Alberta's long-standing Social Credit government.

As noted by Lois Harder, the Conservatives "...ushered the province into a new-found secularism and cosmopolitanism associated with the rapid expansion of the province's cities and wealth generated by the oil boom."[77] Despite the fact that the 1970s were marked by increased government intervention and spending, rectifying social and economic inequality was not a priority.[78] As a result, the women's movement was significantly inhibited during this time in Alberta's history, although perhaps not more so than during the previous Socred era.[79] Women's struggle for equality was constrained by the provincial government's view that the formal equality paradigm that was delineated in provincial human rights legislation adequately recognized women's "political legitimacy."[80] However, as the Alberta courts began to interpret provincial human rights legislation, it became clear that legislative changes were needed to facilitate a conception of equality that responded to the particular needs of women and other marginalized groups.

Initially enacted in 1972, the Alberta Bill of Rights guarantees "equality before the law and the protection of the law" without discrimination because of sex, among other grounds.[81] The Bill of Rights applies to government action and requires that Alberta laws be construed and applied so that they do not abrogate, abridge, or infringe individual rights unless the Legislature expressly declares that legislation operates notwithstanding the Bill of Rights.[82] While a reasonable interpretation of the Bill of Rights would permit, and perhaps even require, courts to declare infringing laws inoperative, it appears no such declaration has ever been made by an Alberta court.[83]

The rationale behind the Alberta courts' cautious approach to the Bill of Rights can likely be explained by the Supreme Court of Canada's similar attitude respecting the application of the Canadian Bill of Rights. As noted by Peter Hogg, the Canadian Bill of Rights is a mere statute and does not provide courts with a constitutional mandate to limit Parliament's sovereignty to create law.[84] Hogg also explains that because the Canadian Bill of Rights does not contain a limiting provision akin to s. 1 of the Charter, the Supreme Court has narrowly interpreted the rights guaranteed to avoid striking down reasonable statutory limits on such rights.[85] Such concerns resulted in a line of jurisprudence that renders the Canadian Bill of Rights ineffective for many individuals, including women.[86] In this same vein, Alberta courts, adopting the reasoning used by the Supreme Court to interpret the Canadian Bill of Rights, narrowly construed the rights afforded individuals under the Alberta Bill of Rights.[87] Although both statutes remain in force, the Canadian and Alberta bills of rights have been superseded in large part by the Charter and its more expansive protection of rights claims against governments.

In addition to enacting the Alberta Bill of Rights in 1972, the government passed the Individual's Rights Protection Act to protect individuals, including women, from private as well as public acts of discrimination.[88] Since its initial inception, the Individual's Rights Protection Act has undergone a number of amendments, including the replacement of "sex" with "gender" as a protected ground, and a change in title to the Human Rights, Citizenship and Multiculturalism Act.[89] Most significant to the development of women's personhood, however, were amendments made in 1985 that expressly recognized discriminatory practices against pregnant women as a form of sex/gender discrimination.[90]

In 1983, prior to such amendments, the Alberta Court of Queen's Bench was asked in *Wong v. Hughes Petroleum Ltd.*[91] to determine whether a dismissal based on an employee's pregnancy was "discrimination because of sex," contrary to section 7(1) of the Individual's Rights Protection Act.[92] In addressing this interpretive question, Justice Tevie Miller noted that the Saskatchewan Human Rights Code was the only human rights legislation in Canada that expressly defined "sex" to include discrimination on the basis of pregnancy.[93] Miller also referred to the Supreme Court of Canada's decision in *Bliss v. Attorney General of Canada*, a 1979 case in which a woman challenged the Unemployment Insurance Act on the basis that it contravened section 1(b) of the Canadian Bill of Rights.[94]

Stella Bliss was denied regular unemployment insurance benefits, despite the fact she had worked the requisite number of weeks to qualify for them, because she was pregnant.[95] Section 46 of the Unemployment Insurance Act stated that a pregnant woman could not claim regular unemployment insurance benefits in the fifteen weeks immediately surrounding the birth of her child.[96] Bliss was also unable to obtain pregnancy benefits because she had not been employed for "...ten or more weeks of insurable employment in the twenty weeks that immediately preceded the thirtieth week before her expected date of confinement," as required by the Unemployment Insurance Act.[97] Because Bliss was unable to obtain benefits of any type, her counsel argued that this amounted to discrimination based on sex.[98] In rejecting her argument and speaking for a unanimous Supreme Court, Mr Justice Roland Ritchie ruled that Bliss's right to equality before the law under section 1(b) of the Canadian Bill of Rights was not violated because pregnancy discrimination did not equate to sex discrimination.[99] Ritchie adopted the following comment from Mr Justice Yves Pratte of the Federal Court:

> Assuming the respondent to have been "discriminated against," it would not have been by reason of her sex. Section 46 applies to women, it has no application to women who are not pregnant, and it has no application, of course, to men. If section 46 treats unemployed pregnant women differently from other unemployed persons, be they male or female, it is, it seems to me, *because they are pregnant and not because they are women.*[100] [emphasis added]

On the basis of this comment, Miller determined in *Wong* that pregnancy was not included in the term "sex" in section 7(1) of the Individual's Rights Protection Act, and he stated:

> I have come to the conclusion that I am bound by the... *Bliss* case and that the term "discrimination because of sex" does not cover a pregnancy. If it is the intention of

our legislators to cover this situation, it will have to do so specifically in its legislation, as has been done by the Province of Saskatchewan.[101]

Bliss and cases that followed it were widely criticized for their formal equality reasoning,[102] and two years later the Alberta legislature added a provision in the Individual's Rights Protection Act deeming pregnancy discrimination in employment to be sex discrimination.[103] A further provision was added in 1990 to specify that "Whenever this Act protects a person from being adversely dealt with on the basis of gender, the protection includes, without limitation, protection of a female from being adversely dealt with on the basis of pregnancy."[104] Alberta women had been lobbying the government for such protection since the early 1970s, and the inclusion of pregnancy in the Individual's Rights Protection Act was seen as a significant victory.[105]

Subsequently, in *Alberta Hospital Association v. Parcels* (1992), the Alberta Court of Queen's Bench re-considered the question of pregnancy discrimination.[106] In the collective agreement at issue in *Parcels*, an employee absent on sick leave was only required to pay 25 per cent of the premium for certain benefits if she or he wished to retain those benefits while absent from work. A pregnant woman, however, was required to prepay 100 per cent of the premium if she wished to retain benefits while on maternity leave.[107] On appeal, the Court upheld the Board of Inquiry's decision that Susan Parcels, a pregnant woman, was discriminated against by her employer and her union.[108] Adopting the reasoning of the Supreme Court of Canada in *Brooks v. Canada Safeway Ltd.*, which overturned the *Bliss* decision in 1989, Madam Justice Marguerite Trussler drew upon this passage:

> It seems indisputable that in our society pregnancy is a valid health-related reason for being absent from work. It is to state the obvious to say that pregnancy is of fundamental importance in our society. Indeed, its importance makes description difficult....If the medical condition associated with procreation does not provide a legitimate reason for absence from the workplace, it is hard to imagine what would provide such a reason....In terms of the economic consequences to the employee resulting from the inability to perform employment duties, pregnancy is no different from any other health-related reason for absence from the workplace.[109]

Trussler specifically noted "...that it is unfair to impose all of the costs of procreation on one half of the population. The function of anti-discrimination legislation is to remove this unfair burden from women."[110] She held that the collective agreement was discriminatory to the extent that it denied to women absent on health-related maternity leave the benefits that were available to other workers on health-related leaves.[111]

In contrast to the philosophy of formal equality that shaped judicial interpretations of bills of rights and human rights legislation in the 1970s and early 1980s, Trussler's ruling reflects an evolution in the Alberta courts' understanding of equality, and it represents a movement toward women's personhood by recognizing the particular needs associated with women's childbearing capacity. While this recognition followed from an amendment to the Individual's Rights Protection Act, Trussler's decision solidified this legislative change with a broad, purposive approach to women's human rights. As the next section will show, her substantive equality analysis stands in marked contrast to the Alberta courts' treatment of women's interests under the Charter.

Charter Case Law

Beginning in the early 1980s, women lobbied vigorously for strongly worded equality provisions in the Charter, because neither the Canadian Bill of Rights nor the common law had facilitated their claims.[112] Specifically, women sought to have s. 15 of the Charter titled "Equality Rights," and they advocated an expansive wording of the rights protected under the section to acknowledge specifically that equality meant more than non-discrimination; women sought this acknowledgement in concert with the consistent use of the word *person* throughout the Charter in recognition of the "symbolic significance" attributed to the word in the Persons case.[113] After two years of effort, in which women relied upon notions of equality reflected in international and domestic human rights law, the drafting of s. 15 of the Charter was completed.[114] Section 15 came into force on 17 April 1985, three years after the other provisions of the Charter, which allowed the federal, provincial, and territorial governments time to bring their legislation into conformity with the new equality requirements.[115]

Considered to be a fundamental evolution in the women's equality movement, the enactment of s. 15 was intended to make a significant contribution to the development of women's personhood throughout Canada. An examination of Alberta jurisprudence, however, reveals that s. 15 may not be facilitating the development of women's equality as was initially contemplated. Indeed, it appears that men are more likely than women to initiate Charter challenges on the basis of sex equality, and courts have often accepted their claims.[116] The following decisions from Alberta courts exemplify this dynamic.

In *R. v. M.L.* (1998), three brothers were ordered to stand trial on charges of rape and incest alleged to have taken place between 1955 and 1964 involving three of their sisters.[117] The accused brothers applied to quash the criminal charges related to the time during which they were, respectively, between the ages of 16 and 18. Their counsel argued that their rights under s. 15 of the Charter were infringed because under the Juvenile Delinquents Act, males were considered adults at age 16 and subject to harsher consequences than were females, who were not considered adults until age 18.[118] Considering the claim of discrimination under s. 15, Justice Eileen Nash of the Alberta Court of Queen's Bench determined the following:

> ...The impugned legislation does draw a distinction between males and females based on gender which results in inequality before the law, inequality under the law, unequal protection of the law and unequal benefit of the law. Females aged 16 and 17 charged with criminal offences were not subject to the same penalties and treatments as their male counterparts. Males and females were not treated equally under the legislation. A female had greater benefit and protection under the [Juvenile Delinquents Act].[119]

In arriving at the conclusion that the Juvenile Delinquents Act violated s. 15 of the Charter, Nash claimed to rely on the principle of substantive equality articulated by the Supreme Court of Canada in *Andrews*, which made this assertion:

> To approach the ideal of full equality before and under the law...the main consideration must be the impact of the law on the individual or the group concerned. Recognizing that there will always be an infinite variety of personal characteristics, capacities, entitlements and merits among those subject to a law, there must be accorded, as nearly as may be possible, an equality of benefit and protection and

no more of the restrictions, penalties or burdens imposed upon one than another. In other words, the admittedly unattainable ideal should be that a law expressed to bind all should not because of irrelevant personal differences have a more burdensome or less beneficial impact on one than another.[120]

Noticeably absent from the Court's decision in *R. v. M.L.* was any discussion of the impact on the three girls allegedly abused by their brothers for almost a decade or, more generally, on other women who had been sexually abused at the hands of men. While Justice Nash purportedly adopted a substantive equality approach, the decision is actually a classic example of the problems inherent in a formal equality approach and the failure to protect historically disadvantaged groups such as women.[121] Moreover, the accused brothers' use of the Charter replicates the trend identified in surveys of equality jurisprudence that men have been more inclined to bring sex discrimination claims under the Charter than women.[122]

In a similar vein, *R. v. Mills* (1997) involved a challenge to provisions of the Criminal Code governing production of personal records in sexual assault cases.[123] These provisions were the result of a concerted effort by feminists and anti-violence activists to prevent fishing expeditions by defendants for diaries, counselling records, and other personal documents in sexual assault trials following the Supreme Court of Canada's general approval of applications for such records in its 1995 decision in *O'Connor*.[124] Parliament subsequently amended the Criminal Code in 1997 to include a detailed set of requirements to be followed by courts in hearing applications for production of personal records.[125] The amendment explicitly referred to women's equality rights and the "prevalence of sexual violence against women and children," and it required courts to balance these considerations against an accused person's right to a fair trial in deciding whether to produce personal records.[126]

In *Mills*, a man accused of sexually assaulting a teenaged girl sought production of her counselling records. Mills's application came before Justice Paul Belzil of the Alberta Court of Queen's Bench two days after the production provisions took effect, and Mills took the opportunity to challenge the amendments to the Criminal Code, arguing that they violated his rights under ss. 7 and 11(d) of the Charter. Belzil agreed, finding that to the extent they departed from the majority decision in *O'Connor*, the amendments were contrary to Mills's

Charter rights to full answer and defence.[127] Raising the spectre of wrongful conviction, Belzil indicated that "the complainant is not a victim unless the Crown proves beyond a reasonable doubt that she is a victim. And even if it is proven that the complainant is a victim, the accused is not the perpetrator unless and until the Crown proves so beyond a reasonable doubt."[128] There was no discussion in the decision of the complainant's equality interests. In a subsequent decision, Belzil found that the production provisions could not be justified under s. 1 of the Charter.[129] Although the judge accepted expert evidence that "the vast majority of complainants of sexual abuse are female,"[130] and found that the potential for disclosure in criminal proceedings "will act as a deterrent for a few complainants not to seek therapy at least until court proceedings have been completed,"[131] he nevertheless struck down the provisions of the Criminal Code. In the end, the production provisions were seen to be a "substantial impairment of the fundamental right to a fair trial,"[132] such that they could not be justified by the government under s. 1 in spite of their positive objective.

As in the *M.L.* case, the Charter challenge in *Mills* was initiated by a man for the purpose of defending himself against criminal acts that have historically victimized women. While *Mills* was not based upon s. 15 of the Charter, the challenge repudiated legislative protections that women had fought to implement and that were intended to further women's equality interests and personhood. These cases exemplify the tension courts confront when balancing the individual rights of criminally accused persons with the rights of those who are victimized by violence individually and as a group. The Charter provides a vehicle for this balancing exercise through s.1, which requires courts to consider reasonable limits on individual rights in the context of broader societal interests (including the rights of women). In the 1990s, the courts were—and still are—becoming accustomed to this role, and as these cases show, judges perhaps erred on the side of ensuring that particular individuals were not convicted in particular cases, regardless of their power to consider historic inequalities under the Charter. This is a phenomenon that extends beyond the Alberta Supreme Court and is reflective of a wider debate in the legal community and society at large about the proper scope of judicial power under the Charter.[133] However, it bears mention that in these decisions the judges could be seen to have taken an "activist" role under the Charter in overturning legislation designed to protect group interests. The Alberta courts' failure to recognize women's equality interests had a particularly harsh impact on women with disabilities, racialized women, young women, and poor women—groups who are more vulnerable to sexual assault and to invasive production applications.[134] Further, it is arguable that the Courts' interpretation of the Charter in these cases undermined the equality values for which so many women strenuously negotiated during the early 1980s even as judges upheld other values protected under the Charter—those relating to fair trials and liberty in the criminal sphere.

Criminal Case Law

While constitutional cases in the realm of criminal law have tended to be brought by men and have threatened women's equality gains, non-constitutional cases in the criminal context have provided more fertile ground for developments in women's personhood in Alberta. This is particularly so in cases involving intimate violence against women.[135] Historically, the law condoned the "chastisement" of women by their husbands.[136] Intimate violence was finally recognized as criminal assault in the late nineteenth century, when more generalized concerns about violent crime rose to the fore.[137] Under the Criminal Code of Canada, wife assault was a separate offence punishable by whipping and incarceration from 1909 to 1953, but conviction required proof of bodily harm.[138] As noted by Strong-Boag, while there were "frequent accounts" of wife battering during this period, women often "made the best of matters" given the problems with divorce and matrimonial property laws.[139] Police, Crown prosecutors, and the judiciary also relegated intimate violence to the "private" family sphere, and charges were rarely laid or were often withdrawn or stayed by the prosecution. Sentences for the rare cases of intimate violence in which convictions were obtained were low compared with those handed down for other violent crimes, and judicial attitudes toward victims could be prejudicial and intimidating.[140]

The women's movement in Canada fought for policies reforming the criminal law during the 1980s, in addition to seeking increased funding for services for battered women.[141] Interestingly, those advocating for reforms in Alberta were not grassroots and academic feminists, as was the case elsewhere in Canada, but "the wives of wealthy oilmen and more traditional women's groups," including religious and professional women's organizations.[142] According to Harder, avoidance of explicitly feminist underpinnings made the issue of combating intimate violence more palatable to the Alberta government and, perhaps, to the broader community.[143] In the criminal law area, Alberta first adopted guidelines for police and Crown prosecutors in 1985 and established specialized justice system personnel and courts beginning in 2000.[144] Further, advocates for battered women were successful in obtaining an increase in government funding to establish more women's shelters.[145]

Turning to the judicial realm, an important case in enhancing the personhood of women in the sphere of intimate violence was *R. v. Brown* (1992).[146] In this case, Justice David McDonald of the Alberta Court of Appeal, writing for himself, Justice Francis Quigley, and Justice Jean Côté, articulated the Court's approach to sentencing in cases involving intimate violence against women.[147] The Court simultaneously rendered judgment in three appeals, all involving men who had pleaded guilty to assaulting their common law wives, resulting in serious injuries to the victims.

In its decision on the appeals of sentence, the Court of Appeal's use of language is especially notable. At the outset of the case, the Court rejected the term "spousal assault" in favour of "wife assault," noting that "it is almost always abusive behaviour by a man toward a woman, not by a woman toward a man."[148] The term *wife assault* was defined broadly to include marriage-like relationships as well as formal marriages.[149] The Court's deliberate choice of language anticipated the 1993 Canadian Panel on Violence Against Women report that articulated the importance of "naming violence against women."[150] The Court's terminology also contrasted with the Alberta government's use of the gender-neutral term *family violence*, which was criticized by anti-violence activists for minimizing the gendered nature of violence in relationships.[151] Later reports have noted that intimate violence against men occurs as well and have sparked a vigorous debate between anti-violence forces (who criticize the statisticians for their methodology and for failing to clarify the differences between assaults against women and men in terms of frequency, severity, and the context of self-defence),[152] and "men's rights" advocates (who argue that the statistics show that women are as violent as men).[153] However, the Court's focus on the gendered nature of intimate violence in *Brown* is very much in keeping with the spirit of the mid-1990s.

Further, the Court cited case law and its own experience to support and reinforce the gendered nature of intimate violence. The Court referred to the Supreme Court of Canada's decision in *R. v. Lavallee* as confirmation that domestic violence against women is a "profound problem."[154] At the same time, it also relied on two previous decisions of Madam Justice Mary Hetherington of the Alberta Court of Appeal that addressed the problems of domestic violence and the Court's lack of sufficient attention to this social problem.[155] Turning directly to *Brown*, the Court made this observation:

> The phenomenon of repeated beatings of a wife by a husband is a serious problem in our society. It is not one which may be solved solely by the nature of the sentencing policy applied by the courts where there are convictions for such assaults. It is a broad social problem which should be addressed by society outside the courts in ways which it is not within our power to create, to encourage, or to finance. But when such cases do result in prosecution and conviction, then the courts do have an opportunity, by their sentencing policy, to denounce wife-beating in clear terms and to attempt to deter its recurrence on the part of the accused man and its occurrence on the part of other men.[156]

The Court's comments on its own limited role in matters of wife assault are critically important. As noted by feminist scholars, courts deal with individual cases, and it is therefore difficult to envision how their actions can fulfill the systemic and structural reforms required to eradicate violence against women.[157] Such evidence is even more elusive in the criminal sphere than in the constitutional realm, where, as indicated above, judges are required to balance individual and systemic interests. Within its own mandate, however, the Court found that it could play an important role in denouncing intimate violence and in efforts to deter future occurrences.

As in previous cases, the Court of Appeal utilized a "starting point" approach in *Brown*, which entails the creation of a base-point for sentences for a particular offence, to be refined based upon aggravating and mitigating factors.[158] In *Brown* the Court's starting point for sentences in wife assault cases was based on what "would be fit if the same assault were against a woman who is not in such a relationship."[159] Clearly meant to categorize assaults in the context of an intimate relationship to be as serious as those between strangers, this signalled a departure from previous cases wherein the domestic context sometimes mitigated against a harsh sentence. In this instance the Court reversed that view and indicated that violence in intimate relationships should actually be treated more harshly than that occurring between strangers. Specifically,

> When a man assaults his wife or other female partner, his violence toward her can be accurately characterized as a breach of the position of trust which he occupies. It is an aggravating factor. Men who assault their wives are abusing the power and control which they so often have over the women with whom they live. The vulnerability of many such women is increased by the financial and emotional situation in which they find themselves, which makes it difficult for them to escape. Their emotional or psychological state militates against their leaving the relationship because the abuse they suffer causes them to lose their self-esteem and to develop a sense of powerlessness and inability to control events.[160]

Again, the Court's thinking and language in this part of the judgment are in tune with that of some feminist authors and anti-violence workers who have focused on male power and control on the one hand, and female vulnerability on the other.[161] Yet at the same time, harsh punitive measures for intimate violence have been critiqued by feminists on the basis that this policy has an adverse impact on marginalized groups, that it cannot fulfil a truly transformative role, and that it pays insufficient attention to victims' agency.[162]

On the latter point, the Court noted that preservation of the parties' relationship was a factor to be considered in fine tuning a sentence for wife assault.[163] However, the application of this factor requires caution for, according to the Court, "the plea of the wife that her husband be returned to her and that she not be further victimized by being deprived of his income should not readily be permitted to prevail over the general sentencing policy that envisages imprisonment of the man as not only an instrument of the deterrence of other men, but also as an instrument of breaking the cycle of violence in that man's family even at the risk of the relationship coming to an end during the enforced separation."[164] This aspect of the case might be criticized for failing to recognize that women do not necessarily support punitive sentences for their abusers even if they want relief from violence, but it clearly comes down on one side of the debate—a side that many feminists supported at the time (and still do).[165]

Brown could also be seen as insufficiently attuned to social context, although much of the literature that brought these concerns to light post-dates the case. For example, while the Court was wary about allowing financial disadvantage to influence a woman's "plea" and her partner's sentence, it did not acknowledge that for many women social services provide inadequate alternatives. Further, feminist literature on intimate violence has argued that disadvantaged women—for example, those from immigrant and refugee communities, those of Aboriginal heritage, those who are poor, and lesbians—confront unique considerations in deciding whether to report violence to the police, whether to testify for the prosecution, and whether to support custodial sentences for their partners. Such women may face pressures from their families and communities to keep their intimate relationships intact; they may also seek to protect themselves and their partners from a justice system that has engaged in discriminatory treatment of men and women from marginalized communities.[166]

One of the three appeals considered in *Brown* involved an Aboriginal man, Highway. Highway's counsel argued that his client's Métis heritage should be a mitigating factor in his sentence. The Court of Appeal rejected this argument in large part because there was no evidence that Highway's community could support his rehabilitation and deter others from committing intimate violence.[167] Further, and more to the point, the Court queried,

> Does the accused's community regard spousal violence as a less serious problem than mainstream society does? Does that community—including the female members of the community—really prefer that serious cases of spousal assault be treated differently when the accused is a member of that community, than if he were a member of the mainstream community?...[T]he courts of this province and of this country should be alert to the risk of moderating sentencing policy in such a case where to do so would mean that some women in Canadian society would be afforded less protection than others.[168]

While a contentious area, some Aboriginal women agree with the position taken by the Court—that they may require the full force of the criminal law to protect their interests in cases of intimate violence.[169] In this respect, the Court's decision can be seen as seeking to ensure the equality and personhood of Aboriginal women who are victims of intimate violence.

The *Brown* case was prescient in recognizing some of the conflicting sentencing principles at play in cases of intimate violence. In 1995, the federal government amended the Criminal Code of Canada to include breach of trust and a spousal context as aggravating factors in sentencing.[170] At the same time, it stipulated that "all available sanctions other than imprisonment that are reasonable in the circumstances should be considered for all offenders, with particular attention to the circumstances of aboriginal offenders."[171] *Brown* was cited directly by the Supreme Court of Canada in *R. v. Stone,* a sentence appeal for a man convicted of manslaughter in the death of his wife.[172] In fact the Supreme Court referred to *Brown* as authority for the principle, even before these amendments to the Criminal Code took effect, that the common law recognized that violence in a spousal context should be treated as an aggravating factor. Case law from other provinces was also cited to support that conclusion.[173] Thus *Brown* was on the leading edge of case law across the country in its treatment of sentencing for wife assault.[174]

Yet despite *Brown's* influence outside of the province, Heather Steinke has argued that the ruling is not consistently followed by lower courts in Alberta or by the Alberta Court of Appeal, and she speculates that this may be because the courts are not convinced that punitive sentences exert a deterrent effect in cases of intimate violence.[175] At the same time, the Court of Appeal has repeatedly reiterated its guidelines for sentencing in cases of wife assault and has harshly criticized courts refusing to follow the guidelines.[176] While *Brown* has its limitations in terms of furthering women's equality, it must be recognized that the judicial response to intimate violence has been the subject of much debate and disagreement within the women's and anti-violence communities. Considering the narrow role of the courts, as articulated in *Brown,* as well as the gender-neutral approach of the Alberta government, *Brown* should be seen as a significant step towards women's personhood in the context of intimate violence in Alberta.[177]

Conclusion

To borrow a metaphor from Brodsky and Day's 1989 study of women's equality, the path to personhood for Alberta women has consisted of some steps forward, some steps back, and some standing still.[178] There have been important legislative gains to women's equality over the past century in the areas of human rights, constitutional and criminal law. Alberta courts have sometimes spurred these changes and, at other times, have been called upon to interpret and apply them. Women have had some victories in the courts, as outlined in our sections on human rights and criminal law, but there have also been defeats, as noted in our section on constitutional law. At other points along the path, women have not stepped as far forward as they might have, as exemplified in our section on civil law. This reflects at least in part the complexity of women's equality claims and the enduring appeal of formal equality reasoning for some judges. Indeed, while some other essays in this collection have treated the Alberta Supreme Court as an institution, we believe it is important to acknowledge the persons who make up the courts. Our review of significant Alberta cases shows that many of the victories won by women occurred in, or were influenced by, cases where women judges presided. This is a qualitative rather than quantitative conclusion, but it supports former Justice Bertha Wilson's argument that women judges do make a difference.[179] For courts to fully play their part in ensuring that women continue toward substantive personhood and equality, they should be peopled with those who can relate to, acknowledge the existence of, and work to eradicate all the dimensions of women's inequalities.[180]

NOTES

1. See for example Married Women's Relief Act, Statutes of Alberta 1910, c. 18; An Act Respecting Infants, Statutes of Alberta 1913, c. 13; Alberta Married Women's Home Protection Act, Statutes of Alberta 1915, c. 4; Dower Act, Statutes of Alberta 1917, c. 14, and An Act to provide for Equal Suffrage, Statutes of Alberta 1916, c. 5. Alberta was the third province to grant equal suffrage, following Manitoba and Saskatchewan. See An Act to amend The Manitoba Election Act, Statutes of Manitoba 1916, c.36; An Act to amend the Statute Law, Statutes of Saskatchewan 1916, c.37. Aboriginal women (and men) did not obtain the right to vote until 1960. See Elections Canada, *A History of the Vote in Canada* (Ottawa: Minister of Public Works, 1997).
2. Sex Disqualification Removal Act, Statutes of Alberta 1930, c. 62.
3. During this time, Alberta was also the first province to have women sit in the legislature when Louise McKinney and Roberta MacAdams were elected in 1917. See T. Brettel Dawson, *Relating to Law: A Chronology of Women and Law in Canada* (North York, Ontario: Captus Press, 1994), 36 [cited hereafter Dawson, *A Chronology of Women and Law in Canada*].
4. *Rex v. Cyr*, Dominion Law Reports [cited hereafter DLR] 38 (1917): 601.
5. On the "Persons case," see Catherine Cavanaugh, "Out of the West: History, Memory, and the 'Persons,' 1919–2000," in *Forging Alberta's Constitutional Framework*, ed. Richard Connors and John M. Law (Edmonton: University of Alberta Press, 2005), 137–64.
6. In the matter of a reference in the meaning of the word "Persons" in s. 24 of the British North America Act, 1867, *Supreme Court Reports* [cited hereafter SCR] (1928): 276. As a reference case on the interpretation of the British North America Act 1867, the matter was never considered by the Alberta Supreme Court.
7. In the matter of a reference in the meaning of the word "Persons" in s. 24 of the British North America Act, 1867, DLR 1 (1930): 98. It was not until 1979 that a woman from Alberta, Martha Bielish, first gained an appointment to the Senate. See Kay Sanderson, *200 Remarkable Alberta Women* (Calgary: Famous Five Foundation, 1999), 88.
8. See Lois Harder, *State of Struggle: Feminism and Politics in Alberta* (Edmonton: University of Alberta Press, 2003), ix [cited hereafter Harder, *State of Struggle*].
9. Gwen Brodsky and Shelagh Day, *Canadian Charter Equality Rights for Women: One Step Forward or Two Steps Back?* (Canadian Advisory Council on the Status of Women, 1989), 11 [cited hereafter Brodsky & Day, *Equality Rights for Women*].
10. See for example a more recent article by Brodsky & Day, "Beyond the Social and Economic Rights Debate: Substantive Equality Speaks to Poverty," *Canadian Journal of Women and the Law* 14 (2002): 185–220.
11. Katharine T. Bartlett, "Feminist Legal Methods," *Harvard Law Review* 103 (1990): 829–88.
12. Databases searched include Quicklaw, Westlaw/ECarswell, CAN LII, and the Alberta Courts website, using terms such as "sex/gender equality," and "sex/gender discrimination."
13. Marie Gordon, "The Marriage of Law and History: Family Law Cases in the Alberta Supreme Courts, 1907–2006," in this volume. See also Dale Gibson,

"The Supreme Court of Alberta Meets the Supreme Court of Canada," in this volume, who discusses *Board v. Board, Western Weekly Reports* 2 (1918): 457, an Alberta Supreme Court case concerning jurisdiction to grant divorces.

14 Veronica Strong-Boag, "Pulling in Double Harness or Hauling a Double Load: Women, Work and Feminism on the Canadian Prairie" [cited hereafter Strong-Boag, "Pulling in Double Harness"], in *The Prairie West: Historical Readings*, ed. R. Douglas Francis and Howard Palmer (Edmonton: University of Alberta Press, 1992), 401–23, 403. See also Catherine A. Cavanaugh and Randi R. Warne, "Introduction," in *Standing on New Ground: Women in Alberta* (Edmonton: University of Alberta Press, 1993), x–xviii. According to Strong-Boag, while many prairie women did work outside the home to bring in extra income, they saw the family sphere as their main site of oppression.

15 Canada, Royal Commission on the Status of Women, Report (Ottawa: Information Canada, 1970).

16 See *Andrews v. Law Society of British Columbia*, SCR 1 (1989): 143; *Ontario Human Rights Commission and O'Malley v. Simpsons–Sears Ltd.*, SCR 2 (1985): 536, and *Canadian National Railway Co. v. Canada* (*Canadian Human Rights Commission*), SCR 1 (1987): 1114, cited in *Andrews v. Law Society of British Columbia*.

17 *Cyr*, 610, 611–12.

18 Dawson, *A Chronology of Women and Law in Canada*.

19 Ibid., 9.

20 See David Bright, "The Other Woman: Lizzie Cyr and the Origins of the 'Persons' Case." *Canadian Journal of Legal Studies* 13, no2 (1998): 99–115. Cyr was sentenced to six months hard labour on the basis of scanty evidence.

21 Alberta Online Encyclopedia, *www.albertasource.ca/lawcases/constitutional/cyrcase/people_alice.htm*

22 *Cyr*, 613.

23 Sexual Sterilization Act, Statutes of Alberta 1928, c.3. See s. 5.

24 Sexual Sterilization Amendment Act, 1937, Statutes of Alberta 1937, c.47, s. 5. See also Sexual Sterilization Amendment Act, 1942, Statutes of Alberta 1942, c.48.

25 Sexual Sterilization Act, Statutes of British Columbia 1933, c. 59. BC had a fraction of Alberta's rate of sexual sterilizations. Angus McLaren, *Our Own Master Race: Eugenics in Canada, 1885–1945* (Toronto: McClelland and Stewart, 1990), 159, writes that it is "impossible" to know the exact number of sterilizations performed in BC because the files of the Eugenics Board "were either lost or destroyed"; however, a recent case puts the number at 188. See *D.E. (Guardian ad litem of) v. British Columbia*, British Columbia Law Reports 4th ser., 45 (2005): 492.

26 Timothy Caulfield and Gerald Robertson, "Eugenic Policies in Alberta: From the Systematic to the Systemic?" *Alberta Law Review* [cited hereafter *Alta LR*] 35 (1996–1997): 59–79, 62. Part of this article is taken from an expert report written by Robertson for the *Muir* case.

27 As noted by Caulfield and Robertson, ibid., 62–66, eugenic policy was implemented not only via sexual sterilization legislation but also through the prohibition of marriage for individuals with mental illnesses or disabilities, and through their segregation and institutionalization.

28 Ibid., 69. For some of the early context of the eugenics movement in Canada,

see Carol Lee Bacchi, *Liberation Deferred? The Ideas of the English Canadian Suffragists, 1877–1918* (Toronto: University of Toronto, 1983), 104–16.

29 Douglas Wahlsten, "Leilani Muir versus the Philosopher King: Eugenics on trial in Alberta," *Genetica* 99 (1997): 185–98, 186.

30 Jana Grekul, Harvey Krahn, and Dave Odynak, "Sterilizing the 'Feeble-minded': Eugenics in Alberta, Canada, 1929–1972," *Journal of Historical Sociology* 17, no. 4 (2004): 358–84, 359. The authors also note the influence of American eugenics policies, which initially targeted "fertile, feeble-minded female paupers" (at p. 360).

31 Ibid., 362, 378; Caulfield and Robertson, "Eugenic Policies in Alberta," 63; *Muir*, 344, para. 97. Wahlsten, "Leilani Muir versus the Philosopher King," 187, notes that it was Murphy's role as a magistrate that brought her into daily contact with persons with mental disabilities or illnesses, which she perceived to be the cause of their criminality "and an enormous cost to the state."

32 Timothy Christian, *The Mentally Ill and Human Rights in Alberta: A Study of the Alberta Sexual Sterilization Act* (unpublished, 1974), Part III, 8–9 [cited hereafter Christian, *A Study of the Alberta Sexual Sterilization Act*]; Caulfield and Robertson, "Eugenic Policies in Alberta," 63.

33 Wahlsten, "Leilani Muir versus the Philosopher King," 187. See also Christian, ibid., 10; Grekul et al., "Sterilizing the 'Feeble-minded,'" 378.

34 Pursuant to its powers, the Eugenics Board heard 4,785 cases, authorized 4,739 sterilizations, and actually performed 2,834 sterilizations between 1929 and 1972. See Grekul et al., ibid., 366–67. These numbers differ somewhat from those cited in other sources (see, e.g., McLaren, *Our Own Master Race*, 159, who states that 2,822 sterilizations were performed out of 4,725 authorized), but Grekul et al. is arguably a more reliable source because the authors' research is based on a case-by-case analysis of files.

35 Christian, *A Study of the Alberta Sexual Sterilization Act*.

36 Grekul et al., "Sterilizing the 'Feeble-minded,'" 373.

37 Ibid.

38 For a thorough discussion of opposition to the legislation, see Christian, *A Study of the Alberta Sexual Sterilization Act*, Part II. In terms of the reasons for the longevity of the Sexual Sterilization Act, particularly in light of the widespread repudiation of eugenics in other jurisdictions following the Second World War, Grekul et al., ibid., 379, point to the authoritarian nature of the government and its weak opposition as one possible explanation; they also note that Alberta was a prosperous place after the Second World War, where citizens were "disinclined to criticize the government." The authors also note the "relative weakness of the Roman Catholic Church in Alberta," ibid.

39 Caulfield and Robertson, "Eugenic Policies in Alberta," 62. See *Muir v. Alberta*, *Alberta Reports* [cited hereafter AR] 179 (1996): 321 ("*Muir*").

40 *Muir*, 330, para. 20.

41 Ibid., 333, para. 40.

42 Ibid., 356, para. 166.

43 Ibid., 339–40, para. 70.

44 Ibid., 332, para. 31.
45 Ibid., 333, para. 35.
46 Ibid., 326, para. 6. See "Joanne Barbara Veit," *Lords of the Western Bench: A Biographical History of the Supreme and District Courts of Alberta, 1876–1990*, Louis A. Knafla and Richard Klumpenhouwer (Calgary: The Legal Archives Society of Alberta, 1997), 184 [cited hereafter *Lords of the Western Bench*, Knafla and Klumpenhouwer].
47 Ibid., 347–48, para. 121.
48 Ibid., 350, para. 138.
49 Ibid., 326, 355–57, paras. 4, 163, 167.
50 Ibid., 351–52, paras. 145–50.
51 Ibid., 352–53, paras. 151–53. The limitation issue has been a live one for sexual sterilization claims in BC. In *D.E. (Guardian ad litem of) v. British Columbia*, the trial judge found the claims for abuse of public office, breach of fiduciary duty, negligence and battery to be statute barred. This was overturned on appeal, and the claims of nine of the plaintiffs were allowed to proceed to trial.
52 *Muir*, ibid., 359–60, para. 182. For a case that takes an approach to loss of future earnings that is influenced by gender equality, see *MacCabe v. Westlock Roman Catholic Separate School District No. 100*, AR 226 (1998): 1, varied AR 293 (2001): 41.
53 Wahlsten, "Leilani Muir versus the Philosopher King," 195.
54 Bill 26, Institutional Confinement and Sexual Sterilization Compensation Act, 2nd Sess., 24th Leg., Alberta, 1998. The Act would have limited compensation against the government to a maximum of $150,000 for sterilization, forced confinement, and sexual assault in Alberta institutions, with no aggravated or punitive damages.
55 Alberta Legislative Assembly, *Alberta Hansard* 2 (1998): 812–13 (11 March 1998, Havelock).
56 Grekul et al., "Sterilizing the 'Feeble-minded,'" 364. The details of the settlements are confidential.
57 *Muir*, 337, 349, paras. 55, 129.
58 Ibid., 348, para. 124.
59 Ibid., 344, para. 98.
60 Ibid., 344, paragraph 96, referring to Professor Robertson's report and pp. 352–53, para. 152. See also references to the evidence of Dr C.M. Hincks at 346–47, para. 116, and to the Chief Commissioner of Mental Institutions in Alberta at 347–48, para. 12.
61 Ibid., 341, para. 79.
62 Ibid., 350, para. 137 (emphasis added), citing *Re Eve*, SCR 2 (1986): 388.
63 *Muir*, ibid., 349, para. 129 (emphasis added).
64 *Kelly v. Lundgard*, Alberta Judgments No. 672 (1996) (Quicklaw).
65 Ibid., para. 49. *Kelly v. Lundgard* was varied on appeal, and the award of damages was reduced to $65,000. However, a majority of the Alberta Court of Appeal affirmed "the significant effect of infertility on a woman's sense of well-being," referring to *Hagan v. Dalkon Shield*, infra. See *Kelly v. Lundgard*, AR 286 (2001): 1, 47, para. 192.

66 *Hagan v. Dalkon Shield Claimants Trust*, AR 231 (1998): 153.
67 Ibid., 181, para. 186. Justice Paperny would have awarded non-pecuniary damages of $70,000 in the circumstances. See also *Adan v. Davis, Canadian Cases on the Law of Torts*, 2nd ser., 43 (1998): 262, 283, where the Ontario Court of Justice cited *Muir* as support for the proposition that "a permanent loss of reproductive capacity can represent a loss of tragic proportions."
68 See Law Commission of Canada, *Restoring Dignity: Responding to Child Abuse in Canadian Institutions* (Ottawa: Minister of Public Works and Government Services, 2001), 3, 40.
69 See Caulfield and Robertson, "Eugenic Policies in Alberta," 61; Christian, *A Study of the Alberta Sexual Sterilization Act*, 122-23.
70 *Muir*, 356, para. 167.
71 Harder argues that feminists' emphasis on difference coalesced with an ideology of "family values" in Alberta that has served to oppress women. *State of Struggle*, 14-15.
72 See for example Jamie Cassels, "(In)equality and the Law of Tort: Gender, Race and the Assessment of Damages," *Advocates Quarterly* 17 (1995): 158-98, 161-62.
73 See *Whiten v. Pilot Insurance Co.*, SCR 1 (2002): 595, a leading case on punitive damages that cites *Muir* as support for circumstances in which such damages are available; *Hagan v. Dalkon Shield; Kelly v. Lundgard; Adan v. Davis. Muir* was also cited by a law reform body considering damages for sexual abuse; see British Columbia Law Institute, *Civil Remedies for Sexual Assault* (Vancouver: BCLI, 2001).
74 Christian, *A Study of the Alberta Sexual Sterilization Act*, 29.
75 Earlier, Alberta passed equal pay laws in 1957. See An Act amending the Alberta Labour Code, Statutes of Alberta 1957, c. 38, s. 41.
76 The Human Rights Act, Statutes of Alberta 1966, c. 39. For discussion of an earlier attempt by Alberta to pass human rights legislation, see Gibson, "The Supreme Court of Alberta Meets the Supreme Court of Canada," in this volume.
77 Harder, *State of Struggle*, 19-20.
78 Ibid., 20.
79 Ibid., 19-43. Harder notes (p. 20) that "the philosophy of governance embraced by the Conservative Lougheed government was not markedly different from its Social Credit predecessor." See also Linda Trimble, "A Few Good Women: Female Legislators in Alberta, 1972-1991," in *Standing on New Ground: Women in Alberta*, ed. Catherine A. Cavanaugh and Randi R. Warne (Edmonton: University of Alberta Press, 1993), 87-114, who argues (p. 97) that "[i]n the period between 1971 and 1986, the Conservatives created few policies designed to help women."
80 Harder, *State of Struggle*, 20.
81 Statutes of Alberta 1972, c. 1; See also Alberta Bill of Rights, Revised Statutes of Alberta 1980, c. A-16; Alberta Bill of Rights, Revised Statutes of Alberta 2000, c. A-14.
82 Alberta Bill of Rights, Revised Statutes of Alberta 2000, c. A-14, s. 2.
83 This issue was addressed in *R. v. Drybones*, SCR (1970): 282 ("*Drybones*"). In *Drybones*, s. 94(b) of the Indian Act made it an offence for an "Indian" to be intoxicated anywhere off a reserve. The Supreme Court held that s. 94(b) was

inconsistent with the equality provision of the Canadian Bill of Rights, and rendered the provision inoperative. This is the only case where the Canadian Bill of Rights was used to this effect by the courts.
84 Peter Hogg, *Constitutional Law of Canada*, 4th ed. (looseleaf) (Scarborough, ON.: Thomson Carswell, 1997), chap. 32, 10-11.
85 Ibid., 11.
86 See for example *A.G. Canada v. Lavell*, SCR (1974): 1349; *Bliss v. A.G. Canada*, SCR 1 (1979): 183.
87 See for example *Regina v. Pennington*, DLR, 3rd ser., 128 (1981): 746; *Marr v. Marr Estate, Alberta Law Reports* [cited hereafter *ALR*], 2nd ser., 71 (1989): 168; *Alberta (Minister of Infrastructure) v. Nilsson*, ALR 4th ser, 8 (2002): 83.
88 Statutes of Alberta 1972, c. 2. The Act also applies to discrimination in the public sphere.
89 Individual's Rights Protection Amendment Act, Statutes of Alberta 1990, c. 23, ss. 2, 4-5, and Statutes of Alberta 1996, c. 25.
90 Individual's Rights Protection Amendment Act, Statutes of Alberta 1985, c.33, s. 3.
91 *ALR*, 2nd ser., 28 (1983): 155 ("*Wong*").
92 Revised Statutes of Alberta 1980, c. I-2.
93 See "Tevie Harold Miller," in *Lords of the Western Bench*, Knafla and Klumpenhouwer, 128-29.
94 SCR 1 (1979): 183 ("*Bliss*"), Statutes of Canada 1970-71-72, c. 48 and *Wong*, 165.
95 *Bliss*, 191-94.
96 Ibid., 188.
97 Ibid., 187-89.
98 Ibid., 189.
99 Ibid., 191-94.
100 Ibid., 190.
101 *Wong*, 165.
102 See Dawson, *A Chronology of Women and Law in Canada*, 9-10.
103 Individual's Rights Protection Amendment Act, Statutes of Alberta 1985, c. 33, s. 3.
104 Individual's Rights Protection Amendment Act, Statutes of Alberta 1990, c. 23, s. 15(c).
105 Harder, *State of Struggle*, 26-27, 68.
106 *ALR*, 3rd ser., 1 (1992): 332 ("*Parcels*").
107 Ibid.
108 Ibid., 335. The Court allowed the appeal in part on other grounds.
109 SCR 1 (1989): 1237-38.
110 *Parcels*, 338.
111 Recognized as a landmark case, *Parcels* has been followed by courts in Alberta and elsewhere; see for example *United Nurses of Alberta, Local 37 v. Alberta (Provincial Health Authorities)*, AR 253 (1999): 57; *Ontario Cancer Treatment and Research Foundation v. Ontario (Human Rights Commission)*, *Ontario Reports* [cited hereafter *OR*], 3rd ser., 38 (1998): 72.
112 Brodsky & Day, *Equality Rights for Women*, 13, citing B. Baines, "Women and the Law," in *Changing Patters: Women in Canada* S. Burt, ed. L. Code and L. Dorney (Toronto: McClelland and Stewart, 1988), 157-83.

113 Penny Kome, *The Taking of Twenty Eight: Women Challenge the Constitution* (Women's Educational Press, 1983), 35-36 [cited hereafter Kome, *The Taking of Twenty Eight*].
114 Brodsky & Day, *Equality Rights for Women*, 15-16.
115 Women also successfully lobbied for the inclusion of s. 28 in the Charter, which guarantees Charter rights and freedoms equally to male and female persons. See Brodsky and Day, ibid., 17; Kome, *The Taking of Twenty Eight*. Surprisingly, this section has never been used by Alberta courts as a direct basis upon which to challenge government action. Instead, it appears to be an occasional fleeting reference in Charter jurisprudence addressing women's equality issues under s. 15.
116 Brodsky & Day, ibid., 49, 56. In Alberta, see for example *R. v. Barrons*, AR 70 (1985): 107; *R. v. Bearhead*, Canadian Criminal Cases, 3rd ser., 27 (1986): 546; *Kastning v. Charles*, AR 80 (1987): 150; *R. v. M.L.*, Alberta Judgments (1998), No. 243 (Quicklaw); *R. v. Brooks*, ALR, 2nd ser., 64 (1989): 229; *R. v. Mills*, AR 205 (1997): 321, further reasons at AR 207 (1997): 161, rev'd SCR 3 (1999): 668. Our research uncovered only three Alberta cases in which women initiated Charter challenges on the basis of sex equality. See *Casagrande v. Hinton Roman Catholic Separate/Separé School District 155*, AR 79 (1987): 241; *Murley v. Hudye*, ALR, 3rd ser., 26 (1994): 91; *Rossu v. Taylor*, ALR, 3rd ser., 68 (1998): 213.
117 *R. v. M.L.*, ibid.
118 Ibid., 9 at para. 42.
119 Ibid., 15 at para. 62.
120 Ibid., 15 at para. 63, citing *Andrews*, 11.
121 While Justice Nash found that the Juvenile Delinquents Act violated s. 15 of the Charter, she reserved judgment on the issue of whether or not the violation could be justified under s. 1 of the Charter. There does not appear to be a reported decision on the s. 1 issue.
122 Brodsky & Day, *Equality Rights for Women*. For more recent studies on s. 15 jurisprudence, see Sheilah Martin, "Balancing Individual Rights to Equality and Social Goals," *Canadian Bar Review* 80 (2002): 299-373; Bruce Ryder, Cidalia C. Faria, and Emily Lawrence, "What's *Law* Good For? An Empirical Overview of *Charter* Equality Rights Decisions" *Supreme Court Law Review* 24 (2004): 103-36.
123 *R. v. Mills*, AR 205 (1997): 321, further reasons at AR 207 (1997): 161 ("*Mills*").
124 See Jennifer Scott and Sheila McIntyre, Women's Legal Education and Action Fund (LEAF) Submissions to the Standing Committee on Justice and Legal Affairs (March, 1997); Diane Oleskiw and Nicole Tellier, Submissions to the Standing Committee on Bill C-46 prepared for the National Association of Women and the Law (March, 1997). Groups representing the rights of criminally accused persons were also consulted. *R. v. O'Connor*, SCR 4 (1995): 411. For an article on the Courts' response to *O'Connor*, see Karen Busby, "Discriminatory Uses of Personal Records in Sexual Violence Cases," *Canadian Journal of Women and the Law* 9 (1997): 148-77.
125 An Act to amend the Criminal Code (production of records in sexual offence proceedings), Statutes of Canada 1997, c. 30. The Bill added sections 278.1-278.91 to the Criminal Code.
126 Ibid., preamble, section 278.5(2).

127 *Mills*, AR 205 (1997): 340, para. 46.
128 Ibid., 342, para. 74.
129 *Mills*, AR 207 (1997): 161.
130 Ibid., 166, para. 20.
131 Ibid., 166, para. 22.
132 Ibid., 173, para. 72. In *R. v. Mills*, SCR 3 (1999): 668, a majority of the Supreme Court overturned Belzil's decision and upheld the production provisions in their entirety, finding that Parliament struck a proper balance between the interests of complainants and accused persons in the Criminal Code. The Alberta Association of Sexual Assault Centres and the Sexual Assault Centre of Edmonton intervened in the case. For an analysis of the Supreme Court's decision, see Jennifer Koshan, "Disclosure and Production in Sexual Assault Cases: Situating Stinchcombe," *Alta LR* 40 (2002): 655–88 [cited hereafter Koshan, "Situating Stinchcombe"].
133 For a classic critique of "judicial activism" under the Charter, see *The Charter Revolution and the Court Party*, F.L. Morton and Rainer Knopff (Peterborough, ON.: Broadview Press, 2000).
134 Koshan, "Situating Stinchcombe," 657, 659.
135 On intimate violence as a women's equality issue, see Kathleen Mahoney, "The Legal Treatment of Spousal Abuse: A Case of Sex Discrimination," *University of New Brunswick Law Journal* 41 (1992): 21–40.
136 Sir William Blackstone, *Commentaries on the Laws of England* (Chicago: Callaghan, 1884), 444.
137 Maeve Doggett, *Marriage, Wife-Beating and the Law in Victorian England* (London: Weidenfeld and Nicolson, 1992).
138 Criminal Code of Canada, Revised Statutes of Canada 1927, c. 36, s. 292, replaced by Statutes of Canada 1953-54, c. 51, s. 231. After the repeal of the separate offence for wife assault, whipping remained as an additional punishment for males convicted of the gendered crimes of rape, incest, and indecent assault, as well as other offences such as robbery.
139 Strong-Boag, "Pulling in Double Harness," 409.
140 Canadian Panel on Violence Against Women, *Changing the Landscape: Ending Violence—Achieving Equality* (Ottawa: Minister of Supply and Services, 1993), 220-21, 223-24; Alberta Law Reform Institute, *Domestic Abuse: Toward an Effective Legal Response* (Edmonton: ALRI, 1995), 36-38.
141 Dawn Currie, "Battered Women and the State: From the Failure of a Theory to a Theory of Failure," *Journal of Human Justice* 2 (1990): 77–96; Gillian Walker, *Family Violence and the Women's Movement: The Conceptual Politics of Struggle* (Toronto: University of Toronto Press, 1990).
142 Harder, *State of Struggle*, 128.
143 Ibid., 112, 128-29.
144 Alberta Justice, *Domestic Violence Handbook for Police and Crown Prosecutors* (Edmonton: Alberta Justice, 2005), 13-18.
145 Harder, *State of Struggle*, 102, 128-29. Funding for shelters suffered cutbacks in the restructuring of the 1990s.
146 *R. v. Brown*, AR, 125 (1992): 150 ("*Brown*").
147 See "Francis Hugh Quigley" and "Jean Edouard Côté," in *Lords of the Western Bench*, Knafla and Klumpenhouwer, 157 and 30-33, respectively.

148 Ibid., 151-52, para. 1.
149 Ibid., 152, para. 2; 156, para. 22.
150 Canadian Panel on Violence Against Women, *Changing the Landscape*, 6-7.
151 Harder, *State of Struggle*, 104. While gender-neutral terminology is more inclusive of violence in same-sex relationships, the Alberta government has typically not recognized such violence. For example, it did not provide civil remedies for abuse in same-sex relationships until 2003. See Protection Against Family Violence Act, Statutes of Alberta 1998, c.P-19.2, amended by the Adult Interdependent Relationships Act, Statutes of Alberta 2002, c. A-4.5, s. 65.
152 See for example Walter S. DeKeseredy and Martin D. Schwartz, "Backlash and Whiplash: A Critique of Statistics Canada's 1999 General Social Survey on Victimization," *Online Journal of Justice Studies* 1 (2003), and Yasmin Jiwani, "The 1999 General Social Survey on Spousal Violence: An Analysis" (Vancouver: The FREDA Centre for Research on Violence against Women and Children, 2000), online: *http://www.harbour.sfu.ca/freda/reports/gss01. htm*, who critique the 1999 General Social Survey on Spousal Violence, in Canadian Centre for Justice Statistics, *Family Violence in Canada: A Statistical Profile, 2000* (Ottawa: Statistics Canada, 2000). See also Holly Johnson, *Measuring Violence Against Women: Statistical Trends, 2006* (Ottawa: Statistics Canada, 2006).
153 This response is discussed in DeKeseredy and Schwartz, ibid.
154 *Brown*, 155, para. 18, citing *R. v. Lavallee*, SCR, vol. 1 (1990), 852 (per Wilson, J.).
155 See *R. v. Coston*, AR 108 (1990): 209 (Hetherington, J.A. in dissent); *R. v. Montgrand*, AR 87 (1988): 221 (Hetherington, J.A). The Court also referred to *R. v. Inwood*, *Criminal Reports*, 3rd ser. 69 (1989): 181 (Ontario Court of Appeal). See "Mary Margaret McCormick Hetherington," in *Lords of the Western Bench*, Knafla and Klumpenhouwer, 71.
156 *Brown*, 155, para. 19.
157 See for example Laureen Snider, "Feminism, Punishment and the Potential of Empowerment," *Canadian Journal of Law and Society* 9 (1994): 75-104.
158 Other cases in which the Court of Appeal established starting points for criminal cases include *R. v. Johnas*, AR 41 (1982): 183 (robbery), and *R. v. Sandercock*, AR 62 (1985): 382 (major sexual assault).
159 *Brown*, 156, para. 20.
160 Ibid., 156, para. 21.
161 A classic work in this vein is Lenore Walker, *The Battered Woman* (New York: Harper & Row, 1979).
162 See for example Dianne Martin and Janet Mosher, "Unkept Promises: Experiences of Immigrant Women with the Neo-Criminalization of Wife Abuse," *Canadian Journal of Women and the Law* 8 (1995): 3-44; Jennifer Koshan, "Sounds of Silence: The Public/Private Dichotomy, Violence, and Aboriginal Women," in *Challenging the Public/Private Divide: Feminism, Law, and Public Policy*, ed. Susan B. Boyd (Toronto: University of Toronto Press, 1997), 87-109; Joanne Minaker, "Evaluating Criminal Justice Responses to Intimate Abuse through the Lens of Women's Needs," *Canadian Journal of Women and the Law* 13 (2001): 74-106; Janice Ristock, "And Justice for All?...The Social Context

of Legal Responses to Abuse in Lesbian Relationships," *Canadian Journal of Women and the Law* 7 (1994): 415-30, 429. Also see Laureen Snider, "Feminism, Punishment and the Potential of Empowerment."

163 *Brown*, 157, para. 26. Other factors include whether or not the assault was serious, and whether it was an isolated event.
164 Ibid.
165 See Minaker, "Evaluating Criminal Justice Responses to Intimate Abuse through the Lens of Women's Needs."
166 See Martin and Mosher, "Unkept Promises"; Koshan, "Sounds of Silence"; Ristock, "And Justice for All?"
167 *Brown*, 158, para. 29. The Court does seem open to entertaining this point in the future if it is more fully argued.
168 Ibid.
169 See for example Emma La Roque, *Violence in Aboriginal Communities* (Ottawa: National Clearinghouse on Family Violence, 1994); Anne McGillivray and Brenda Comaskey, *Black Eyes All of the Time: Intimate Violence, Aboriginal Women, and the Justice System* (Toronto: University of Toronto Press, 1999).
170 An Act to amend the Criminal Code (sentencing) and other Acts in consequence thereof, Statutes of Canada 1995, c. 22; s. 6, enacting s. 718(2) of the Criminal Code.
171 Ibid.
172 *R. v. Stone*, SCR 2 (1999): 290.
173 Ibid., 409-10, para. 241, citing *R. v. Doyle, Nova Scotia Reports*, 2nd ser., 108 (1991): 1 (Court of Appeal); *R. v. Pitkeathly, Criminal Reports*, 2nd ser., 29 (1994): 182 (Ontario Court of Appeal); *R. v. Edwards, OR*, 3rd ser., 28 (1996): 54 (Court of Appeal). *Brown* was also referred to as a "leading case" in Alberta Law Reform Institute, *Domestic Abuse: Toward an Effective Legal Response*, 22.
174 *Brown* was cited with approval by the Ontario Court of Appeal in *Pitkeathly*, ibid., as well as by other jurisdictions in numerous other cases.
175 Heather Steinke, "Starting-Point Sentencing for Domestic Assault: A Critical Review of the Brown Guidelines," *Alta LR* 35 (1996-97): 785-94, 792.
176 See for example *R. v. Crazybull*, AR 141 (1993): 69; *R. v. Ollenberger*, AR 149 (1994): 81; *R. v. Bonneteau*, AR 157 (1994): 138; *R. v. Heavyrunner*, AR 346 (2003): 74.
177 In this respect, *Brown* can be contrasted with other criminal cases of the Alberta courts in the area of violence against women, both before and after this 1992 decision. See for example *R. v. Sandercock*, AR 62 (1985): 382, where the Court of Appeal established a sentencing starting point for cases of major sexual assault without any explicit gender analysis; and *R. v. Ewanchuk*, AR 212 (1998): 81, where Justice John McClung of the Court of Appeal used language influenced by gender stereotypes to describe a sexual assault. See also *R. v. Piche*, AR 145 (1993): 233 (Court of Appeal), where Justice McClung upheld a sentence departing from the *Brown* guidelines in a case where the sentencing judge found that the accused "seems to have the good fortune to be married to a woman who has her feet on the ground" for agreeing to reconcile with her husband.
178 Brodsky & Day, *One Step Forward or Two Steps Back?*

179 Bertha Wilson, "Will Women Judges Really Make a Difference?" *Osgoode Hall Law Journal* 28 (1990): 507-22. For an analysis of whether women have made a difference in the Alberta legislature, see Trimble, "A Few Good Women."
180 While the Alberta courts have achieved a degree of gender parity, there is still a great distance to travel with respect to the appointment of judges with disabilities, judges who are racialized, gay and lesbian judges, and judges from impoverished backgrounds.

APPENDIX

Judges of the Supreme Court of Alberta, 1907–2007

SCC = Supreme Court of Canada
SCT = Supreme Court Trial
SC = Supreme Court of Alberta
SCA = Supreme Court of Alberta Appeal
QB = Queen's Bench
CA = Court of Appeal

A = Active
R = Retired
S = Suppernumerary
* = Deceased

LAST NAME	FULL NAME	APPOINTMENT	COURT	STATUS
Acton	Leora-Alice Darlene	1 Dec. 1998	QB, Edm.	(A)
Agrios	John Andrew	3 July 1982	QB, Edm.	30 Oct. 2007 (R)
Allen	Gordon Hollis	12 May 1966	CA, Cal.	28 May 1978*
Andrekson	Alexander	22 Aug. 1985	QB, Edm.	12 Dec. 1997*
Beck	Nicholas Du Bois Dominic	23 Sept. 1907 15 Sept. 1921	SC SCA, Edm.	14 May 1928*
Belzil	Roger Hector	30 June 1979 18 June 1981	QB, Edm. CA, Edm.	26 Dec. 1996 (R)
Belzil	Roger Paul	19 Dec. 1995	QB, Edm.	(A)
Bensler	Suzanne Margo	3 Feb. 1994	QB, Cal.	(A)
Berger	Ronald Leon	22 Aug. 1985 20 June 1996	QB, Edm. CA, Edm.	(A)
Bielby	Myra Beth	24 Dec. 1990	QB, Edm.	(A)
Binder	Melvyn A.	20 Feb. 1996	QB, Edm.	14 July 2007 (R)
Bowen	Donald Haines	20 Jan. 1972 30 June 1979	SCT, Edm. QB, Edm.	14 Sept. 1986*
Boyle	John Robert	27 Aug. 1924	SCT, Edm.	15 Feb. 1936*
Braco	John David	30 June 1979 31 Dec. 1987	QB, Cal. CA, Cal.	3 Aug. 1991 (S)*

333

LAST NAME	FULL NAME	APPOINTMENT	COURT	STATUS
Brennan	William Robert	8 April 1976 30 June 1979	SCT, Cal. QB, Cal.	7 Nov. 1995 (S)*
Brooker	Cameron Scott	20 June 1996 18 Jan. 2005	CA, Cal. ACJ, QB, Cal.	(A)
Burrows	Brian Russell	29 Jan. 1998	QB, Edm.	(A)
Cairns	James Mitchell	24 Mar. 1952 15 Feb. 1965	SCA, Cal. CA, Cal.	25 Oct. 1977 (R)*
Cairns	Robert MacMillan	22 Mar. 1991	QB, Cal.	22 Mar. 2006 (S)
Cavanaugh	James Creighton	18 May 1973 30 June 1979	SCT, Edm. QB, Edm.	31 Dec. 1990 (R)*
Cawsey	Robert Allan	27 Nov. 1979	QB, Edm.	11 Nov. 1992 (S)*
Chrumka	Paul Stephen	28 Jan. 1982	QB, Cal.	19 Sept. 2007 (S)
Clackson	Terrance David	1 Jan. 2000	QB, Edm.	(A)
Clark	Peter MacDonell	25 April 1995	QB, Cal.	(A)
Clarke	Alfred Henry	15 Sept. 1921	SCA, Cal.	30 Jan. 1942 *
Clarke	Charles Philip	25 April 1995	QB, Cal.	(A)
Clement	Carlton Ward	12 Feb. 1970 30 June 1979	SCA, Edm. CA, Edm.	7 Jan. 1982 (R)
Conrad	Carole Mildred	10 Nov. 1986 24 June 1992	QB, Cal. CA, Cal.	(A)
Cooke	Alan Thomas	10 Nov. 1986	QB, Edm.	30 Mar. 2005 (R)
Cormack	John Spiers	30 June 1979	QB, Edm.	21 Feb. 1985 (R)*
Costigan	Peter Thomas	1 Dec. 1994 25 Aug. 1999	QB, Edm. CA, Edm.	(A)
Côté	Jean Edouard Leon	30 Oct. 1987	CA, Edm.	(A)
Coutu	Jacqueline Claire	3 July 1997	QB, Cal.	15 Feb. 2007 (R)
Crighton	Michelle Gay	27 April 2007	QB, Edm.	(A)
Crossley	Arthur William	30 June 1979	QB, Edm.	9 Sept. 1991*
Cullen	Alan Joseph	12 Feb. 1970	SCT, Cal.	23 April 1975*
Dea	John Berchmans	30 June 1979	QB, Edm.	5 Sept. 2003 (R)
Dechene	André Miville	15 Feb. 1965 30 June 1979	SCT, Edm. QB, Edm.	25 Mar. 1987 (R)*

LAST NAME	FULL NAME	APPOINTMENT	COURT	STATUS
Decore	John Nickolas	30 June 1979	QB, Edm.	9 April 1984 (R)*
Decore	Lionel Leighton	1 Aug. 1983	QB, Edm.	5 Mar. 1984 (R)
Deyell	Roy Victor	31 Dec. 1987	QB, Cal.	23 April 1997 (R)
Dixon	Russell Armitage	23 Oct. 1980	QB, Cal.	27 April 1995 (S)
Egbert	William Gordon	25 Jan. 1950	SCT, Cal.	8 Feb. 1960*
Egbert	William Gordon Neil	27 Nov. 1979	QB, Cal.	15 Sept. 1997 (R)*
Eidsvik	Kristine Marie	27 April 2007	QB, Cal.	(A)
Erb	Marsha Colleen	15 Nov. 2001	QB, Cal.	(A)
Ewing	Albert Freeman	27 Jan. 1931 13 Jan. 1941	SCT, Edm. SCA, Edm.	21 Aug. 1946 (R)*
Farthing	Hugh Craig	7 April 1960	SCT, Cal.	18 July 1967 (R)*
Feehan	Joseph Bernard	30 June 1979	QB, Cal.	11 Feb. 2004*
Foisey	René Paul	30 June 1979 1 Jan. 1987	QB, Edm. CA, Edm.	25 Aug. 1999 (R)
Ford	Clinton James	19 April 1945 25 Jan. 1950 17 Jan. 1957	SCT, Edm. SCA, Edm. CJ Alberta	1 Mar. 1961 (R)*
Ford	Frank	3 May 1926 3 Nov. 1936	SCT, Edm. SCA, Edm.	13 Oct. 1954 (R)*
Forsyth	Gregory Rife	26 Mar. 1979 30 June 1979	SCT, Cal. QB, Cal.	16 Sept. 2002 (R)
Foster	James Lambert	13 Sept. 1991	QB, Red Deer	13 Sept. 2006 (S)
Foster	Nina Leone	18 April 1984	QB, Edm.	16 Aug. 1994 (R)*
Fraser	Catherine Anne	7 Mar. 1989 1 Mar. 1991 12 Mar. 1991	QB, Edm. CA, Edm. CJ CA	(A)
Fraser	Robert Patrick	21 June 1991	QB, Cal.	10 Oct. 2004 (R)
Fruman	Adelle	6 May 1993 1 Dec. 1998	QB, Cal. CA, Cal.	(A)
Gallant	Tellex William	21 June 1984	QB, Edm.	21 June 1999 (S)
Germain	Adam Wilson	5 Nov. 2003	QB, Edm.	(A)
Gill	John Joseph Michael	18 Jan. 2005	QB, Edm.	(A)

Appendix: Judges of the Supreme Court of Alberta, 1907–2007

LAST NAME	FULL NAME	APPOINTMENT	COURT	STATUS
Girgulis	William James	18 June 1981	QB, Edm.	10 Nov. 2005 (R)
Graesser	Robert Alexander	15 Dec. 2006	QB, Edm.	(A)
Greckol	Shelia Joy	15 Nov. 2001	QB, Edm.	(A)
Greschuk	Peter	17 Jan. 1957 30 June 1979	SCT, Edm. QB, Edm.	14 Nov. 1983 (R)*
Haddad	William Joseph	29 Nov. 1974 30 June 1979	SCA, Edm. CA, Edm.	26 Nov. 1990 (R)
Harradence	Asa Milton	26 Mar. 1979 30 June 1979	SCA, Cal. CA, Cal.	23 April 1997 (R)
Hart	Dennis	3 Feb. 1994	QB, Cal.	(A)
Harvey	Horace	15 Sept. 1907 12 Oct. 1910 15 Sept. 1921 27 Aug. 1924 27 Aug. 1924	SC, Edm. CJ SCT SCT, Edm. SCA, Edm. CJ Alberta	9 Sept. 1949*
Hawco	Gerald Cantwell	20 June 1996	QB, Cal.	(A)
Hembroff	Willard Vaughan	23 Dec. 1991	QB, Leth.	23 Dec. 2006 (S)
Hetherington	Mary Margaret McCormick	30 June 1979 4 April 1985	QB, Cal. CA, Cal.	31 Dec. 2000 (R)
Hillier	Stephen Don	9 April 2003	QB, Edm.	(A)
Holmes	Jack Kenneth	30 June 1979 1984	QB, Cal. QB, R. Deer	2 Jan. 2003 (S)
Hope	John McIntosh	23 Dec. 1976 30 June 1979	SCT, Edm. QB, Edm.	26 Feb. 1992 (R)*
Horner	Karen Mae	12 Dec. 2002	QB, Cal.	(A)
Howson	William Robinson	2 Mar. 1936 6 May 1942 20 Oct. 1944 20 Oct. 1944	SCT, Edm. SCA, Edm. SCT, Edm. CJ SCT	25 June 1952*
Hughes	Elizabeth Anne	15 Nov. 2001	QB, Cal.	(A)
Hunt	Constance	23 Dec. 1991 26 April 1995	QB, Cal. CA Cal.	(A)
Hutchinson	Ernest Arthur	30 Sept. 1985	QB, Cal.	9 June 1999 (S)
Hyndman	James Duncan	11 July 1914 15 Sept. 1921	SC, Edm. SCA, Edm.	15 Jan. 1931 (R)*
Irving	Howard Lawrence	15 Feb. 1985	CA, Edm.	28 Dec. 1999 (R)

LAST NAME	FULL NAME	APPOINTMENT	COURT	STATUS
Ives	William Carlos	11 July 1914 15 Sept. 1921 25 Sept. 1942	SC, Cal. SCT, Cal. CJ, SCT, Cal.	16 Aug. 1944 (R)*
Johnson	Horace Gilchrist	16 Dec. 1954	SCA, Edm.	20 Dec. 1973 (R)*
Johnstone	Cecilia Irma	21 Feb. 1996	QB, Edm.	15 April 2006*
Jones	Lionel Locksey	28 April 1995	QB, Edm.	18 June 2001 (R)
Kenny	Colleen Lynn	25 April 1995	QB, Cal.	(A)
Kent	Caroline Adele	11 Feb. 1994	QB, Cal.	(A)
Kerans	Roger Philip	30 June 1979 23 Oct. 1980	QB, Edm. CA, Cal.	2 April 1997 (R)
Kidd	James George	30 June 1979	QB, Cal.	1 Nov. 1983 (S)*
Kirby	William John Cameron	18 Oct. 1960 30 June 1979	SCT, Cal. QB, Cal.	12 Jan. 1984 (R)*
Kryczka	Joseph Julius	3 July 1980	QB, Cal.	11 Jan. 1991*
Langston	James Hilton	29 Nov. 1994	QB, Leth.	
Laycraft	James Herbert	31 July 1975 26 Mar. 1979 30 June 1979 20 Feb. 1985	SCT, Cal. SCA, Cal. CA, Cal. CJ Alberta	31 Dec. 1991 (R)
Lee	Donald	3 Feb. 1994	QB, Edm.	(A)
Lefsrud	Erik Sigurd	29 Nov. 1991	QB, Edm.	25 Aug. 2003 (S)
Legg	Sidney Vincent	30 June 1979	QB, Edm.	22 Sept. 1992 (S)*
Lewis	James Lester	1 Feb. 1993	QB, Edm.	21 Dec. 2003 (S)
Lieberman	Samuel Sereth	12 Feb. 1970 23 Dec. 1976 30 June 1979	SCT, Edm. SCA, Edm. CA, Edm.	15 April 1987 (S)
Lomas	Melvin Earl	28 April 1981	QB, Cal.	30 Sept. 2003 (R)
LoVecchio	Salvatore Joseph	25 April 1995	QB, Cal.	(A)
Lunney	Henry William	23 May 1928	SCA, Cal.	6 Oct. 1944 (R)*
Lutz	Arthur Morton	4 Nov. 1982	QB, Cal.	3 Feb. 2002 (S)
MacCallum	Edward Patrick	22 Dec. 1983	QB, Edm.	2 Jan. 2001 (S)
MacDonald	Hugh John	20 Oct. 1944 17 Jan. 1957	SCT, Edm. SCA, Edm.	2 Mar. 1965*

Appendix: Judges of the Supreme Court of Alberta, 1907–2007

LAST NAME	FULL NAME	APPOINTMENT	COURT	STATUS
MacDonald	Hugh John	25 Mar. 1968 30 June 1979	SCT, Cal. QB, Cal.	11 April 1986 (R)*
MacDonald	William Alexander	6 May 1942 20 Oct. 1944	SCT, Cal. SCA, Cal.	17 Jan. 1957 (R)*
MacKenzie	John Horace	22 Dec. 1983	QB, Red Deer	1 Sept. 2002 (R)
Macklin	Eric Frank	18 April 2002	QB, Edm.	(A)
MacLean	Lawrence David	21 Dec. 1978 30 June 1979	SCT, Leth. QB, Leth.	30 June 2002 (R)
MacLeod	Donald Ingraham	14 Mar. 1990	QB, Cal.	14 Mar. 2005 (S)
Macleod	Alan Douglas	22 Nov. 2005	QB, Cal.	(A)
MacNaughton	Frederick Richards	19 Dec. 1980	QB, Edm.	17 July 1987*
MacPherson	Jack Leon	15 Mar. 1985	QB, Cal.	2 April 1991*
Mahoney	Bryan Ernest	15 Nov. 2001	QB, Cal.	(A)
Major	John C.	11 July 1991 13 Nov. 1992	CA, Cal. SCC	25 Dec. 2005 (R)
Manning	Marshall Edward	18 Aug. 1959 30 June 1979	SCT, Edm. QB, Edm.	28 Dec. 1979 (R)*
Marceau	Joseph Richard Phillipe	19 Dec. 1995	QB, Edm.	(A)
Marshall	Ernest Arthur	16 June 1986	QB, Edm.	13 Jan. 2002 (S)
Martin	Peter Walter Lambert	12 June 1998 22 Nov. 2005	QB, Edm. CA, Edm.	(A)
Martin	Sheilah Louise	24 June 2005	QB, Cal.	(A)
Mason	David Blair	22 Aug. 1985	QB, Cal.	31 Mar. 2001 (S)
Matheson	Douglas Randolph	15 Mar. 1985	QB, Edm.	6 May 1996 (R)
McBain	Ross Thomas George	22 Dec. 1983	QB, Cal.	5 April 2001 (R)*
McBride	James Boyd	30 Oct. 1946 17 Jan. 1957	SCT, Edm. SCA, Edm.	2 Jan. 1960*
McCarthy	Maitland Stewart	11 July 1914 15 Sept. 1921	SC, Edm. SCT, Edm.	3 May 1926 (R)*
McClung	John Wesley	22 Dec. 1977 30 June 1979 19 Dec. 1980	SCT, Edm. QB, Edm. CA, Edm.	21 Oct. 2004*
McDermid	Neil Douglas	14 Aug. 1963 30 June 1979	SCA, Cal. CA, Cal.	5 June 1986 (R)

LAST NAME	FULL NAME	APPOINTMENT	COURT	STATUS
McDonald	David Cargill	1 Jan. 1974 30 June 1979 1 Jan. 1996	SCT, Edm. QB, Edm. CA, Edm.	7 April 1996*
McDonald	John David Bruce	18 Sept. 2006	QB, Cal.	(A)
McFadyen	Elizabeth Ann	30 June 1979 1 Feb. 1993	QB, Cal. CA, Cal.	1 Sept. 2005 (S)
McGillivray	Alexander Andrew	8 May 1931	SCA, Cal.	12 Dec. 1940*
McGillivray	William Alexander	5 Dec. 1974 30 June 1979 5 Dec. 1974	SCA, Cal. CA, Cal. CJ, CA, Cal.	16 Dec. 1984*
McIntrye	Peter Joseph	29 Nov. 1994	QB, Cal.	(A)
McLaurin	Colin Campbell	23 Sept. 1942 27 June 1952	SCT, Cal. CJ SCT, Cal.	1 Sept. 1968 (R)*
McMahon	Terrence Frederick	4 Sept. 1992	QB, Cal.	4 Sept. 2007 (S)
Medhurst	Donald Herbert	30 June 1979	QB, Cal.	17 Dec. 1999 (R)
Miller	Dallas Keith	23 Dec. 2006	QB, Leth.	(A)
Miller	Tevie Harold	8 July 1976 30 June 1979 24 Feb. 1984	SCT, Edm. QB, Edm. ACJ QB, Edm.	21 Aug. 1996*
Milvain	James Valentine Hogarth	18 Aug. 1959 26 Sept. 1968	SCT, Cal. CJ SCT, Cal.	14 Feb. 1979*
Mitchell	Charles Richmond	13 Mar. 1926 3 Nov. 1936	SCA, Cal. CJ SCT, Cal.	16 Aug. 1942*
Moen	Andrea Beverly	1 Jan. 2000	QB, Edm.	(A)
Moir	Arnold Fraser	18 May 1973 30 June 1979	SCA, Cal. CA, Cal.	24 Sept. 1987*
Montgomery	Robert Archibald	4 Nov. 1982	QB, Cal.	31 Jan. 1998 (R)
Moore	John Stanley	27 Nov. 1992	QB, Cal.	15 Sept. 2006 (R)
Moore	William Kenneth	20 Jan. 1972 30 June 1979 28 April 1981 24 Feb. 1984	SCT, Cal. QB, Cal. ACJ, QB, Cal. CJ, QB, Cal.	5 Dec. 2000 (R)
Moreau	Mary Teresa	29 Nov. 1994	QB, Edm.	(A)
Morrow	William George	28 May 1976 30 June 1979	SCA, Cal. CA, Cal.	13 Aug. 1980*

Appendix: Judges of the Supreme Court of Alberta, 1907–2007

LAST NAME	FULL NAME	APPOINTMENT	COURT	STATUS
Moshansky	Virgil Peter	27 May 1976 30 June 1979	SCT, Cal. QB, Cal.	14 Sept. 1993 (R)
Murray	Alec Thirlwell	30 Oct. 1997	QB, Edm.	7 Aug. 2007 (R)
Nash	Eileen Margaret	1 Feb. 1993	QB, Edm.	5 Dec. 2001*
Nation	Rosemary Elizabeth	23 Dec. 1997	QB, Cal.	(A)
Neilson	Kenneth G.	27 April 2007	QB, Edm.	(A)
O'Brien	Clifton David	13 May 2005	CA, Cal.	(A)
O'Byrne	Michael Brien	19 Sept. 1967 30 June 1979	SCT, Edm. QB, Edm.	9 Sept. 2000 (R)*
O'Connor	George Bligh	13 Jan. 1941 30 Oct. 1946 25 Jan. 1950	SCT, Edm. SCA, Edm. CJ Alberta	13 Jan. 1957*
O'Leary	Willis Edward	22 Dec. 1983 27 Sept. 1994	QB, Cal. CA, Cal.	6 Sept. 2006 (R)
Ouellette	Joseph Omer	18 April 2002	QB, Edm.	(A)
Paperny	Marina Sarah	20 June 1996 6 Feb. 2001	QB, Cal. CA, Cal.	(A)
Park	Alexander Graham	1 Dec. 1998	QB, Cal.	(A)
Parlee	Harold Hayward	19 Dec. 1944 9 April 1945	SCT, Edm. SCA, Edm.	28 Feb. 1954*
Patterson	Henry Stuart	30 June 1979	QB, Cal.	3 Nov. 1988 (R)*
Perras	Delmar Walter Joseph	4 Oct. 1989	QB, Edm.	4 Oct. 2004 (S)
Phillips	Carolyn Susanne	29 Nov. 1994	QB, Cal.	(A)
Picard	Ellen Irene	1 Jan. 1986 27 April 1995	QB, Edm. CA, Edm.	1 Mar. 2006 (S)
Porter	Marshall Menzies	1 Sept. 1954	SCA, Cal.	12 Oct. 1969 (R)*
Power	Peter Charles Garneau	27 Nov. 1979	QB, Cal.	16 April 2005 (R)
Primrose	Neil Phillip	1 Sept. 1954	SCT, Edm.	15 Sept. 1977 (R)*
Prowse	David Clifton	1 Sept. 1972 30 June 1979	SCA, Cal. CA, Cal.	26 July 1988*
Prowse	Hubert Samuel	27 Nov. 1979	QB, Cal.	8 Dec. 1993 (S)*
Purvis	Stuart Somerville	3 July 1980	QB, Edm.	25 Sept. 1986*

LAST NAME	FULL NAME	APPOINTMENT	COURT	STATUS
Quigley	Francis Hugh	28 Nov. 1974 30 June 1979	SCT, Cal. QB, Cal.	31 Dec. 1995 (R)*
Rawlins	Bonnie Leigh	8 Mar. 1989	QB, Cal.	(A)
Read	Donna Lynn Carson	18 April 2002	QB, Edm.	(A)
Ritter	Keith Gregory	1 Feb. 1993 18 April 2002	QB, Edm. CA, Edm.	(A)
Romaine	Barbara Ellen Catherine	27 Aug. 1997	QB, Cal.	(A)
Rooke	John Daniel	22 Mar. 1991	QB, Cal.	(A)
Roslak	Yaroslav	31 Dec. 1987	QB, Edm.	3 May 1995*
Ross	June Marie	5 Nov. 2003	QB, Edm.	(A)
Rowbotham	Henry Slater	30 June 1979	QB, Cal.	30 Sept. 1985 (S)
Rowbotham	Patricia Adele	8 June 1999	QB, Cal.	(A)
Russell	Anne Helen	27 Nov. 1992 27 Nov. 1994	QB, Edm. CA, Edm.	1 May 2006 (R)
Sanderman	Sterling Michael	20 June 1996	QB, Edm.	(A)
Scott	David Lynch	16 Sept. 1907 15 Sept. 1921 15 Sept. 1921	SC, Edm. SCA, Edm. CJ Alberta	26 July 1924*
Shannon	Melvin Earl	18 May 1973 30 June 1979	SCT, Cal. QB, Cal.	5 June 2002 (R)
Shelley	Donna Lee	15 Dec. 2006	QB, Edm.	(A)
Shepherd	Simpson James	3 Nov. 1936	SCT, Leth.	6 Feb. 1952 (R)*
Sifton	Arthur Lewis	16 Sept. 1907 16 Sept. 1907	SC, Cal. CJ Alberta	25 May 1910 (R)*
Simmons	William Charles	12 Oct. 1910 15 Sept. 1921 27 Aug. 1924	SC, Cal. SCT, Cal. CJ, SCT, Cal.	1 Sept. 1936 (R)*
Sinclair	William Robert	26 Sept. 1968 25 Jan. 1973 22 Feb. 1979 30 June 1979 24 Feb. 1984	SCT, Edm. SCA, Edm. CJ, SCT, Edm. CJ, QB, Edm. QB, Edm.	18 Dec. 1985 (R)*
Sirrs	Douglas Albert	9 June 1999	QB, Red Deer	(A)

Appendix: Judges of the Supreme Court of Alberta, 1907–2007

LAST NAME	FULL NAME	APPOINTMENT	COURT	STATUS
Sisson	Kirk Leader	27 Oct. 2006	QB, Red Deer	(A)
Slatter	Frans Felling	1 Mar. 2001 27 Oct. 2006	QB, Edm. CA, Edm.	(A)
Smith	Pamela Lawrie Jean	29 Nov. 1991	QB, Edm.	(A)
Smith	Sidney Bruce	8 Jan. 1959 7 April 1960 15 Mar. 1961	SCT, Cal. SCA, Cal. CJ Alberta	5 Dec. 1974 (R)*
Smith	Vernor Winfield MacBriare	19 Dec. 1980	QB, Edm.	13 June 2000 (R)
Steer	George Alexander Cameron	28 Nov. 1974 30 June 1979	SCT, Edm. QB, Edm.	16 Dec. 1979*
Stevenson	William Alexander	30 June 1979 23 Oct. 1980 17 Sept. 1990	QB, Edm. CA, Edm. SCC	6 June 1992 (R)
Stratton	Joseph John Walker	23 Oct. 1980 30 Oct. 1987	QB, Edm. CA, Edm.	13 Dec. 1995 (R)
Stuart	Charles Allan	16 Sept. 1907 15 Sept. 1921	SC, Cal. SCA, Cal.	5 Mar. 1926*
Sulatycky	Allen Borislaw Zenoviy	4 Nov. 1982 28 Aug. 1997 13 Dec. 2000	QB, Edm. CA, Cal. ACJ QB, Cal.	12 Dec. 2004 (S)
Sullivan	William Patrick	25 April 1995	QB, Cal.	(A)
Sulyma	Doreen Anastasia	23 Dec. 1997	QB, Edm.	(A)
Thomas	Dennis Roland Gwynne	24 June 2005	QB, Edm.	(A)
Topolniski	Juliana Elizabeth	9 April 2003	QB, Edm.	(A)
Trussler	Marguerite Jean	7 Nov. 1986	QB, Edm.	16 April 2007 (R)
Turcotte	Louis Sherman	30 June 1979	QB, Leth.	10 Sept. 1979 (R)*
Tweedie	Thomas Mitchell March	15 Sept. 1921 16 Aug. 1944	SCT, Cal. CJ, SCT, Cal.	4 Oct. 1944*
Veit	Joanne Barbara	18 June 1981	QB, Edm.	9 Sept. 2007 (S)
Verville	Gerald Albert	1 Dec. 1998	QB, Edm.	(A)
Virtue	Charles Gladstone	9 Oct. 1985	QB, Cal.	15 June 1997 (R)*

LAST NAME	FULL NAME	APPOINTMENT	COURT	STATUS
Wachowich	Allan Harvey Joseph	30 June 1979	QB, Edm.	(A)
		1 Feb. 1993	ACJ, QB, Edm.	
		13 Dec. 2000	CJ QB, Edm.	
Waite	John Hilary	2 Feb. 1978	SCT, Cal.	12 April 2003 (R)*
		30 June 1979	QB, Cal.	
Walsh	William Legh	3 April 1912	SC, Cal.	1 May 1931 (R)*
		15 Sept. 1921	SCT, Cal.	
		27 Jan. 1931	SCA, Cal.	
Watson	Jack	27 July 2000	QB, Edm.	(A)
		18 Sept. 2006	CA, Edm.	
Wilkins	Lloyd David	3 Feb. 1994	QB, Cal.	(A)
Wilson	Ernest Brown	27 June 1952	SCT, Edm.	10 Dec. 1958*
Wilson	William Ernest	1 Mar. 1991	QB, Edm.	17 June 2003 (S)
Wittmann	Neil Charles	9 June 1999	CA, Cal.	(A)
		19 Jan. 2005	ACJ, CA, Cal.	
Yanosik	Clarence George	30 June 1979	QB, Leth.	20 April 2001 (R)

Index

Aberhart, William, government
  monetary legislation (*Alberta Statutes*),
    100, 107–10
Aboriginal people
  spousal abuse and, 319–20
  See also First Nations, treaty hunting
    rights
Acadia judicial district, 31, 55
accretion. *See* water law, riparian
Adams v. McLeod, 286
adoption rights and same-sex couples,
  276–77
adult children, support for, 280
AEUB. *See* Alberta Energy and Utilities
  Board
agriculture and water drainage, 211–19
Alberta, history
  immigration, 52–53, 71–72
  natural resources law, 112–17, 227–29
  population growth, 47–49
  populism, 174, 178
  settlement and water law, 194–98
Alberta Act, 30, 113
Alberta Bill of Rights Act (1946), 110–12,
  117
Alberta Bill of Rights Act (1972), 112,
  307–11
Alberta Energy and Utilities Board
  creation of, 244–45
  "extricable" legal principles (*ATCO*),
    248–51
  judicial review, exceptional
    circumstances (*Rozander*), 246
  judicial review, factors, 245–48
  regulatory powers (*Spooner*), 232
  sour gas plant, challenge to (*Coalition
    of Citizens, Caroline*), 251–52
Alberta Farmers' Union, 163

Alberta Game Act (1907), 142–44
Alberta Hospital Association v. Parcels,
  310–11
Alberta Law Reports (ALR), 56–57
Alberta School Trustee Association, 163
Alberta Treasury Branch, 107–12
"Alberta Trilogy" child support cases,
  282
Allen, Gordon, 109–10
American and English Encyclopedia of Law,
  58
American law. *See* United States
Anabaptists, 160
Anderson v. Amoco Canada Oil and Gas,
  239–41
Andrews v. Law Society of B.C., 300, 312–13
Andriet v. Strathcona (County) No. 20,
  210–11
Anglin, Francis Alexander, 78, 84
Annual Practice of the Supreme Court, 54
Appellate Division, Supreme Court
  of Alberta. *See* Supreme Court of
  Alberta, history (1905–1921)
Armstrong v. McLaughlin Estate, 276
assault, spousal, 315–21
assimilation
  and First Nations people, 141, 150
  and Hutterites, 162–63, 174, 178
ATB Financial, 107–10
*ATCO Electric Limited. v. Alberta (Energy
  and Utilities Board)*, 248, 250–51
*ATCO Gas and Pipelines Ltd. v. Alberta
  (Energy and Utilities Board)* [ATCO
  Gas 2004], 248, 251
*ATCO Gas and Pipelines Ltd. v. Alberta
  (Energy and Utilities Board)* [ATCO
  Gas 2005], 248
Athabaska judicial district, 31, 55

B. v. B., 266
Bailey, Stella, 271
Baker v. Baker, 280
Bank Act, 110
Bank of Montreal v. Dynex Petroleum Ltd., 254
banks
    ATB Financial (*Breckenridge/Long*), 107-10
    reference of Bill of Rights Act, 111-12
Barber v. Barber, 284
Barka v. Barka, 285
Bastarache, Michel, 251
battered women, 315-21
beaver dams
    water drainage (*Farnell*), 214-16, 219
Beck, Nicholas D.
    biographical notes, xvii, 11, 31, 32, 33, 39-40, 44-47
    on independence of SCA, 31
    judicial districts, 50, 53
    as legal editor, 30, 56
    religion and, 39-40, 59, 105
    use of legal resources, 55, 58
    views of, generally, 16, 44-47
Beck, Nicholas D., cases
    child custody (*O'Leary*), 282
    conscription (*Lewis/Norton*), 75-78, 83, 85, 88, 101-03
    divorce (*Board*), 59, 105, 268
    political dissent (*Felton/Trainor*), 52, 54-55
    water law (*Clarke*), 199-200, 218
Belzil, Paul, 313-14
Bennett, R.B., 38, 40, 46, 76, 101
Berger, Ronald, 280
Big Bear, trial of, 34
Biggar, O.M., 78
Bill of Rights, Alberta, 110-12, 307-11
bison, 137, 140
Bliss v. Attorney General of Canada, 309-11
Blue Sky Colony (Hutterite), 182
Board v. Board
    Beck on, 59, 268-69
    Beck on Catholicism and, 105
    divorce law jurisdiction, 38-39, 104-05, 264-66
Borden, Robert, government
    conscription exemptions (*Lewis*), 37-38, 71-75, 101
    Union coalition, 73-75
Borys v. Canadian Pacific Railway and Imperial Oil Ltd., 228, 237-41

Bowen, Donald H., 262
Bowker, Wilbur, 43, 79, 81, 95n54
Boyle, John, 267
Breach, E.F., 165, 167-68, 175-77, 179-80, 183
Breckenridge Speedway Ltd. v. Alberta, 108-10
Breen, David, 228, 230-31
Bright, David, 10
British Columbia
    appeals and trial divisions, 32
    justices in, 46
    legal resources, 57
    patronage appointments, 33
    sexual sterilization legislation, 302
British law. *See* England
British North America Act (1867)
    Constitution as supreme law, 99-100
    judicial independence and, 69
    jurisdiction over banking, 108
    jurisdiction over divorce, 104, 264
    jurisdiction over Indians and Indian lands, 135, 138, 143, 149
    jurisdiction over natural resources, 135, 137, 138
    local legislation on local matters, 29
    Persons case, 297-301
    Resources Amendment, 244
    taxation powers and NEP program, 243-44
Broder v. Broder, 288
Brodsky, Gwen, 298, 320
Brookes v. Strohschein, 279
Brooks v. Canada Safeway Ltd., 310-11
Brownlee, John, 119-20
Burrell, Martin, 81
Burroughs, 56-57
Burrows, Brian, 274
Burwash v. Mirosh, 287

Cairns, Robert M., 271
Calgary judicial district
    caseloads and population, 47-51
    courthouses, xviii, xxi, 32
    creation of, 30-31
    en banc sittings, 6
    law library, 58
    trial judges, 53
Calliou, Brian, vii
    on treaty hunting rights, 12, 133-57
Campbell, R., 54
Canada, government of
    Order-in-Council for conscription

(*Lewis/Gray*), 11, 37-38, 70-71, 74-79, 82, 85, 101-03
Canada (*Director of Investigation and Research*) *v. Southam Inc.*, 247
Canada Law Book Company, 57
Canadian Bill of Rights
  application of, 308
  communal property challenge, 170
  pregnancy (*Bliss*), 309-11
Canadian Charter of Rights and Freedoms
  contextual and formalist approaches, 86
  gender and Charter challenges, 312
  habeas corpus, 86
  SCA and, 12, 117-18, 125-26
Canadian Charter of Rights and Freedoms, cases
  cohabitational relationships, 276-77
  family law cases, 273-75
  Lord's Day Act (*Big M. Drug Mart*), 118
  publication limits (*Edmonton Journal*), 119-20
  same-sex relationships, 276-77
  search warrants (*Hunter*), 118, 126
  sexual equality, 311-15
  substantive equality (*Andrews*), 300, 312
Canadian Encyclopedic Digest, 57
Canadian Northern Railway, 47
Canadian Pacific Railway
  early SCA cases, 47
  prairie fire ordinances, 29
  sale of mineral rights, 201, 237
  Simmons as critic of, 41
Carson, J.M., 78
Carswell, 56
Cassell, William, 54
Castor, communal property, 174-77
Catholic Church. *See* Roman Catholic Church
Cavanaugh v. Ziegler, 274
Chapman, Terry, 266
Charter of Rights and Freedoms. *See* Canadian Charter of Rights and Freedoms
children
  access rights (*Csicsiri*), 286
  adoption rights re same-sex couples (*Re C.*), 276-77
  "best interests" test, 283-86
  born to unmarried parents, 273-75
  child custody, 268, 282-88
  child support, 279-82

child support guidelines, 274
history of family law, 288-90
history of law re, 263, 267-68, 282, 284
joint custody, 287-88
parallel parenting (*Broder*), 288
parenting orders, 288
recent court initiatives, 283-84
support for adult children, 280
tender years doctrine, 286-87
Child Support Guidelines, 273-74, 280-82
Christian, Tim, 302
Chuckery v. the Queen (Manitoba), 205-06, 210
Cipperly v. Cipperly, 271
civil liberties
  hate propaganda (*Keegstra*), 122-24
  political dissent (*Felton/Trainor*), 52-54
  reference of Bill of Rights Act, 110-11
civil matters
  caseloads of SCA, 47-52
  early history, 7, 47-48, 59-60
Clark, Peter M., 182-83
Clarke, Alfred Henry
  biographical notes, 32
  contract interpretation (*Majestic*), 234
  jurisdiction over inheritance law, 113
  treaty hunting rights (*Wesley*), 147
Clarke, C. Philip, 277
Clarke v. Edmonton (City), 199-201, 218
climate change, 211
C.M. v. C.M., 274
coal, 114, 202, 241
coal bed methane, 241
Coalition of Citizens Impacted by the Caroline Shell Gas Plant v. Alberta (Energy and Utilities Board), 251-52
Colborne, F.C., 164
Coleman v. Coleman, 265
Colonial Laws Validity Act, 107
Combines Investigation Act, 118, 126
commercial cases
  ATB Financial (*Breckenridge/Long*), 108-10
  banks in reference of Bill of Rights Act, 111-12
  early years, 47
Communal Property Act
  amendments to, 166, 168-69
  constitutional challenge (*Hatch*), 164-65, 169
  constitutional challenge (*Walter*), 169-75

Index 347

Communal Property Act (*continued*)
  legislative review of, 167-69, 171-72, 174, 176-77
  provisions in, 164-69, 178
  repeal of, 159, 166, 176-77
  SCC on, 13, 173-77
Communal Property Control Board
  history of, 165-66, 168-69, 175-79
Conflict of Laws (Dicey), 54
conscription
  exemption process, 73-74
  exemptions (*Lewis*), 37-38, 71-75, 101-03
  judicial independence and, 81-85
  legislation re, 70-75
consortium, loss of, 271-72
Constitution Act (1867). *See* British North America Act (1867)
Constitutional Act (1982)
  Constitution as supreme law, 99-100
  NEP and, 244
contextual and formalist approaches, 86-87
Conybeare, Charles, 43
Cook v. Cook and the Attorney General of Alberta, 266
Corpus Juris, 58
Côté, Jean E.L., cases
  communal property, 181-82
  intimate violence (*Brown*), 316
courthouses
  construction of, xviii-xxi, 32
  libraries in, 55, 58
Court of Appeal
  Charter and, 117-18
  first female justice, 17
  First Nations and, 134
  judges, list of (1907-2007), 337-47
  number of justices, 7-8
  reorganization of courts, 8
  use of term, 6, 23n26
court officials, 31
Court of Queen's Bench
  family law initiatives, 283
  First Nations and, 134
  judges, xxvi
  judges, list of (1907-2007), 337-47
  number of justices, 7-8
  reorganization of courts, 8
  use of term, 6, 23n26
Crawley, Hector, 146
criminal matters
  appeals to JCPC, 106
  caseloads, 47-52
  differential ages for adulthood, criminal (*R. v. M.L.*), 312-14
  early history, 7, 29, 37, 41-42, 47-50, 315
  execution of murderers, 32
  hate propaganda (*Keegstra*), 121-24
  Prohibition, impact of, 106-07
  search warrants, Charter challenge (*Hunter v. Southam*), 118
  sexual assault cases, records (*Mills*), 313-15
  spousal assault, 315-21
  voluntary confessions, 29
Crowsnest Pass rumrunners, 41-42
Csicsiri v. Csicsiri, 286
Cullen, Alan Joseph, xxv, 285
custody of children. *See* children
Cyclopedia of Procedure and Practice, 58

Daly, T. Mayne, 139-41
dams
  beaver dams (*Farnell*), 214-16, 219
  to prevent drainage (*Makowecki*), 212-16
  rights of lower owners (*Molden*), 216
Dart, J.H., 54
Davidovich v. Davidovich, 285
Dawson, Brettel, 301
Day, Shelagh, 298, 320
Dechene, André, 278
Decore, John, 174-77, 184
deed registry land titles system, 204
Department of Indian Affairs
  First Nations game laws, 135-45
development appeal boards
  zoning and communal property, 177-84
Dewdney, Edgar, 28
Dicey, A.V., 54
Dickson, Brian, 121-24
Digest (Cassell), 54
disabilities, people with, 304, 306-07
dissent, public. *See* free speech
District Courts
  communal property cases, 165-66, 168, 174-75
  history of, 165
Divorce Act (1968), 278
Divorce Act (1985), 279, 281, 287, 288
Divorce and Matrimonial Causes Act (1857), 39, 265, 266
divorce law
  adultery as grounds for divorce, 267-68

child support (*Olsen*), 270
domicile issue (*Coleman/McCormack*),
   265–66
grounds for divorce cases, 266–67
history, pre-1918 period, 263–70
history, post-1918 period, 263–64,
   270–72, 278, 288–90
jurisdiction (*Board*), 38–39, 104–05,
   264–66, 268–69
loss of consortium (*Fediuk*), 271–72
marriage validity, 264
open court requirement (*McPherson*),
   119–20, 269
publication limits (*Brownlee/
   McPherson*), 119–20
religious views (*Board*), 59
spousal support cases, 269–71, 277–79
See also matrimonial property law
Doherty, Charles, 79–80
Domestic Relations Act, 271–72, 276, 288
domestic violence, 315–21
domicile in divorce, 265–66
Dominion Lands Act, 204, 236
Dominion Land Survey, 204, 207–08
Dominion Petroleum Regulations
   (1906), 234
Doukhobors, 162, 164, 171, 174
Down syndrome
   policies of Eugenics Board, 303–04
drainage, water. *See* water law
Driedger, Elmer, 86
Duck Lake conflict, 34
Duff, Lyman, 113–14
Dumas v. Dumas, 279

Eaton, R.B., 79
Eddy v. Eddy, 279
Edmonton, City of
   employment law (*Gallagher*), 38, 64n77
Edmonton Journal v. Alberta, 118–20
Edmonton judicial district
   caseloads and population, 47–49, 51–52
   courthouse, xix, xxiv, 32
   creation of, 30–31
   en banc sittings, 6
   law library, 55, 58
   trial judges, 53
Edmonton Roman Catholic Separate
   Schools
   francophone education (*Mahe*), 120–21
Egbert, William G.N., 239–40
Eliason v. Alberta, 201–03
Emery, Edward Corrigan, 39

Energy and Utilities Board. *See* Alberta
   Energy and Utilities Board
energy law, 227–60
   coal and coal bed methane, 241
   contract interpretation (*Majestic*),
      233–35
   Crown ownership, 202–03, 229–30
   "extricable" legal principles (*ATCO*),
      248–51
   history of, 14–15, 112–17, 227–31
   impact of NRTA, 227–29
   interpretation of language, 233–35, 238,
      252–54
   jurisdiction (*Mercury*), 231–32
   NEP tax on gas (*Re Proposed Federal
      Tax*), 115–17, 242–48, 255
   oil and gas unit agreements (*Prism*),
      239–40
   provincial jurisdiction under
      Amendment to BNA, 244–45
   regulation of private development,
      229–30
   regulatory boards (Turner Valley),
      230–31
   regulatory powers of boards (*Spooner*),
      228–32, 246, 255
   rights to accreted land (*Eliason*), 201–03
   royalties, future (*Huggard*), 114–15, 228,
      233–37, 255
   royalties as "free an common socage"
      tenure, 235–36
   royalty system cases, 254
   SCA and, 227–29, 254–55
   split ownership, oil and gas (*Anderson*),
      239–41
   split ownership, oil and gas (*Borys*),
      228, 237–41
   use of American authorities, 253
   See also Alberta Energy and Utilities
      Board; Natural Resources Transfer
      Agreement
England
   laws of 1870, use in Canada, 28, 31, 195
   legal resources from, 56–58
   See also Judicial Committee of the
      Privy Council
English Reports Annotated, 58
English Reports Reprint, 58
environmental issues
   gas flaring, 230–31
   sour gas plant (*Coalition of Citizens,
      Caroline*), 251–52
   treaty hunting rights, 139

Index   349

equality
　Charter challenges, 311–15
　in family law, 273–74, 276–77
　formal equality, 305, 307, 310
　formal equality, definition, 299–300
　formal equality and communal
　　property, 183
　formal equality and populism, 174
　substantive equality, definition, 300
　See also same-sex relationships;
　　women's equality
Equity Jurisprudence (Pomeroy), 54
Esau, Alvin J., 160
escheat, principle of, 112–13
Eugenics Board
　decisions of (*Muir*), 303–07
　powers of, 301–02
evidence, rules of, 37
execution of murderers, 32

family law, 261–96
　Charter and, 273–75
　cohabitational relationships, 276–77
　definition of family, 273–74
　female judges and, 16–17, 283–84, 321
　history of, 15, 263–72, 288–90
　judicial activism, 283–84
　publication ban (*Janfield*), 274–75
　recent court initiatives, 283–84
　same-sex relationships, 276–77
　SCA and, 263–64, 288–90
　See also children; divorce law;
　　matrimonial property law
Family Law Act
　children born to same-sex parents, 277
　children born to unmarried parents,
　　275
　child support guidelines, 274
　equality-based law in, 273–74
Family Relief Act, 276
"Famous Five," 302
Farmers' Union of Alberta, 167
Farnell v. Parks, 214–216
Federal Child Support Guidelines,
　273–74, 280–82
federal-provincial relationships
　divorce law, 264
　early history of SCA, 30
　First Nations game laws, 135–46
　mineral rights ownership, 201, 227–28
　See also Natural Resources Transfer
　　Agreement
Fediuk v. Lastiwka, 271–72

Feir, Elmore B., 165–66
Feldman v. Feldman, 278
feminism. *See* women's equality
First Nations, treaty hunting rights,
　133–57
　federal-provincial relationships, 135–46
　Game Act (1907) and, 142–44
　Game Ordinance (1894) and, 139–43
　hunting as traditional life, 139, 141,
　　148–49
　NRTA and (*Wesley*), 145–49
　numbered treaties, 135–36, 139–40, 143,
　　146
　"Queen's promises" and, 136, 139–40,
　　144–45, 148–51
　SCA and, 133–34, 149–51
　sport hunters and, 138–40, 148
　See also R. v. Stoney Joe; R. v. Wesley
First World War. *See* World War I
fishing rights, treaty, 135–36
　See also First Nations, treaty hunting
　　rights
Fitzpatrick, Charles, 82
Flewelling v. Johnston, 198
forced confinement (*Muir*), 306–07
Ford, Clinton, 270
Ford, Frank, 235
formal equality. *See* equality
formalist and contextual approaches,
　86–87
Fort Macleod Provincial Courthouse,
　xviii
　See also Macleod judicial district
Foster, Nina, 120
Fraess v. Alberta, 277
Fraser, Catherine, 17
free speech
　hate propaganda (*Keegstra*), 121–24
　political dissent (*Felton/Trainor*), 53–55
Freeze, Frank, 80–81
French Canadians
　animosity toward, 174
　against conscription in WWI, 72–75, 83
　control of francophone education
　　(*Mahe*), 120–21
Frog Lake Massacre, 34
Fruman, Adelle, 240–41

Gallagher v. Armstrong, 38, 64n77
Game Act (1907), 142–44
Game Ordinance (1894), 139–43
gas, natural. *See* energy law
Gas Tax Reference (NEP). *See* Reference

350　*The Supreme Court of Alberta*

Re Proposed Federal Tax on Exported Natural Gas
gays and lesbians. *See* same-sex relationships
gender equality
   child custody cases
   gender and Charter challenges, 312
   sexual assault cases, records (*Mills*), 313–15
   sexual sterilization (*Muir*), 303–07
   See also women's equality
Gibson, Dale, vii
   on constitutional law and SCA, 12, 99–131
Gonthier, Charles
   hate propaganda (*Keegstra*), 124
   judicial independence, 83–84
Gordon, Marie, vii
   on family law, 15, 261–96
Gordon, Robert, 1, 3, 4
Graham, F.M., 79–81, 101–03
Grand Prairie judicial district
   caseloads, 7, 47, 49
   courthouses, xxi, xxiii
   law library, 55
Grand Truck Railway, 47
Great War. *See* World War I
Guaranty Trust Co. v. Hetherington, 254

habeas corpus
   Charter-protected remedy, 86
   Civil War, suspension of habeas corpus, 81
   conscription (*Lewis*), 76–78, 80, 85, 101
   conscription (*Norton*), 37–38, 78, 80, 85
Hagan v. Dalkon Shield Claimants Trust, 305–06
Haismann v. Haismann, 281
Hall, Emmett, 110
Handhills Colony (Hutterite)
   communal property cases, 178–84
Hanna judicial district
   caseloads, 48–49, 52
   creation of, 31
   law library, 55
   trial judges, 53
Harder, Lois, 307, 315–16
Harradence, A. Milton, 179–80, 287
Harring, Sidney, 133–34, 150
Harvey, Horace
   biographical notes, xvii, 7, 11, 33, 36–38, 44–46
   as Chief Justice, 28, 31, 32
   claim to title of Chief Justice, 7
   dispute over title of Chief Justice, 7, 46
   on impact of SCNWT, 31
   judicial districts, 53
   judicial independence, 81, 84–85
   on rule of law, 82
   use of legal resources, 55, 58
   views of, generally, 16, 44–46
Harvey, Horace, cases
   conscription (*Lewis*), 11–12, 37–38, 77–84, 89–91, 101–03, 126
   conscription (*Norton*), 37–38, 78, 80
   divorce jurisdiction (*Board*), 104
   political dissent (*Felton/Trainor*), 54
   water law (*Clarke*), 199–200, 218
Hatch v. East Cardston Hutterian Colony, 164–65, 169
hate propaganda (*Keegstra*), 121–24
Hawco, Gerald, 254
Hetherington, Mary, 17, 317
Hiemstra v. Hiemstra, 282
history, legal. *See* legal history
history of Supreme Court of Alberta. *See* Supreme Court of Alberta, history
Hodge v. The Queen, 144
Hogg, Peter, 308
homestead land titles, 204, 209
homosexuality. *See* same-sex relationships
Housen v. Nikolaisen, 247–50
Howson, William, 238
Hudson, Albert, 235
Hudson's Bay Company
   marriages and Native customs, 29
   sale of mineral rights, 201
Huggard Assets Ltd. v. Attorney General of Alberta, 114–15, 228, 233–37, 255
human rights
   of children, 283–84
   formal equality communal property, 183
   formal equality issues, 305, 307, 310
   history after WWII, 110, 177, 184, 272
   human rights legislation, 307–11
   SCA and, 125–26
   tolerance and immigration, 53
   See also Alberta Bill of Rights; Canadian Charter of Rights and Freedoms
Human Rights, Citizenship and Multiculturalism Act, 308
Human Rights Act, 307

Hunt, Constance
  equality and same-sex relationships
    (*Vriend*), 9, 124-25
  interpretation of language, 252-53
  use of American authorities, 253
Hunter v. Southam, 118, 126
hunting, First Nations. *See* First
  Nations, treaty hunting rights
hunting, sport, 138-40, 148
Hutterites, 159-92
  antipathy toward, 13, 162-63, 167, 169,
    174-78, 183-84
  branches of, 162, 178, 183
  communal property beliefs, 13, 160-61,
    164, 173
  government liaison office, 177
  history of, 159-64, 183-84
  Land Sales Prohibition Act and,
    162-64, 167
  legislative reviews of Acts re, 163-64,
    167-68, 171-72, 174, 176-77
  Starland colony cases, 159, 177-84
  statistics on land holdings, 163, 172, 183
  See also Communal Property Act
Hyndman, James Duncan
  biographical notes, 32, 33, 42
  conscription exemptions (*Lewis*), 75-76,
    82, 88, 101
  divorce jurisdiction (*Board*), 104
  judicial districts, 53
  jurisdiction over inheritance law
    (Ultimate Heir), 113

Iacobucci, Franck, 86
Idington, John, 88
immigration
  human rights and, 53
  promises to Hutterites, 162, 170
  and SCA, 52-53
  and WWI military service, 71-72
Imperial Oil Ltd., 237
Income War Tax Act, 87
Indian Act, 138-139, 141-43
Indian hunting rights. *See* First Nations,
  treaty hunting rights
Individual's Rights Protection Act,
  308-11
In re Lewis
  conscription legislation, 70-75
  events in case, 37-38, 75-81
  formalist and contextual approaches,
    86-87

judicial independence and rule of law,
  11-12, 81-91, 100-03
physical force and, 88-91
In re Norton, 37-38, 75, 78, 80, 88-91
intimate violence, 315-21
Irrigation Act, 198
Irwin, Robert, 137, 145
Ives, William Carlos
  biographical notes, xvii, 32, 33, 43
  energy jurisdiction (*Mercury*), 231-32,
    245-46
  judicial districts, 53
  jurisdiction over inheritance law
    (Ultimate Heir), 113

Jamieson, Alice (*Cyr*), 37-38, 297-301
Janfield v. Foote, 274-75
JCPC. *See* Judicial Committee of the Privy
  Council
Johnson, Horace G.
  ATB Financial validity (*Breckenridge*),
    109-10
  communal property (*Walter*), 171-74,
    184
Johnson v. Sand, 276-77
Johnstone, Cecilia, 280
joint custody, 287-88
Judicature Act (1873), 28
judicial activism
  in child custody cases, 283-84
  in SCNWT, 28
  Stuart as activist, 38-39, 142
  See also judicial independence
Judicial Committee of the Privy
  Council
  abolishment of appeals to, 99, 105-07
  dispute over title of SCA Chief Justice,
    7, 46
  as final court of appeal, 56, 99-100,
    105-06
  future energy royalties (*Huggard*),
    114-15, 228, 236-37
  jurisdiction for divorce (*Board*), 38-39,
    104-05, 265
  jurisdiction over inheritance law
    (Ultimate Heir), 113-14
  open court for divorce (*McPherson*),
    119-20, 269
  Persons case, 9-10, 297-301
  power to hear appeals (*Nadan*), 106-07
  pre-1930 federal dispositions (*Western
    Canadian Collieries*), 114-15

reference of Bill of Rights Act, 111-12
split ownership, oil and gas (*Borys*),
  228, 239, 240
judicial districts
  creation of, 30-31
  law libraries, 55, 58
  trial judges, 50, 53
judicial independence
  conscription (*Lewis/Norton/Gray*),
    11-12, 37-38, 69-70, 78, 81-91,
    100-103
  early history, 69-70, 100-01
  individual, 69-70
  institutional, 69-70
  physical force and, 88-91
  protection of legal norms and, 84-85
  public and private influences on, 83-86
  rule of law and, 81-82
  See also judicial activism
Juvenile Delinquents Act, 312

Kalman, Laura, 4
Kane, Edward W.
  ATB Financial validity (*Breckenridge*),
    109-10
  communal property (*Walter*), 171
Kelly v. Lundgard, 305
Kerans, Roger
  hate propaganda (*Keegstra*), 122-24
  minority language education (*Mahe*),
    121
  tender years doctrine (*R. v. R.*), 286-87
Kerr, W.W., 54
Kerwin, Patrick, 235
Kirby, William J.C.
  child custody (*Mullen*), 284-85
  loss of consortium (*Fediuk/Wener*),
    271-72
  review of court system, 8
Klein, Ralph, government
  sexual sterilization liability, 304
K.(M.M.) v. K. (U.), 287
Knafla, Louis, vii
  on criminal law history, 2
  on formative years of SCA, 27-68
Kopfman, R., 175
Koshan, Jennifer, viii
  on women's equality, 15-16, 297-332
Kraus v. Kraus, 278
Kwasniak, Arlene, viii
  on water law, 14, 193-26

L. (V.) v. L. (D.), 288
La Forest, Gérard, cases
  freedom of expression (*Edmonton Journal*), 120
  hate propaganda (*Keegstra*), 124
Laird, David, 136-37, 141, 148
lakes. *See* water law
Lakeside Colony (Hutterite), 178-84
Lamer, Antonio, 84
Land Sales Prohibition Act (1942)
  ban on sales to Hutterites, 162-64
  legislative review of, 163-64, 167
Land Titles Act, 208-09
land titles systems
  deed registry system, 204-05
  river course changes (*Robertson*),
    207-09
  Torrens system, 14, 204-05, 208-09, 211
  water law, accretion and, 203-05
language
  formalist and contextual approaches,
    86-87
  interpretation of, 233-35, 238, 252-53
language rights
  minority control (*Mahe*), 120-21
Laskin, Bora, 262
Laurier, Sir Wilfrid, government
  conscription (*Lewis/Norton*), 37-38
  wartime coalition, 73-75
law libraries, 55, 58
Law of Fraud and Mistake (Kerr), 54
Law of Legislative Power in Canada
  (Lefroy), 144
*Law relating to Vendors and Purchasers
  of Real Estate* and Chattels Real
  (Williams), 54
*Law relating to Vendors and Purchasers of
  Real Estate* (Dart), 54
Law Society of Alberta
  early years, 60
  legal resources, 55, 56-57
Law Society of the North-West
  Territories
  legal resources, 55
  officers of, 39
Laws of England (Halsbury), 58
Lawyer's Reports Annotated, 58
Laycraft, J.H., 271
*Leading Cases in Various Branches of the
  Law* (Smith), 54
legal history
  of Aboriginal traditions, 133-34

Index   353

legal history (*continued*)
 approaches to, 1-6
 formalistic and historical views, 3-4
 history in law and *law in history*, 4-5
 studies of court systems, 2-3
legal resources
 law reports, 30, 39
 legal publishing, 56-57
 list of early titles, 54
 use in early years, 54-58
lesbians and gays. *See* same-sex relationships
Lethbridge, treaty hunting rights, 138-40
Lethbridge judicial district
 caseloads and population, 7, 47-51
 courthouse, xx
 creation of, 30-31
 trial judges, 53
Levesque v. Levesque, 280-81
Lloyd v. Lloyd, 267-68
Lord's Day Act
 Charter challenge (*Big M. Drug Mart*), 118, 126
Lougheed, James Alexander, 39
Lougheed, Peter, government
 human rights law, 307-308
 NEP gas tax (*Re Proposed Federal Tax*), 115-17, 244-48, 255
 repeal of Communal Property Act, 176-77
 repeal of Sexual Sterilization Act, 303
 review of courts (Kirby commission), 8
Low, Frederick, 85
Low, Solon, 162-63
Lucas, Alastair, viii
 on energy law, 14-15, 227-60
Lunney, William
 treaty hunting rights (*Stoney Joe/Wesley*), 147, 149-51

M. (T.C.I) v. U. (L.), 274
MacDonald, D.C., 261-262, 285-86
MacDonald, William A., 234
MacKenzie, John Horace, cases
 child custody (*Davidovich*), 285
 spousal support (*Brookes*), 279
Mackintosh, Charles H., 140-41
Mackin v. New Brunswick, 83-84
Macleod, James F., 28, 34
Macleod judicial district
 caseloads and population, 47-52
 courthouse, xviii

 creation of, 30-31
 law library, 55
 trial judges, 53
MacMillan v. Brownlee, 119
MacMinn v. MacMinn, 282
magistrates
 early history, 28, 61n2
 females as (*Cyr*), 9-10, 37-38
 females as (Persons case), 297-300
Mahe v. Alberta, 120-21
Maintenance and Recovery Act, 276
maintenance of children. *See* children
Majestic Mines Ltd. v. Attorney General of Alberta, 233-35
Major, John C.
 spousal support (*Cipperly*), 271
 xxx, 84-85
Major, John C., cases
 equality and sexual orientation (*Vriend*), 125
 split ownership, oil and gas (*Borys*), 241
Makowecki v. Yachimyc, 212-16
male equality. *See* men
Manitoba
 appeals and trial divisions, 7, 32
 First Nations treaty hunting rights, 137-38, 145
 Hutterite colonies, 162, 185n2
 land titles (*Chuckery*), 205-06, 210
 legal resources, 57
Manning, Ernest, government
 communal property legislation, 164, 166, 169, 176-79
 reference of Bill of Rights, 111-12
Maple Creek, treaty hunting rights, 138-40
marriage
 HBC employees and Native customs, 29
 marriage validity law, 264
 same-sex marriage, 277
 WWI impact on marriage, 265
 See also divorce law
Marriage Act, 277
Martin, Peter, 276
Martland, Ronald
 ATB Financial validity (*Breckenridge*), 110
 communal property (*Walter*), 173
Mason, David, 273-74
Matrimonial Causes Act (1857), 104
Matrimonial Property Act (1979), 262
matrimonial property law
 division of property (*Murdoch*), 261-63

McBride, Boyd, 233-34
McCardle, Bennett, 138
McCarthy, Maitland Stewart
  biographical notes, 32, 33, 44, 45-46
  judicial districts, 50, 53
  political dissent (*Felton/Trainor*), 53-54
McCarthy, Peter, 36, 38
McCaul, C.C., 28
McClung, John W., 60
  equality and same-sex relationships (*Vriend*), 9, 124
  views of, generally, 16
McClung, Nellie, 302
McCormack v. McCormack, 265-66
McCormick, Peter, 84, 86, 90
McDermid, Neil D., 171-72, 173
McDonald, David
  on Charter rights, 126
  intimate violence (*Brown*), 316
McFadyen, Elizabeth, 16-17
McGillivray, William Alexander
  treaty hunting rights (*Stoney Joe/Wesley*), 12-13, 133, 147-51
  views of, generally, 16
McGuire, Thomas Horace, 35
McKinney, Louise, 302
McLachlin, Beverley, 124
McLean, J.D., 141
McLeod, Jay
  children born to unmarried parents (*T. [P.] v. B.[R.]*), 275
McLeod, treaty hunting rights, 138-40
McMurtry, R. Roy, ix
McPherson v. McPherson, 119, 269
Medicine Hat judicial district
  caseloads, 7, 48-49, 51
  courthouse, xix
  creation of, 31
  law library, 55
  trial judges, 53
men
  differential ages for adulthood, criminal (*R. v. M.L.*), 312-14
  gender and charter challenges, 312
  policies of Eugenics Board, 302, 303-04
  sexual assault case, personal records (*Mills*), 313-14
  See also gender equality
Mennonites, 162
Mercury Oils v. Attorney General of Alberta, 231-32, 245-46
methane, coal bed, 241

Métis, 319
Metropolitan Electric Supply Co., 149
Military Service Act (1917)
  conscription (*Lewis/Gray*), 11, 37-38, 73-77, 83, 85
Militia Act (1906), 70, 73, 76
Miller, Tevie H.
  informal family law trials, 284
  pregnancy rights (*Wong*), 308-11
Milne (Doherty) v. Alberta (Attorney General), 273-74
Milvain, J.V.H.
  ATB validity (*Long*), 110
  biographical notes, xxv
  child custody (*Barber*), 284
  communal property (*Walter*), 170-71
mineral resources. *See* coal; energy law; Natural Resources Transfer Agreement
Mines and Minerals Act
  accreted land rights, 202-03
Mitchell, Charles, 147
Moge v. Moge, 279
Moir, Arnold F., 278
Molden v. Kirkeby, 216
Moore, Lt. Col., 78-81, 101-03
Moose Jaw, Sask., treaty hunting rights, 138-40
Morrow, William George, 59
Muir, James, 80
Muir, Lellani, 303-07
Mullen v. Mullen, 284-85
municipalities
  expropriation (*Red Deer v. Pitt*), 209
  zoning and communal property, 177-84
Munroe, Karen M., 285, 286
murder, 29, 32
Murdoch v. Murdoch, 261-63
Murphy, Emily, 37-38, 302

N. (P.F.) v. N. (A.), 280
Nadan v. The King, 106-07
Nash, Eileen, 312-13
Nastajus v. North Alberta, 206-07
Nation, Rosemary, 207-09
National Council of Women, 302
National Energy Program
  impact of, 115-17, 228, 241-54
  reference re taxation (*Re Proposed Federal Tax*), 115-17, 242-48, 255
Native people, hunting rights. *See* First Nations, treaty hunting rights

natural gas, NEP tax. *See Reference Re Proposed Federal Tax on Exported Natural Gas*
natural resources law. *See* energy law
Natural Resources Transfer Agreement
   First Nations hunting and fishing rights, 135, 145-46
   history of oil and gas law, 227-30, 236
   NEP reference and, 244
   oil and gas royalties under, 233, 236
   provisions re pre-1930 land transactions, 114-15, 201
   treaty hunting rights (*Wesley*), 145-49
   water law and, 197
Nelson, William, 4
North West Game Ordinance, 139
North-West Irrigation Act (1894), 196-97, 216
North-West Territories
   continuation of law after 1905, 30
   First Nations treaty hunting rights, 135-42
   land survey system, 204
   origins of SCNWT, 27-30
   treaty hunting rights (*Wesley*), 147-48
   water law, 195-96
Nova Scotia, land titles system, 204-05
NRTA. *See* Natural Resources Transfer Agreement
numbered treaties. *See* First Nations, treaty hunting rights
NWT. *See* North-West Territories

O'Connor, George, 234, 236
oil and gas. *See* energy law
Oil and Gas Conservation Act, 232
O'Leary, Willis, 124
O'Leary v. O'Leary, 282
Olsen v. Olsen, 270
Olynyk v. Olynyk, 270
Oosterhoff, A.H., 254
Osgoode Society for Canadian Legal history, ix-x
Osgoode Society for Canadian Legal history, publications, 333-36
Ostrom v. Sills (Ontario), 213
Owram, Douglas, 241

Palliser, John, 195
Palmer, Howard, 174
Panel on Violence Against Women (1993), 316

Paperny, Marina, 305-06
Parentage and Maintenance Act, 274-75
parenting orders. *See* children
Parlee, Harold, cases
   future energy royalties (*Huggard*), 235-36
   split ownership, oil and gas (*Borys*), 238-40
Peace River judicial district
   caseloads, 7, 49
   creation of, 31
Peacock, M.B., 146-47
Pearce, William, 196, 218
Percy, David, 217
Perras, Delmar, 276-77
persona designata, judge as, 165
Persons case, 9-10, 37, 297-01
petroleum. *See* energy law
Petroleum and Natural Gas Conservation Board, 231-32
Picard, Ellen, 17, 286
Police Court, 48
policing, 90-91
populism, 174, 178
Porter, Marshall, cases
   ATB Financial validity (*Breckenridge*), 108-10
   communal property (*Walter*), 172-74
Poundmaker, trial of, 34
Power, Peter, 276
Power, W. Kent, 56-57
Power's Western Practice Digest, 57
Pratte, Yves, 309-11
pregnancy and women's equality, 308-11
Prendergast, James E.P., 39
Primrose, Neil, cases
   ATB Financial validity (*Breckenridge*), 108
   loss of consortium (*Fediuk*), 271-72
Prism Petroleum Ltd. v. Omega Hydrocarbons Ltd., 239-40
Privy Council. *See* Judicial Committee of the Privy Council
Prohibition, impact of, 106-07
Provincial Court, 7
Provincial Lands Act, 201
Provincial Training School for Mental Defectives, Red Deer, 303-07
Provincial Treasurer of Alberta v. Long, 110
publication bans, 275
Public Lands Act, 201-03
puisne (junior) justices, 28, 31, 35

Purvis, Stuart
    hate propaganda (*Keegstra*), 121-24
    minority language education (*Mahe*), 121

Quigley, Francis (Frank), xxv
    hate propaganda (*Keegstra*), 122-23
    intimate violence (*Brown*), 316

R. v. Big M. Drug Mart Ltd., 118, 126
R. v. Brown, 316-20
R. v. Cyr, 9-10, 37-38, 297-01
R. v. Felton, 54-55
R. v. Keegstra, 121-24
R. v. Lavallee, 316-17
R. v. Mills, 313-14
R. v. M.L., 312-314
R. v. O'Connor, 313-14
R. v. O'Rourke, 144
R. v. R., 286-87
R. v. Robertson (Manitoba), 137, 145
R. v. Stone, 320
R. v. Stoney Joe
    approach to rights in, 12-13, 134
    suppression of publication, 39, 64n79
    treaty hunting rights, 142-46, 148-51
R. v. Superintendent of Vine Street Police Station, 85
R. v. Trainor, 39, 54-55
R. v. Wesley
    approach to rights in, 12-13, 134
    McGillivray on decision, 133
    treaty hunting rights, 146-51
R. v. Wilson (1919), 44
racial issues
    discrimination against Blacks, 267
    human rights legislation, 307-11
    people of colour on judiciary, 17
    policies of Eugenics Board, 302
railways, 29, 44, 47, 100
Raymond, Hutterite colonies, 162
Rayner, W.B., 254
Re C., 277
Re Communal Property Act, 174-77
Red Deer, treaty hunting rights, 138-40
Red Deer (City) *v. Pitt*, 209
Red Deer judicial district
    caseloads, 7, 47, 49
    courthouse, xxii
    creation of, 31
    trial judges, 53
Red Deer River, 209

Reed, Hayter, 139-41
Re Eve, 305
Reference Re Alberta Bill of Rights Act, 111-12
Reference Re Alberta Statutes, 100
Reference Re Proposed Federal Tax on Exported Natural Gas, 115-17, 242-48, 255
Registration of Title to Land Throughout the Empire (Hogg), 58
Re Gray, 11-12, 75, 77-78, 84, 103
Reid, John Phillip, 3-5
Reid, Richard, government
    publication ban on divorces, 119-20
religion
    "Catholic Seat" on early SCA, 40
    definition, communal property (*Walter*), 173-74
    divorce (*Board*), 105
    Eugenics Board decisions and, 302, 305
    hate propaganda (*Keegstra*), 121-24
    human rights legislation, 307-11
    Lord's Day Act (*Big M. Drug Mart*), 118
    Lord's Day Act challenge (*Big M. Drug Mart*), 126
    provincial power to legislate (*Walter*), 171, 173-74
    SCA justices and, 41, 59, 105, 268-69
    SCC on religious tracts (*Saumur*), 171
    separate school systems, 40
    See also Hutterites
Renke, Wayne, viii
    on judicial independence (*Lewis/Gray*), 11-12, 69-98
Riel, Louis, trial of, 34, 105
Riley, Harold, 270
riparian law. *See* water law, riparian
Ritchie, Roland, 309-10
rivers. *See* water law
Robertson v. Wallace, 207-09
Rock Lake Colony (Hutterite), 169
Roman Catholic Church
    "Catholic Seat" on SCA, 40
    divorce law jurisdiction (*Board*), 59, 104-05, 268-69
    sexual sterilization (eugenics), 302
Roman Catholic Schools
    francophone education (*Mahe*), 120-21
    separate school systems, 40
Rosario v. Rosario, 279
Rowbotham, Harry Slater, xxv
Rowley, communal property, 174, 178-84

Row v. Row, 279
Royal Commission on the Status of
    Women, 299
royalties, natural resources
    future oil and gas royalties (*Huggard*),
        114-15, 228, 233-37, 255
    pre-1930 federal dispositions of coal
        (*West Canadian Collieries*), 114
*Rozander v. Alberta (Energy Resources
    Conservation Board)*, 246
Rudiak v. The Public Trustee, 270
rule of law
    early years, 38, 59-60
    First Nations treaty hunting rights,
        150
rules of court, 31, 37
Ruling Cases (Campbell), 54
Russell, Anne, cases
    equality and same-sex relationships
        (*Vriend*), 9, 124-25
    joint guardianship (*L. [V.] v. L. [D.]*),
        288
Russell, David, 180
Rutherford, Alexander, 30, 36

same-sex relationships
    equal protection (*Vriend*), 9, 124-25
    family law, 276-277
Sanders, Douglas, 145
Saskatchewan
    appeals and trial divisions, 7, 32
    early history of Supreme Court, 28-29
    First Nations treaty hunting rights,
        135, 141, 145
    Hutterite colonies, 167
    legal resources, 57
    use by SCA of law of, 46, 110, 309
Saskatchewan Act, 30
Saumur v. City of Quebec, 171
SCA. *See* Supreme Court of Alberta
SCC. *See* Supreme Court of Canada
SCNWT. *See* Supreme Court of the North-
    West Territories
Scott, David Lynch
    biographical notes, xvii, 7, 30-35, 38,
        45-46
    as Chief Justice, 7, 34
    claim to title as Chief Justice, 7
    dispute over title of Chief Justice, 7, 46
    divorce (*Lloyd*), 267-68
    judicial districts, 53
    Persons case (*Cyr*), 37-38

use of legal resources, 55, 58
views of, generally, 45-46
Scurry-Rainbow Oil Ltd. v. Galloway Estate,
    252-54
Scurry-Rainbow Oil Ltd. v. Kasha, 254
search warrants
    Charter challenge (*Hunter v. Southam*),
        118, 126
Second World War. *See* World War II
sexual orientation. *See* same-sex
    relationships
sexual sterilization
    accidental sterilization (*Kelly v.
        Lundgard*), 305
    eugenics theories and, 301-03
    forced sterilization (*Muir*), 303-07
    IUDs (*Hagan v. Dalkon Shield*), 305-06
    value of conception (*Re Eve*), 305
Sexual Sterilization Act, 301-04
Shepherd, S.J., 40
sheriff, powers of, 79-81, 90
Sherlow v. Zubko, 280
Short, James, 38
Sibbald, Andrew, 142
Sifton, Arthur Lewis
    biographical notes, 31, 33, 35-36, 38, 45
    as Chief Justice, 35-36
    judicial districts, 53
    as premier, 31, 36
Sifton, Clifford, 40
Simmons, William Charles
    biographical notes, 31-33, 40-41
    conscription exemptions (*Lewis*), 75-76,
        82, 88, 101
    judicial districts, 50, 53
    political dissent (*Felton/Trainor*), 54-55
Sinclair, William Robert, 8
sloughs. *See* water law
Smith, Bruce, 42
Smith, John W., 54
Smith, Sidney, 109-110
Snell, James, 267
Social Credit governments. *See*
    Aberhart, William, government
Sosin, J.M., 3-4
*Spooner Oils v. Turner Valley Gas
    Conservation Board*, 228-32, 246, 255
sport hunters and treaty hunting rights,
    138-40, 148
spousal assault, 316-21
spousal support, 269-71, 277-79
Spring v. Spring, 267

358   *The Supreme Court of Alberta*

Starko v. Starko, 286
Starland, M.D., Hutterite colonies, 159, 177–84
Statute of Westminster (1931), 107
Statutes at Large, 58
Steinke, Heather, 320
sterilization, sexual. *See* sexual sterilization
Sterilization Act. *See* Sexual Sterilization Act
Stettler judicial district
 caseloads, 48–49
 creation of, 31
 law library, 55
 trial judges, 53
stipendiary magistrates, 28
stockbroker "bucket shops," 43
Stoney Indians and game laws, 138, 140–41
 See also R. v. Stoney Joe; R. v. Wesley
Stratton, Joseph, 287
Stricker v. Stricker, 278
Stuart, Charles Allan
 biographical notes, xvii, 11, 30–33, 38–39, 44–45, 47, 142
 judicial activism, 38–39, 142
 judicial districts, 50
 judicial districts, service in, 53
 judicial independence, 84–85
 use of legal resources, 55, 57
 views of, generally, 31, 39, 44–45, 47
Stuart, Charles Allan, cases
 beaver dams (*Farnell*), 215–16, 219
 conscription (*Lewis*), 75–76, 78, 82, 87–88, 101–03
 conscription (*Norton*), 75
 divorce domicile (*McCormack/Cook*), 265–66
 divorce jurisdiction (*Board*), 38–39, 105
 personal liability (*Wilson*), 44
 Persons case (*Cyr*), 9–10, 38, 300–01
 political dissent, 52
 political dissent (*Felton/Trainor*), 54–55
 treaty hunting rights (*Stoney Joe/ Wesley*), 12–13, 39, 142–46, 148–51
substantive equality, 300
 See also equality
Sulatycky, Allen, 287
support of children. *See* children
support of spouses. *See* divorce law
Supreme Court Act (1907), 30, 90
Supreme Court of Alberta

Constitutional cases, 99–100
courthouses, xxi–xxiv, 32, 55, 58
female judges, 16–17, 283–84, 321
judges, xxiii, xxiv–xxvi
judges, list of (1907–2007), 337–47
media and public views of, 9, 16–18
reorganization of court (1970s), 8
use of term, 6, 23n26
See also Court of Appeal; Court of Queen's Bench; judicial activism; judicial independence; *names of individual justices*
Supreme Court of Alberta, history (1905–1921), 27–68
 Appellate and Trial Divisions, 6–8, 31–33, 46, 49, 105–06
 assize courts, 31
 caseloads, 47–53
 chief justice, dispute over title, 7, 46
 chief justice, office of, 30–31, 46
 Constitutional cases, 99–100
 continuation of SCNWT, 30–31
 courthouses, xviii–xxi, 28, 32, 55
 court officials, 31
 early decisions, 92–107
 early history and origins, 27–33, 59–60
 en banc sittings, 6–7, 28, 31, 45–46
 first Supreme Court, 31–33
 formalist and contextual approaches, 86–87
 increase in number of justices, 7, 47
 judges, list of (1907–2007), 337–47
 judicial districts, 6, 30–31
 justices, biographical notes, xvii, 30–47
 justices, personal qualities of, 9–12, 16–17
 justices, residency of, 7
 justices, views of, 6–7, 39, 44–47, 59–60
 law libraries, 55, 58
 legal resources, 34–35, 54–58
 patronage and, 33
 politics and, 40, 45
 puisne justices, 31, 35
 religion and, 40, 41, 59, 105
 rule of law, 59
 rules of court, 31, 37
 use of common law, 59–60
 use of legal resources, 40, 46
 views on common law, 39
 WWI impact on

Index 359

Supreme Court of Alberta, history
    (*continued*)
    See also In re Lewis; In re Norton; judicial
        activism
Supreme Court of Canada
    Charter and, 12, 125-26
    constitutional law and, 99-100
    contextual and formalist approaches,
        86
    reference of Bill of Rights, 111-12
    regulatory review standards, four
        criteria, 246, 249-50
Supreme Court of Canada, cases
    ATB Financial validity (*Breckenridge*),
        108-10
    child support cases, 282
    communal property (*Walter*), 173
    conscription exemptions (*Gray*), 38,
        77-78, 82-84, 103
    domestic violence (*Lavallee*), 316-317
    energy royalties (*Dynex*), 254
    first Alberta Charter case (*Hunter*), 118,
        126
    freedom of expression (*Edmonton
        Journal*), 119-20
    future energy royalties (*Huggard*),
        114-15, 235-36, 255
    hate propaganda (*Keegstra*), 121-24
    judicial independence (*Mackin*), 83-85
    jurisdiction over inheritance law
        (Ultimate Heir), 113
    minority language education (*Mahe*),
        120-21
    mixed fact and law (*Housen*), 247-50
    NEP natural gas tax (*Re Proposed
        Federal Tax*), 115-17, 242-48, 255
    ownership of public land (*Trusts and
        Guarantee*), 112
    Persons case, 100, 301
    provincial powers re monetary
        schemes (*Alberta Statutes*), 107-10
    regulatory power of boards (*Spooner*),
        231
    religious tracts (*Saumur*), 171
    sexual assault, evidence (*O'Connor*),
        313-14
    spousal assault (*R. v. Stone*), 320
    sterilization (*Re Eve*), 305
    substantive equality (*Andrews*), 300,
        312-13
    water law cases, 200-01, 205-06, 210-11
Supreme Court of the North-West
    Territories

continuation after 1905, 30-31, 33
courthouses, xviii
justices, 34, 36, 39
origins of, 27-30
rule of law, 59-60
Swainger, Jonathan, viii, 1-19

T. [P.] v. B.[R.], 275
Taylor, Gordon, 179
Taylor, William Pentlowe, 56
Taylor v. Rossu, 276
Territories Law Reports, 30, 39
The Queen v. Charcoal, 29
Thompson, Sir John, 147
Torrens land title system, 14, 204-05,
    208-09, 211
Tory, Henry Marshall, 57
trading and trapping rights. *See* First
    Nations, treaty hunting rights
Treasury Department Act, 107
treaties, First Nations
    numbered treaties, 135-36, 139-40, 143,
        146
    traditional life and, 135-36, 139, 141,
        148-49
    See also First Nations, treaty hunting
        rights
*Treatise on the Anglo-American System of
    Evidence in Trials at Common Law*
    (Wigmore), 54
Tremblay v. Tremblay, 287
Trial Division, Supreme Court of
    Alberta. *See* Supreme Court of
    Alberta, history (1905-1921)
Trudeau, Pierre, government
    National Energy Program, 115-17
Trussler, Marguerite
    child custody (*Burwash*), 287-88
    child support arrangements, 279-80
    family law initiatives, 283-84
    parallel parenting (*Broder*), 288
    pregnancy and human rights (*Brooks*),
        310-11
Trusts and Guarantee Co. v. Canada, 112-13
Tupper, Allan, 9
Turcotte, L.S. (Louis Sherman), xxv
Turner Valley Gas Conservation Act, 231
Turner Valley Gas Conservation Board,
    230-31, 244-45
Tushner, Mark, 4
Tweedie, Thomas Mitchell, 32, 113

Ultimate Heir Act, 112-14

Unemployment Insurance Act
  pregnancy benefits (*Bliss*), 309-10
United Farm Women of Alberta, 302
United States
  Canadian use of decisions in energy
    law, 253
  Civil War, judicial independence, 81,
    102-03
  impact on SCA, 60
  legal resources, 58
  political dissent, decisions, 52
  rule of law case, judicial independence,
    102
  use of land survey grid, 203-04
  WWI, military service law, 73
Universal Declaration on the
  Independence of Justice, 83-84
University of Alberta, 36, 39
University of Alberta, Law Faculty, 57
University of Calgary, Law Faculty, 57
Utilities Board, Alberta Energy and. *See*
  Alberta Energy and Utilities Board

Vankoughnet, Lawrence, 139
Veit, Joanne
  adult child support (*N.[P.F.] v. N. [A.]*),
    280
  child support (*C.M.*), 274
  publication ban (*Janfield v. Foote*),
    274-75
  sexual sterilization and forced
    confinement (*Muir*), 303-07
  spousal support (*Row*), 279
  views of, generally, 16
Verdant Valley Colony (Hutterite),
  179-84
Veterans Land Act (1942), 164
Victoria, Queen, and treaties, 136,
  139-40, 148-51
violence
  domestic violence, 315-21
  judicial independence and, 79-81,
    88-91
Vriend v. Alberta, 9, 124-25

Wahlsten, Douglas, 302
Wahl v. Wahl, 280
Walkden v. Walkden, 267
Walsh, William Legh
  biographical notes, 31, 32, 33, 41-42, 53,
    60
  use of legal resources, 57
Walsh, William Legh, cases

divorce law (*Board*), 265
jurisdiction over inheritance law, 113
political dissent (*Felton*), 54
Walter v. Attorney-General of Alberta,
  169-74
War Measures Act
  emergency powers (*Lewis*), 37-38, 70-71,
    74-78, 85, 87-88, 101-03
water law, 193-26
  common law and, 193
  Crown rights, 196
  dams, beaver (*Farnell*), 214-16, 219
  dams and drainage (*Makowecki*), 212-16
  domestic and extraordinary uses, 195
  drainage, regulatory controls, 216-19
  drainage and common law, 193-94, 197,
    211-13
  "first in time, first in right," 196-98
  history of water law, 14, 194-99, 217-19
  hydrology of province, 197, 212-16, 219
  land titles systems, 203-05
  NRTA and, 197
  SCA and, 193-94, 203, 211, 217-19
  Torrens land title system, 14, 204-05,
    208-09, 211
  Water Act (1999), 197, 217
  Water Resources Act (1931), 197, 217
  See also water law, riparian
water law, riparian, 198-211
  access and common law, 196-97
  accretion and common law, 14, 193,
    196-211
  accretion and recessed lands (*Nastajus*),
    206-07
  accretion and timeframes (*Clarke*),
    199-01, 218
  climate change and, 211
  expropriation (*Red Deer v. Pitt*), 209
  history of law, 14, 195-201
  land titles (*Flewelling*), 198
  land titles systems, 203-09, 211, 217-19
  mineral rights (*Eliason*), 201-03
  recessed lands (*Andriet*), 210-11
  river course changes (*Robertson*),
    207-09
Watson, Henry, 175-77
Watson, Jack, 17, 275
Watson Hamilton, Jonette, viii
  on regulation of Hutterite expansion,
    13, 159-92
Wener v. Davidson, 272
Wener v. Wener, 278
Western Canadian Collieries v. Alberta, 114-15

Western Law Reporter (*WLR*), 56
Western Stock Growers' Association, 169
Western Weekly Reports (*WWR*), 56
Wetaskiwin judicial district
    caseloads and population, 7, 47-49, 51-52
    courthouse, xxii
    creation of, 30-31
    law library, 55
    trial judges, 53
wetlands, loss of, 217
    See also water law
Wetmore, Edward Ludlow, 28-30
Whitsett, Elizabeth, viii
    on women's equality, 15-16, 297-332
wife assault, 315-21
Wigmore, John H., 54
Wildman, Don, Sr., 146
Williams, T.C., 54
Wilson, Bertha, 321
Wilson, H.J., 147
WLR. *See Western Law Reporter* (*WLR*)
women's equality, 297-332
    eugenics movement and, 301-04
    female judges, impact of, 17, 283-84, 321
    feminist perspectives, 298-99
    formal equality issues, 305, 307, 310
    history of, 15-16
    human rights law, 307-11
    invisible inequality in conditions, 298-99
    Persons case (*Cyr*), 9-10, 37-38, 297-301
    pregnancy, 308-11
    sexual sterilization (*Muir*), 303-07
    wife assault, 315-21
    women judges and, 17
Wong v. Hughes Petroleum Ltd., 308-09
Wooldridge v. Wooldridge, 279
World War I
    animosity toward Hutterites, 162
    conscription and rule of law (*Lewis*), 37-38, 70-75, 86-87, 101-03
    impact on marriage and divorce, 265
    impact on SCA, 59-60
    military service exemptions, 37-38, 101-03, 162
    political dissent (*Felton/Trainor*), 52-54
World War II
    animosity toward Hutterites, 162, 163
Wright v. Wright, 267

Publications of the Osgoode Society for Canadian Legal History

2007

Robert Sharpe & Patricia McMahon, *The Persons Case: The Origins and Legacy of the Fight for Legal Personhood*
Lori Chambers, *Misconceptions: Unmarried Motherhood and the Ontario Children of Unmarried Parents Act*
Jonathan Swainger, ed., *The Alberta Supreme Court at 100: History & Authority*
Martin Friedland, *My Life in Crime and Other Academic Adventures*

2006

Donald Fyson, *Magistrates, Police and People: Everyday Criminal Justice in Quebec and Lower Canada, 1764–1837*
Dale Brawn, *The Court of Queen's Bench of Manitoba 1870–1950: A Biographical History*
R.C.B. Risk, *A History of Canadian Legal Thought: Collected Essays*, edited and introduced by G. Blaine Baker & Jim Phillips

2005

Philip Girard, *Bora Laskin: Bringing Law to Life*
Christopher English, ed., *Essays in the History of Canadian Law, Vol. IX: Two Islands, Newfoundland and Prince Edward Island*
Fred Kaufman, *Searching for Justice: An Autobiography*

2004

John D. Honsberger, *Osgoode Hall: An Illustrated History*
Frederick Vaughan, *Aggressive in Pursuit: The Life of Justice Emmett Hall*
Constance Backhouse & Nancy Backhouse, *The Heiress versus the Establishment: Mrs. Campbell's Campaign for Legal Justice*
Philip Girard, Jim Phillips & Barry Cahill, eds., *The Supreme Court of Nova Scotia, 1754–2004: From Imperial Bastion to Provincial Oracle*

2003

Robert Sharpe & Kent Roach, *Brian Dickson: A Judge's Journey*
George Finlayson, *John J. Robinette: Peerless Mentor*
Peter Oliver, *The Conventional Man: The Diaries of Ontario Chief Justice Robert A. Harrison, 1856–1878*
Jerry Bannister, *The Rule of the Admirals: Law, Custom and Naval Government in Newfoundland, 1699–1832*

2002

John T. Saywell, *The Law Makers: Judicial Power and the Shaping of Canadian Federalism*
David Murray, *Colonial Justice: Justice, Morality and Crime in the Niagara District, 1791–1849*
F. Murray Greenwood & Barry Wright, eds., *Canadian State Trials, Volume Two: Rebellion and Invasion in the Canadas, 1837–8*
Patrick Brode, *Courted and Abandoned: Seduction in Canadian Law*

2001

Ellen Anderson, *Judging Bertha Wilson: Law as Large as Life*
Judy Fudge & Eric Tucker, *Labour Before the Law: Collective Action in Canada, 1900–1948*
Laurel Sefton MacDowell, *Renegade Lawyer: The Life of J.L. Cohen*

2000

Barry Cahill, *'The Thousandth Man': A Biography of James McGregor Stewart*
A.B. McKillop, *The Spinster and the Prophet: Florence Deeks, H.G.Wells, and the Mystery of the Purloined Past*
Beverley Boissery & F. Murray Greenwood, *Uncertain Justice: Canadian Women and Capital Punishment*
Bruce Ziff, *Unforeseen Legacies: Reuben Wells Leonard and the Leonard Foundation Trust*

1999

Constance Backhouse, *Colour-Coded: A Legal History of Racism in Canada, 1900–1950*
G. Blaine Baker & Jim Phillips, eds., *Essays in the History of Canadian Law, Vol. VIII: In Honour of R.C.B. Risk*
Richard W. Pound, *Chief Justice W.R. Jackett: By the Law of the Land*
David Vanek, *Fulfilment: Memoirs of a Criminal Court Judge*

1998

Sidney Harring, *White Man's Law: Native People in Nineteenth-Century Canadian Jurisprudence*
Peter Oliver, *'Terror to Evil-Doers': Prisons and Punishments in Nineteenth-Century Ontario*

1997

James W. St.G. Walker, *'Race,' Rights and the Law in the Supreme Court of Canada: Historical Case Studies*
Lori Chambers, *Married Women and Property Law in Victorian Ontario*
Patrick Brode, *Casual Slaughters and Accidental Judgments: Canadian War Crimes and Prosecutions, 1944–1948*
Ian Bushnell, *The Federal Court of Canada: A History, 1875–1992*

1996

Carol Wilton, ed., *Essays in the History of Canadian Law, Vol. VII: Inside the Law— Canadian Law Firms in Historical Perspective*
William Kaplan, *Bad Judgment: The Case of Mr. Justice Leo A. Landreville*
Murray Greenwood & Barry Wright, eds., *Canadian State Trials, Volume I: Law, Politics and Security Measures, 1608–1837*

1995

David Williams, *Just Lawyers: Seven Portraits*
Hamar Foster & John McLaren, eds., *Essays in the History of Canadian Law, Vol. VI: British Columbia and the Yukon*
W.H. Morrow, ed., *Northern Justice: The Memoirs of Mr. Justice William G. Morrow*
Beverley Boissery, *A Deep Sense of Wrong: The Treason, Trials and Transportation to New South Wales of Lower Canadian Rebels after the 1838 Rebellion*

1994

Patrick Boyer, *A Passion for Justice: The Legacy of James Chalmers McRuer*
Charles Pullen, *The Life and Times of Arthur Maloney: The Last of the Tribunes*
Jim Phillips, Tina Loo, & Susan Lewthwaite, eds., *Essays in the History of Canadian Law, Vol. V: Crime and Criminal Justice*
Brian Young, *The Politics of Codification: The Lower Canadian Civil Code of 1866*

1993

Greg Marquis, *Policing Canada's Century: A History of the Canadian Association of Chiefs of Police*
Murray Greenwood, *Legacies of Fear: Law and Politics in Quebec in the Era of the French Revolution*

1992

Brendan O'Brien, *Speedy Justice: The Tragic Last Voyage of His Majesty's Vessel Speedy*
Robert Fraser, ed., *Provincial Justice: Upper Canadian Legal Portraits from the Dictionary of Canadian Biography*

1991

Constance Backhouse, *Petticoats and Prejudice: Women and Law in Nineteenth-Century Canada*

1990

Philip Girard & Jim Phillips, eds., *Essays in the History of Canadian Law, Vol. III: Nova Scotia*

Carol Wilton, ed., *Essays in the History of Canadian Law, Vol. IV: Beyond the Law: Lawyers and Business in Canada, 1830–1930*

1989

Desmond Brown, *The Genesis of the Canadian Criminal Code of 1892*

Patrick Brode, *The Odyssey of John Anderson*

1988

Robert Sharpe, *The Last Day, the Last Hour: The Currie Libel Trial*

John D. Arnup, *Middleton: The Beloved Judge*

1987

C. Ian Kyer & Jerome Bickenbach, *The Fiercest Debate: Cecil A. Wright, the Benchers and Legal Education in Ontario, 1923–1957*

1986

Paul Romney, *Mr. Attorney: The Attorney General for Ontario in Court, Cabinet and Legislature, 1791–1899*

Martin Friedland, *The Case of Valentine Shortis: A True Story of Crime and Politics in Canada*

1985

James Snell & Frederick Vaughan, *The Supreme Court of Canada: History of the Institution*

1984

Patrick Brode, *Sir John Beverley Robinson: Bone and Sinew of the Compact*

David Williams, *Duff: A Life in the Law*

1983

David H. Flaherty, ed., *Essays in the History of Canadian Law, Vol. II*

1982

Marion MacRae & Anthony Adamson, *Cornerstones of Order: Courthouses and Town Halls of Ontario, 1784–1914*

1981

David H. Flaherty, ed., *Essays in the History of Canadian Law, Vol. I*